THE NEW ETHICS

THE NEW ETHICS

A TOUR OF THE 21ST-CENTURY MORAL LANDSCAPE

Anita L. Allen

MIRAMAX BOOKS

Printed in the United States of America. For information address Hyperion, 77 West 66th Street, New York, NY 10023-6298

ISBN 0-7868-6897-X

FIRST EDITION

10   9   8   7   6   5   4   3   2   1

To Cynthia, Monica, Grover, Michael, and André

CONTENTS

Introduction: The New Ethical Landscape   xi

LAY OF THE LANDSCAPE · WITHOUT A PULPIT ·
CIRCUMSPECT MORALISTS · STILL A PLACE FOR
JUDGMENT · JUDGING OURSELVES · ETHICAL FAILURE,
AMERICAN STYLE · RESOURCE RICH: SO, WHY AREN'T
WE BETTER? · NOVEL OPTIONS FOR THE DESIGN OF
LIFE · FROM COPING WELL TO CHOOSING WELL ·
COMPLACENT ISLANDS SYNDROME · FOR THE SAKE OF
COMMUNITY

PART 1: WHAT IS WRONG

1. Running From Blame   1

TRYING TO BE PERFECT · MY MORAL BREAKDOWN ·
WHY BE MORAL? · TRAGEDY, UNCERTAINTY, AND
WILLPOWER · WON'T POWER · THEY CALL IT *AKRASIA* ·
UNETHICAL ETHICISTS · GETTING TO TUT · TOO
SMART FOR ETHICS · LENIENT ETHOS · OUR ETHICAL
DIVERSITY · COST OF COMPASSION

2. Cheating, The Big Mistake   28

A DISHONEST ECONOMY · UNIVERSITY OF CHEATING ·
BAD SPORTS · WHY CHEATING IS WRONG · GETTING

CAUGHT · MAKING EXCUSES · RACE TO THE TOP ·
FACING OUR PROBLEM

PART II: IMPROVING THE PICTURE

3. The Challenge of Moral Education   61
IMMATURE MORALISTS · MORAL DEVELOPMENT
DEBATES · RELIGION FIRST · COUNTING ON
CHARACTER · FIGHTING OVER CHILDREN · SUBSTANCE,
PLEASE · SCHOOLING PATRIOTISM · INSIDE YOUNG
HEADS

4. Ethics Go to College   90
HIGHER ED HEARS THE CALL · THE ACADEMIC MISSION ·
CAMPUS LIFE · MEDICAL ETHICS · BUSINESS ETHICS ·
LEGAL ETHICS · DEADLY FORCES · THE INSTITUTIONALIZATION
OF ETHICS · RE-EDUCATING SOCIETY FOR GOOD

5. An Ethic of Work   109
HARD AT WORK · WORKPLACE ETHICS · WORK/HOME
FIREWALLS · SEXY AT WORK · SLEEPING IN CLASS ·
WORKING WOMEN CHOOSE

6. Real Ethics for Business   128
A RESPONSE TO SCANDAL · "IT'S ONLY ETHICS, NOT
MORALS!" · "UNETHICAL, BUT NOT FROM A BUSINESS
POINT OF VIEW" · THE WISDOM OF SELF-REGULATION ·
THE ETHICS REGULATION STAVE-OFF STRATEGY ·
ETHICAL CONSULTANTS · PRODUCING PROUD VALUES

PART III:
CHOOSING WELL ON NOVEL GROUND

7. The Child I Always Dreamt About   149
   DESIGNING A FAMILY · GENETIC ARTISTRY · PICKY
   PARENTS · STRONGER THAN YOU THINK

8. Consumption Ethics   169
   GETTING OFF DOPE · GETTING ON MEDS ·
   EATING RIGHT

9. Living Beautifully   187
   ADORNMENT · BOTCHED JOBS · ETHICAL LONGEVITY ·
   A BROKEN HEART

10. The Best Way to Die   206
    PLANNING FOR THE INEVITABLE · FALSE ALLURE OF
    SUICIDE · KIND UNTIL THE END

PART IV: JUST LIVING TOGETHER

11. Beyond Your Own Kind   223
    NEO-SEGREGATION · IMMIGRATION TO SEGREGATION ·
    STICKING TO YOUR OWN KIND · ISLAND NATION ·
    WORKING FOR AN ITALIAN · YOU STICK, THEREFORE I
    STICK · ODD, POROUS BOUNDARIES · UN-NEIGHBORLY
    NEIGHBORS · THE JEWISH CEMETERY · EXTREME BIAS:
    WE CAN DO BETTER

12. Leave Home on Election Day   244
    A REASON TO VOTE · DISENFRANCHISEMENT ·
    EMBRACING CIVIC DUTIES · SPEAKING FOR YOURSELF

Conclusion: An Agenda for Better Ethics   256
    HOW TO FIGHT ETHICAL FAILURE · HOW TO MAKE
    NOVEL CHOICES WELL · HOW TO BUILD BETTER
    COMMUNITIES · A FINAL WORD

ENDNOTES   277

INDEX   301

THE NEW ETHICAL LANDSCAPE

I magine America. Cities, towns and farms come quickly to mind. Images of rivers, lakes and seashores follow, then deserts, mountains and woods. The features of the nation's geographical terrain are easily conjured. Now take a moment to visualize another vast American expanse, the ethical landscape. What do you see? People are everywhere in the picture, of course, because human character and conduct are what ethics is all about. But what are these people doing? Some are taking responsibility for their families and helping needy strangers. Some are lying and cheating for personal gain. Some are busy designing character lessons for school children or debating tough new regulations for corrupt businesses. Activities like these comprise our country's wide-ranging panorama of ethical values: caring for others, making big mistakes, and trying to marshal ethical resources to produce better character.

Living well requires responsible choices and adherence to the common virtues. Trustworthiness, for example, is vital to every facet of just and humane lives. Every personal and professional relationship, every financial transaction and every democratic institution thrives on trust. Openly embracing ethical standards and consistently living up to them remain the most reliable ways for individuals and businesses to earn the respect on which all else depends.

The ethical standards Americans embrace are a dynamic blend of personal belief, religion, public morality and law. Plainly we need to be clear as individuals about the mix of standards for which we personally stand. However, we also need to recognize the diverse standards for which our fellow citizens, communities and nation stand. Because the United States is such a large, diverse and changeable society, it is hard to keep abreast of ethical trends. Yet responding in constructive ways to contemporary problems—from teenage drinking and sex in the workplace to corporate fraud and pulling the plug on comatose kin—depends upon an ability to see ethics in a broad perspective.

Indeed, just as you master the features of the most traveled geographical terrain, you must also conquer the ethical realms that you negotiate daily. Behind the wheel of your car, you are unlikely to make the mistake of driving headlong into the Grand Canyon; but when it comes to practical ethics, Americans make disastrous wrong turns and fall victim to the monstrous derailments of others all the time. Things go better if you understand the lay of the land. We get more things right in our lives when we pause to take long, wide views. Think of this book as a comprehensive guided tour of the ethics scene. I am an eager docent, ready to escort you from place to place.

LAY OF THE LANDSCAPE

Our contemporary ethical landscape is marked by three especially challenging features that I want to journey in some detail. The first is widespread ethical failure against the background of a culture rich with moral resources. We seem to have everything we need for exemplary character and conduct, and yet wrongdoing flourishes in every sector. Why are we not better? How can we become better?

The second feature is the emergence of an array of novel options for the design of life. We are repeatedly called on to embrace far-reaching opportunities presented by modern medicine, science and technology. Moreover, a constitutional system of enhanced equality and liberty, new to recent generations, has further multiplied our options. We are now empowered by law to choose where we live, with whom we live, and how we make a living. Public health, public safety and homeland security measures qualify our freedom, but still we are left with choices aplenty. In what manner should the power of choice be exercised? What options have ethical implications for which we should be held to account?

The third feature is insular complacency toward nation and community, at odds with high aspirations of justice and citizenship. We are lately too content to sit out national elections and let other people do the work of democratic self-government. We are also too content to live segregated among our own kinds on exclusive islands of race, ethnicity and income. What matters? Whose voices are determining public policies? Where is community?

These three features—visible ethical failure, demanding new choices, and insular complacency—are barriers to the common good. But they are surmountable. Fortunately we come equipped with a towering ethical capacity. First, we can make judgments about what to do and how best to live; and second, we can choose to act on the basis of those judgments. A sense of responsibility for conduct emerges early in life and continues until we can no longer think, remember and feel. When properly nurtured, educated and disciplined, our ethical capacity becomes a powerful springboard to better lives.

WITHOUT A PULPIT

At first I hesitated to write a book in my own voice about the vast sweep of contemporary ethics. I was concerned about the appearance of hubris, but even more so about hypocrisy and moralism, a pair of forceful seducers. In one respect, though, taking on the subject seemed entirely natural. Ethics had captured me about the same time that Barbie dolls loosened their tiny grips.

The year I turned eleven, standing especially tall in a pink dress, white gloves, and sky blue shoes, I was baptized into the United Methodist Church. The minister sprinkled a few drops of water onto my freshly curled hair by way of sacrament. For weeks before baptism, I attended a required course of Christian instruction that piqued my curiosity about the reasons behind the rules of biblical morality. Why should you honor your father and mother, if they don't honor you back? Why shouldn't you covet your neighbor's ox, if his ox is better than yours? Why should you love your enemy, if your enemy bombs your cities?

My enthusiasm for ethics eventually extended to second-guessing the advice that columnist Ann Landers offered readers of the daily newspapers. Maybe that jobless mama's boy should be allowed to move back home, even if hard-working hubby will pout for a while! I could not get enough of the steamy dilemmas posed in my mother's *True Confessions* magazines. Now that they have set their wedding date, should virgin Victoria go to bed with randy Ralph to help keep him faithful? My first publication was a letter to the editor of *Revealing Romances*.

As a teenager, I moved beyond ethical issues inspired by ingenue fancy. I hunted for answers to serious questions in the stacks of the public library. I began reading philosophy and its spiritual cousin, theology. Any newly encountered worldview might command my attention: egoism, pacifism, socialism, existentialism, pantheism, atheism. Works by Søren Kierkegaard and the radical theologian Paul Tillich made my head spin. I puzzled over foundation-shaking questions posed by Bertrand Russell, Friedrich Nietzsche and Jean-Paul Sartre. Is God really dead? Is morality just herd behavior? Is adherence to prescribed values bad faith?

College and graduate school brought some intellectual discipline. Under the direction of first-class scholars, I learned systematic approaches to the study of ethics and the other branches of philosophy. Physical discipline was a craving, too, in those days, so I loaded up with ballet and modern dance classes during my ample spare time at the University of Michigan. I learned the José Limón technique sweating next to Madonna, who was enrolled full-time in the dance department.

Notwithstanding the distractions of dance, by the age of twenty-five I had earned a doctorate in philosophy. I landed a job at Carnegie Mellon University that entailed teaching a required ethics course to throngs of truculent actors and engineering students. After fleeing to Harvard for a law degree, I briefly practiced corporate law in New York City. Cravath,

Swaine & Moore was down on Wall Street then, and David Boies of *U.S. v. Microsoft,* Napster, and *Bush v. Gore* fame was a legendary young partner at the firm.[1] At thirty-two I resumed academic life, this time happily as a law professor. In addition to teaching, I have served as an ethics consultant to government and business, led seminars for professionals, and lectured widely. Ethics and law have kept me busy.

I have the right background for surveying the ethical landscape, a task others with similar backgrounds have performed for general audiences in the past.[2] But writing a *personal* book recommending my vision of better ethics required extra gumption. It is no small matter to invite strangers to peer into your intimate moral universe. Indeed, my credentials qualify me as an expert in an academic discipline or two but not as a saint beyond reproach. And with a history of error like mine, I am not entitled to cast stones at other people's ethics. Yet the consoling cliché is correct: People do learn from their mistakes. Ethical understanding flowers in the fertile fields of transgression and redemption. Moreover, ethical truths become more vivid when they have undergone the test of experience. We have good reason to be ethical; and when we fail, we have an even better reason to try again.

CIRCUMSPECT MORALISTS

Both liberal and conservative Americans tend to agree that smug, intrusive moralism gives the entire ethical enterprise a bad name. Inhabitants of a country in which individual, religious and cultural differences are the norm, Americans increasingly demand moral toleration. In 1958 the committed moral philosopher Kurt Baier began his book *The Moral Point of View* this way: "Moral talk is often rather repugnant. Leveling moral accusations, expressing moral indignation, passing moral judgment, allotting the blame, administering moral reproof, justifying oneself, and, above all moralizing. Who can enjoy such talk? And who can like or trust those addicted to it?"[3]

Moralism is still suspect, and the United States has grown wary of dictating morality through law. Accordingly, our courts and legislatures have begun to put an end to the legislation of morals. The prohibition of alcohol early in the last century was both a moral fiasco and a law enforcement nightmare: People kept getting drunk. More than merely impractical, the legislation of morality can violate the Constitution. Citing ideals of equality and essential Fourteenth Amendment liberty, the Supreme Court recently struck down a controversial morality ban on consensual adult gay sodomy. The landmark case, *Lawrence v. Texas* (2003), thrust a sword in the side of a category of legal moralism that stationed police in the bedroom.[4]

Not all morals laws violate the Constitution. Police caught a young woman named Lauren Mueller selling sex to an adult customer in her home in Hawaii. Mueller protested that she had a constitutional right to do as she pleased in the privacy of her own apartment. Upholding her criminal conviction, the unsympathetic judge wrote: "A large segment of society undoubtedly regards prostitution as immoral and degrading."[5] Like commercial sex, public nudity remains an area of legal prohibition. The owners of the Kitty Kat Lounge and the Glen Theater in South Bend, Indiana, wanted their erotic dancers to perform totally nude. They believed the women—and their clubs—would earn more money that way. However, because an Indiana state statute banned public nudity, dancers were required to wear pasties and G-strings to avoid arrest. Club owners went to court arguing that the ban on nude dancing violated performers' First Amendment guarantee of free expression. The owner fought a long legal battle and ultimately lost in the Supreme Court. In *Barnes v. Glen Theater* (1991), the Court concluded that the no-nudity statute was perfectly constitutional: "[T]he statute's purpose of protecting societal order and morality is clear from its text and history."[6] At present, public nudity and prostitution are prohibited on moral grounds without protest in most jurisdictions. However, few ordinary Americans have to lose sleep anymore worrying about the legal consequences of the sodomy, fornication or adultery that their neighbors may disapprove.

STILL A PLACE FOR JUDGMENT

Old-time morals legislation is headed out, but the practice of evaluating conduct and character remains in.[7] This is as it should be. As a society, Americans place special public emphasis on moral education. Schools, universities and workplaces are taking on the task of building character. Moreover, compliance with ethical standards in government, business and the professions has become an urgent public priority. Prurient moralizing about the private lives of public officials and celebrities gets out of hand, but our overall reemphasis on ethical character and personal accountability is warranted by the recent meltdown of values and the grave responsibilities of modern choice.

Americans need to make value-driven choices. But based on what? How is an expanding public emphasis on values workable in a country in which the moral and ethical values that individuals hold are shaped by diverse ethnic and religious backgrounds? Don't Americans disagree about fundamentals? We certainly fight as though we disagree. We fight about what we eat, smoke and wear. We fight about abortion, the death penalty, stem cell research, same-sex marriage, taxes and war. We fight about drugs, prayer, flags, race, music, and guns. We fight about many things; yet we do not disagree about everything. We recognize difference and disagreement but make a bold presumption that a foundation of national and global values, firm enough for praising and blaming one another, exists.

Unethical acts violate recognized standards of conduct and character. The worst unethical conduct simultaneously offends important social, professional and legal standards. Although "unethical" is the term of choice in recent public discourse about right and wrong, "immoral" is also in daily use. Americans tend to speak of business and professional *ethics* rather than business and professional *morality*. "Moral" otherwise covers much of the same territory as "ethical." We refer to positive character traits both as ethical virtues and as moral virtues. Honesty, for example, is both ethical and moral.

A hundred years ago, the British philosopher G. E. Moore neatly summed up the wide spectrum of ethics this way: "In the vast majority of cases where we make statements involving any of the terms 'virtue,' 'vice,' 'duty,' 'right,' 'ought,' 'good,' 'bad,' we are making ethical judgments; and if we wish to discuss their truth, we shall be discussing a point of Ethics."[8] Today, making ethical judgments and discussing their truth is going on all over the place. It is happening in bedrooms and boardrooms. It is occurring in classrooms and courtrooms. In fact, in response to a mass of controversies and scandals, discussing ethics in all its recent guises has become something of a national mandate and obsession. American society is immersed in spiritual and political debates about every imaginable category of ethics—from sexual ethics to business and professional ethics; from government and environmental ethics to bioethics and the ethics of citizenship.

No one needs to feel overly squeamish about calling the people who lie, cheat and defraud their way into the hands of the law unethical. But being called unethical is not a fate reserved for law breakers. We openly call those wrongdoers whose misconduct falls short of a broken regulation, civil injury, or crime "unethical," too. For example, duplicitous romancing is legal, but a married man who pretends to be single and proposes marriage to a lonely woman he met on the Internet is freely branded. Wholesale dishonesty in intimate relationships violates just about everyone's standards. The quip that "Morality consists of suspecting other people of not being legally married," attributed to George Bernard Shaw, dates itself.[9] Nonetheless, the person who knowingly violates widely shared ideals of right, good, virtue or justice courts the moral condemnation of the community.

JUDGING OURSELVES

Ethical judgment extends beyond critical assessment of other people's conduct and character. It is, in addition, a matter of self-assessment. What should I choose? What are my responsibilities? How could I be a better person? How ought I contribute to a more just society? We are

proud when we get things right, and we condemn ourselves for ethical failure. Like self-sacrifice, self-condemnation can get out of hand. But ethical
ambition, a keen desire to do what is right, is normal, healthy and
admirable. We have succeeded in meeting high ethical ambition in the past
and we can work together to improve our chances of meeting it more fully
in the future.

Caring for others and putting moral convictions to work is a test of
mettle. The responsibilities of ordinary life may press the limits of
patience and altruism. To start, families are full of moral demands. I am a
married woman with a preteen daughter and a teenage son to care for at
home. I am constantly making judgments about what is best for us and
trying to find the time and courage to do what I believe I should. Extended
families are demanding, too. One of my six siblings used to be a crack
addict. Others close to me are among the alcoholic, suicidal and abusive
mentally ill. Cousins have gone to prison, and cousins have died of AIDS.
Friends have invited me to share lifestyles and politics that cut against the
grain of my instincts; and I have asked some of them to act against the grain
of theirs. But these are not grounds for global pessimism.

Philosophy's most famous pessimist lamented what he thought professionals serving the general public observe about human character. "The
doctor sees all the weakness of mankind, the lawyer all the wickedness, the
theologian all the stupidity," Arthur Schopenhauer wrote.[10] My knowledge of the traits seen by doctors and theologians is secondhand, but I am
sure they observe more than weakness or stupidity. As a lawyer turned law
professor, I know firsthand the virtues and vices that lawyers see. Attorneys witness abundant charity and enterprise; however, in our work as liti-
gators, prosecutors and judges, we do encounter plenty of the worst
sorts—including the worst of our own profession.

Ethical capacity is uniquely human. Animals display affection and
care. But the loyal hound is not a self-conscious agent of morality, nor is
the gentle mother cat licking her sticky newborn brood. Only the human
animal is blessed with ethical capacity and ethical ambition to boot. We
can be ethical. Most of us want badly to try, and many of us succeed.

We seem to have everything we need for exemplary character and conduct, and yet wrongdoing flourishes in every sector. Why are we not better? How can we become better?

═══════════════

Philosophies of pessimism can be postponed for the improbable day when vistas of inhumanity cease to dishearten.

ETHICAL FAILURE, AMERICAN STYLE

The past twenty-five years have told an especially disheartening tale of American values. I know many good people, and a few who are exceptionally good. Yet ethical vice upstages ethical virtue in every sector. Ethics appear to be beyond the reach of our leaders, sports heros, and elite professionals. Ethics scandals in the corporate world have robbed countless individuals of jobs, pensions and savings. Ethics breaches by government employees and public officials have threatened to undermine public trust. Revelations of dishonesty in amateur and professional sports have repeatedly assaulted ideals of integrity and fair play. Sex abuse cloaked by esteemed religious institutions has mocked the concepts of clerical chastity and pastoral care. Lately some of our best scholars have turned out to be plagiarists; our prized researchers, frauds; our bold young journalists, creative liars.

Ethical failure plagues every sector, including government and politics, where it is especially worrisome. Although we must rely on the leadership of public officials and politicians, they are not above malice, greed, sexual impropriety, recklessness or dishonesty. Some highly publicized lapses of virtue in government and politics have been close to incredible for the lack of judgment they suggest. For example, in 1998, Byron "Low Tax" Looper tried to get elected by eliminating his competition—he shot and killed incumbent Tennessee state senator Tommy Burks.[11] Looper was convicted of murder and sentenced to life in prison without parole. A few years later Congressman James Traficant, a nine-term Democrat from Ohio was convicted on federal charges of bribery, racketeering and tax evasion. By a vote of 420 to 1, Traficant was expelled from Congress on the recommendation of the House Committee on Standards of Official Conduct. Bizarre is the only word to describe the congressman's comments as he faced expulsion in 2002, including these: "I'm disgusted, busted, can't be trusted."[12]

President Clinton's affair with former White House intern Monica Lewinsky was a matter of private adultery and high-level public deception that combined to place the president's morals on trial. The former president was acquitted of perjury and obstruction of justice in a three-week impeachment trial in the Senate that analyzed his relationship with Lewinsky in pornographic detail. The morality of the president remained on the public agenda until he settled sexual harassment charges, stemming from an encounter with Paula Jones in a hotel room while he was governor of Arkansas, for close to a million dollars. Surprisingly, former California Congressman Gary Condit repeated President Clinton's central mistake of having sex with a young intern. The married congressman had an affair with Chandra Levy while she was working as an intern with the Federal Bureau of Prisons in Washington.[13] He might have kept the romance a secret, had Levy not mysteriously disappeared in the spring of 2001. She later turned up dead. After Levy's disappearance made the news, a second and third woman came forward claiming to have been Condit's lover. Condit went on television to deny their allegations, but the ethically clouded congressman lost his bid for reelection as representative for Modesto, California. Condit has never been officially linked to Levy's homicide.

Poor judgment takes many forms. In August 2003, William J. ("Bill") Janklow, a first-term Republican congressman and a former governor of South Dakota, was driving recklessly and speeding on a rural road near Sioux Falls when he collided with motorcyclist Randy Scott, a Vietnam veteran and volunteer firefighter. Sadly, Scott died as a result of the congressman's negligence, leaving behind a family and a flourishing trucking business. The South Dakota State's Attorney charged Representative Janklow with several misdemeanors—speeding, running a stop sign, reckless driving and second-degree felony manslaughter. Janklow resigned from Congress following his conviction. He was sentenced to one hundred days in jail and fined $5,400.

A final example: Harvey Pitt resigned from his post as chairman of the Securities and Exchange Commission on November 5, 2002, brought down by two major ethics blunders. First, Pitt made the mistake of meeting with Eugene D. O'Kelly, the chairman and CEO of KPMG, a former client when Pitt was a partner at the Washington law firm Fried, Frank, Harris, Shriver & Jacobson. O'Kelly said he asked Pitt to drop an SEC investigation of KPMG for auditing fraud in connection with work performed on behalf of the Xerox Corporation. Pitt admitted meeting with O'Kelly but denied that O'Kelly made the audacious request for special treatment. In a second error of judgment, Pitt failed to disclose pertinent information about William Webster, the man he originally selected to head the high-profile accounting oversight committee established by the Sarbanes-Oxley Act of 2002. The oversight committee is responsible for enforcing ethical accounting rules, yet Webster had headed an audit committee at U.S. Technologies, a company accused of fraud and nearly bankrupt. Pitt resigned in direct response to public outrage over his concealment of material facts about Webster.

RESOURCE RICH: SO, WHY AREN'T WE BETTER?

I gnore all the violent crime. Set aside moral concerns about the role of the United States and its citizens in international arenas. Catalogue just the most memorable nonviolent ethics scandals on the domestic front. Nonetheless America appears to be in the midst of a downward spiraling ethical crisis. But appearances can be deceiving. Exaggerated fears of precipitous moral decline have dogged earlier generations, and they dog ours, too. We have some real problems, but we are not clearly worse in the moral fiber department than our great-grandparents were. We channel more services to the disabled and the poor than they did. We are more attentive to the needs of children. We do a better job of respecting the rights of women and ethnic minorities.[14]

A heightened sense of moral decline is an understandable response, though, to what we hear and read about every day. Unprecedented national publicity is given to crime, negligence and other wrongdoing: bad guys make good news. A hundred years ago—when we were a nation without television, the Internet and cell phones, an ethics violation in one community might go unreported in another. Thanks to the many print and electronic modes of mass communication now in use, news of folly, greed, and mayhem gets widely and rapidly disseminated. It could have been a purely local story, but we all heard about Wanda Webb Holloway, the Texan convicted of murder solicitation for asking her former brother-in-law Terry Harper to find a hit man to murder Verna Heath, the mother of her daughter's cheerleading rival, Amber Heath. And that was in 1991, when the Internet was only being used by a few nerds. After a 1996 retrial, Holloway was sentenced to ten years behind bars.

Rapid mass communication amplifies the news of wrongdoing. It is hard to prove that we are in an unprecedented state of overall moral decline. Still, the volume of publicized ethical failure is discouraging. Faced with so much ethical failure, you would almost think Americans lack ethical resources. Yet the opposite is true. We may have more than we know what to do with. The United States is saturated with resources designed to educate the conscience. Ethical resources permeate every sector of American society. The nation drips with sources of ethical guidance; ethics discourse, ethics rules, ethics laws. Ethics teachers, ethics advisors, ethics consultants. Ethics lectures, ethics institutes, ethics books, ethics journals, ethics Web sites. Ethics on television, ethics on the radio. Ethics is a stated priority of schools, universities, professional associations, business and government.

In the 1990s former comedian Randy Cohen began answering ethics questions in an entertainment-oriented advice column for the *New York Times Magazine*. Ethics is even a form of recreation. The Association for Practical and Professional Ethics has turned ethics into a spectator sport. The association sponsors an annual ethics competition for young people, the Intercollegiate Ethics Bowl. The Sears, Roebuck and Company's Office of Ethics and Business Practices has funded the Ethics Bowl since 1996. Teams of three to five students answer questions about "classroom topics (e.g., cheating or plagiarism), personal relationships (e.g., dating or friendship), professional ethics (e.g., engineering, architecture, business, the military, law, medicine), or social and political ethics (e.g., free speech, gun control, etc.)."[15] Judges determine winners based on soundness of reasoning, clarity, focus, and depth.

With so many ethical resources to educate and guide, Americans seem to have everything a people could plausibly need for exemplary character and conduct. Yet ordinary vice and extraordinary ethical scandal abound. We expect a return on our investment in moral resources, and seem not to be getting it. Just about everyone believes that dishonesty for personal gain is unethical. But in the past two decades, hordes of public officials, athletes and business executives—including acclaimed role models, spiritual leaders and public intellectuals—have been caught deceiving for gain with flair.

There are reasons the nation's abundant moral resources have not protected it from the likes of Enron. For one thing, some ethical failure is inevitable. A certain number of people who know right from wrong and understand the ethical standards of their professions will experience moral weakness and fall prey to temptation. They have conscience but give in to impulse and rationalization. It is easier to teach, preach, study, advocate, debate and publish ethics than to practice ethical living. I know from personal experience that it is easier to talk the talk than to walk the walk. Although we cannot hope to eliminate the problem of failed moral resolve, we can work to reduce the problem with approaches to moral education that convey ethical know-how as powerfully as they convey ethical knowledge.

Another reason ethical failure occurs despite abundant ethical resources is that people will temporarily cast aside the ethical point of view and deliberately pursue self-interest when doing so seems smart. Businessmen and -women, for example, often view financial objectives as paramount and knowingly violate ethical and legal rules that stand in their way. When facing great financial and personal losses, individuals from all walks of life will bracket ethical principles they believe they cannot afford. Moreover, a number of unscrupulous people will always prefer to free ride on civil society, secure in the knowledge that as long as most people are fair, honest and charitable, they do not necessarily have to be. A certain number of people in any society will be opportunistically selfish, discriminatory and cruel.

A final reason ethical failure occurs despite abundant ethical resources is that some of our vaunted resources—for example, student honor codes, professional association codes, industry standards and ethics laws—are poorly designed to deter wrongdoing. The quantity of resources is less of a problem for Americans than the quality. Honor codes are a bad way to build character if they predictably invite cheating among unsupervised students.[16] Ethics laws will not work if they are craven compromises between government regulators and business or industry groups. The case for self-regulation is that in many instances the real experts about the rules a sector needs are the people closest to it. However, some self-regulating is ineffective in protecting the public's interest. Ethics codes adopted by professional groups are often high-toned pronouncements aimed at reassuring the public rather than effectively addressing the complex causes of professional misconduct.

Viewed in one light, the wealth of ethics resources one finds in the United States is an ironic symptom of ethical failure rather than proud evidence of ethical success. Pure moral idealism has not prompted pragmatic problem solvers to proliferate ethical standards. Instead, the worse we think we are, the more we scramble to create additional mechanisms of public education, professional training and law. In gloomier moments we look like a society continually churning out ethical resources in an effort to avoid the shame of indifference to vast private and public immoralities we feel helpless to abate. Yet I believe we are not helpless to address costly ethical failures. As we will see, it is possible to improve our approaches to moral education, revitalize the work ethic and, where necessary, buttress industry and professional self-regulation with strict, well-enforced ethics laws.

NOVEL OPTIONS FOR THE DESIGN OF LIFE

Ethical failure is one hazard on the new ethical landscape. Dozens of new kinds of ethical choices comprise a second hazard. How are choices a hazard? More than ever before, we are compelled to make a great many choices with consequences that reach far beyond our own lives. Developments in science and law have brought about this fundamental change in the number and range of high-impact personal choices. What ought I do?—a simple-sounding question—can actually be a daunting call to complex ethical engagement and self-education. In some of our choices, the biological future of the human race and of mother Earth, our habitat, is at stake; in others, the fundamental nature of national social life and the political order that sustains it is on the line.

Science is transforming the kinds of lives individuals in the United States and other wealthy nations can expect to live. Thanks to medical science and technology we have unprecedented power to master biological limitations. Technology has presented new options for the food we eat, the clothing we wear and the cars we drive. Medical science has diminished the peril of illness and injury. Innovation has enhanced our ability to determine for ourselves how we will look, feel and reproduce. It has transformed the ways we are born, cared for and die. We can expect to live longer, in better health and with a more complete understanding of human nature. Physicians have the know-how to treat serious diseases, save lives and make normal but imperfect bodies looks perfect. Cosmetic plastic surgery can give anyone who wants it a movie-star profile. Pharmacists dispense drugs that allow us to control our moods and limit the size of our families. A recently introduced drug called Seasonale allows women to reduce the frequency of their menses from once a month to four times a year.

As a consequence of these awesome powers, typical individuals can expect to have a bigger say than ever before over the design of their futures. Because of innovations in science, we do not have to settle for the suboptimal lives of regret dished up by Fate or Nature. In a world remade by genetic or other science, however, we face pivotal and often uncertain ethical responsibility for personal health, family health and the health of the shared natural environment. We know the right thing to do in familiar circumstances. For example, it is clearly wrong to set up a phony business to cheat people out of hard-earned money with lies and broken promises. So is betraying the trust of a close friend. But the new ethical landscape is characterized by many unfamiliar circumstances. In fact, the field of bioethics was born in the 1970s to cope with issues of morality and professional ethics raised by new techniques and technologies in clinical medicine, research and the life sciences.

Suppose Jim discovers that his widowed mother is certain to die in a few weeks' time of an invasive cancer. Her death and Jim's loss are inevitable. He cannot heal her. He cannot avert his grief or the grief of others who love her. He simply has to cope. From an ethical perspective, coping well would require sticking to moral principles and displaying the moral virtues called for by unavoidable personal loss: courage in the face of death; patience with others' emotions; fidelity to the wishes and expectations of the dying and deceased; justice to heirs.

But there is more to modern death than coping appropriately with the hand Fate has dealt. One is also called upon by medical practice to view oneself as an active moral agent and make certain specific choices. Hence, Jim could be called upon as next of kin to decide whether to continue palliative chemotherapy or to attempt to resuscitate his mother should her heart stop. It could be up to Jim to decide when to discontinue life support. Jim might be called on to help his dying mother choose whether or not to participate in cancer research that offers her no therapeutic benefit but could someday benefit others like her. From an ethical perspective, choosing well would entail making caring decisions that reflect due consideration of the rights and interests of everyone concerned. We no longer primarily cope with death; we make major choices about its time, manner and meaning.

In unfamiliar situations brought on by science and technology we may need to make ethical choices about which we are understandably uncertain or clueless. There is no shame in the fact that most of us are baffled by novel biomedical options. Should you donate a kidney to a brother whose chances of survival are lower than average for transplant recipients? Physically abusing a child is clearly wrong, but what about conceiving a child to serve as a source of umbilical cord stem cells or bone marrow for a sibling with leukemia? Could that amount to mistreatment, too? We cannot afford to assume that ethical traditions born in antiquity equip us to easily discern obligation and responsibility in every setting, including those wholly unheard of a mere generation ago.

Several years ago couples seeking the children of their dreams quickly lined up to clone a baby using unknown, unproven techniques under study by a team of international researchers including Severino Antinori and Panayiotis Zavos, based in Rome. For these couples, "I can clone" seemed to mean "I should clone." Yet "I can clone" may not entail that it is ethical for me to clone. Faced with the problem of infertility and ideals of human perfection, should you make a baby by cloning yourself? Would it be any better to purchase the eggs of a tall Ivy League coed with good teeth and perfect SAT scores? Would it be best of all to reject medically assisted reproduction and adopt an existing child of another race in need of a good home?

In some novel situations, you may fail even to recognize that the options presenting themselves have significant ethical dimensions. Does it matter if you choose to eat meat or prefer illegal drugs to the latest prescription antidepressants? It is easy to be uncertain or clueless about the multifaceted ethics of what we consume for fun, health and survival. And what about high-tech cosmetic enhancement of our bodies? Is cosmetic surgery a matter of prudent well-being or ethical well-being? The last ten years have been filled with reports of people flocking to surgeons for fat removal, breast augmentation, nose jobs, vision improvement, face lifts, breast reductions, calf reductions, eyelid surgery, collagen and Botox injections, and even circumcision reversal. Cosmetic surgery has hidden ethical dimensions. And should you aim to live as long as possible, even if it means exploiting embryonic stem cells, manipulating your genes, living with a mechanical heart or accepting a new lung transplanted from a healthy friend? What about the quality of life and the sweeping economic implications of a longer-lived population?

Along with science, law has radically changed the context of ethical decision making. The egalitarian law of a democratic society committed to civil rights and civil liberties has resulted in lives with heightened freedom of choice. Because of twentieth-century legal reforms, including the civil rights reforms of the last half century, individuals in the twenty-first century have greater control than ever before over the social roles and political responsibilities they undertake. The United States' legal system does not officially lock its citizens into a certain way of life based on caste, class, race or gender. Everyone can aspire to opportunities and rewards once reserved for a privileged few. We have unprecedented power to defy the limitations of birth, income, gender, color, disability or religion. We are no longer stuck simply coping with predetermined roles and responsibilities with moral grace. On the whole, poor people, women of all races and racial minorities have meaningful options. Women and minority groups enjoy a new status in society, altering familiar old social expectations, housing patterns, employment opportunities and social hierarchies. Legal reforms have outlawed discrimination, reducing the number of intractable prohibitions. Neither race nor gender nor family income limits social freedom and political participation as it did in the 1950s.

It would be easy to overstate American justice. Many of us still enjoy too little freedom, equality and opportunity. Women working in the corporate sector are still paid twenty percent less than men, and are still caged in by glass ceilings. Civil liberties have been constricted by homeland security measures. Insular lives of vulnerability and victimization are still the fate of too-low-income Americans. Yet to stand in my shoes is to stand in special appreciation of the ways that the rule of law has been fulfilling some of its most ambitious promises. Had I been born twenty years earlier, there is a good chance I would have wound up as a housemaid. Supreme Court Justice Clarence Thomas might have been a bellhop. Diversity policies and legal equality have changed the ethical, no less than the social and political, landscape. They have added choices, altered the stakes, increased the competition and magnified the difficulty of deciding what to do.

Each of us bears a great ethical responsibility for the life we must design as a participant in a free democracy. Family law reforms and liberal social attitudes have made it possible for me to decide for myself, engaging my own moral beliefs, whether to remain single, marry or divorce. Because I can choose to live mainly among people of my same ethnic group or in a more diverse community, I am responsible for making a good choice about the matter. Today, a parent like me who considers enrolling her son in the Boy Scouts is expected to take a stand on the broad ethical implications of supporting an organization intolerant of gay men.[17] Considerations of religious freedom, equal treatment and role modeling bear on ethical decisions about membership.

FROM COPING WELL TO CHOOSING WELL

In centuries past, the direction of your life would have been well settled before you emerged from the womb. Social structures—political economy, law and custom—constrained opportunity. Politics fixed caste, class and social roles. Men had a certain set of options, women had their own set. Sons of artisans faced certain possibilities, sons of wealthy merchants others. Masters followed one path, slaves a different path. Not yet tamed by modern science, nature functioned as a powerful constraint on opportunity, too. Neither the politically privileged nor the politically subordinated could reliably escape the ravages of disease and disaster for long. You played the hand you were dealt in the game of life for as long as you could. You may not have been all that happy; you may have sometimes faced tragic moral dilemmas, but you would not have been routinely overwhelmed by a vast array of ever-changing options requiring responsible individual choice.

Living an ethical life used to amount to coping well with the social disadvantages and biological perils Fate sent one's way. Ethics primarily required taking the high road called for by virtue, good and right. The correct path was generally clear—all you had to do was muster the will to follow it. In recent decades, the situation has changed. The pace of life is swifter and the problems with which we cope are more complex. Living an ethical life increasingly requires choosing well, not merely coping well. Of course, coping well was never the whole story of moral life. People have always had to make uncertain and tragic choices. Imagine the difficult choices families short on food have had to make over the centuries about feeding their children and elderly. But today typical American families choose in contexts in which they have more options, with farther-reaching implications. As in the past, ethics requires self-control and good intentions, but more than ever before, ethical living requires readiness to confront thorny issues. Ethical living requires that we be thoughtful and well-informed.

The volume and novelty of ethical choices means that we cannot understand ourselves simply as ethical day hikers cautioned to take the high road. We are more like ethical trailblazers bound to traverse perilous terrain, some mapped, a good deal unmapped. To this end, we need an updated, practical understanding of what ethical living requires. If we are to do a better job of getting things right, we need to do a better job of preparing ourselves for familiar and novel challenges that together comprise the new ethical landscape. To the degree that simple old-fashioned integrity eludes us, prospects look poor for meeting the challenge of right and wrong in the complex contexts of choice presented these days. If we cannot responsibly handle the ethics of cheating, how can we handle the ethics of cloning humans and diverse communities? A society that cannot manage day hiking through well-traveled ethical terrain will be ill-equipped for trail blazing through new ethical terrain.

COMPLACENT ISLANDS SYNDROME

Through our own choices, we Americans create the third perilous feature of the present ethical landscape. I imagine it this way: groups of people, backs to one another, clustered by creed and ancestry on their own turfs, tending to their business in complacent coexistence. I believe we need to step off our turfs and turn to face one another. We can redesign the landscape by rejecting the complacent islands syndrome and replacing it with inclusive, participatory community.[18] Complacent insularity—sticking to yourself, or sticking to your own kind—is troubling from an ethical point of view. The trouble relates to social justice.

Justice is an ethical virtue with a long history. For many of its central understandings of justice, the western world owes a debt to Aristotle. His philosophy erects justice as a preeminent virtue for humankind, a social animal. In fact, responsibility for the invention of western ethics as a systematic study of all of human virtue is attributed to Aristotle.

Born in 384 B.C., Aristotle was the most distinguished pupil of his older Greek contemporary, Plato. Justice also played a central role in Plato's thought. When Plato died in 348 B.C., he left as his enduring legacy a set of philosophical conversations in dramatic form. In his best-known dialogues, Plato's irascible protagonist, Socrates, perplexes everyone he meets with ethical dilemmas, including whether a man like him, accused of a crime he did not commit, should attempt to avoid legal punishment. Plato's questions of justice and loyalty to the state no doubt enthralled Aristotle, who moved to Athens to study at Plato's Academy when he was a boy of seventeen.

Aristotle originated a striking account of intellectual and moral virtues as the essence of human excellence. Moral virtue, he explained, is a matter of habit: repeatedly doing what is conducive to happiness creates a disposition to do so. Within this framework, Aristotle explained the virtues as habitual avoidance of extremes. A man of virtuous character avoids extremes of behavior and emotion. He aims at a "Golden Mean." Virtuous individuals will habitually avoid the extremes of timidity and temerity, both vices; they will aim at courage, the mean between the two opposing extremes. Virtuous people are neither utterly self-indulgent nor utterly self-sacrificing, but seek temperance. The just man or woman gives and takes in mathematical proportion to what is due. Other Aristotelian virtues include generosity, pride and friendliness. For Aristotle, happiness is the lot of people who habitually live their roles in the virtuous middle between the polarities of human vice.

Influenced by Aristotle, a number of important modern philosophers have understood virtues as habitual dispositions. The early-twentieth-century British philosopher G. E. Moore, for example, defined the virtues as "habitual dispositions to perform actions which are duties."[19] Ordinary people think of the virtues less exactly, as simple lists of positive character traits. In his influential book *After Virtue,* the Notre Dame philosopher Alasdair MacIntyre stressed the diversity of the virtues praised by great writers and world religions.[20] Jane Austin stressed consistency and integrity; Benjamin Franklin, industry and silence; the New Testament of the Bible, faith, hope and charity. The Catholic Church teaches that justice, along with prudence, fortitude and temperance are principal or "cardinal" virtues; while faith, hope and charity are the core, theological virtues that pertain directly to a person's relationship with God.

Tempered with mercy, justice is a popular virtue. *A Small Treatise on the Great Virtues* became a European bestseller for French philosopher

André Comte-Sponville. He undertook an examination of a winsomely long list of desirables that included politeness, fidelity, prudence, temperance, courage, generosity, compassion, mercy, gratitude, humility, simplicity, tolerance, purity, gentleness, good faith, humor, love and, of course, justice. American academic philosophers are more parsimonious, offering a handful of traits sufficient for good character; but justice always makes philosophers' short list of critical virtues for democratic governments. John Rawls's monumental *Theory of Justice* and *Political Liberalism* identify justice with fairness, liberty and equality. American character educators tend toward parsimony, too. The Josephson Institute of Ethics offers its audiences "Six Pillars of Character." Its selections are trustworthiness, respect, responsibility, fairness, caring and good citizenship. Justice is not a separate "pillar," but blending fairness, responsibility, and good citizenship gets us pretty close to what justice is thought by most to entail.

Justice requires many things, and the more specific the conceptions of its requirements, the more controversy they excite. I believe justice requires establishing a democratic rule of law that respects all persons as equals. It requires compensating losses and punishing crime. Modern civil societies allocate to government the power to secure criminal retribution and civil correction. Justice also requires sharing surplus bounty with the less fortunate. In the United States, we empower government to collect taxes that redistribute wealth to benefit the poor and finance public programs. Another kind of sharing that justice requires is a type that must be performed directly by individuals. Sharing the burden of securing a politically fair and egalitarian nation is something just men and women have an ethical obligation to try to do. Previous generations of Americans worked hard to establish a more just society through individual, as well as collective action. We must likewise sustain and extend justice with our personal voices and contributions.

Two contributions are of special concern to me. One is direct participation in democratic self-government, which begins with exercising the right to vote in national elections. We should be more attentive to the communal, deliberative demands of legitimate representative government. The other is continuing to desegregate and integrate communities.

FOR THE SAKE OF COMMUNITY

Voting is fundamental to democracy and well-informed public policy, yet, according to U.S. Census Bureau survey data, in 2000, only sixty percent of eligible voters cast a ballot in the presidential election. At the same time, one of the larger groups that finally won the right to vote in the last century is feeling shut out, segregated on islands of disadvantage. The right to vote has special value to African Americans still seeking to share power and affect the direction of public policy. African Americans enjoy the same responsibility for choice that other Americans enjoy, thanks to civil rights innovations of the 1960s. But limitations on full citizenship remain for many minority groups. The NAACP protested that African American Floridians were intimidated at the polls and denied a chance to vote in the 2000 presidential election. In a more resistant problem for the black vote, African Americans are locked out of the polls by prison records. The prison population is now disproportionately composed of African American and Latino men, contributing to minority disenfranchisement. Our laws deny the vote to men and women with prison records. We are threatening to become a nation of voluntary nonvoters who aggressively seek to keep willing fellow citizens from voting.

The second contribution to a more just society is abandoning insular lifestyles. This is much harder to do than showing up at the polls on election day and casting a reasonably well informed vote. The historic experience of the United States has been one of voluntary and involuntary group segregation based on snobbery, prejudice and racism. Furthering justice and completing the civil rights agenda requires an extreme bias against tolerating neo-segregation today. Yet Americans seem barely capable of living in the same neighborhoods and attending the same schools. We live apart now, as if on separate islands, clustered by race, ethnicity, language and income.

My experience as an African American of a certain age heightens my personal moral discomfort with communities that are less than communal. I have taught at Harvard, Yale and Princeton, but I grew up with an African American father who had not gone to college and an African

American mother who dropped out of high school at age sixteen to have a baby. One of six children, I lived as an army brat, for a time on the Hawaiian island of Oahu, but for longer stretches on bleak southern and midwestern army depots behind barbed wire fences. The spartan military neighborhoods were racially integrated havens I grew to love. However, I also attended kindergarten in Alabama under demeaning segregation and then survived the scary process of court-ordered school desegregation in Georgia. I was the first and only black pupil in my seventh grade classroom at Forest Park Junior High in Forest Park, Georgia. I attended Newt Gingrich's alma mater, Baker High School, in Columbus, Georgia, under the terms of a court-ordered desegregation plan. With the benefit of affirmative action, I was one of only two blacks—and the only black girl—in my freshman class at New College, in Sarasota.

College admission was an incomplete release from the prison of unbelonging. A New College professor so doubted my ability that he accused me of plagiarizing a translation of the poet Lucretius and urged me to abandon college to become an airline stewardess. To prove that I had mastered the dead language he taught, I translated paragraphs of ordinary English into classical Latin. During my years as a scholarship student, I got by on low-paying jobs that white employers offered me with the implicit threat that I would be fired if I acted my color—that is, if I conformed to the stereotype of young black women as lascivious, lazy and dishonest. After scoring 100 percent on a written employment test that normally kept blacks out, Woolworth's begrudgingly hired me to stock shelves and make change. The Wackenhut company gave me a better job as an airport security guard at the Sarasota-Bradenton Airport and was impressed that I could ask foreign tourists to open their suitcases in both German and Italian. But the big boss called me into the downtown office one day to express his sincere hope that rumors I was dating a white boy were untrue. The boy in question is the man to whom I am currently married.

Wackenhut is in the distant past. We need to let old wounds heal and strive to live in the present. But the United States is still trying to close the book on the era of mandatory segregation. A Louisiana desegregation lawsuit brought in the 1950s remained unsettled until 2003. In 1956 a group of black families sued to integrate the Baton Rouge, Louisiana, public schools.[21] Two years before, the Supreme Court had decided *Brown v. Board of Education*, bringing a formal end to the concept of "separate but equal" public accommodations and calling for white schools to open their doors to black children, "with all deliberate speed."[22] African Americans wanted access to exclusive white schools because they were better-equipped facilities and because legal exclusion implied black moral and intellectual inferiority to whites. Today Baton Rouge's formerly white schools are 75 percent black. All but 25 percent of the whites bailed out of the public schools in the years after blacks enrolled. Now, those formerly coveted white schools are majority black schools, decrepit with age and neglect, scantily attended by mainly low-income whites. This same story has been repeated in cities all over the country. Most black and Hispanic children live in neighborhoods and attend schools in which people of color are in the majority.

Deep down, every sane person wants to live among others in harmony and security with his or her dignity intact. The frustration of this basic, near universal desire is a leading cause of human conflict. Unfortunately, in too many contexts, one person's dignity is believed to depend on another person's degradation. One group's security is believed to require another group's extermination. Torture, political rape, genocide and terrorism are unbearably common, perpetrated under the banners of self-protection and just desserts. Atrocities happen not only in faraway Europe, Asia, Africa and South America, but in our own cities and towns. New York City is one of the places where diabolical foreign terrorists struck hard; it is also where in August 1997 police officer Justin Volpe brutally sodomized Haitian immigrant Abner Louima in a 70th Precinct station bathroom with a broken stick. I do not believe Mr. Volpe would have committed this horror against a man he humanized as belonging to his own kind.

Legal segregation is over, but we still lead remarkably divided, insular lives. We enjoy calm and complacency most of the time, but all is not right. We need to take responsibility for what is wrong and do something about it. The problem is not just black and white islands. There are Chicano islands, Native American islands, and Arab American islands; rich people islands and poor people islands; Filipino immigrant islands and Orthodox Jewish islands. Our stubborn insularity is historically grounded in injustice, yet the desire to preserve it in its historical forms is itself an unjust sentiment. A segregated America has historically meant that society's benefits and burdens are unequally distributed. People are emotionally undercut by reasonable suspicions that they are being excluded solely by virtue of morally arbitrary traits such as sex, race and ethnicity, not to mention disability and obesity. Segregated lifestyles means we are less well prepared to work in multiracial, multicultural employment settings. It is hard to work next to, over or under someone you cannot comprehend. We need to learn to live effectively with people of diverse origins and beliefs in order to appreciate their equal worth as fellow citizens.

We are supposed to participate in self-government, and yet we cannot make competent public policy if our familiarity with other groups is shallow and distant. Wise, fair public policies require knowledge of the people for whom the policies are designed. When social life is segregated, political life is more divisive and less trusting than it should be. We have seen, too, that patterns of law enforcement reflect racial bias based on harmful stereotypes that persist in part because of ethnic, race and class segregation. Diversity education is moral education. Things are better than they used to be because minorities share power with whites in cities and states around the country. But we are still badly disabled on our isolated turfs. We need to have meaningfully better choices about where, how and with whom to live. A more throughgoing diversity, combined with more extensive civic participation in self-government, would mean that the talent, knowledge, and experiences of all groups are incorporated and preserved as contributions to public life. We owe this moral debt to ourselves and to the common good. Truly cohabiting the nation is too an element of getting it right on the new American landscape.

PART I

WHAT IS WRONG

CHAPTER 1

RUNNING FROM BLAME

You can care too much about doing the right things. When I was a teenager, I wanted to be a better person, so I went to the extreme of inventing my own strict ethical code. I called it "perfectionism." Although I did not know it then, philosophers sometimes classify as perfectionism any moral theory that follows the Aristotelian tradition of identifying moral virtue with habitual excellence. My naive code did not stop with a demand for mere excellence, though. It was a call for infallibility.

Although perfectionism was supposed to improve upon what I knew of existing value systems, I took my cue from a conventional source, the Gospel according to Saint Matthew. The story goes that Jesus once stood on a mountainside and preached a sermon. He ended by challenging the crowd to love its enemies. Love your enemies as yourself. "You must be perfect," he further instructed, "even as your God in heaven is perfect." The summon to Godlike perfection inspired me to come up with a perfectionist creed that I recorded in my diary. My creed required that I be perfectly honest, perfectly faithful, perfectly generous, forgiving, courageous, kind, modest, loving and so on, down a list of Western and Judeo-Christian virtues. Believing I had major vices to conquer, I earnestly undertook a campaign of self-improvement. I would stop harboring resentment of adult authority! I would never lie about where I went on dates! I would give up stealing coins from my mother to buy candy bars!

TRYING TO BE PERFECT

It is one thing to want to be a good person, something else to want to be perfect. At first glance it is difficult even to comprehend why anyone, let alone a red-blooded American teenager, would want to be perfect. It is pointless to strive for perfection, arrogant to think you know what it takes to achieve it—to err is human, as the saying goes. Everyone makes mistakes. We have compassionate metaphors for referring to moral failure. People who make mistakes "fall prey to temptation." They ignore the "voice of conscience," the "better self," and the "Good Angel."

Notwithstanding the Sermon on the Mount, none of the world's great religious or secular moral traditions expect literal perfection, and few bother demanding it. Dr. Eugene C. Bay is one of the nation's preeminent Presbyterian pastors. Before his retirement, the urbane cleric shepherded a well-heeled congregation some three thousand strong near my home outside Philadelphia. After I discovered his church, I often went to hear him preach his Sunday sermons. The one time I met privately with Dr. Bay, I asked him about perfectionism. Bay explained that the New Testament command to be perfect is a bad translation. The Greek word usually translated into English as "perfect" is the Greek word for "purpose." "You must be perfect" or "be ye perfect" actually means something closer to "you must fulfill your ultimate purpose." Jesus was imploring followers to set aside animosity and aim for humanity's high spiritual *teleios*. Faultlessness was never the plea. The Presbyterians, like other Protestants, regard both the church and individual as fallible. In fact, one of the rituals in the weekly order of worship at Bay's church is the "Assurance of Pardon," in which the congregation is reminded that their merciful God forgives sincerely confessed sin.

Dr. Bay regrets the misinterpretation of Christ's sermon. In his experience, perfectionism makes people judgmental, harsh, and even fanatical. Research lends support to Bay's observations. Counseling experts say religious perfectionism impairs the genuine spiritual growth that comes with self-acceptance.[1] As a personality trait, psychologists regard perfectionism as a downright dangerous disposition. Dr. Sidney Blatt of the department of psychiatry at Yale Medical School associates perfectionism with clinical depression. Other research links perfectionism in teenage girls to anxiety and the deadly starvation disorder, anorexia nervosa. It seems that perfectionism makes for bad ethics, bad religion and bad mental health. As the basis of a human ethic, rigid perfectionism has got to be taken off the table.

MY MORAL BREAKDOWN

You can care too much about doing the right things, but you can also care too little. When I was twenty-one, I was a full-time graduate student studying moral philosophy. My academic work was intellectually stimulating, but I was no longer focused on being a better person in the intense way I had been as a teen. Ethics was a study, not a daily practice. My major preoccupations included dance classes and a wide circle of friends that for a time centered around "Amy" and "Lennie."

Amy was my new best friend and Lennie was her lover. I saw Amy and Lennie nearly every day. Lennie liked to cook, so the three of us often gathered in his kitchen at dinnertime. When Amy and I were alone, she confided in me about all of the important things in her life, including her unhappy relationship with Lennie. Amy wanted Lennie more than Lennie wanted her, and that made her sad. Our conversations about Lennie's unwillingness to make a commitment sometimes went on for hours. But we had time on our hands. We were university students without jobs or families of our own.

Eight months into my friendship with Amy, I was alone in my apartment one night when the doorbell rang. My surprise midnight visitor was Lennie. Tipsy after drinking more than a few beers, he plopped down on the sofa in the pint-sized living room and revealed why he had come by. He was attracted to me, he wanted to be with me, he said. Although this was not a possibility I had previously considered, I was fond enough of Lennie to begin an intimate affair that night. We agreed not to tell Amy what had happened.

Amy, Lennie and I continued to spend time as a threesome. Amy continued to confide in me. Amy's relationship with Lennie deteriorated. She was so miserable that she decided to leave the university and get a job back in her hometown. One afternoon, sitting with me in my apartment, Amy was ruminating about Lennie with a painful combination of adoration and regret. She mentioned that he had an endearing appendectomy scar low down on the right side of his abdomen. "It looks just like a row of telephone poles," she sighed. "Yes," I agreed, "that's exactly what it looks like." Amy and I were both astonished by what had slipped out. "How could you possibly know that?" She screamed, "You've been sleeping with Lennie, haven't you!?" I was trapped. I had betrayed my best friend and gotten caught. I had placed pleasing Lennie and myself above my regard for Amy's feelings. A student of ethics, I had set aside loyalty, trust and honesty in an important relationship. At the time, I felt twinges of a guilty conscience about my misconduct. In an attempt to assuage my guilt I offered myself uneasy justifications like these: "All three of us are adults. No one is married. Lennie and I are really good friends. Amy and Lennie have a dead-end relationship. I am not really hurting Amy, since she will never find out." With the benefit of hindsight, I see my justifications for what they were; self-interested rationalizations. I had no genuine justifications for breaking my own moral rules, and I had no excuses, either. I was not mentally incompetent. I was not brought up in an amoral home with neglectful parents. I simply blundered. Miraculously, Amy forgave us both and moved on.

WHY BE MORAL?

Close to retirement, Professor William Frankena was thin, stooped, soft-spoken. You had to strain to hear him speak. I sat in rapt attention in his Angell Hall classroom at the University of Michigan, positioned up front near a chalkboard blanketed with definitions, distinctions and arguments. His ethics course was designed to answer the question of the ages: "Why should I be moral?" On the last day of the term, after weeks of wading through the dense history and logic of Anglo American and European ethical theories, Frankena finally gave us his answer. The reason to be moral is not happiness, security or peace. It is not wealth or wisdom. None of those are guaranteed to follow from doing what is right. "Why then should I be moral?" he asked with genuine drama in his quiet voice. "Because I care," he answered. The reason to be moral is that you care. This was an astoundingly simple answer, and a bit innocent-sounding to his students, a generation hardened by Vietnam and Watergate.

However, care *is* a dynamic moral beacon. In fact, after Frankena's death, a new school of ethics was born with care as its guide. Educational psychologist Carol Gilligan and philosopher Nel Noddings were key among the founders of the ethics of care movement. Care ethicists conceive of responsible human relationships as bonded by mutual accountability, trust and caregiving. When people attend to one another in the special way a care ethic demands, "we must temporarily suspend our own projects, set aside our own agendas and bracket our *a priori* expectations; we do this in order to apprehend another's reality on their own terms."[2] Whereas Frankena offered care as an ethical motive, contemporary care ethicists offer care as the organizing theme of ethics, its central attitude and method. Care is not just why you should be moral; care is what right conduct and the virtues are all about. Thinkers outside the care-ethics school privilege ideals of care, too. I especially like the way another soft-spoken Michigan philosopher, Alan Gibbard, once described the way people care about themselves and other people: "We wish others well, and we care about fairness. We want to deal with others in mutual respect. We carry a sense of our own moral value."[3] Care now appears on many character educators' lists of top moral virtues. They recognize too that "caring expresses ethically significant ways we matter to each other...beyond...necessity or brute survival."[4]

Suppose you do not care, though? What then? Do ethics have a point for you? Like a lot of moralists, Bill Frankena preferred to minimize the practical rewards that can flow from morality. The great Immanuel Kant prescribed duty for duty's sake as an expression of an individual's rational moral autonomy.[5] Free men and women of good will do what is right simply because they know it is right. Myriad moralists are drawn to Kant's lovely idea that there is inherent dignity in willingly following categorical moral rules. But not everyone is.

The idea that we should be good for goodness' sake leaves some people cold. They want assurance of tangible reward. Precisely for this reason, centuries of religious moralists have said we have to look to Heaven for ethics' reward. When the reasons ethics provide for choosing the right course fail to convince, "religion helps us to put our hearts into it," philosopher of science Stephen Toulmin reminded his readers.[6] But discernible prizes lie here on earth, too. Honesty, fairness and generosity—some of the core of what we have long considered as ethical regard for others—contribute to a cooperative society in which personal satisfaction and security are more readily achieved. The value of ethically good choices is often evident to the eye. It is obvious why you should not steal your coworker's wallet: if you get caught, you might get beaten up or lose your job or prompt others to steal from you. You are likely to have more of what you want if you and others consistently live by ethical principles. Longtime University of Pittsburgh philosopher Kurt Baier thus answered the question "Why should we be moral?" in this succinct way: "We should be moral because being moral is following rules designed to overrule reasons of self-interest whenever it is in the interest of everyone alike that such rules should be followed."[7]

There is a big problem, however. The tangible rewards of individual moral acts are often indistinct to those called upon to perform them. It is hard to be motivated to act ethically on general principles when it does not appear to you that the ethical options on the table are in your best interest. Doing what others say is the right thing can seem foolish. Yet judgment is fallible, and so is will. Experience has shown that what seems like foolish ethical compliance today can tomorrow prove wise. The business executive bent on profit is sure his unethical high flying will make shareholders better off. He believes he has carefully assessed the risks, but then it turns out his seemingly shrewd business moves were not so smart. He loses money, the company's reputation suffers, and as a consequence of his actions, innocent people get hurt in ways the self-absorbed executive did not even fathom.

We are all abundantly capable of bad judgment. We are all prone to weak wills when temptations appear. We can all lose full control. "There is something like a dizziness which leads from weakness to temptation and from temptation to fall," French philosopher Paul Ricoeur said of human fallibility.[8] Rather than trying to out-think ethics to get the best deal for ourselves, we ought to commit to the venerable enterprise with more humility. We do better for ourselves and, at the same time, for our communities by striving to cultivate ethical dispositions.

The struggle for consistent ethical conduct is helped along by faith. I do not necessarily mean religious belief. Nor do I have in mind blind trust. I am proposing an eyes-open, rational faith that gives the benefit of the doubt to morality. Frankena's answer to the what's-in-it-for me question about morality turns out to be close to the mark. If for no other reason, you should do what is right, good and virtuous because you have faith enough in the output of ethics to participate in the enterprise. Concern in the face of attenuated material reward is the soul of faith, ethical faith. Being ethical is not a program of perpetual individual profit, nor is it a demand for inevitable self-sacrifice. Ethics is not a regime of strict utility maximization, as Jeremy Bentham advocated in nineteenth-century England; nor is ethics the regime of absolute individual rights sought by Ayn Rand, high priestess of twentieth-century utopian libertarianism. It is a lifelong quest to respond to others with a willingness to forego brazen self-interest. What makes the quest worthwhile is that we are social creatures compelled by nature to inhabit an interdependent social world. That same nature equips us to judge how to live in peace. Selfishness and partisanship are ultimately self-destructive, philosopher Sissela Bok portends in *A Strategy for Peace* (1989).[9] With thought, practice and training—the materiel of a good, lifelong program of moral education—we can learn to make judgments conducive to social harmony, and then live by them.

TRAGEDY, UNCERTAINTY, AND WILLPOWER

The new ethical landscape includes the challenge of meeting familiar old ethical requirements. Do not cheat. Do not lie. Do not steal. Do not break promises. Do not harm the innocent. Be fair. Be inclusive. And by all means, do not betray deserving friends. To meet the challenge of these routine demands, you have to muster the willpower to do what you were probably reared to believe are the plainly right things—although the right thing to do is not, of course, always plain.

In situations of moral tragedy, ethical ideals pull in contradictory directions. You are stuck, stymied. No matter which of the available alternatives you elect, deeply held principles are offended. Sophocles' *Antigone* may be the most famous western moral tragedy of all. Passionate young Antigone is torn by competing expectations that she be a dutiful citizen of Thebes and a dutiful sister to her slain brother Polynices, who has committed treason against Thebes. As a dutiful citizen, she is required by King Creon to leave the corpse of Polynices for the vultures. As a dutiful sister, she is required by custom and the gods to bury the corpse.

Moral tragedy can be distinguished from moral uncertainty. In situations of moral uncertainty, you would like to do the right thing, but you are genuinely unsure which course of action would be best. What to do is not obvious. To dispel uncertainty, thoughtful people try a variety of tactics. They discuss their options with family and friends. They consult moral teachings, clergy and their hearts. They conduct research to clarify the facts.

Moral uncertainty is common. Carla, the victim of a horrifying rape, was uncertain about whether to keep her new baby girl or place the infant for adoption. I believe pregnant victims of rape or incest find themselves in positions of legitimate moral uncertainty. By contrast, I was not in a position of moral uncertainty with respect to Lennie and Amy. If anyone had asked me, I would have said that it is wrong to enter into a relationship with your best friend's boyfriend behind her back. It is hurtful, disloyal, dishonest.

"Getting it right" begins with a commitment to core ethical ideals. Honesty is one such ideal. It is core by consensus: the world's major ethical traditions universally commend honesty. (I have yet to hear anyone say, "I'm for dishonesty as a general principle.") We have all been brought up in families, schools or religions that instruct us to avoid dishonesty in all of its forms. Accordingly, cheating, lying, stealing, and breaking promises number among the core ethical prohibitions. Ethical ideals like honesty in personal and business relationships are expressions of our capacity to care for fellow human beings. Being honest with others is an important way to show that you are mindful of their interests, just as you, reciprocally, want them to be mindful of yours.

In order to pursue our own well-being, we all need a more or less accurate picture of who and what we are dealing with. Likewise, if your best friend is sleeping with your boyfriend behind your back, she may not be an ideal person to advise you about your personal life. If your business partner is secretly siphoning off profits you have relied on to pay the debts of the partnership, you need to know so you can dissolve the partnership and start looking for a good lawyer.

WON'T POWER

We often fall short of our own ideals, as I did. Mobilizing the better self to comply with straightforward ethical demands can be difficult. It must be difficult, because decent people regularly fail in the attempt. At times, decent people cannot even get themselves to try. Faced with what should be simple choices, many of us turn our backs on our own professed standards. The ethical standards of the groups and professions of which we are proud and willing members go unheeded. It is as if our moral, religious and legal traditions have outlived their usefulness as ethical guides; families, schools and professional associations have somehow fallen down on the job. We know unethical behavior is not costless, yet the risk of a guilty conscience, disappointed family and friends, public condemnation and even serving time in prison is insufficient to consistently motivate us to do the obviously right things.

I believe ethical failure is normal and often avoidable. Obsessed as so many of us are with personal success and satisfaction, we can still do much to fortify ourselves against ethical failure. A key obstacle to routine ethical compliance is mustering the willpower to do what we know we should. We can bolster will by added attention to what tends to weaken it. This requires self-knowledge and freedom from self-deception. A part of me, the part I consider my better self, wanted to preserve a Platonic relationship with Lennie. But I was overcome by what ethicists refer to as "weakness of will." Sometimes, basically good people find themselves in a situation in which they lack willpower. They know perfectly well what is ethically right, but they cannot bring themselves to do it. Weakness of will is an explanation for many commonplace ethics violations, but it is not a justification or an excuse. We are not altogether helpless in the face of common temptations. Many people successfully avoid them all the time. They mobilize ethical resources at hand, like conscience, distractions, advice, role models, or sacred scripture. They are practical. They quickly distance themselves from foreseeable temptation to dim its allure. I could have called my drunk friend Lennie a cab that first night and sent him packing. And I should have.

THEY CALL IT *AKRASIA*

Philosophers use a Greek word to refer to the struggle to do right in the face of knowledge of right and wrong: *akrasia*. According to the *Stanford Encyclopedia of Philosophy*, akrasia literally means "lack of mastery" or "incontinence." The "akratic" person is one who has failed to exercise sufficient mastery over impulse or will to do what he or she otherwise appears to know is right. When the akratic errs he or she could be mistaken for someone who is motivated by evil or who lacks practical knowledge of right and wrong. But the akratic is generally decent and morally educated, not evil and ignorant.

Akrasia is weakness of will. Impulsivity is one kind of akrasia. Who has not committed an unkindness unthinkingly, or in the heat of anger? These we quickly come to regret, marveling at our lack of emotional self-control. However, akrasia is not always a matter of acting in the moment. Moral weakness can be the outcome of an extended set of Faustian reflections about whether to give in to temptation.

Two angels visit Christopher Marlowe's Dr. Faustus, Good Angel and Evil Angel. Good Angel calls him "Sweet Faustus" and begs him to "think of heaven and heavenly things." But Evil Angel tells him to think instead of honor and wealth. In a tug-of-war between the better self and the less good self, the better self persistently urges with passion and reason for the right thing. A hardworking retail cashier goes back and forth for months about whether to take money from the register to pay off a debt.

Should I? Should I not? Dare I? Dare I not? She knows it is wrong (and illegal). One day she ignores the advice of her better self and slips a few hundred dollar bills into a pocket. Instead of listening to the advice of the good angel sitting on the right shoulder, she follows the advice of the bad angel sitting on the left.

Philosophers have debated akrasia for centuries in a literature that presents the intriguing phenomenon as something of a paradox. The puzzle is how rational, informed people who seem to know what is right, who know what virtue and goodness require, nonetheless do the wrong thing. Aristotle suggested in Book VII of the *Nicomachean Ethics* that akrasia should be impossible.[10] After all, he reasoned, someone with real, practical knowledge of what is good would have no trouble doing good to reap the benefits of goodness. The Roman Emperor and Stoic moralist Marcus Aurelius agreed. "Begin the morning by saying to yourself, I shall meet with the busybody, the ungrateful, arrogant, deceitful, envious, unsocial," his *Meditations* advise. Referring to human fault and foible, he continued, "All of these things happen to them by reason of their ignorance of what is good and evil."[11] However, the gap between ethical knowledge and ethical conduct is a common reality. With all due respect to the ancients, there are no philosopher kings whose appreciation of the good and habitual virtue immunizes them from error.

UNETHICAL ETHICISTS

Ethical knowledge is not ethical know-how. Even seasoned ethics experts fall prey to old-fashioned vices. William Bennett, education secretary under President Ronald Reagan and drug policy czar for the elder President George Bush, published nearly a dozen books on ethics for both adults and children. After the publication of the best-selling *Book of Virtues,* his name became synonymous with regard for traditional moral traits like self-discipline and compassion for the less fortunate. But then it was revealed in the media that the devout Catholic moralist was a lavishly self-indulgent casino gambler. Bennett had spent $8 million on casino gambling in a single decade. In light of criticism from religious and political supporters, Mr. Bennett was forced to disavow his gambler's life, saying he had "done too much gambling" and promising to give up the Las Vegas scene to avoid setting a bad example.[12]

The list of prominent religious moralists in public life who have committed what they themselves eventually admit are ethical blunders is long. The Reverend Jesse Jackson went on that list a few years ago when it came to light that the married minister and civil rights leader had fathered a child by another woman. As the number of Catholic priests now on the list for sexual offenses becomes astounding, the agony of the Roman Catholic Church is nearly audible. Rabbi Fred Neulander, who was convicted of hiring a hit man to murder his wife, once led one of New Jersey's largest synagogues. Although he may belong to a special class of spiritual offenders, people make mistakes, even learned moral advisors.

GETTING TO TUT

A*krasia* is a major stumbling block to ethical compliance. Another stumbling block to good choices is the tendency to temporarily disengage ethics and act from calculated self-interest to get what you badly want. When it is easy and sensible to comply with ethical rules, you do. Suppose, for example, you are an art buff, and it means everything to you to see a certain temporary art exhibit at a museum. You go to the museum, take your place in a mercifully short line and purchase tickets. The thought of lying your way to the front of the line by claiming to be a museum member entitled to special privileges never crosses your mind.

Now imagine that you arrive at the museum and the line is quite long. You figure you will have a wait of at least two hours. You briefly consider subterfuge to cut to the front of the queue. But after thinking it over you decide against it as a matter of ethics and etiquette. You know subterfuge is not right. You also know you would be embarrassed if dishonesty failed, and that you will eventually get into the museum anyway. Patiently awaiting your turn seems most sensible.

But what about when complying with familiar ethical rules does not appear at all smart? In 1977, five friends and I took a late night train from

I had no genuine justifications for breaking my own moral rules, and I had no excuses, either. I was not mentally incompetent. I was not brought up in an amoral home with neglectful parents. I simply blundered.

=================

Ann Arbor to Chicago to see the spectacular Treasures of Tutankhamen exhibit of Egyptian artifacts at the Field Museum. The King Tut show set the standard for all future blockbuster museum exhibitions. During its four-month run, 2.2 million people turned out to see the show. We arrived at the museum in the wee hours of the morning, only to find that about two thousand other art-lovers had gotten there first and were waiting in a thick, drowsy line many blocks long. Some had tents and sleeping bags. If my group had taken our rightful place at the end of the line as we ought, we would never have been admitted to the museum that day. So, taking advantage of a certain amount of mob confusion that erupted near the entranceway as the museum's opening drew near, we insinuated ourselves into the line near the front and were rewarded with precious entry tickets. Breaking line had been the only way to get into the building, so we cut line, we "smart" university students, like a bunch of middle schoolers at a first-run Saturday matinee movie, without much by way of serious internal moral struggle. No little angels at war that time.

Hundreds who had waited in line for hours longer than we had were turned away, unable to obtain tickets. My group, on the other hand, had a fabulous time. The dazzling exhibit was everything we hoped it would be. Some in my group were moved to tears to at last see the objects of rare African beauty we had only read about. We went home with souvenir posters and postcards, completely satisfied. My friends were socially cooperative and morally decent people, but we were motivated by calculated self-interest rather than a desire to do what was right. When ethics stand in the way of what people consider important personal goals, like prestige or higher incomes, many of us become pragmatists. Not impulsive or agonized wrongdoers, but wrongdoers who have judged it clever to temporarily sidestep the ethical domain.

TOO SMART FOR ETHICS

Very few ethical rule breakers are simply uncaring, evil people. For that reason, I am not interested here in addressing the small number of morally bankrupt individuals who intentionally flout ethical standards out of complete indifference to others. (The existence of evil in the world is a daunting concern in its own right. Philosopher Susan Neiman examines natural and human evil in riveting detail in an award winning book, *Evil in Modern Thought: An Alternative History of Philosophy.*[13]) My focus is people like you and me, who are generally well-meaning but who stumble when advancing our interests in the face of other values. Decent people will do the wrong thing when the voice of the better self is drowned out by the din of impulse. But decent people also do the wrong thing in a more calculated, clearheaded fashion. We do wrong when it seems like the sensible, pragmatic thing to do. We all have our King Tut exhibits. The demands of ethics clash with the seemingly smart demands of rational self-interest, and we elect to do what is "smart."

This is how I understand the actions of corporate officers, accountants, bankers and brokers whose ethical misconduct has recently come to light. They were too smart to be held back by mere ethics. On smaller scales, many of us do what those business executives have done. We set aside ethics and seize the opportunity for financial or other gain, for example, when our better, ethical self says "submit a truthful tax return." Some of us will wage an internal battle at that moment and others with similar needs will simply take self-interest as a conclusive reason to act: "Lie, because everyone does it; your chances of getting audited are very low, and you badly need a new car."

Akrasia is a philosopher's puzzle about reconciling practical reason and action. But both weakness of will and "smart" situational pragmatism are much more. They are also key practical concerns for personal morality and public policy. We have to worry, as a society, that educating children and professionals with ethical facts and norms will not protect us from costly ethics scandals like Enron. We teach rules, we enact and promulgate ethics laws, and people are still overpowered by temptation and driven by self-interest. Our lenient ethos backfires.

LENIENT ETHOS

Mainstream American ethics have a lenient quality. We are compassionate. We embrace ethical judgment but recoil at moralism. Tolerance is the pervasive ethos of American ethics. For example, mainstream ethics tolerate individuality and nonconformity, setting many aspects of lifestyle aside from the province of moral governance. Although many American families and individuals embrace far-reaching moral regimes mandated by religions that closely dictate clothing, eating and sexuality, those ways of life fall to varying degrees outside of the secular mainstream. The Amish of Lancaster County live a nineteenth-century lifestyle with neither automobiles, television sets, nor electricity. As such they dwell considerably outside the secular mainstream and are unique among American religions as well.

Mainstream ethics, both secular and religious, are also slow to blame people for erroneous but heartfelt choices. "They mean well," we say. For many years, the complex issue of "spanking" and "beating" children was like this for me. I did not want to blame parents. "They are trying to do what is best," I reasoned. Although I viewed physical discipline as harming the innocent, I knew most members of my own family and ethnic group felt differently. Many African Americans adhere to the Old Testament warning that parents who spare the rod spoil the child. Moreover, African Americans have heightened concerns about the consequences for their children of social deviance. Although I readily condemn spanking children today, I was slow to blame loving parents who believe it best to spank their children, and I felt they might even be justified in the choice they made, especially if they had listened to all sides of the controversy and sorted through the evidence.

However, the case against striking children has grown compelling. A number of countries have moved to outlaw corporal punishment of children: in 2000 Israel joined a group that also includes the Scandinavian countries, plus Austria and Italy. The state of Minnesota has banned corporal punishment, as have two dozen others. Some psychologists believe hitting children fosters fear, resentment and abusive personalities. Michigan

State University law professor Susan H. Bitensky advocates tougher anti-spanking laws on the ground that corporal punishment is state-sanctioned violence.[14] Her view is shared by many child welfare advocates. I certainly have memories of morally incomprehensible childhood whippings. Once, when I was six, I sneaked a bit of ham from the refrigerator, knowing it was forbidden. I got caught by my great-grandmother, who whipped me with a switch I had to pull from a peach tree. On another occasion, when I was seven, my mother called upstairs and asked me to throw her a bed pillow. I took her literally and tossed a pillow down the stairs. She had expected me to bring the pillow to her and therefore beat me with a jumping rope so hard that I went to school with welts on my legs the next day.

Americans are too comfortable with violence and may therefore not be disposed to subject it to the full moral scrutiny it deserves. A passion for nonviolence once got me knocked silly. In an attempt to prove that physical retaliation is human nature, a college classmate, with whom I had been debating the possibility of pacifism, slapped me hard in the face. He was sure I would strike him back. Maybe I should have, but I won the argument with Harry Underwood by walking away horrified.

To further complicate matters, ethical obligation is ultimately more subtle than categorical statements of familiar imperatives like "Do not cheat" or "Do not lie" reveal. General ethical rules have exceptions. For example, deception is wrong, but fooling the enemy about strategic troop movement is not considered unethical. Lying to a mugger about the contents of one's wallet is not considered unethical either (trying to deceive a mugger might be less safe, though, than handing over a wallet in silence). Moralists have debated the question of lying to the unjust for centuries and nearly all agree that it is morally permissible to use deception to protect oneself and other innocent people from dangerous wrongdoers.

In addition to *exceptions*, ethical obligation is also open to *excuses* and *justifications*. Small children, for example, have an excuse for not living up to society's standards. The mentally retarded do as well, a sentiment reflected in the decision of the Supreme Court in *Atkins v. Virginia* (2002) to disallow the execution of retarded persons convicted of serious crime.[15] Illness and mental illness are bona fide excuses: not keeping a promise is forgiven in a person with Alzheimer's; an impulsive theft or a grandiose lie by a person suffering from active schizophrenia is not recognized as wrongdoing but as mental illness. Criminal law also incorporates mental illness as an excuse for wrongdoing. In July 2001, former Congressman Edward M. Mezvinsky, an Iowa Democrat, pled not guilty by reason of insanity to dozens of counts of fraud and other financial and professional crimes. Mezvinsky spent his clients' money, passed bad checks and fabricated financial documents to back up bogus African investment schemes. Over a ten-year period Mezvinsky cheated family members, banks and acquaintances out of more than $10 million. Lawyer Mark E. Cedrone said his client's "bizarre financial investments" resulted from untreated bipolar disorder, worsened through use of the antimalarial drug Lariam.[16] Mezvinsky pled guilty after a federal judge ruled that he could not plead mental illness because his expert witnesses had not linked his alleged brain abnormalities to his capacity to deceive. Mezvinsky was eventually sentenced to six and a half years in prison. Most people with bipolar disorder do not appear ill to casual onlookers, and lead fairly typical lives. Those like Mezvinsky who admit to having the illness for the first time to escape criminal conviction are bound to look suspect—good excuses are not always believable. The ones to watch out for are the routinely bad excuses we offer ourselves.

Honest ignorance can be a legitimate excuse for wrongdoing. People sometimes cheat without knowing that what they do is cheating. Consider the young adult who does not realize that hobby earnings are taxable income and that the law defines nonpayment as unlawful. Although the error, if detected, could result in a tax penalty, nonpayment in that case would not be considered unethical or prosecuted as a crime.

Moral diversity is sometimes offered as an excuse for violating ethical principles. It is a bad excuse, though, when it is opportunistic. Genuine nonopportunistic moral diversity exists in the United States. For example, we have immigrants from countries where polygamy is lawfully practiced and who genuinely believe polygamy is good. Polygamy is part of their culture and the structure of their beliefs about family life. I had a law student in my constitutional law class a few years ago who defended polygamy. She herself was the fourth wife of an African. She said she enjoyed the freedom of being married without the responsibilities of her husband's first and second wives, whose dutiful performances back home allowed her the freedom to pursue her education in the United States. A better example of American moral diversity may be the fact that some people believe drinking alcohol is wrong and others do not. We tend to be tolerant of moral diversity concerning legal acts like drinking and premarital adult sex. We can respect people who say, "It's okay for you, but it's not for me. I have different values." An aspect of the lenient tendency in American ethics has been an openness to moral relativism of this sort.

However, wrongdoers are prone to run from blame using a broadbrush appeal to diversity: "What I did was not wrong; I have different values than you." An argument like this has to be suspect when the person making it has otherwise always seemed to share values with the rest of the community. But arguments like this are not suspect when the person making it is a stranger to the community. A few years ago Danish actress Annette Sorensen left her baby in a carriage outside of a New York City restaurant while she and the baby's American father, Exavier Wardlaw, dined. The police were called when locals assumed the baby had been abandoned. Sorensen and Wardlaw claimed cultural differences as an excuse for their violation of New York child protection standards, which landed them in jail for two nights and their fourteen-month-old daughter in foster care for four days. I found Sorensen's explanation for abandoning her daughter credible only because on a visit to Scandinavia a dozen years ago, I observed the trusting practice of parking perambulators outside of shops on busy city streets. Manhattan authorities eventually bought the cultural difference argument and dropped criminal charges. However, an angry Sorensen filed a $20 million civil suit against the city for false arrest and malicious prosecution.

In the United States, Americans of diverse backgrounds share a great many basic values that provide a common framework for assessing right and wrong. This should not be surprising. To begin with, the structure of our lives is similar. In youth and middle age, families, friends, schools, religions and jobs crowd the days. At retirement, medical care and leisure take over. Exposure to popular culture is a lifelong homogenizing force, contributing to commonly held values. The television we watch, movies we see and music we listen to convey messages about how we ought to treat one another and discharge our duties. Children and adolescents are especially receptive. Parents like me complain that our stern moral messages are drowned out by the din of ubiquitous advertising.

Law shapes shared values. A nation tends to internalize the standards of appropriate and inappropriate conduct imposed by its laws. Legal values become moral values. The opposite is also true. Moral values also become legal values. "In civilized life, law floats on a sea of ethics," Chief Justice Earl Warren once wrote.[17] Law is a human creation that reflects the moral or ethical values of its creators. The law we are glad to live under inspires and reinforces moral prohibitions against killing, theft, assault, fraud, negligence and discrimination. Of course, law need not reflect public morality perfectly. Driving faster than the posted limit, smoking marijuana, and assisting the suicide of a terminally ill partner are illegal acts that not everyone would deem immoral.

Developments in biomedical science influence values in commonly experienced ways. What people can do affects what people will do. What people do in turn shapes communal beliefs about what people ought to do. Now that safe, affordable medicines are effective against common illnesses, for example, we think it best to readily administer them. Most everyone would view it as reprehensible for a parent to let a child who would benefit from antibiotics suffer through a bout of strep throat without treatment. Parents who do not seek medical care face moral disapproval and possible intervention by child welfare authorities.

Developments in technology also influence values in commonly experienced ways. For example, the multicultural, teched-up practice of carrying cell phones has had a norm-shaping impact. The invention of small affordable mobile phones led Americans to begin purchasing them in droves. In 2003, the Cellular Communications and Internet Association estimated that half of all Americans—148 million people—had cell phones. The phone booth is virtually a relic. Now that we carry phones, we are all beginning to believe that we ought to carry phones. It feels selfish to turn the phone off and irresponsible to leave home without it. We are supposed to remain in close touch with family and friends at all times.

OUR ETHICAL DIVERSITY

Genuine moral diversity introduces complexity into assessing con-duct and character. It cannot be swept under the rug to make things seem easier than they are. For all the similarity in our values, at least four broad dimensions of ethical disagreement pervade our communal lives. We disagree about where to look for guidance; about ideal lifestyles for ourselves and our families; about priorities for the use of our time and money; and—if and when we turn our minds to it—about ethical theory.

First, we disagree about where to look for ethical guidance because we live by different spiritual philosophies. We mine discrepant texts and great books for truth. Fortunately, people with dissimilar lodestars can share similar moral and ethical concerns. One person may find inspiration in modern Western philosophies, another in traditional Eastern philoso-phies; and yet both can conclude that kindness is a moral imperative. One person may rely on the Koran, another, the Bible; and yet both value char-ity. One person may keep *Bullfinch's Mythology* on her night table, another the Egyptian *Book of the Dead,* a third the *Kabbalah*; yet all three can seek to better understand the moral meanings of life and death.

We do hold meaningfully divergent, even antagonistic, beliefs. Eth-nic and religious differences provoke substantive moral disagreement that cannot be ignored in an effort at civility. Distinctive religions are vital to the ways many of us believe we must mark our happiest occasions, including childbirth and marriage. Religion is also vital to the way we manage the saddest moments of our lives. This was confirmed on September 11, 2001. In response to an unprecedented American disaster, people flocked to churches, synagogues and mosques for days. Dr. Eugene C. Bay, Pres-byterian pastor in Bryn Mawr, Pennsylvania, was not surprised that his congregation crowded into the sanctuary on the Sunday after 9/11. "I knew you would be here," he preached that Sunday. "Where else would you go?" Strikingly, in terrible times not only our own religions but other people's religions may be a great source of comfort. On September 15, 2001, the first person in line to attend the memorial mass at Saint Patrick's Cathedral celebrated for the victims of September 11 was not a Roman Catholic but a man who said he was Jewish. He arrived five hours early to secure entry. I was not a member of the Presbyterian church at the time (I have subsequently joined), but I sat among Dr. Bay's faithful the Sunday after the Twin Towers went down. I was seeking the comfort of community to ease my fear and grief.

A second dimension of moral disagreement is the divergence of lifestyles—clothing, diet and intimacy—some tied to membership in religious or cultural groups, some not. Sally is a strict vegetarian. She, her husband, Steve, and their two children do not eat meat or wear leather. But they are tolerant of people who do; our families have spent happy hours together in my meat-eating, leather-wearing home. I have photographs of her children romping with mine on the big brown leather sofas in my family room. Sally and Steve do not turn their visits into moral confrontations over the ethical treatment of animals.

Peaceful ethical variety about lifestyles persists through minority-group assimilation. I was recently reminded of this when I listened to Peter, an Asian American colleague, describe Buddhist principles and Chinese traditions that dictated arrangements for the funeral and burial of his beloved grandmother. I was reminded again when a Cuban American whom I was helping with a legal problem told me he would seek a favorable resolution to his case by sacrificing live chickens in the name of a spirit with whom he believes I have an affinity. I was reminded yet again when my congenial research assistant turned down an invitation for lunch. She keeps kosher but does not think ill of me because I eat shellfish. She dresses modestly, and I wear short skirts. But Ruth does not expect a Gentile to live the life of an Orthodox Jew. She is content to live and let live when it comes to such matters.

A third dimension of disagreement is disagreement about priorities. Even individuals from the same ethnic group or social class clash over ethical priorities, which leads them to differ about what should be done in individual cases. Marta and I are alike in many ways. We are about the same age, are married to lawyers, have children who play soccer, and live in the suburbs of Philadelphia. I believe in kindness toward animals and so does she. But Marta is willing to spend serious money on surgery for an aging house pet that is like a member of her family, whereas I have no pets and channel my extra time and cash toward human charities.

Finally, there is widespread disagreement about ethical theory. In the 1970s the University of Michigan boasted three top senior ethicists on its faculty. Their presence made the Ann Arbor campus something of a Mecca for anyone interested in ethical theory. I found the Michigan moral philosophy crew intriguing. They shared basic moral beliefs. They each opposed lying, cheating, stealing, racial discrimination and so forth. But each held a contrasting theory of morality. They mainly agreed about "normative" ethics—the term philosophers used at the time to denote conceptions of what people in concrete situations should and should not do. But they mainly disagreed about "meta-ethics"—the term used for abstract theories of moral truth and knowledge.

One member of the faculty, Charles Stevenson, propounded an emotive theory of ethics. He argued that moral value judgments are neither true or false; they are emotional expressions of approval or disapproval. "Lying is wrong" means something akin to "I disapprove of lying" or "I do not like lying." My teacher Bill Frankena nicknamed his colleague's emotive approach the "Yeah!/Boo!" theory of morality. Yeah, honesty! Boo, lying! Frankena defended morality as a vital enterprise encompassing duties and virtues, motivated by care. Frankena rejected the view that moral evaluations are simply expressions of personal pro or con feelings; however, he also rejected the view that moral evaluations like "lying is wrong" are statements of fact like "snow is white." He argued that we are expressing approval or disapproval when we make moral judgments; but we are also making statements that we believe everyone who takes the moral point of view and is clearheaded ought to agree with.

The third ethicist, Richard Brandt, was the man who supervised my dissertation. Brandt rejected the belief that ethical judgments are reducible to subjective or shared feelings. He argued instead that moral assertions are best modeled as rational utilitarian judgments about whether particular moral codes promote welfare.[18] After I got my Ph.D. and he retired, Professor Brandt and I became friends, but he never persuaded me to adopt his moral theory. In fact, most days he seemed to me like a walking advertisement against the interest-maximizing school. For example, once he phoned me to ask whether he had a moral obligation to pick up his grandchildren at the airport, even though he preferred not to go out. (He said he decided to consult me because I had written a dissertation on children's rights.) I urged my friend to put aside cost/benefit analyses when it came to dealing with his personal life. Pick up the grandkids! But Brandt was incorrigible, and I learned that he applied utilitarianism to dating, too. I once asked him why a man of seventy like himself preferred to pursue women decades younger. The question put a twinkle in his eye. "I get turned down a lot," he admitted, "but the pleasure I get from each rare success outweighs the pain of frequent failure."

For specialists, ethics has the engaging elements of an unsolved mystery that invites dispute. Centuries of disputation preceded ours and centuries will surely follow. Many Western philosophers have argued that in making sound ethical judgments we rely on feeling, instinct or intuition; others have stressed the centrality of learning or reason. Some posit a divine origin for ethics, and others locate the basis of ethics in human nature, history or custom. While there are those who view ethics as an impartial, principled appeal to categorical absolutes, there are also those who view ethics as narrative, situational and contextual. A number stress the need to follow rules and principles; others stress the display of virtue. While some say we should judge conduct and outcomes, others say we need to consider inner motivations. On the subject of the ultimate motivations behind ethical conduct, moral philosophers also part company. Some insist on the possibility of pure, selfless altruism, while others theorize that strategic self-interest is the ultimate basis of what we exalt as human morality. Indeed, social scientists have hypothesized that if the human animal does not more often deceive, rob and kill, it is only because it knows human society takes punishing revenge.

Ethical theory, like music theory and literary theory, has value as a humanistic discipline that occasionally produces enduring cultural products. Ethical theory also has social value as a platform for reform. The nineteenth-century British utilitarians John Stuart Mill and Jeremy Bentham defended controversial ethical theories and were also some of the most notable social innovators of their day. Bentham took a special interest in the criminal law; Mill, in civil liberties and women's rights. Neither Bertrand Russell, Jean-Paul Sartre nor Hannah Arendt were content to work purely in the realm of abstract theory.

Leading contemporary philosophers debate theory but also actively seek to engage the real world about matters of importance. The premier legal philosopher in the United States, Ronald Dworkin, has defended affirmative action, abortion rights and the right to die. The daughter of Nobel Prize winners Alva and Gunner Myrdal, philosopher Sissela Bok has been a voice for personal integrity, humane science and peace. Philosopher Douglas Husak has taken on drug policy; Preston Covey, gun control; and Eva Kittay, caregiving. The controversial Princeton ethicist Peter Singer is famous for making a moral case for animal rights and infamous for making a moral case against the rights of some severely and hopelessly disabled humans. When it comes to animal rights, he can be persuasive. A guiltless meat-eater, I gave up veal for years after reading one of Singer's early articles in *The New York Review of Books* describing cruelty toward calves destined for the dinner plate.

The four dimensions of ethical disagreement just described— divergence of lodestar, lifestyle, priority and theory—loom large. They reflect the diversity of people in the world. To be sure, there is cultural variation: a gratuity in one country is considered a bribe in another. One country's interrogation is another's torture. One country's female circumcision is another's genital mutilation. Yet societies enshrine shared ethical ideals of freedom, nonviolence and fairness into law. Honesty, loyalty, courage and other ethical ideals reign internationally as imperatives of social life. The consensus found in the world's recognized ethical standards could stand as evidence that the most important values are timeless and universal. Philosophers conjecture that societies around the world and throughout time have settled upon similar ethical ideals to address commonly experienced human problems. I, too, believe the moral rules that elicit cooperation in one society faced with greed, indifference, envy and scarce resources will look a lot like the moral rules required in neighboring and distant societies faced with the same impediments to well-being. Our diversity and disagreements are real, but they will not typically undermine the fairness of the expectation that the people around us adhere to basic principles of human cooperation.

COST OF COMPASSION

In the light of the many widely embraced exceptions, excuses and justifications to general rules, any notion that being ethical requires unwavering adherence to strictly construed general rules is out of sync with contemporary ethical theory and popular practice. Ethical leniency makes for a compassionate realm of practical responsibility. Compassion is good; yet the atmosphere of moral leniency potentially invites running from blame. When contemplating or committing wrong, we can be eager to believe we fall into some category of blamelessness that makes our ethical rule breaking acceptable. When unethical options begin to look attractive, every layperson is liable to become a lawyer. The better self is overwhelmed by a dazzling brief of logical exceptions, excuses and justifications that really amount to mere rationalization.

The foundation of ethical know-how is knowledge of applicable ethical standards. But more is required if weakness of will and deliberate self-interested deviance from standards are not to undermine ethics. Every responsible moral agent needs to be familiar with the catalogue of typical reasons we give ourselves for deviating from common ethical rules. The ability to live in accord with ethical values requires self-awareness of the characteristic intellectual moves of the weak will and the calculating heart.

Despite our differences, contemporary Americans have a thick bedrock of shared ethical expectations. We therefore can join in collective efforts to turn the tide on wrongdoing. Stronger on ethical knowledge than ethical know-how, we need to emphasize workable approaches to making ethical breaches less attractive and less likely. Cheating is the perfect illustration of a major category of ethical failure that we as individuals and a society can do something about. The ethical case against cheating is weighty, and the fact that cheating often involves unethical lying and promise breaking only adds to its low standing. Ethical know-how can reduce the incidence of weak-willed cheating, "smart" cheating, and all sorts of running from blame.

CHAPTER 2

CHEATING, THE BIG MISTAKE

I f we were to make a list of the top ten moral rules, "do not cheat" would have to be somewhere on the list. Our laws and public policies condemn cheating. Our religions and moralities condemn cheating.[1] "Do not cheat" failed to make an explicit appearance on the stone tablets Moses brought down from the mountain.[2] However, cheating is a major category of ethical transgression today, and contemporary moralists often speak out against it. The moral philosopher Bernard Gert includes "do not cheat" on his list of imperatives.[3] The anticheating rule clearly belongs with Gert's nine other choices: do not kill; do not cause pain; do not disable; do not deprive of freedom; do not deprive of pleasure; do not lie; keep your promises; do not commit adultery; and do not steal. Gert argues that cheating is the paradigm of all moral misconduct. Cheating, Gert concludes, "provides in miniature the nature of immoral action."[4] Immoral persons knowingly violate rules of social cooperation that apply impartially to all. So do cheaters.

To cheat is to intentionally gain advantage over other people by violating standards of fair play.[5] Standards of fair play include laws, as in the statutes violated by insider traders and tax evaders; nonlegal rules, as in the strictures of chess or baseball; and moral or ethical principles, such as the promise keeping principle violated by adulterers. The provisions of codes of conduct, such as a university's honor code or a profession's code of ethical responsibility, are also standards of fair play.

We know cheating is not right, but we do it anyway. Cheating is not simply prevalent. In some sectors cheating has begun to look like a moral epidemic. Most ethicists agree that dishonesty is justified in an extreme situation: it is fine to thwart a kidnapper or to depose a ruthless dictator. Contemporary Americans, however, commonly cheat and rarely face kidnappers or dictators. Americans cheat in entirely ordinary circumstances. We are starting to look like a culture of cheaters, unwilling or unable to reign in the vice.

A DISHONEST ECONOMY

In recent years the media has been filled with stunning examples of cheating that involve billions of dollars, major institutions and national leaders. While only the people who profit big-time to further selfish ends earn the label "cheater," nearly everyone cheats a little in some corner of their lives. Many of us supplement our wealth by breaking the law. Any serious attempt to describe the U.S. economy must understand the structures that allow workers to "rob, cheat, short-change, pilfer and fiddle customers, employers, subordinates and the state."[6]

Placed in charge of deciding where to invest Connecticut pension funds, former state treasurer Paul J. Silvester invested in companies that paid him kickbacks. A federal investigation led to criminal charges of money laundering and racketeering, and a guilty plea; in November 2003, Silvester was sentenced to jail. Other Connecticut employees have done more than take home paper clips, too. At the University of Connecticut's Environmental Research Institute lab employees stole tens of thousands of dollars while the chief laboratory director, Professor George Hoag was preoccupied with his lucrative, $1.3 million outside consulting gigs. According to a report of the state attorney general, employees solicited charitable donations from the public that never went to fund the lab as promised. Lab employees Robert Carley and Shili Liu were convicted of charging unsuspecting international students rent for housing that had already been paid for, hoarding thousands of dollars in extorted cash on lab premises.

Cheating was part of the old economy and it is a part of the new economy.[7] Cheating a business partner can mean secretly taking more profits from the company than allowed under contract. Cheating a customer can mean intentionally overbilling for services or skimping on construction materials. In June 2003, Sprint paid $5.5 million to settle accusations that it had fraudulently overbilled the Justice Department. In August 2003, the Sprint company was accused by the General Services Administration of overbilling the federal government by $2 million for its telephone services. Sprint said the jumbo billing error was inadvertent and no punitive action was taken. Cheating on the job can mean obtaining employment with a padded resume. It can involve claiming to have worked unworked hours, taking bribes, selling stock on insider information, or "late day" trading within the $7 trillion mutual fund industry.[8]

The scale of corporate bankruptcies in which cheating by management played a causal role is enormous. The WorldCom bankruptcy, the largest in history at the time, involved billions in admitted accounting irregularities. Insider trading, sham transactions and accounting irregularities amount to massive unethical cheating by executives, shareholders, accountants and bankers. Judging by the public reaction to its bankruptcy, the cheating of which Enron executives were accused violated the public's ethical values as well as the laws. But the business world often seems to operate with its own standards. Cheating in business occurs in part because businesspeople's decisions and ultimate conduct are shaped not only by society's general culture but also by "company, personal, situational and industry standards."[9] The sad truth may be that the general culture tolerates cheating, and business culture tolerates what I sardonically call "smart" cheating even more.

Research on business students carries grave implications for the ethics of corporate managers.[10] Research by Donald L. McCabe suggests that business majors cheat more than other students.[11] A study of business students in which a large number of students admitted cheating but only a small number reported cheating by peers, "should be sobering for managers" who might like to count on whistle-blowing to curb corporate misconduct.[12]

That the elite business world is still dominated by men is an interesting fact to ponder in light of what research suggests about the gender differentials among cheaters. Although some researchers say women lie more often than men because they engage in more social interactions on average than men, several studies suggest that men may be more likely to cheat. In one study, little boys cheated more often than little girls on a puzzle-completion task promising a prize at task's end.[13] The most typical college cheaters are younger males with low grades. Surveying the period following September 11, 2001, Professor Anita Hill noted that the most high-profile government and corporate whistle-blowers to emerge had been women. Three women, Cynthia Cooper, Coleen Rowley and Sherron Watkins, were named "Persons of the Year" in 2002 by *Time* magazine for bringing to light troubles at WorldCom, the FBI and Enron, respectively. Hill's theory is that women remain marginalized in the corporate hierarchy to such a degree that they do not develop strong bonds of loyalty to wrongdoers and are therefore more likely to turn in unethical peers. She herself was one of the most famous whistle-blowers of the twentieth-century, appearing before Congress in 1991 to accuse Supreme Court nominee Clarence Thomas of sexual harassment.

UNIVERSITY OF CHEATING

Many colleges and universities have proud student honor codes. The honor codes of the U.S. Military Academy and the U.S. Air Force Academy state "We will not lie, steal or cheat, nor tolerate among us anyone who does."[14] But can students be trusted? With the help of a cheat-detector computer program of his own design, University of Virginia physics professor Lou Bloomfield uncovered 122 cases of plagiarism among his science students in 2001.[15] The professor subsequently erected a "Plagiarism Resource Site" on the Web to help other teachers ferret out student misconduct. The World Wide Web may be a better resource for cheaters than cheat detectors, however. A Web seminar on electronic plagiarism erected by Le Moyne College librarian Gretchen Pearson of Syracuse, New York, lists more than two dozen Web sites that offer academic papers for sale. The total number of free cheat sites may number in the thousands. Students of history, philosophy, politics, literature and African American studies can easily copy term papers on standard topics. Students of religion and ethics have their cheat sites, too.

Cheating is prevalent in secondary schools, colleges and universities. Cheating in higher education is an especially well studied phenomenon. Researchers have investigated whether, how, when and why students cheat. They have examined how one can be sure students have cheated, what students perceive as cheating and what we can do to reduce the incidence of cheating.[16] Student cheating is lavishly studied in part because most social-science researchers are university professors with easy access to student subjects. The youngest college and university students are less mature than typical adults; nevertheless, what social scientists learn about student ethics may have important implications for our understanding of the ethics of the mature adult professionals, parents and citizens that students quickly become.

Surveys conducted by the Josephson Institute of Ethics suggests student dishonesty has been on the rise. Eight out of ten high school students say they cheat. Academic researchers worry that contemporary students may have "a diminished sense of academic integrity."[17] A number of academic studies of students in the natural and social sciences indicate significant increases in unauthorized collaboration and serious exam cheating in the past thirty years. However, we need to be careful when interpreting cheating studies, some of which draw broad conclusions from data relating to a single examination or homework exercise. Student research subjects may over-report cheating among their peers because they view cheating as the favored response on survey questionnaires.[18] Although no one knows for sure whether the percentage of cheaters or the frequency of cheating is increasing overall, experts agree that cheating is pervasive and accepted as normal by students in American colleges and universities.

While American law, professional ethics, religion, secular morality and common sense are united in opposition to nearly all forms of cheating, their combined influence has been inadequate to stop academic dishonesty. Calling greater attention to cheating as an ethical issue could conceivably lead some student cheaters to refrain from dishonesty, although nearly all schools have adopted rules, codes, and policies that plainly condemn cheating. Handbooks, brochures and Internet materials detail what counts as cheating and how failures of academic integrity are harmful. However, students need to know not only that cheating is unethical but also how to avoid cheating when the pressure is on and so many others seem to be doing it without getting caught. A number of schools have tried to address that problem, but some students are determined to cheat and keep cheating.

In a study of 663 undergraduates at a southern university, 56 percent of whom identified themselves as cheaters or potential cheaters on two actual exams, the "cheaters indicated that they would continue cheating." The cheaters even suggested that "the teacher should ignore cheaters."[19] Luckily for unreformed cheaters, many professors do ignore cheating. The results of a national survey of psychology professors suggest that professors ignore cheating to minimize stress, to cope with fears of retaliation or legal challenges, and to avoid thankless drains on time and wasted effort. Professors also disregard cheating to avoid punishing the easily detected bumblers while the more clever offenders go free.[20]

I can attest to the price paid by faculty who hold college cheaters accountable. Early in my career, I once spent days dealing with what should have been a simple cheating case. Two Carnegie Mellon undergraduates in my required *ethics* class swore they had not cheated, even though the two not-so-clever young men turned in papers identical in every way, down to elaborate doodles in the margins. I flunked the pair after listening to hours of denials and plaintive pleas. Cheaters often run from blame by taking advantage of their procedural due process rights under university disciplinary rules. Indeed, I have spent months as defense counsel and also as a prosecutor in proceedings brought against law student cheaters caught red-handed. The wrongdoers could have pled guilty but chose to prolong their cases looking for every conceivable loophole in the student honor code.

College seniors and recent graduates have found the temptation to cheat on standardized tests irresistible. The GRE, (Graduate Record Examination) administered by the New Jersey-based Educational Testing Service is a standardized test required for admission to universities offering masters and doctoral degrees in the sciences and humanities. Columbia University students were arrested as principals in a GRE cheating ring in 2002, the same year the ETS suspended computer-based GRE testing in Asia due to apparent widespread security breaches. In 1996, test takers paid thousands to a cheating ring headed by Po Chieng Ma (a.k.a. George Kobayashi), who pleaded guilty to conspiracy and obstruction of justice. With the help of coded pencils and cell phones, questions and answers were transmitted to university applicants who took three exams, the GRE, the GMAT (Graduate Management Admissions Test) required of elite business schools, and the TOEFL (Test of English as a Foreign Language) required of some non–U.S.-born university applicants.

BAD SPORTS

An article in the February 1, 1999, *Sports Illustrated* magazine bore a disturbing headline: "Lying is Sweeping the Nation."[21] Published ten years after Pete Rose was banned from baseball for gambling on his sport, the article identified numerous examples of duplicity and dishonesty in professional, collegiate and amateur sports. The sports world is full of fair competitors and a few too many cheaters—cheating athletes, cheating coaches and cheating administrators.

In 2003, the president of Saint Bonaventure University resigned after revelations that he had permitted his school to recruit an ineligible player to play NCAA basketball. Late in 2001, an ethics scandal sent Notre Dame's newly hired head football coach out looking for a new job: George O'Leary resigned after an investigative journalist uncovered that he had lied for years about a supposed three-year football career at the University of New Hampshire and a master's degree from New York University.[22] The 2002 Salt Lake Olympic Games were ethically tainted before they opened. Utah organizers paid extravagant incentives to members of the

International Olympic Committee charged with selecting the host city. Lloyd Ward, former head of the U.S. Olympic Committee, was forced out in March 2003 for fraud. Investigating Republican Senators Ben Nighthorse Campbell of Colorado and Ted Stevens of Alaska uncovered evidence that Ward channeled business and perks to his family. Six other members of the troubled committee had been previously forced to step down for wrongdoing.

Olympic figure skating has been rife with ethics scandals, none more memorable than Tonya Harding's facing ethics charges under the amateur athletes' code of ethical behavior after her ex-husband Jeff Gillooly and bodyguard Shawn Eckardt conspired to bash ice skater Nancy Kerrigan in the knees. Some of Harding's friends said she was in on the plot to secure a spot for herself on the 1994 U.S. Olympic figure skating team. Harding never admitted a role larger than obstruction of justice. She was placed on probation and ordered to pay fines. She was allowed to participate in the Lillehammer Winter Olympics, but her performance was miserable.

Florence Griffith Joyner died suddenly at the age of thirty-eight after a brilliant Olympic career. She won three gold medals as well as a silver one amid allegations that she took human growth hormone and other drugs to achieve her meteoric rise.[23] It is not known for sure whether Griffith Joyner used prohibited drugs, but plenty of athletes reportedly do, and most are never caught. In 2003, four members of the Oakland Raiders football team tested positive for the steriod tetrahydrogestrinone (THG), a drug that, until recently, escaped detection using routine testing methods.

Basketball's good guys and bad guys have floundered off the court. The classy Michael Jordan faced the embarrassment of an extramarital affair with a woman to whom he paid $250,000 to keep quiet. Allen Iverson barely escaped a weapons charge after showing up armed at a relative's home looking for his wife. In July 2003, married superstar Kobe Bryant was charged with sexually assaulting a nineteen-year-old hotel employee with whom the star admitted to having had adulterous sex.

In 2004, national controversy erupted over the use of performance enhancing drugs by Major League baseball players. Even wholesome Little League baseball has not been exempted from ethical tarnish. On a hot summer day in 2001, a cool young New Yorker from the Dominican Republic named Danny Almonte pitched a perfect game for the Bronx-based Rolando Paulino All-stars. It was only a child's game, but this boy's team had a shot at the Little League World Series championship. Nearly fifty years had passed since a Little League pitcher had thrown a perfect game, and this twelve-year-old's rare performance happened in the play-offs, live, on national television. Fanfare and adulation followed the boy's achievement. But the celebrations were cut short by a shocking revelation; the boy was not twelve years old, as his coach and parents claimed, but fourteen—much too old to play in the Little League division he had just conquered. It appears that Danny's parents and team manager wanted the talented, ineligible teenager to play for the team so badly that they knowingly used a falsified birth certificate obtained from the Dominican Republic to get around the rules. They cheated. Little League officials swiftly moved to invalidate the team's Little League World Series third-place tournament finish and to ban the boy's father and team manager Rolando Paulino from further participation in Little League ball.

Newspapers soon reported that the team manager had been banned from play at least once before for similar infractions of the rules. You have to wonder: was this man a repeat offender because he thought age qualifications were unimportant when compared to giving talented minority youth an opportunity to develop their potential for college sports scholarships and lucrative careers as professional athletes? Or was he a recidivist because he was a self-aggrandizing competitor determined to win at any cost? According to Little League president Stephen D. Keener, "Clearly, adults have used Danny Almonte and his teammates in a most contemptible and despicable way," this, in a sport whose motto is "character, courage and loyalty."[24]

Dominican youth have few of the opportunities enjoyed by counterparts living in affluent U.S. suburbs. In the Dominican Republic, boys play baseball with sticks and with balls made of rags. Behind many instances of cheating is a strong desire to compete to victory against formidable contestants in a high stakes arena for scarce rewards and opportunities. Fairness would call for a level playing field and clean, honest competition. In an "our kind" versus "their kind" world lacking a consistent tradition of social justice, people may doubt that there really are level playing fields, or resent the level fields as barriers to victory craved by self-esteem, cheating to compensate.

WHY CHEATING IS WRONG

What we ourselves define as cheating, many of us do anyway. On the one hand, we share a deep-seated hatred of the cheat, colorfully described by journalist Natalie Angier as, "the transgressor of fair play, the violator of accepted norms, the sneak who smiles with Chiclet teeth while ladling from the community till."[25] On the other hand, cheating and cheaters are deeply rooted in American culture. It is hard to escape childhood with a clean record on cheating, and adulthood is a forest of fresh temptation.

Most of us are taught at a very early age that cheating is wrong, but it takes a while to figure out what counts as cheating. I innocently cheated as a first grader. I used to finish my classwork quickly and then allow other children to copy. I had no consciousness of wrongdoing. One minute I would break my snack-time cookies into tiny pieces to share them with classmates seated around me and the next minute I would slide my answers around the table to share them, too. As we grow up, we learn that sharing schoolwork is sometimes cheating. We also learn that life is full of opportunities to cheat, and that many otherwise good people are cheaters.

We do not like cheaters and may be hardwired not to. Sociobiologists speculate that human beings have evolved into a species with a rational dislike of individuals in our midst who take more than their fair share and give less than their fair share in return.[26] Cheaters force us to work harder or consume less for their benefit. We may also be hardwired to respond to cheaters in a way that reflects social hierarchy. One study concluded that we are three times less likely to look for cheaters when checking on individuals who are lower-ranking than equally high, equally low, or higher-ranking.[27] So executives suspect and detect cheating secretaries, who suspect and detect cheating mail clerks, who suspect and detect interns. This makes sense. It is easier to blow the whistle on someone perceived as less powerful.

The anticheating ethic presupposes that cheating is a moral wrong in personal life, an ethical failing in business and professional life. Behind this supposition are powerful conceptions of fairness. One major conception of why cheating others is wrong is that it is an injurious lack of reciprocity. By deviating from standards that others stick to, cheaters exempt themselves from standards of fair play, thereby injuring the legitimate interests of others, including others' equal interest in wealth, opportunity and self-respect. Whether in isolation or as part of a collusive group, cheaters violate reciprocity by exploiting others' compliant behavior to their own advantage. Cheaters are free riders. And some free riders simply do not care. Although "humans are remarkable within the animal kingdom for the extent to which they become involved in cooperative exchange,"[28] strategies of asocial conduct and free riding are also potentially rational strategies.[29] If cheating is potentially rational, calculating individuals will be tempted by it.

When "everyone" cheats—say, a whole classroom of test takers or an entire industry of auto dealerships—the problem goes beyond a failure of reciprocity. Communities of cheaters rebuff standards that frame schemes of cooperation, trust and merit. If a whole class of medical students cheats on a chemistry examination by passing around a stolen answer sheet, the class violates institutional trust. Through collusive deception, the students manage to cooperate with one another, but by the same token fail to cooperate with teachers and administrators. They also undermine the system of merit through which prospective physicians are evaluated and rewarded. Plainly, cheaters sometimes lack a sense of collective responsibility.[30] Since cheating is not always the rationally optimal strategy, social scientists agree that cheaters fail to understand that their own rational self-interest may require cooperation with authorities. "Smart" cheating may not be as smart as the rational calculator thinks.

The anticheating ethic mainly targets the practice of cheating other human individuals. Cheating oneself can also be an ethical concern. The Enlightenment philosopher Immanuel Kant maintained that we have a duty to show ourselves the same moral respect we show others. Consequently, we should no more victimize ourselves than we should victimize others. Under a Kantian worldview, grounds exist for moral concern about people who cheat themselves, whether by taking less than they are due or by forgoing opportunities. The extreme altruist is thus a potentially worrisome self-cheater. When told the story of an Asian American woman who won a midwestern state lottery but gave the money to Washington University in Saint Louis for a new law library, I wondered if she had not perhaps cheated herself by being imprudently generous. She subsequently went bankrupt. Perhaps the philanthropic-minded men who have made the news in recent years because they wanted to donate a second kidney, relegating themselves to a life of dialysis, wanted to cheat themselves out of good health.

For the theologically inclined, "cheating God" is a significant ethical failing, as serious as cheating a human competitor, the government or oneself. I recently heard someone argue that cloning body parts for lifesaving organ transplants would "cheat God" by extending the normal human life span. If cheating God is blameworthy, "cheating death" sometimes elicits praise and admiration, as we describe the lucky passenger who walks away unharmed from the fireball of an automobile collision.

On a more practical front, in addition to cheating flesh-and-blood human beings, the anticheating ethic targets cheating the government, companies and "the system," for the obvious reason that cheating those targets takes advantage of other people, too. The doped-up sprinter is taking unfair advantage both of the institution of sporting and of other individuals running her race. The tax evader is taking unfair advantage of the government and the individuals who comprise the political community. Both the sprinter who uses prohibited performance enhancing drugs and the tax evader are dishonest. At the core of the anticheating ethic is condemnation of unfair advantage-taking that victimizes either flesh-and-blood human beings or the valued institutions that serve flesh-and-blood human beings.

In the United States we are forced to compete with other people for many of the good and necessary things in life, so the playing field of competition should be level. This is a requirement of basic fairness. When I was a small child, the American system of government was something of a cheater. The nation's constitutional principles of liberty and equality were unfairly applied, giving whites and men undeserved advantages. The playing field was not level—not even close. Members of racial minority groups were barely allowed in the game, and white women faced enormous obstacles. The system was radically unfair to the poor. Eventually, tax-financed government programs distributed modest resources to the needy, especially after the mid-1960s. Landmark antidiscrimination laws passed by Congress, starting with the Civil Rights Act of 1964 and continuing into the 1990s with the Americans with Disabilities Act, greatly improved the situation of women, racial minorities and the disabled. State and local antidiscrimination measures have contributed to an even more broadly egalitarian legal order. For example, although federal statutes do not specifically prohibit discrimination based on sexual orientation, many local laws do.

Civil rights laws function as leveling devices. Prohibit discrimination in employment, and people of any race, gender, national origin, orientation, disability or age can compete as equals for jobs and professions. Prohibit discrimination in housing, and everyone who wants a new home can make their bid. Prohibit discrimination in public office, and any candidate has a shot at becoming mayor. Prohibit discrimination in education, credit, sport, contracts and public accommodations, and you are well on your way to a society of thoroughgoing equality of opportunity. The remarkable body of federal, state and local antidiscrimination law has not eradicated extremes of wealth and poverty, sexism or ethno-racial prejudice, but it has made things unquestionably better. Someone like me, whose African American and Cherokee great-grandmothers were maids and washerwomen, can attend Harvard Law School alongside men and women of genteel Caucasian ancestry.

Legal equality is a wonderful thing—and a necessity—but it does bring about problems of its own. Now that the number and variety of competitors for economic and social goods is greater, the pressure is on to resort to Hobbesian modalities of self-interest. Put everyone together so that men and women, blacks and whites, gays and straights, Spanish speakers and English speakers leave the starting blocks in unison in a fair race for the same prize, and people greedy for victory, bent on getting ahead of a crowded field, will cheat their way to the front of the pack. People accustomed to privilege may cheat to insure that they hold on to their lead, and people accustomed to exclusion may cheat out of self-doubt, a sense of superior need or a suspicion that the field is still somehow rigged against them. Both the Jayson Blair and the Danny Almonte cases looked to me like a case of this sort—doubt, need and suspicion.

Americans can take pride in the fact that some egregious forms of cheating are not a part of our mores. For example, bribing judges and other public officials is not a routine business norm in the United States the way it seems to be in parts of Latin America, Europe and Asia. Moreover, government-paid physicians in the United States do not exact "tips" as a condition of care, as sociologists report they have done in Hungary.[31] Not only do Americans not engage in such practices, we puzzle over anthropological claims that seek to characterize what would be "cheating" in our towns and cities as something else abroad.

There is, though, a striking prevalence and curious persistence to cheating in the United States, a nation of religion, opportunity and bounty. We need a better understanding of why Americans resort to cheating when we do not have to—and when we've been taught that it is wrong. The competitive ethos of our society, its acquisitiveness and the vulnerability some of us feel about losing out and being left behind are important dimensions of the problem. We need a better understanding of how to tackle the cheating our ethos encourages but our ethics condemn.

GETTING CAUGHT

Cheating is typically clandestine and has to be.[32] Get caught cheating in a Las Vegas casino, and you are escorted to the door—you may even be arrested. Tax cheating and Medicare fraud can get you arrested, too. The most skillful cheaters escape the label by avoiding detection. Few will suspect just how much disrespect the clever cheater really has for the rules. Because the cheater pretends allegiance to the norms that regulate the activities in which he or she participates, others trust the cheater to their detri-

When a ten-year-old asks whether it is okay to cheat, it may be time for a long conversation, rather than an occasion to recite an unadorned black-letter rule.

———————

ment. I know a Washington white collar crime lawyer who wrote his son's law school admission essays and managed not to get caught. He should have known better. His son entered law school on fraudulent terms.

Cheating does come to light. Cheaters often get caught. Detected cheating need not, however, ruin a life or a career.[33] Sammy Sosa returned to applauding crowds after being suspended for using a corked baseball bat.[34] Former New York Mayor Rudy Giuliani was named "Man of the Year" for the brilliance with which he handled the terrorist attacks on the World Trade Center, despite an unseemly adultery scandal. The general public may forget and forgive, but the Internal Revenue Service, the Securities and Exchange Commission, and some spouses are not terribly forgiving. The fact that one has managed to avoid cheating most of the time may mean little to a humiliated spouse, a government regulator or a hard-nosed judge and jury.

In some lines of work, people are on the lookout for cheaters. Writers, scholars and scientists often get caught because vigilant colleagues and competitors in their field suspect and expose them. Considerable fact checking and peer-policing by investigative journalists uncovers cheating among fellow journalists. In 2003, the *New York Times* fired two top editors under whose watch the paper published stories fabricated and plagiarized by reporter Jayson Blair. In 1998, the *New Republic* fired Stephen Glass, an associate editor and former fact checker, for fabricating stories out of whole cloth. Blair and Glass had learned nothing from the disgrace of Janet Cooke. In 1980, *Washington Post* journalist Janet Cooke made up a news story about a drug-addicted eight-year-old. Cooke's elaborate fiction won her paper a Pulitzer Prize for investigative journalism. Cooke, who, the *Post* learned, had doctored her resume to get hired in the first place, resigned, and the *Post* returned the Pulitzer. Cooke later explained that she concocted her sensational report under pressure. After hearing rumors of a drug-addicted child, she wanted to be the first to report it.[35]

The late historian Stephen Ambrose plagiarized Thomas Childers's *The Wings of Morning* in his best-selling book, *The Wild Blue,* and failed to get away with it. Doris Kearns Goodwin was detected after copying and sloppily footnoting portions of her 1987 book, *The Fitzgeralds and the*

Kennedys. Another acclaimed historian was disgraced in 2000 when Emory University Professor Michael Bellesiles published *Arming America: The Origins of a National Gun Culture*, which won the 2001 Bancroft Prize. The book came under attack after other researchers could not locate archives Bellesiles cited in support of his controversial thesis that fewer Americans owned guns in the past than previously assumed. In response to the attacks, an investigation by a panel of independent experts convened by Emory University concluded that Bellesiles faked archival data. Bellesiles denied wrongdoing but resigned his faculty post in October 2002. American Enterprise Institute affiliated–researcher John Lott has also denied deliberate wrongdoing in research on gun ownership. Yet top scholars, including Stanford professor John J. Donahue, have found errors in Lott's books and articles alleging that "right-to-carry" gun laws reduce crime. When critics asked to see data backing up some of his conclusions, Lott said the data in question had been lost in a computer mishap. In an attempt to defend his flagging reputation for integrity, Lott deceptively created a fictitious fan named "Mary Rosh." Between 1999 and 2003, Lott flooded the Internet with statements commending his character and abilities, all signed "Mary Rosh."

Historians and social scientists take dishonest shortcuts, and so do natural scientists. Bulgarian-born scientist Victor Ninov was on the staff of the prestigious Lawrence Berkeley National Laboratories when he announced the discovery of a new atomic element. In the summer of 1999, Ninov reported sightings of a brand-new building block of the universe, element number 118. The scientific community greeted this and other unique accomplishments Ninov claimed with high praise. But subsequent researchers inside and outside Lawrence Berkeley could not corroborate Ninov's momentous findings, and investigators concluded in 2001 that Ninov had deliberately fabricated research. Ninov lost his job in May 2002. A year after Ninov's uncloaking on the West Coast, University of Connecticut and Connecticut state officials disclosed that employees of the University of Connecticut Environmental Research Institute in Mansfield Depot had been routinely falsifying test reports on toxins. "Sound scientific research and practices were often abandoned for convenience," the

New York Times reported.[36] Laboratory manager Dr. Jianshi Kang admitted that he had knowingly changed results for toxic compounds found in air, soil and water samples "from unacceptable to acceptable levels."

One standard form of cheating can survive public disclosure: sexual infidelity often continues unabated after its discovery. However, since victims of flagrant, persistent cheating in personal relationships may understandably feel humiliated, cheating out in the open can be as or more wounding than cheating on the sly. From the cheater's point of view, openly cheating in relationships, like running a perpetual personals ad, may make it easier for the cheater to attract additional casual lovers. But the reputation as a cheater may make it harder for the cheater to someday secure a trusting new partner for a committed relationship. So even if a person feels he or she can get away with overtly cheating on a partner, there are incentives to keep cheating clandestine.

MAKING EXCUSES

The anticheating ethic admits bona fide exceptions and excuses, such as letting your guests win a tennis match. In the context of playing otherwise competitive games with young children, clandestine rule breaking is a way to teach children to be gracious winners and losers. I used to cook the outcomes of various board games to insure that I lost. I did it to model for my preschool daughter (she threw tantrums whenever she lost) how to be a good-humored loser. I also openly removed the "go backward" cards from the board game Candyland to spare her the pain of too frequently losing this popular game of chance that teaches taking turns and counting. In Chutes and Ladders we sometimes ignored the chutes that are supposed to force players to move backward and just attended to the ladders that give players the right to move ahead. On a related front, when my twelve-year-old son went to the Internet to get what are popularly known as the "cheats" for new video games to advance more quickly through the maze of perils, he was not really cheating in an ethically significant way. The video games are not serious, everyone has access to the "cheats," and the rules of the game serve no inherent moral or ethical purposes. Youthful and adult gamers who rely on "cheats" are not participating in an institution or practice colored by reciprocal expectations of unaided fair play. By contrast, when my son is on the field playing league soccer or lacrosse, he knows that the rules of play matter and strictly adheres to them. Context is everything.

Cheating is a paradigm ethical failing and therefore gives rise to a paradigm set of excuses. Poor excuses for cheating recur so often that they ought to have their own names: the "I just cheated a little" excuse; the "I'm not bad, the rule's bad" excuse; the "It's for a good purpose" excuse; the "I am just taking what I deserve" excuse; and the "Everyone else is doing it" excuse. These are the top excuses for cheating, but similar excuses are used for other ethical failings.[37]

I Just Cheated a Little

The "I just cheated a little" excuse is the excuse of employees who pad expense accounts by a few dollars every now and then. Lawyers who overstate the number of hours spent on a wealthy client's case implicitly rely on the excuse, too. The habit of viewing some cheating as worse than other cheating can feed into the tendency to make excuses for oneself: "What I did was bad, but tiny when compared to what others do." Some types of cheating *are* genuinely worse than others, depending on a range of factors that include the motive for cheating, the consequences of cheating, and the context. Cheating in the context of employment is generally worse than cheating in the context of purely recreational sport. Because of the number of victims and the size of the losses, cheating in the context of big business is often worse than cheating in the context of small business. However, even in small businesses, misconduct can exceed the bounds of decency. Throughout the 1990s Tri-State Crematory in Georgia casually dumped at least 334 corpses on its property and then provided relatives with urns of "ashes, sticks, insects, sand, gravel, ground masonry particles and other things."[38] These ghoulishly unethical business practices came to light in the winter of 2002, as the victims of September 11 terrorist attacks were still being mourned.

Cheating in government seems worse than cheating in most other contexts because public trust in the rule of law is one of the most essential needs of modern societies. Cheating in intimate relationships may hurt only the three people directly involved, whereas cheating in international finance may hurt tens of thousands. As a general rule, though, even tiny cheating can be big. Cheating in recreational sports can cause accidents, but has also been known to incite violence. Cheating in intimate relationships can have wide consequences beyond the principals; a single extramarital affair has been known to have a profound effect on the rejected spouse, on children, in-laws, and an entire network of angry and disappointed kin and friends. The adulteries of a political leader can shake a nation, as in the cases of Gary Hart, Bill Clinton and Gary Condit.

I'm Not Bad, the Rule's Bad

The "I'm not bad, the rule's bad" excuse has sophisticated applications to tax evasion. In grade-school civics, Americans learn that responsible citizenship means following the rules and working within the system to bring about change. To get rid of legal obligations that you believe are unfair or ineffective, you are supposed to use democratic political processes. Speak out at town meetings! Write your Congressman or Congresswoman! Run for office! But this lesson in democracy and change only goes so far. Americans' behavior suggests a willingness to simply skirt unwelcome legal and ethical standards. There are far more surreptitious tax evaders than there are bold tax protesters.

Taxpayers who underreport income year after year may feel justified in their failure to comply with the tax code, by virtue of a sincere belief that the system of taxation imposes undue burdens on income earners. But they may underpay for other reasons. They may underpay (or not file) because the forms and rules are too complicated, or because their peers do not pay. If the people you know do not file, it may seem to you that "nobody files" and therefore that you would be a sucker to file.

I asked Michael Graetz, an expert on tax compliance and member of the Yale University law faculty, what he thought about tax evasion, and in particular about the "I'm not bad, the rule's bad" excuse for not paying taxes.[39] Graetz originally got interested in tax cheating as a particular kind of law enforcement problem. He hoped general theories of law enforcement would illuminate the problem of tax law enforcement. Against the grain of leading economic theories, Graetz concluded that the IRS's responses to nonpayment, both to the legal kind (loopholes and shelters) and the illegal kind (under-reporting income) were critical factors in the pattern of tax compliance. He is disturbed that—in the words of an April 8, 2000, *Wall Street Journal* headline—the "IRS Rides the Ups and Downs of Congressional Whim."[40] The IRS seems to get tougher or more lax as the politics of Washington demand.

Graetz speculates that tax cheating is becoming more common, especially among younger taxpayers, and that this may be part of a larger trend toward cheating in schools and sports. Professor Graetz thinks little of the excuses people give for not paying taxes. "People should pay their taxes. We have the fairest tax system in the world," he said. Graetz agrees that the system is too complicated, but views needless complexity as a reason to press for change rather than to break the law. I asked Graetz why a low-income family whose tax payments equal the cost of sending their child to preschool should not skip taxes and pay for preschool. I believe many in the United States would say that poor families are right to do what they have to do to cope with unfairness in the system. His reply was pointed. "Why shouldn't they go into the grocery store and steal groceries? It's the same thing." People think stealing groceries is worse because of the risk involved. It is riskier to steal $500 in groceries than to under-report by $500 wages earned as a maid. But either way you are taking someone's property, Graetz explained. The injury in the one case is more impersonal and distant, but it's the same injury. I agree with Graetz but would be outraged if the IRS allocated its scarce enforcement dollars into prosecuting the poorest tax evaders, or if fellow citizens rushed out to become citizen tax enforcers targeting low-income families. Graetz, too, was unenthusiastic about tax whistle-blowing that amounted to turning in one's neighbors.

Like taxpayers, students and employees use the "I'm not bad, the rule's bad" excuse. They will ignore requirements with which they disagree, if the requirements feel too burdensome. Studies show that college students who cheat on exams report thinking that cheating is justified when a professor's requirements have been unreasonably onerous.[41] In 2001, Montgomery County, Maryland, schoolteachers leaked test answers to students taking standardized tests. Their defenders pointed to the unreasonable pressure teachers experience when government lays down unrealistic performance standards. To avoid penalties, teachers and administrators resorted to cheating, feeling okay about themselves because they could offer the "I'm not bad, the rule's bad" excuse. Although they may have acted from altruistic rather than selfish motives, their own students blew the whistle.

It's for a Good Purpose

The Maryland educators who gave their students test answers may have rested, in addition, on a different excuse, the "It's for a good purpose" excuse. They may have thought it more important that their pupils make a good showing on the tests than that the state know the students' actual level of preparation. Why waste time "teaching to the test" or coping with the institutional consequences of underperformance when you can simply let your students practice actual test questions? The dangers of the "It's for a good purpose excuse" are clear. An election official would not have the right to toss ballots into the trash in a close election just because a larger margin of victory would spare the county an expensive runoff. The candidate who loses by a small margin is entitled to a recount to uncover errors—and so is the voting public, notwithstanding the expense. Public officials who accept illegal gifts may save taxpayers money, but they do so at the cost of public interests that are as important as money. Short-term economic utility is not the measure of right and wrong.

Frustrated professionals charged with the care of vulnerable people—children, patients, indigents—sometimes come to believe that the system is rigged against them. They conclude not only that they can cheat the system, but that they must. Lawyers find ways to bend and stretch rules so that people can get what they want without technically cheating. But a lawyer, like any professional who believes unjust rules are standing in the way of getting to a fair, humane outcome, may be tempted to cheat the system. Cheating rarely loses its unethical quality, though, when motivated by an individual's beneficent motive to get the best of an unfair bureau-cracy. Even if cheating is not likely to be detected, relying on the "bad rule" and "good purpose" excuses may be self-serving. Moreover, it is risky to individuals to presume to know which social policy rules are "bad" and what conduct will in the aggregate, redound to the public good. Mistaken judgments have potentially enormous social costs that can be avoided by seeking relief through established channels.

I'm Just Taking What I Deserve

The "I'm just taking what I deserve" excuse is equally troublesome. Suppose you are a whiz in biology. You have never scored less than 95 percent on an assignment because you study hard before each test. Before this week's test, though, you get food poisoning and cannot study. If you cheat by bringing in a crib sheet, you will surely get the score that you always get. If not, you will get a much lower score. The wrongness of cheating in such a situation is clear if you subscribe to a blanket principle that cheating is always wrong. But if you run from blame with the "I'm just taking what I deserve" excuse, the cheating looks acceptable. From a prudent point of view, the biology whiz should not cheat because there is some chance she will be detected, placing her future career in jeopardy. From a moral point of view, the would-be cheater's conduct implies the untenable principle that unlucky people should break inconvenient ethical rules. Suppose you have been a top law student and would surely ace the bar exam. But the month before the exam you suffer an emotional blow—a divorce—and are unable to adequately prepare. Had you prepared, you would have passed with flying colors. Should you cheat to insure that you get the score you would have gotten but for the fortuitous bad timing of a personal problem? Not from an ethical standpoint. You could postpone taking the test and plan to sit for the bar exam when it is next offered in six months' time.

Some people who use the "I'm just taking what I deserve" excuse are busy, not unlucky. Historians who intentionally plagiarize other historians know how to write and conduct research, but they are not consistently willing to invest the time it takes to do it: they copy instead. Some users of the "I'm just taking what I deserve" excuse are neither unlucky nor busy.

They are lazy. They do not want to bother with the kind of careful preparation that assures success. The lazy cheater's cheating rewards two vices: sloth and deception. Moreover, lazy cheating hurts fellow test takers who are denied the opportunity to be top scorers. A law license is supposed to certify knowledge. Credentials awarded to bright but lazy cheaters misstate their accomplishments to the world.

People who feel cheated may be motivated to engage in anticipatory, compensatory, or retributive cheating. If you feel you are likely to be cheated, you may cheat first. If you feel you have been cheated by others, you may cheat them back, thinking, "I'm just taking what I deserve." Paradoxically, both cheating and feeling cheated are ethical failures. Cheating is failure to respect others as equals with needs and interests similar to one's own; while allowing oneself to feel cheated is an ethical failure when it amounts to unproductive self-pity or an ungenerous, uncooperative, cheating spirit. The competitiveness of American society may incline everyone toward a bit of paranoia about being cheated.[42] Since we are fallible judges of fairness, it is prudent for the ethically fair-minded to play by the rules rather than cheat out of fear of being cheated. Playing by the rules curbs the contagion of cheating by denying another an excuse for competitive cheating.

Everyone Else Is Doing It

The final excuse I want to consider is "Everyone else is doing it." With respect to doped-up athletes, noted bioethicist Thomas H. Murray observes that "[i]f they could be assured that their competitors were free of performance-enhancing drugs, the pressure to use such drugs themselves would dissipate."[43] There is a strong element of pride in the psychology of cheaters who cheat because they believe everyone else is doing it. If people think all of their peers or competitors are cheating, the point of cheating may be to preserve reputation and standing.[44] To not cheat is to risk being a wimp (a weakling afraid of risk) or a fool (too dumb to care about self-interest). Cheating out of pride in some settings is peculiar, because deep down inside the cheater knows that his or her achievement is illusory; yet the felt need to maintain a facade of genuine achievement is satisfied even by false victory.

RACE TO THE TOP

In many cases, we Americans cheat because we are hell-bent on getting ahead. We know that this desire to get ahead is not a valid excuse to cheat, though it sometimes feels like a very practical justification. Cheating to get ahead seems "smart." Getting ahead today is unlike getting ahead fifty years ago, a hundred years ago, or centuries ago, when most of the moral and ethical traditions to which Westerners subscribe originated. An intense desire to get ahead coexists with the most diverse set of competitors in history. As observed, no one's race or sex absolutely predetermines his place. No one's identity or status takes her out of the race to the top. Playing a little dirty can seem like a rational strategy for success in competitive domains of education, employment and business. Undetected cheating can easily be the more lucrative alternative to honest competition. Risk takers prefer to cheat, profit and then deal later with any guilty conscience. A mildly guilty conscience is a lighter burden for some people to contemplate than living modestly like a loser. And there may be no guilty conscience to speak of where an individual believes cheating was the overwhelmingly smart and sensible thing to do under the circumstances.

A sense of fairness is a preeminent virtue and requirement of caring for others in a liberal democratic society. Fairness gets deliberately shoved into the closet by people who feel a strong need to run with the pack, if not at the front. Cheating is one way to get the diploma, then the job, the second home, the extramarital sex and the early retirement. Only a few Americans of any age are desperate enough to murder their political rivals or cripple the athletic competition; however, more than a few resort to serious, nonviolent forms of cheating. "Getting ahead" is the familiar story of cheating in the United States, but our complex motives for wanting to gain advantage deserve a fuller account.

Two things make "the top" seem desirable: the emotions one expects to feel and the material rewards one expects to reap. The people who cheat hoping to ascend to the top may be most interested in the inherent pleasures and rewards of knowing that they have achieved success; but much more cheating is doubtless motivated by a quest for material rewards. Money, a job, a glistening trophy, proud families and adoring friends. The monetary rewards that flow from cheating can be ends in themselves, or they can be a means to an end, like paying off debts or getting a parent into a better nursing home.

Cheating to experience the top is in some cases just a vintage form of greed. We want more than we are entitled to, so we violate well-established rules to get it. We need things we cannot acquire through honest means, so we resort to dishonesty. A certain amount of cheating among the poor results from unmet needs for vital resources, yet most of the cheating we read about is not committed by the poor and does not relate to vital needs like food, medicine or minimum-wage jobs. Physicians convicted of Medicare reimbursement fraud are not impoverished or unemployable. The standard of living is so high in the United States that most people have more than they need. Cheating is not, therefore, primarily a means of garnering essential resources. If need does not explain cheating, greed might come closer. Greedy people want more wealth, status and power than they believe they could as easily accumulate without cheating.

Many young adults cheat for reasons other than greed. They go to college and discover the campus cheating norm. Students enter college understanding that the wider society professes an anticheating ethic but feel impelled by the campus cheating norm to cheat anyway. They plagiarize because peers plagiarize, especially when they believe the opportunity to cheat without detection is presented. If it is easy to cheat, students may even conclude that authorities do not really care about cheating and that the expectation some people will cheat sometimes is somehow built into the system. At many schools, students take most final examinations in large rooms without proctors. We do it this way at the University of Pennsylvania Law School, where the students are as honest as anywhere else. Examinees are told at the start of each exam that they are on their honor not to cheat and are asked to report cheaters. Cheating is rarely reported. Many schools have similarly optimistic honor systems.

In the university, young adults sometime break the rules against plagiarism because they are insecure about their ability to succeed. I have had to play the role of prosecutor in student misconduct cases, a downside of being a law professor. One of my reluctant prosecutions at Georgetown University led to the expulsion of a first-year student who had stolen a copy of his roommate's legal writing exercise. He had hoped that the professor and her teaching assistants would not notice that two of the six hundred papers they had to grade were identical. This first-generation college-educated Hispanic cheated out of insecurity. He lacked confidence in his ability to meet the demands of a top law school and was afraid of disappointing his family. I am sure he could have done the work.

Students cheat when they are anxious about not performing as well as their peers and the work they are asked to do is difficult or onerous. They cheat because they believe competition for good jobs requires that students do whatever it takes to graduate on time. A 1980s study concluded that a tight job market contributed to cheating. According to David Callahan, economic pressures are partly responsible for the cheating epidemic.[45] Indeed, I believe some of the cheating in the academy can be attributed to stiff competition for rewards that were once the exclusive provinces of white men. Whites may cheat to stay atop the heap, and minorities may cheat to get what they believe they will be wrongly denied by the "system."

I attended a large public high school. Each quarter, shortly after report cards were issued, one person from each grade was designated "top scholar." The top scholar was the person with the highest grade point average in his or her grade. The rewards of this designation were a form letter sent home to the top scholar's parents, and the announcement of the award over the intercom system during the principal's morning news. Senior year I was competing against two or three others to be named top scholar, and I wanted this designation badly. No African American had ever been a top scholar. I was a high achiever who had already been permitted to skip the tenth grade. A virtually straight-A student, I feared my one non-A mark in an advanced-placement math course would put "top scholar" out of reach. The day arrived for reporting our grade point averages for the current quarter to our homeroom teachers. We were supposed to do the math ourselves in accord with a set formula. Conveniently "forgetting" that A's in physical education did not count as much as A's in academic courses, I reported a higher score to my homeroom teacher than I had actually earned. The mistake was in plain view. My teacher had all my grades and courses in front of her but did not have time to double-check a classroom of thirty pupils' math. She reported to the principal's office the scores we gave her. My misconduct was never detected. I became that quarter's top scholar.

I relished the admiration that came my way the day Principal Oscar P. Boyles announced my "achievement." As a black teenager in a newly integrated white school, my need for recognition was especially keen. I lived in fear of being, as I would have said, once again overlooked. With respect to the top scholar award, I exemplified the type of "high self-esteem, high need for approval" child identified by researchers as more likely to cheat than other high self-esteem children and as likely to cheat as low self-esteem children.[46] In general though, my high need for approval did not lead me to cheat. I loved reading and writing, and possessed an enviable memory. Indeed, I memorized the entire periodic table of elements to win a seventh grade science bee. Most of the time I willingly lavished the kind of attention on schoolwork that earns high marks the honest way.

FACING OUR PROBLEM

Many young people seem to think cheating in school is justified or innocent, like fibbing. Mature adults seem to think cheating in personal relationships is to be expected—the inevitable seven-year itch. In fact, many committed or married people will have an affair in their lifetimes, even if, as priest and novelist Andrew Greeley observes, "the monogamous bond...is far more powerful in this country than is the propensity...to adultery."[47] Corporate executives seem to think cheating in business is playing to win, something you are supposed to do. They do not bring fair-mindedness into the picture. And the fact of the matter is, a lot of people do not think cheating is really all that unfair, since anyone who wants to do it can. At issue here is the logic of cheating.

To address the logic of cheating that is turning us into a society of cheaters, we need to confront it openly. If people are deep down comfortable with cheating, they will probably keep on doing it. And if they are going to keep doing it, we should try to understand the reasons why and prepare for the societal consequences. Leaders and moralists who ought to know better often talk as though wrongdoing were the rare exception, as if it were easy to follow moral rules. Just do it! Just say no! Right is right and wrong is wrong! But it is not easy to do what is right. Good people frequently fail. We need to speak publicly to one another about why misconduct has appeal. We need more open discussion and debate about the norms of advantage taking under which we actually live.

As a polity, Americans rarely have thorough conversations about the cheating we accept and practice. Typical ethical discussions in public life are simplistic: cheating is bad; catch, expose and punish the cheaters; toughen standards. Episodes like the Gary Condit and Jesse Jackson marital infidelities lead us to opportunistically label particular people as bad guys and to reap the political benefits of doing so. Public scandals do not, however, do much to get us talking about our rich understandings of what moral decency really requires of emotionally needy, overworked, married men holding high public office. The Enron scandal led to loud expressions of outrage and tougher laws, but to no better understanding of why cheating big remains so attractive throughout the business and financial services communities.

Calling attention to cheating for the sake of public education and discussion can backfire. No one wants to appear to be defending, let alone promoting, what others may consider cheating. The fear is that one's own morality will be called into question, and one's own conduct and accomplishments rendered suspect.[48] Yet, honest disagreement exists about what counts as cheating, and when cheating is excused or "smart."[49] To ignore disagreement, to continue talking as though the cheating imperatives are categorical, simple and obvious, when they are contextual, complex, and contested, limits the ability to effect change. The discussions we need to have would accept that cheating is a normal, though morally compromised, response to need, want, suspicion, fear and competition.

Because cheating is out of hand in our society, an anticheating ethic has got to be brought front and center. We can reduce cheating and the temptation to cheat by taking responsibility for revising the policies, practices and laws that discourage fair play. As an adjunct to character training, we need tough laws that make cheating harder and less profitable. Through well-designed approaches to character training, we can both curb our own personal cheating and also take responsibility for curbing cheating in the institutions in which we work and learn. We need to focus on the practical aim of teaching and learning honesty as a requirement of ethical virtue. When a ten-year-old asks whether it is okay to cheat, it may be time for a long conversation, rather than an occasion to recite an unadorned black-letter rule. To improve the picture of moral failure, we need to approach the moral education of youth with conviction, but as a realistic, dynamic process that takes personal and cultural limitations seriously.

PART II

IMPROVING THE PICTURE

CHAPTER 3

THE CHALLENGE
OF MORAL EDUCATION

I have witnessed untutored goodness emanating from my children, both of whom were adopted as infants. Perfect angels! However, goodness that seems untaught may be just mimicry. Children do tend to copy the positive behavior they observe in loving caretakers. To our delight, though, children are sometimes kinder and wiser than we adults around them.

From the age of three my son, Adam, was a determined but fair competitor and a remarkably cheerful loser. He was generous, too. The first time Adam saw a homeless person, he was about four years old. We were walking a few blocks from the Smithsonian's Air and Space Museum in Washington, D.C., when he noticed a man sitting on the curb of a busy street. Adam stopped dead in his tracks and looked the man over from a respectful distance. He asked me why the grown-up was sitting on the ground. I told him the man was poor and had nowhere else to go. Adam stuck a chubby hand into the pocket of his orange-and-blue Gymboree shorts and pulled out some precious coins. Over my strenuous objection, he insisted on giving his money to the needy stranger. The homeless man, who had not been panhandling, was effusive with thanks.

My daughter, Ophelia, was only three the day she stroked my brow and made a loving, unsolicited promise: "I will take care of you when you are old." When she was still in diapers and barely able to speak in sentences, Ophelia had an uncanny understanding of the requirements of civil cooperation. A few days after her second birthday, her father and I took her to what was planned as the final meeting with her birth parents until she reached the age of eighteen. We four adults sat awkwardly, sad and stony-faced around a table. Sensing our mood, Ophelia turned to each of us separately and insisted, "You hold hands! You hold hands! You hold hands! You hold hands!" We were startled into obedience, laughing at her precocious mediation, which broke the ice and enabled us to amicably work out a plan for Ophelia's future.

"It is possible for a person to want to be moral," G. J. Warnock concluded in the final paragraph of *The Object of Morality*, "and a person is moral, by and large, exactly in proportion as he really wants to be so."[1] Unfortunately, we are not born wanting to be moral. Experts agree that we are mostly born with raw ethical potential and an urgent need to learn everyday morals. Human young need what has often been termed "moral education"—"character education" lately—if they are to develop into persons who are reliably drawn to benevolent duties and virtues. Whether tied to home, religious institutions or schools and whether formal or informal, the basic purposes of moral education in the United States have been to cultivate moral feeling, convey moral requirements, train moral reasoning and fortify moral resolve. The production of these qualities is a major responsibility of the adult world.

Character training is not a one-shot deal, accomplished in childhood, like a vaccination against the chicken pox. It is a slow, continuous endeavor. Although typical parents are completely in the dark about it, recent efforts at moral education in the schools have been shaped by competing theories of moral development, competing conceptions of moral truth and partisan politics. Moreover, although the United States has a stated national commitment to character education, as reflected in numerous private and public initiatives, the federal investment in character education programs has been surprisingly recent and modest. A significant portion of the millions awarded to some school districts has been earmarked for programs not yet fully under way.

IMMATURE MORALISTS

The enterprise of human morality can build on the spontaneous gestures of little children but cannot stand on that basis alone. Children lack overall judgment. They seem pervasively egocentric when small, and in adolescence may come to believe that their peers have all the answers. Bright, charming children can make demands on others that are spine-chillingly thoughtless. My friend Justine's teenage daughter Marcy wanted her own car and expected her mother to buy her one. Justine told Marcy that she had no money for a car. "Why don't you sell your wedding ring?" Marcy blithely suggested.

Our becoming and remaining ethical will depend on developmentally appropriate moral education, followed by continuing moral education to help master social roles. There is a place for morality in all the roles we play throughout the life cycle—whether student, caretaker, employee, public official or simple citizen. School curricula, workplace codes of conduct, professional ethics devised by associations of learned professionals and ethics laws are all mechanisms for the lifelong production of values. As adults, we take ultimate responsibility for moral education into our own hands. Moral self-education is the critical talking, listening, reading, and reflecting about matters of importance that we should undertake to inform and train the capacity to care. Through moral education and moral self-education, we cultivate what Warnock termed "nonindifference" to the varieties of human need that comprise our common predicament. Ideal moral education engages the everyday moral concerns of society, in addition to contemporary understandings of global human values. With moral education, people are more likely to display the minimal virtues of honesty, fairness, beneficence and nonmaleficence that Warnock and so many other ethicists have described as crucial. And hopefully a little bit more.

Without moral education, children can develop into adults who are indifferent to the demands of family, community and work. Moral education is the foundation of both responsible civic involvement and business and professional ethics. Society needs morally competent children to carry on its just and humane institutions. Likewise, children need to possess moral competence for their own peaceful survival. We adults have an obligation to equip the young with our best-defended, most enduring conceptions of good and bad. Adults willy-nilly convey ethical conceptions to children in the ordinary course of daily life. But that is not enough. The moral training required of a complex modern state is too important to be left to chance. A commitment to ethical living requires practices through which the deliberate production of values begins in earnest in childhood.

Structured ethical training is a routine part of the home, religion and school-based educations of American youth. A bounty of varied public and private ethics resources is available. Our laws and social customs entrust primary care of young children to their parents. Responsibility for selecting from among the available ethical resources and orchestrating an appropriate moral education for children thus falls primarily to parents. In the absence of parents, other designated caregivers assume the tasks. My friend Jeannie sent her daughter to a feminist leadership camp one summer, whereas other parents would prefer Vacation Bible School or Outward Bound for their girls. On the surface, parental choices may appear radically at odds with one another. Yet typically parents are guided by common underlying concerns. We all want our children to learn the basic virtues of honesty, integrity, fairness and kindness. We want them to understand the obligations of caretaking, charity and citizenship. We urgently want them to steer clear of crime, violence, illegal drugs, excessive alcohol and unsafe sex. And we want them, finally, to grasp the values that underlie the social, economic and political structures of their nation and world.

Like anything else, teaching ethics depends upon readiness to learn. The typical one-year-old is not ready to learn to use the toilet. Trying to teach bladder control before a child is ready is both useless and unkind. At what age, though, are typical children ready to begin learning ethical habits? "Start teaching them when they are young," would seem to be good advice for any parent. But can parents teach one-year-olds to share their toys? Can a three-year-old be taught to keep promises and tell the truth? Can a ten-year-old learn not to cheat?

Those of us who raise children—or care about how others raise them—crave practical advice for discharging obligations of moral training. When can moral education begin? What can parents expect of their children? Will a child's development follow a universal pattern? What will children need from their schools and communities? Many experts say there are important developmental milestones to mind, and built-in limitations on what we can expect from our girls and boys. Competing experts say there is hardly a bad time to teach character. Listening to experts can be valuable even if, as in this case, they disagree with one another about fundamentals.² The disagreements reveal the range of possibilities every parent and teacher should consider.

MORAL DEVELOPMENT DEBATES

M oritz Schlick's book *Problems of Ethics* is eerie, given when and where it was written: Vienna, 1930. The book speaks of altruism as the essence of moral disposition, of "considerateness for one's fellow man," and of "accommodation to and friendly understanding of their needs."³ According to Schlick, "Man is noble because he enjoys such behavior." The virtues "signify the highest joys."⁴ Unfortunately, nothing Schlick wrote could have convinced the Third Reich to have a "friendly understanding" of European Jews. In fact, Schlick was shot dead by an irate Nazi student as punishment for belonging to the famed Vienna Circle of philosophers, which included Ludwig Wittgenstein and other logicians of Jewish descent. A collective Aryan self-centeredness was the coin of the realm in Austria at that time.

The experience of the Holocaust places the potential for evil in bold relief. That is not what we want for our children. But how can we make them good? Leading psychologists of human moral development have theorized that human children begin life self-centered. A sense of reciprocal fairness and altruistic concern for others is said to come later. Starting in the 1960s, Harvard psychologist Lawrence Kohlberg devoted classic research to finding out how much later. "How," he asked in an essay published in 1964, "does the amoral infant become capable of morality?"⁵

Whence comes the penchant for honesty, service, self-control and friendliness? How does genuine morality grow from mere "adjustment to the group" which is "no substitute for moral maturity" and can lead to slavish compliance with the orders of a Hitler or a Stalin?[6] As parents on a practical mission, we want to know the answer to Kohlberg's probing questions.

Kohlberg built on the cognitive tradition of the Swiss researcher Jean Piaget. During a long career that ended with his death in 1980, Piaget watched and listened to children, hoping to better understand how they develop moral knowledge. He came to believe children's moral lives display a logical structure. He thought he discerned patterns and stages of moral understanding. "Our problem, from the point of view of psychology and the point of view of genetic epistemology," Piaget wrote in 1968, "is to explain how the transition is made from a lower level of knowledge to a level that is judged to be higher."[7] Kohlberg was drawn to Piaget's theory that children progress through separate stages of moral development, and that the conceptual framework of moral thinking may change over time. Based on empirical studies of the pattern and content of moral judgments conducted in the 1960s, Kohlberg identified six distinct stages of human moral development. He contended that these stages predictably occur over the course of three periods that he labeled the "preconventional" period, the "conventional" period, and the "postconventional" period.

In Kohlberg's preconventional period, we humans are typically egocentric. At Stage 1 of the preconventional period, people (typically, very young children) do what they have to do to avoid pain and earn rewards dealt out by power holders; at Stage 2, people (typically, school-aged children) think instrumentally, weighing the costs and benefits—mainly to themselves, of alternative courses of action. In the next period, the "conventional period," human actors (typically, older children and adults) begin to focus on social expectations, rather than merely on their own wants and interests. At Stage 3, people try to please others. They are a "good boy" or "good girl," in relation to others' expectations. At Stage 4, people are oriented toward obedience to authorities who enforce law and order. The final, "postconventional" period, consists of two stages of moral development that Kohlberg doubted many people ever fully achieve, even as mature adults. At Stage 5, people believe morality requires more than adherence to existing social conventions. It requires adherence to principle. Those who achieve this stage begin to view obligations to others in contractarian, legalistic terms of mutual, rationally acceptable standards. In Stage 6, people are in full possession of autonomous conscience. They are willing to make independent reasoned judgments about the objective principles of conduct applicable to behavior.

Kohlberg's theories have implications for moral education. If a program is to be successful, it must take into account a child's stage of moral development, the expected duration of that stage, and proven methods of facilitating a child's healthy progress from lower to higher stages. Kohlberg's theory of moral development attracted critics. Philosophers questioned whether Kohlberg had a solid basis for claiming that his moral stages were universal. Maybe they were culturally relative, merely the stages of development in the particular cultural groups he actually observed. In addition, philosophers balked at the possibility that Kohlberg's theory might mislead people into ranking some ethical theories as more highly evolved than others. Emotivism (understanding good as subjective or intersubjective approval), utilitarianism (understanding good as what promotes the most pleasure or happiness) and conventionalism (understanding good as a matter of prevailing custom or opinion) are all low-stage tendencies under Kohlberg's scheme. Never mind that John Stuart Mill was a utilitarian and David Hume a conventionalist.

Elliot Turiel, a fellow social scientist, was one of Kohlberg's most astute critics. His work posed a significant challenge to Kohlberg's model. Turiel asked the following question. Suppose one or more of what Kohlberg calls stages of moral development are actually just parallel frameworks, capable of existing simultaneously? Kohlberg maintained that conventionalism is the predominant mode of moral thinking for many children and adults. He classified the tendency to heavily weigh conventional social expectations as simply one stage of moral thinking. Rather than depicting conventionalism as a stage of moral development, as Kohlberg had done, Turiel argued that young children learn to differentiate the domain of morality, a context of thinking about well-being and justice, from the domain of mere convention, a context of thinking about laws, customs and mores that can sometimes be violated without harming people. Children figure out that wearing a shirt in public is a conventional expectation, whereas telling the truth is a moral one.

A Kohlberg student and later colleague at the Harvard School of Education, Carol Gilligan mounted a potent attack against Kohlberg's research in her widely influential book, *In a Different Voice* (1982). This book was a major force behind what has come to be known as the "ethics of care" school. Gilligan's empirical research suggested that women and girls have a different overall moral orientation than boys. When Gilligan interviewed women and girls about moral dilemmas and recorded their narrative responses, her female research subjects appeared to explain their choices by reference to relationships and care. Females reasoned most often in a moral language of responsible care and relationships, whereas males reasoned mainly in a moral language of rights and justice. As Mary Jeanne Larrabee explains, the different voice Gilligan discovered is a voice also possible for men: "This voice was one of care and responsibility, of concern and connection with other people, and Gilligan claims that it stems from a self which is intrinsically related to other people."[8] Gilligan did not hide the limitations of her studies. Some of her work was based on interviews with a small number of females from similar backgrounds. Yet excited readers were prepared to generalize her conclusions to a flat-out claim that Kohlberg got it all wrong: females and males do not exhibit the same pattern of moral development—moreover, they operate with distinct ethical frameworks, whether because of social differences, biological differences or some combination of the two. Responsibility-fulfillment is the moral orientation of females; rights protection, the orientation of men.

Kohlberg's research methods left him vulnerable to gender-focused critics like Gilligan. His crucial empirical studies were conducted almost entirely on male subjects, yet he generalized his conclusions to both sexes and people of all backgrounds. A single-sex pool of male research subjects introduces the spectre of "sex bias" and raises the possibility—yet to be definitively proven—that girls and women might exhibit their own unique patterns of moral development. This was the conclusion of researcher Lawrence Walker in an 1984 article in the journal *Child Development*. Walker admits the possibility of sex bias in Kohlberg's research but denies that existing studies support Gilligan's claim of gender differences in moral development.[9] However, two years later in the pages of the same journal, Diana Baumrind concluded that a number of studies discounted by Lawrence do support the thesis of different male and female ethical voices.[10] The hypothesis of gender differences lives on.

There may be different voices of race, class and experience, too. Mainly Caucasian subjects participated in both Gilligan's and Kohlberg's early research. Carol Stack's research suggests that race and social experience have a bearing on moral orientation. She studied African Americans' return migration from the urban Northeast to the rural South in the 1970s and 1980s. This work led her to conclude that "under conditions of economic deprivation there is a convergence between women and men in their construction of themselves in relationship to others, and that these conditions produce a convergence also in women's and men's vocabularies of rights, morality, and the social good."[11]

Kohlberg's influence continues to inspire important research. A recent book by European Georg Lind, *Can Morality Be Taught?* (2002), reports research building on Kohlberg's seminal ideas and drawing a notable conclusion about the duration of moral education.[12] Lind believes his studies corroborate Kohlberg's claim that morality is a matter of cognitive development; but whereas Kohlberg believed most people develop moral competence through moral education over time, initially in age-linked progressions, Lind's empirical work suggests that it is possible to regress from higher to lower stages of moral competence. In Lind's studies, having a college education is associated with developing and sustaining superior moral competence, an interesting conclusion, since some Americans cannot afford to attend college and many who do attend lack academic integrity. Yet, for all their moral mistakes, college and university students may come out at the other end of the experience as better people. Perhaps, as James Rest pointed out, it is in the years after high school that shifts to principled moral thinking are most likely to take place.[13]

Although ultimately the psychological realities of children's moral development and capacities remain undetermined, the moral development debates convey two extremely important messages. First, to know right and wrong is to gradually assimilate knowledge over time. Caregivers and educators must be patient with what is surely a *gradual* emergence of consistent other-regarding virtues in children. One should not write youngsters off as incorrigible too soon. Harsh punishments will not hasten the process. Ethical understanding and habits take a while to develop. Adolescents are still going to be unfolding when they head to college. Second, the moral development debates encourage listening carefully for possibly distinct ethical voices in children reflecting their gender and social experience. I have only heard whispers of difference so far between my "girly" brown girl and my "all boy" brown boy, but they are continuing to grow in their own ways.

RELIGION FIRST

Some parents rely heavily on religious instruction to convey ethical messages. Despite the tarnish of recent child abuse scandals and homophobia, religion is a splendid jewel in the treasure chest of America's moral education resources. Not everyone practices a religion, but religion is pervasive in the United States. The country is dotted with flourishing churches, mosques, temples and shrines, all symbols of moral and spiritual missions. Some of these are modest sites of worship and meditation. Others are large, affluent institutions with political influence and broad social services agendas. Notwithstanding its declining impact on daily life in our secular society, organized religion responds to the needs many people have for ethical and spiritual guidance. It is also a focal point for ethically motivated caretaking. Churches, synagogues, and temples house schools. They feed the poor and shelter the elderly. They sponsor immigrant families. They facilitate adoptions. They open their doors for public lectures, public elections and community meetings.

Years ago my parents used to pack all six of their children off to Sunday school and elaborately celebrate Christian holidays. They made religious observance look easy. Now that I am a parent myself, I wonder whether it was as easy as it seemed to pull off one-size-fits-all moral instruction. I have had to approach my children's early moral education individually. My daughter attended Sunday school and belonged to a church choir starting at age four. She responded well to religious education and wanted more. Her brother was more responsive to homeschooling through conversation, stories and music, one-on-one. I sang to him from my tattered copy of the Armed Forces hymnal, from the opus of Burt Bacharach, from the Canadian folksinger Raffi—whatever it took to get across my point. He was happier with a secular introduction to values, and after the age of six could only be dragged into a church when food was being served.

COUNTING ON CHARACTER

M ost American children leave home for school at the age of five, at which time their parents entrust their education substantially to others. Already shaped by the values of their families and communities of origin, schoolchildren are further molded by the moral values of teachers, school administrators and peers. Today children may be offered formal moral education curricula. Indeed, formal character education has been a national priority for over a decade. The existence of the Character Education Partnership (CEP), whose board of directors includes leaders from the corporate and education sectors, is one of many signs that the concept of school-based character education has come of age. CEP is a private not-for-profit organization based in Washington, D.C., established to foster effective character education for youth.

President Ronald Reagan appointed philosopher William J. Bennett to the post of secretary of education. Bennett shared Reagan's desire to reintroduce concerns about morality and personal responsibility into national discourse. For Bennett, the time seemed right to focus on traditional conceptions of character. Under his leadership, the United States Department of Educaton initiated an awards program to recognize schools for exemplary efforts at character education. By 1993, more than 250 schools had been honored.

Washington stepped up its involvement with school-related character education in the mid-1990s. Through the Partnerships in Character Education Program in 1994, the Department of Education began channeling millions of federal dollars into character-building initiatives in nearly every state. Between 1994 and 1998, the Department awarded $8 million. For example, the California State Department of Public Instruction was awarded $1 million in 1995 to implement character education models in ten elementary and middle schools. Under recent federal guidelines, for the Partnerships in Character Education Program, grant applicants may select which elements of character to emphasize: "Elements of character may include caring, civic virtue and citizenship, justice and fairness, respect, responsibility, trustworthiness, giving, and any other elements deemed appropriate by the eligible applicant."[14]

President Bill Clinton and Congress declared the week of October 16–22, 1995, "National Character Counts! Week." The declaration heralded the arrival of a new focus on moral education in the United States, and symbolized the success of efforts by many, (including communitarian sociologist Amitai Etzioni, education professor Thomas Lickona, and California philanthropist Michael Josephson) to get character education on the public agenda. In an October 10, 2003 proclamation President George W. Bush urged American educators to celebrate the third full week of October as a "National Character Counts! Week."

In 1992, Josephson first organized a Character Counts Coalition as a project of the Marina del Rey–based Joseph and Edna Josephson Institute of Ethics, a nonprofit organization named for his parents. The Character Counts Coalition was established in response to, in Josephson's words, "excessive violence, drug use, drunk driving, teen pregnancy, theft and cheating."[15] An impressive group of prominent liberals (like lawyer Marian Wright Edelman, founder of the Children's Defense Fund) joined conservatives to kick off the Coalition's effort to introduce character education into the lives of schoolchildren. Many school districts initiated character education programs as a result of Josephson's efforts, some inspired by his methods.

Josephson promotes practical methods for teaching about ethics. He has harsh words for snobs who believe ethics can only be taught with

. . . like adults, youth experience fear and temptation. Like adults they need to be familiar with the idea that moral life is full of ambiguity, uncertainty, cluelessness and expectations.

obscure Great Books by academics with Ph.Ds. His own approaches to teaching young children and corporate executives center on conveying the "Six Pillars of Character": trustworthiness, respect, responsibility, fairness, caring and citizenship. These Six Pillars were initially developed in 1992 as the Aspen Declaration on Character Education traits at a conference of educators, philosophers and community leaders held in Aspen, Colorado, and are widely employed today in character training. For example, the $2 million federally funded character-education program under way in New York's District 3 schools will restructure its curriculum to focus on the Six Pillars.

In 1998, Congress found that "record levels of youth crime, violence, teenage pregnancy, and substance abuse indicate a growing moral crisis in our society."[16] These findings prompted an enhanced federal commitment to character education. George W. Bush campaigned for the White House in 2000 on a promise to increase federal spending on character education by $25 million. True to his promise, grants are now available to broader categories of recipients for public schools, faith-based schools, higher education and community partnerships. The Department of Education awarded a total of $25 million in 2001 and at least $16.7 million in 2002.[17] A grant of $2.5 million went to the Caring School Community Character Education Program of the San Francisco Unified School District and the Developmental Studies Center of Oakland. Philadelphia won a four-year $2 million grant for plans to reach students in sixty-four of its public schools. An additional $3 million went to eight additional school districts in 2003, raising to ninety-three the number of state and local education agencies that have received character education grants.[18]

It is much too soon to assess the efficacy of the new federal character education subsidies; some grantees have yet to complete their multi-year projects, and others have yet to implement them. It is important to point out, though, that while the overall federal commitment to character education is in the millions of dollars, the per-pupil expenditure of under a dollar in 2001 and 2002 may not buy a lot of practical virtue. Michael Josephson supports the premise of federal funding for character education but told me in a November 13, 2003 telephone interview that he is "concerned about the lack of public access to information about precisely what is being done with federal dollars." If it seems that federal subsidies for school-based character education are too modest and mysterious, there is encouragement to be found in Thomas Lickona's point of view.[19] In a November 25, 2003 interview he suggested viewing the federal awards as symbolic gestures: "The real measure of the American commitment to values is at the grassroots level, where schools denote time and attention of their own initiative to the tasks of character education."

With federal dollars pouring into character-education projects all over the country, men and women are being trained to teach our children moral virtues and moral reasoning skills. "Teaching the teachers is key," Josephson observes. University-based institutes at the University of California, Penn State University and many other colleges and universities are currently devoted to developing research-based methods of character education. One of the better-known institutes, Professor Thomas Lickona's Center for the Fourth and Fifth Rs, affiliated with the State University of New York at Cortland, designs childhood moral-education programs. Simplified, its premise is that children need lessons, not just in the three R's (reading, 'riting and 'rithmetic), but in a fourth and a fifth R—respect and responsibility. Lickona promotes sex education as essential to character training and maintains that youth should be taught the wisdom of sexual abstinence. Lickona's Center and Syracuse University's Project LEGAL, run by James J. Carroll, provide the main models for the federally funded New York City District 3 programs that also incorporate Josephson's Six Pillars.

Like many institutes, the Bonner Center for Character Education at the California State University, Fresno, does more than pure research. Along with local school authorities it publicly recognizes middle schools that "demonstrate outstanding efforts" on behalf of their pupils' character education.[20] To earn recognition in 2003, a school was expected to "promote core ethical values as a basis of good character," "foster an intentional, proactive, and comprehensive approach to its core values in all phases of school life," and provide "students with opportunities for moral action." The Bonner Center's statement of criteria interprets the second requirement to mean that a candidate school "ensures a clean and secure learning environment free from drugs, alcohol, crime and violence and promotes healthy student behaviors and positive character traits."

One way to get an overview of what American children are being taught under the rubric of character education today is to take a look at what their teachers are being taught to teach them. Dr. Kevin Ryan, Director Emeritus of the Boston University Center for the Advancement of Ethics and Character surveyed American university programs that teach teachers approaches to childhood moral education. He identified eleven different emphases in the programs he analyzed. Specifically, teachers are being taught about methods of value clarification introduced by psychologist Carl Rogers in the 1960s, about moral reasoning and cognitive development, typified by the Kohlberg research debates, and about traditional moral virtues. They are taught methods of conveying practical life skills required of responsible adults, the fundamentals of good citizenship and the value of public service. They are taught how to create caring classroom and school communities, and health education focusing on drugs, pregnancy and violence prevention. Finally, they are taught conflict resolution and peer mediation methods, ethics and moral philosophy and, at religiously affiliated universities, approaches to religious education. Not every teacher's college or university education department offers each emphasis. And not every teacher will study every subject his or her school offers.

One emphasis Dr. Ryan found in an overwhelming majority of every category of education schools, whether housed in a public, private or religiously affiliated university, is caring community. This approach conveys practical knowledge classroom teachers need concerning how to encourage courteous, respectful behavior in the community of the classroom and school. At my daughter's public elementary school on the Philadelphia Mainline, a respectful school community free from bullying appears to be the main goal of the second graders' limited ethics education.

Most parents and taxpayers have only a very indirect, limited role in shaping character-education programs. I believe many parents would be comfortable with all eleven of the broad categories of moral education just mentioned, however. They would no doubt applaud ambitious efforts at their children's schools to incorporate the eleven areas on Dr. Ryan's list in addition to other required subjects. Yet some parents have strong moral and psychological views about whether particular subjects should be taught, and at what age. School-based sex education, for instance, is controversial and politically charged. Some parents do not want it for their young children, and some parents do not want it for their children at all. Many parents approve of sex education, but only if it equates good character with abstinence or heterosexuality. Sex education is just the beginning. Members of our community who take an interest in education have opposed "values clarification" training on the grounds that it presupposes moral relativism. They have also opposed "good citizenship" training on the grounds that it inevitably teaches uncritical patriotism. We fight mightily over the hearts and minds of our children.

FIGHTING OVER CHILDREN

With competing input from a few parents, diverse communities, school boards, legislators and federal agencies, politics is inevitable. Political battles over character education get us off track, always to the detriment of unified efforts to address children's vital needs. It seems off track, for instance, to fight over the semantics of what we seek to accomplish, but people do. I have used the term "moral education" freely here. But it turns out that the term is old-fashioned and politically sensitive. "Moral education" sounds too sectarian and judgmental to some ears, compared to "character" or "ethics" or "values" education. One has to stick to the thesaurus of political correctness to evade the appearance of indoctrination.

Another way of getting off track is to claim partisan ownership of moral education for one's own group or party. Indeed, the very idea of "character" education plays out as a partisan issue, at times, with conservatives seemingly more committed to traditional values and character than moderates and liberals. In the popular Zeitgeist, President Ronald Reagan, a conservative Republican, symbolized character, personal responsibility and traditional family values. By contrast, President Bill Clinton, a moderate Democrat, symbolized alternative lifestyles and modern liberal values. As a presidential candidate, George W. Bush pledged major increases in character-education funding, Al Gore did not. Yet it bears remembering that the original Character Counts Coalition attracted support from liberals and conservatives.

Regardless of political affiliation, Americans share many core moral notions about child rearing and education. As previously noted, we want many of the same things for our children. We do go about protecting our children in very different ways, but as often as not our differences are idiosyncratic; they do not track categories of national partisan politics. For example, I am as perplexed as the most conservative parent by adults who try to control their children's vices by enabling them; for instance, parents who provide alcohol and motel rooms for their children's prom nights.

The parents of younger children can be enablers, too. A warm-up to Halloween, October 30 is Mischief Night. Adolescents in my community go out after dark pulling pranks. I told my eleven-year-old son he could not participate. I was especially concerned that he, one of the few African Americans in the neighborhood, not be involved in anything the police could view as a crime. On Mischief Night 2002, a jolly parent pulled up in my driveway with an SUV full of middle-school children inviting my eleven-year-old to go out for naughtiness. Her kids were armed with rolls of toilet paper and cans of Silly String. "It's so much fun!" the perky mom said. "They remember it all their lives." Too black of skin to lighten up about the white mother's proposed vandalism, I politely demurred. She looked embarrassed. "I can respect that," she said, "I tell my kids to only spray nice things on people's windows, like 'Jesus loves you.'" Never mind that many of our neighbors are not Christians, and that I woke up the next morning with wet toilet paper and Silly String all over my shrubs. The children who had had such a great time putting it there were nowhere in sight for the cleanup, a messy chore left to party poopers.

SUBSTANCE, PLEASE

I have had at least one child in public or private school continuously for a decade, and yet no teacher or school administrator has ever asked my opinion about educating my children's characters, or presented me with a description of his or her formal character-education curriculum. During this same decade, though, policymakers prioritized character education, and battles have raged within education policy about whether moral education should be packed with substance—specific notions of right and wrong values; or whether it should be focused on process—techniques for identifying and thinking about the values children happen to have. Educators committed to teaching substantive notions of right and wrong face the question of whether childhood moral education should include sex education, abstinence values, religion or respect for homosexuals. Moral educators also face concerns over whether substantive moral education should rely on the corpus of classic Western literature or on a broader array of texts that include recent literature and multicultural selections.

I was puzzled when I discovered that the basic options—substance and process—are often presented by the experts as mutually exclusive. Were I asked, I would say that I want my son and daughter to learn *both* what values to hold *and* how to think and reason about the values they in fact hold. On the surface, combining the options looks like a viable alternative. Yet teaching the Six Pillars, for example, is seen by some as inconsistent with teaching what is known as "values clarification," a nonjudgmental method of recognizing personal values. Parents who care about the moral educations their children may receive in the coming years, whether as a consequence of the No Child Left Behind Act character-education funding initiatives or other curricula, will want to make a special effort to penetrate the reasons that values clarification and similar process-oriented moral education is condemned by influential character educators, including Josephson and Lickona. These two men have similar historical views about how three particular trends—positivism, relativism, and atheism—purportedly contributed to an unwillingness to teach American school children any substantive ethical values. In an article published in August

2002 in *The State Education Standard,* Josephson cites the impact of those schools of thought to explain why substantive character education was not emphasized in the United States between the 1920s and the early 1990s. Lickona tells essentially the same historical story on his Center's Web site and in a 1991 book.[21]

Positivism for Ethics

The story is unconvincing in important respects. For a start, it is unlikely that the philosophical movement known as "logical positivism" had a material affect on American moral education. Logical positivism gathered steam between World War I and World War II. Moritz Schlick, the Vienna Circle member murdered in 1936 for associating with Jews, was one of the founders of logical positivism. The positivists' main agenda was to understand the connections among language, truth and meaning. Schlick defended a verification theory of meaning: "We know the meaning of a proposition when we are able to indicate exactly the circumstances in which it would be true." Moreover, "the description of these circumstances is the only way in which the meaning of a sentence can be made clear."[22] Schlick meant something like this. The sentence "The baby took the candy" has meaning because its truth value can be determined by appealing to empirical realities: baby, candy, and act of taking. By contrast, the sentence "Taking candy from a baby is wrong" does not have a truth value that can be ascertained in the same way by empirical fact.

The logical positivists believed that ethical assertions cannot be verified in the same way statements of nonethical fact are verified. However, they did not recommend that parents and schools cease to educate their children about right and wrong. Several of the positivists had a special interest in the transmission of ethical values. Moritz Schlick wrote a book expressing his practical commitments to human morality, and those commitments cost him his life. G. E. Moore, one of the great moral philosophers of the twentieth century, was a cofounder of logical positivism, along with Bertrand Russell, a man of strong if controversial ethical beliefs.[23] My undergraduate thesis on the work of logical positivist Rudolph Carnap was inspired by the invitation to values I discerned in the exhortation that appears at the end of one of his best-known essays, "Let us be cautious in making assertions, but tolerant in permitting linguistic forms."[24] In any case, it is hard to believe that American policymakers in an era of economic depression and mounting fascism and totalitarianism would let up on character education simply because a dozen European philosophers segregated facts and values into realms of cognitive and noncognitive meaning. There has to be more to the story.

Atheism

I became curious about atheism when I was a teenager living in a part of the country where admitted atheists were as scarce as hen's teeth. I won third prize in a social science fair for a research paper "Atheism in America." Activist atheists and civil libertarians have made religion in public schools politically untenable. The atheists have had help from the First Amendment and the Supreme Court, though. Religious character education in public schools is unconstitutional. I believe it belongs elsewhere, such as in parochial schools, optional off-site after-school programs, and in the home. In 2004, the Supreme Court will decide whether public-school children can be permitted to recite the words "one nation, *under God*" in the daily pledge of allegiance to the flag, and the Court could decide that the words must be omitted.

For a while, I attended a Christian prayer session held in my public high school. It was a voluntary before-school activity led by fellow students. I never mentioned to my parents that I was praying in school, but had I, they would have heartily approved. I do not think the prayer meetings were harmful, and they helped me to steel myself for the day. However, religion in public schools can inadvertently disparage the moral traditions of a child's culture and religion. I doubt that my school would have welcomed a before-school atheism club meeting on the premises, or even meetings of Muslims, Jews and Buddhists. In my southern Christian-dominated high school, teachers unthinkingly used the term "Christian" as a synonym for "good," wounding the feelings of the students of other backgrounds and beliefs. "Do the *Christian* thing," they would say. *Character* meant "Protestant Christian character." You can see the problem.

Relativism and Values Clarification: Dirty Words?

The view of ethics known as "cultural relativism" teaches that what is right for a person depends upon that person's cultural background; "moral relativism" or "subjectivism" teaches that what is right for a person depends upon that person's individual beliefs. Much as logical positivism does not logically dictate an end to moral education, neither would the truth of either cultural or moral relativism. Suppose relativism were true. Would you not still want to impart your cherished ideals to your children? I would. If educators and politicians believed right and wrong depended upon individual perspective, they would have no reason to give up on moral education designed to cause the young to treasure what they treasure. A society would still be warranted in attempting to promulgate what it understands to be important values, even if values are not subscribed to universally.

However, it is possible that with enough relativism or positivism in the air, the political will to make substantive character education a priority would not have existed in the middle of the last century. It is also true that some particular theorists of that era who believed relativism is true concluded that we should not be judgmental in our dealings with other people. They concluded that teachers should teach children to understand and express their own desires and values.

Take for example, Carl Rogers. Rogers was a humanistic psychologist whose ideas first were popular in the late 1960s and early 1970s. Humanistic psychology's trademark was facilitating individuals to discover who they are and to accept themselves. Collaterally, humanistic psychology promoted ideas of toleration and acceptance of diverse perspectives. Translated into an approach to moral education, "values clarification" is a method of moral training that deemphasizes the transmission of values and emphasizes helping individuals get in touch with their own internal value systems. The popularity of "values clarification" did not undercut the case for moral education as such. It pointed the way to less judgmental approaches to moral education, approaches that minimize finger-pointing and maximize efforts at self-understanding.

"Values clarification" are dirty words in some quarters, because they emphasize process (the process of gaining clarity about one's own internal values, whatever they may be) rather than substance (knowledge of specific ethical rules, principles and virtues deemed genuine and important). Although everyone should learn to recognize their own values, critics of "values clarification" correctly observe that children need an approach to moral education that loads them up with guidance on what they ought to do in a variety of familiar circumstances and how to do it. They need to be taught conceptions of right and wrong, and the rationales behind them, as soon as they develop the capacity to take in this kind of knowledge. Discussing feelings and preexisting values is only part of what children need. Although "values clarification" skills should not be a child's entire moral education, I believe they are a plausible adjunct to more directive modes of school- and home-based instruction. Many philosophers argue that critical moral reasoning begins, in fact, with an ability to figure out what one internally values and why. Teaching undergraduates to identify the premises of their beliefs is a standard exercise in college philosophy courses.

Multiculturalism

William K. Kilpatrick has an interesting, politically charged take on why character education was not an emphasis in public schools until the 1990s. He, too, is an enemy of all that smacks of relativism. Kilpatrick lamented children's ignorance of traditional morality in a 1992 book, *Why Johnny Can't Tell Right from Wrong*.[25] Kilpatrick attributed moral deficiencies in youth to timidity about passing on culturally specific substantive moral values. Writing from the perspective of the day, Kilpatrick argued that schools and parents actually avoid ethics instruction. Schools approach the responsibility of passing on substantive moral values with a reticence born of misplaced respect for children's diverse cultural origins. Believing that ethics vary from group to group, schools are afraid of stepping on toes. Multiculturalism has come to imply moral relativism, Kilpatrick concluded. Kilpatrick charged that liberal parents and schools assume that, uncorrupted by adults, children are by nature innocent and good. They assume that to produce moral persons, we simply need to allow children to flourish on their own. Children are not naturally good, though, Kilpatrick contended, nor is cultural diversity a reason to shy away from teaching children traditional Western ethics to guide the development of their characters. In short, relativism and process-oriented moral education, bad; substantive education based on traditional values, good.

Kilpatrick introduced late-twentieth-century dichotomies of American politics that threaten to get us nowhere: traditional vs. modern; conservative vs. liberal, Western vs. multicultural. He is asking us to fight over the hearts and minds of children, and the terms of the debate require that we take sides with one camp or the other. Side with the conservative pro-Western traditionalists or with the liberal multiculturalist, he asks. Kilpatrick aligned himself with the first camp, wildly exaggerating, I believe, the need for exposure to specific literature. Kilpatrick picked a fight over children when what we should really be about is fighting for them.

Children need a lot of substance, and process on the side is good, too. But once the door is open to substantive moral education, parents do have to face the hard question of what substance. Whose values get taught? And how do we teach them—via Great Books or comic books? The latter question is the easier of the two. Comic books are fine if they can get the job done. I am a fan of the Great Books literature Kilpatrick recommends for the cornerstone of American moral education. I think reading Aesop and Greek myths are fun and important texts. Yet literacy in the humanities, not learning right from wrong, provides the best argument for making sure we expose Johnny (and Johanna, by the way) to the traditional Western literary canon. There is no necessary connection between knowledge of the Western ethical canon and subsequent good conduct or character. Even after decent role models, *Bullfinch's Mythology,* Aristotle's *Nicomachean Ethics* and the holy *Bible,* Johnny may fail to recognize right. Worse still, recognizing right, Johnny may still choose to do wrong. Adults who know the Western moral canon and who understand moral reasoning can be ethical disasters in their personal and professional lives. We cannot expect more of little Johnny the school kid than big John, Sr., his classically well educated but federally indicted dad.

The ethical training children need can derive from any number of sources, high and low. Ethics is too important for elitism. Maybe all some children need is a focused caregiver armed with an ethics pamphlet downloaded from the Internet. I believe it is important to give extremely careful thought to the specific methods and materials we employ in the moral education of children in the public schools. But it would be wrong to overrely on the "classics" to raise ethical standards and to waste public resources in fights over whether traditional vs. multicultural texts are superior. We need a realistic understanding of what we want our children to value, the variety of human resources and media we can use to convey those values, and how to mobilize those values in everyday life.

SCHOOLING PATRIOTISM

I want to return, though, to the harder question of which—whose—values should be taught in substantive character education. One answer that seems plausible is that we should teach the values we all have in common. We can take the lead from Congress on this. Congress has asserted in its public laws that "trustworthiness, respect for self and others, responsibility, fairness, compassion, and citizenship... are universal, reaching across cultural and religious differences." Yet teaching the values we all have in common requires interpreting the values we all have in common. Beyond a certain point, interpreting the values we all have in common can get ugly. We teach nonviolence and then discover that we differ over how to teach the ethics of the death penalty and our nation's latest wars. Patriotic respect for country seems like a subject everyone can agree on, until current events make the interpretation of patriotism contentious. Some parents have objected to what they perceive as overly patriotic moral education lately. They fear their children will become uncritical of national policies.

One man's skeptical response to calls for civic education that followed 9/11 and the start of the "War on Terrorism" provide an instance of what I am talking about. On the anniversary of 9/11, Dartmouth government professor James Bernard Murphy published an article criticizing attempts to teach civic morality.[26] Teaching children patriotism is not something schools should try to do, he urged, because they cannot do it well. The mission of schools is academic and should be confined to the teaching of intellectual virtues of "thoroughness, perseverance and intellectual honesty." Why can't schools teach civic morality well, according to Murphy? "The aim of teaching students to love (or, more recently, to criticize) their nation has all too often prompted textbook authors and teachers to falsify, distort and sanitize history and social studies." But politics, not competence, is Murphy's real concern. He is not just a snob. He thinks teaching intellectual virtues is something typical teachers can handle. Teaching intellectual virtues is not exactly for dodos. Murphy's underlying worry is that civic education is either going to be politically acceptable and therefore probably intellectually unsound, or intellectually sound, but politically impossible to get into public school classrooms. He just does not trust politicians and other policymakers to put the interest of children first.

Again, the political aspect of debates over childhood moral education shines through. Debates about civic education, school prayer, sex education, and vouchers are often political battles that adults—not children—win or lose. Clearly children need a robust civic education that includes patriotism, an understanding of the basis of patriotism, and the rationale for critical modes of citizenship. Lost in the politics is the importance of responding with care to the drama of children's actual moral lives.

INSIDE YOUNG HEADS

Children have busy inner lives and serious moral quandaries beyond the cardinal temptations. Children inhabit the same morally ambiguous world of risk, social competition and politics that adults inhabit. Some children "see too much."[27] I grew up in the 1960s, a scary and confusing decade, though by no means the most scary and confusing our nation has known. While I lived in Hawaii I attended a military-run school at Wheeler Air Force Base. In addition to fire drills, we elementary schoolchildren practiced hurrying from our classroom, flinging ourselves onto the ground, and hiding our faces from the flash of nuclear explosions. I did not understand why. Were we still at war with Japan? In October 1962, at the height of the Cuban Missile Crisis, I cowered in fear inside a coat closet, wondering whether it was really right to drop bombs on innocent civilians.

When I was sixteen, I was a high-stepping pom-pom girl in the high school band, cheering at local ball games. I marched the streets of New Orleans in the 1969 Sugar Bowl Parade with jingle bells on my toes. I knew how to enjoy myself. I also knew how to don the happy-go-lucky affect expected of young girls when they are not enjoying themselves. Underneath the mask of girlish ease, I was bothered by the moral priorities of the adult world and what they meant for me. The news was full of nuclear threats, assassinations, body counts, riots and protests. Maybe for some teenagers war seemed remote, and inequality was a vague abstraction. The situation was completely different for me. My father was a noncommissioned officer with the United States Army stationed in Vietnam. My prom date faced the draft but chose to enlist in the military instead, taking with him the belief that his white American neighbors trained their pet dogs to chew up the limbs of "Negroes" like us. To comply with a court-ordered desegregation plan, my education required a daily bus ride to a public school in Columbus, Georgia. Some of my closest kin numbered among the Deep South's poor. The middle-class exceptions, I recently learned, worked alongside Martin Luther King, aided Operation Push and kept counsel with Malcolm X.

Although my intellectual abilities matched those of privileged white men, my early opportunities did not. Because I was a female with dark skin, no one would have been surprised had I gotten pregnant and dropped out of high school. By 1969, however, black girls were suddenly being offered the newly invented birth control pill and scholarships to formerly exclusive colleges. I wanted to be grateful for the liberating innovations of medical science and egalitarian politics. Yet after baby dolls, Barbie dolls and segregation, the national about-face on race and gender seemed suspect, promising me choice and opportunity for which I was simply not fully prepared. (My first years of college were emotional disasters. Depression and anorexia accompanied my struggle to fit in to the remade world.) Popular culture dished up wholesome distractions from all this, but who could tune in to *The Brady Bunch* for long when there was so much to figure out and decide?

Children are complex, their moral lives are complex and therefore the substantive demands of their moral education are complex. There are so many ways a well-meaning adult can miss the mark. One can falsely assume that exposure to Great Books and good role models will automatically result in character and conscience, when more is required to nurture moral capacity. One can oversimplify. We adults who engage in moral instruction often try to shelter the young with oversimplified rules and commandments. Do right, get a happy-faced sticker. Do wrong, get a frown. But like adults, youth experience fear and temptation. Like adults, they need to be familiar with the idea that moral life is full of ambiguity, uncertainty, cluelessness and exceptions. And while temptation is a problem included in standard moral lessons, the broader parameters of children's internal struggles are often ignored. Who is eager to set aside political differences to write the lesson plans children deserve?

There is another challenge: steering children away from moral and political extremism. Like adults who come to take ethics seriously, children may see illusory or dangerous ethical innovation as part of the solution to problems overwhelming their communities and country. Moral extremism is as dangerous as no morality at all. The men who flew airplanes into the World Trade Center, the Pentagon, and the Pennsylvania countryside claimed to be on a moral mission. The snipers who terrorized metropolitan Washington, D.C., in the autumn of 2002 called themselves God. One of the two, Lee Malvo, was a teenager, now sentenced to life in prison. In July 2003 an Oaklyn, New Jersey police officer arrested three teenagers who had attempted a carjacking. The boys were armed with a duffle bag full of guns, ammunition and knives and, according to the *Philadelphia Inquirer,* had made plans to murder several of their peers. Oaklyn Detective Craig Stauts quoted the eighteen-year-old ringleader, Matthew Lovett: "There are six billion people in the world. A few less would not hurt anything."[28]

The tumultuous decade of the 1960s was rife with moral turmoil and the millennium decade of September 11 is troubled in its own way. Civil rights and alleviating poverty have receded as domestic policy priorities, yet now, as then, national problems include the proliferation of weapons of mass destruction and war on foreign soil. Now, as then, Americans are called to embrace technology and demographic diversity. We cannot know for sure the ethical refuge youth privately sought following the September 11 attacks, the bombing of the Oklahoma City federal building, the Columbine school shootings and the Washington snipers. We can only surmise what ethical ambitions arose in response to anthrax in the mail, multi-billion-dollar corporate corruption, bold child predators, and high-profile hate crimes targeting Jews, gays and Arab Americans. It is difficult to discern what tragicomic episodes like President Bill Clinton's impeachment trial, the presidential election antics of *Bush v. Gore* or the circus surrounding the California gubernatorial recall election in 2003 said to young people about the relevance or possibility of integrity in public life.

Perhaps teenagers in the decade of September 11 conclude, as I did thirty years earlier, that Americans need stronger moral values. But I suspect teenagers today are less naive than I was about what secret individual moral resolve can accomplish. With any luck, most young people understand that deficient values are not the complete explanation for every social problem and that moral severity is not a plausible remedy. With luck, they know that moral deficiencies are real, but that neither thoughtlessly spouting conventional moral clichés nor holding ourselves to impossibly high or fanatical standards are laudable approaches to opposing modern forms of evil and inequity.

CHAPTER 4

ETHICS GO TO COLLEGE

M oral education cannot end with grade school. A significant percentage of young adults in the United States attend college, and about 26 percent of those who attend wind up staying for four years. Higher education sees understanding, improving and enabling ethics as one of its core missions. American colleges and universities acknowledge responsibility for moral education. The men and women who go to college become the adult managers and professionals who mind our nation's store. Their values and conduct matter.

HIGHER ED HEARS THE CALL

O n an evening in September 2003, when the school year had barely begun, Princeton University convened a campuswide assembly on integrity. The keynote speakers at the event were big guns, suggesting an institution genuinely committed to character. University president Shirley M. Tilghman was on the program, joined by former U.S. senator Bill Bradley. "You'll need your moral compass long after you've signed your last honor pledge at Princeton," Bradley said. "It takes a lifetime to build a reputation and only one false step to call it into doubt."[1]

The students of Princeton were eager to hear these messages at an event they themselves had requested. Student members of the Discipline and Honor Committees and Undergraduate Student Government had asked the university to sponsor an event for members of the community to focus on the importance of integrity.[2] The day after the assembly, I spoke to an eighteen-year-old Princeton freshman about his perceptions of the well-attended event: serious or pro forma? "Definitely serious," he replied. "And we had many similar events throughout orientation week about ethics and the Princeton Honor Code." He then rattled off the history of the code and the procedures it requires. Established in 1893, the honor code remains relevant. Examinations are administered to Princeton students without faculty supervision or proctors. Freshmen agree on their honor, in writing, not to cheat and to report cheaters. When I taught a course at Princeton in the fall of 2003, all of my students included a signed statement at the end of their written assignments: "This paper represents my own work in accordance with University regulations."

THE ACADEMIC MISSION

Higher education began focusing intently on exposing college and university students to the study of ethics in the late 1960s and early 1970s. It was a morally engaged era. On the one hand, students' moral idealism was fueled by the civil rights movement, women's rights, poverty programs and the first buds of consumer advocacy and environmentalism. On the other hand, young people were skeptical of ethical traditions saluted by the leadership of what campus radicals disparaged as the military industrial complex. The country was reeling from the disappointments of war and defeat in Vietnam. National military leaders had failed us. General William C. Westmoreland would fight for years to recover a reputation for honesty and military judgment. Trust in civilian government was assaulted by the astonishing Watergate break-in and cover-up. The resignation of President Richard M. Nixon was a lesson in stark moral realism. Infamous tape recordings of White House conversations exposed the president as a coarse, mocking and deceitful man. Nixon's sneaky then legalistic efforts to keep incriminating tapes out of the public domain compounded his moral failures.

I was a college and university student from 1970 through 1978. My peers and I found it hard to believe in lofty visions of ethical value, yet revisiting moral values seemed to be all that could save us from corruption at home and inhumanity on foreign soil. Many of my classmates were drawn to gentle philosophies of peace, inspired by Eastern ethical traditions; others found hope in militant philosophies of community.

In response to the times, the ethics curricula at American colleges and universities underwent a striking transformation. Academic ethics was reinvented as a more practical endeavor. The giant University of Michigan, for example, offered an array of courses seemingly designed to persuade the disillusioned counterculture that traditional morality was more than a bunch of arbitrary rules dictated by society and perpetuated by cynical power holders to keep the unprivileged and underprivileged in line. New courses in professional ethics sprouted up as requirements for students of business, public policy, medicine and law. Undergraduates flocked to relevant philosophy courses with titles like "Contemporary Moral Problems" to debate the ethics of civil disobedience, war, capital punishment and abortion.

In the 1970s "applied ethics"—practical ethics relating to specific areas of worldly concern—sprouted like a tree of hope from the dark, bitter ground of national moral crisis. By 1980, the prominent Hastings Institute of Society, Ethics, and the Life Sciences was estimating that at least 11,000 courses in applied ethics were being offered at the undergraduate and professional levels.[3] Applied ethical studies blossomed in the final decades of the last century and bear fruit today. Ethics is found in every corner of standard college and university curricula. University scholars teach and research the history, theory, methods and applications of ethics.

At the present time, the military service academies and other public and private institutions of higher learning are home to ethics centers, institutes, departments and programs. Many, like Princeton's University Center for Human Values, Cornell's Program on Ethics and Public Life, the University of San Diego's Values Institute, and the University of Maryland Institute for Philosophy and Public Policy have broad missions relating to ethically informed public policy. Others have a special focus on business, science, engineering or medicine: the University of Pennsylvania's Department of Bioethics, DePaul University's Institute for Business and Professional Ethics, Loyola Marymount's Center for Ethics and Business, and the Illinois Institute of Technology Center for the Study of Ethics in the Professions come to mind. But these are just examples, selected arbitrarily. One could fill a page or two with just the names of noteworthy academic ethics enterprises.

In 1998 Congress formally announced its commitment to "support and encourage character building initiatives in schools across America and urge colleges and universities to affirm that the development of character is one of the primary goals of higher education."[4] Through its Fund for the Improvement of Postsecondary Education, the Department of Education has funded a variety of projects geared toward responsibility in specific professional roles as well as in professional life in general.

CAMPUS LIFE

Higher moral education aims to teach ethical humanities, but also to train ethical persons. Today, programs like the Center for Academic Integrity at the Kenan Institute for Ethics at Duke University are dedicated to making fundamental values a part of the entire college and university experience. The Kenan Institute for Ethics emphasizes honesty, trust, fairness, respect and responsibility. Beyond the resources within higher education itself, the public and the private sectors are devoting additional resources to postsecondary moral education. For example, the John Templeton Foundation has established a national College and Character Initiative, offering grants in the area of higher education character development. Its philosophy is a variant of Martin Luther King's words that "Intelligence plus character—that is the goal of a true education."[5] Templeton's way of putting it: "By inspiring students to lead ethical and civic-minded lives, colleges fulfill their educational mission and prepare their graduates to meet the challenges of tomorrow."[6]

Academic communities are awash with ethical resources, and yet student misconduct flourishes. The research on the prevalence of campus cheating suggests that our colleges and universities are not completely successful at conveying ethical know-how in the areas of honesty and fairness. There are multiple forms of ethical disregard plaguing campuses, including violence.

Hazing incidents show that male and female college students are capable of grotesque acts of violence against peers. In 1993 my nephew Christopher Allen Powell reluctantly reported that he was paddled for days while pledging the Zeta Iota chapter of Kappa Alpha Psi at the University of Georgia.[7] State law, official fraternity policies and campus rules prohibited the secret male bonding ritual. Chris's battered buttocks bled, blistered and became infected. Though he was feverishly ill, members of the fraternity allegedly locked him in a bathroom to prevent him from going to the hospital. They released him just in time for life-saving emergency surgery. One of Chris's assailants privately admitted to the beatings and promised compensation. Yet when confronted by campus authorities and the police, the fraternity denied wrongdoing. Chris was offered a small out-of-court settlement but turned it down. I helped my nephew launch an ultimately unsuccessful lawsuit; as a rule, individual local fraternity chapters and members are judgment proof, while national fraternities and universities that officially oppose hazing are not held legally responsible.

The brutish hazing that I traveled the country speaking out against in the early 1990s continues today with more beatings and hospitalizations. There have been deaths, too. Hazing violates the official policies of Kappa Alpha Psi's national organization, but hazing continues among the Kappas. In 1999 Ray Austin was hospitalized with severe injuries to his buttocks, stomach and legs following a beating that Austin attributed to Kappa Alpha Psi initiation rituals at Georgia State University in Atlanta. In 2000 the Lambda Delta chapter of Kappa Alpha Psi at the Georgia Institute of Technology in Atlanta was placed on a minimum three-year suspension after being found guilty of violating the Fraternity Conduct Code and the Interfraternity Council's hazing policy. A third Kappa hazing was reported at the University of Arkansas in March 2003. This list is not exhaustive. The contorted logic of the underground practice was explained to me by an African American law student who had belonged to a fraternity in college. "We have to prove we can take from one another what our ancestors survived at the hands of the men who enslaved them." Hazing is by no means limited to black men; young men of other racial and ethnic groups undoubtedly have equally troubling rationalizations for their acceptance of hazing, including the oft heard argument that hazing is essential to create bonds of trust and community.

Morehouse College, in Atlanta, Georgia, takes special pride in the nonviolent philosophy of Martin Luther King, Jr. The African American men's college has produced generations of outstanding leaders and appears on a Templeton Foundation list of exemplary campuses for promoting moral integrity. Yet even Morehouse has made the news for failures of kindness and trust. Morehouse junior Gregory Love was severely beaten by a fellow student wielding a baseball bat. Aaron Price said he was showering when Love entered the bathroom and deliberately looked in on him. Love's explanation was that he was searching for his roommate. Price interpreted Love's act as homosexual aggression and later confronted Love with the bat. Love, who says he is not a homosexual, told authorities that Price spewed hateful antigay epithets as he beat him. Price was convicted of aggravated assault and battery, though not of a separate hate crime.

The hazing, the hate speech, the illegal drugs, the alcohol abuse, the sexual harassment, the date rape, the attacks on gays, lesbians and minorities—these things happen. The problems of violence and excessive alcohol consumption on campuses have been so severe that in 2003 the Department of Education made $2.2 million available for projects to "Prevent High-Risk Drinking and Violent Behavior Among College Students." Some of these problems are not inherent to college campuses. Violent hazing, for examples, is practiced among high school students. The Mepham High School varsity and junior varsity football team traveled from Long Island, New York, to Preston Park, Pennsylvania, for a preseason training camp in late August 2003. While there, three boys sodomized three younger boys with "pine cones, a broom stick and golf balls."[8] The suspects were expelled from school and placed on criminal probation.

In the spring of 2002, the University of Pennsylvania held its annual convocation to celebrate the ascension of juniors to seniors, as seniors prepared for graduation. The president of the Ivy League institution, Dr.

Judith Rodin, rose to the podium to speak. Something then occurred which was not part of the program but that had happened every year since a *woman* took on the job of running the university. "Show us your breasts!" shouted a jubilant crowd of undergraduates. In April 2003, negative advance publicity about the insulting ritual led students concerned for the school's reputation in the media and for Dr. Rodin's feelings to refuse to participate, reducing the number of taunting undergrads to a handful.

In raising these cases I am, of course, pointing to the worst behavior. There is a tremendous amount of ethically motivated public service donated by college and university students; at times the service is global. A few years ago a group of Penn students took up the cause of low-paid laborers in distant Asian sweatshops licensed by American schools to produce the logo apparel sold in bookstores and souvenir shops. The students were successful in persuading a committee of Penn administrators and faculty, on which I served, to support organizations set up as watchdogs against human rights abuses by the apparel industry's foreign operations. Sometimes the students teach the teachers.

MEDICAL ETHICS

In 1972, the federal government's Tuskegee Syphilis Experiment came to light. The public learned that hundreds of poor rural African American men had participated in research to follow the course of untreated syphilis—without informed consent—for forty years. Incredibly, U.S. doctors and public health authorities ignored the autonomy of research subjects as boldly as Nazi physicians had ignored the autonomy of the Jews. In 1973, the United States Supreme Court handed down *Roe v. Wade*, legalizing abortion and galvanizing a "pro-life" movement.[9] Other biomedical controversies erupted in this period. "Informed consent," "right to privacy," and "right to die" became household words. Biomedical technology enabled physicians to save and prolong life. Godlike doctors with their new machines could preserve life at the expense of death with dignity. In 1976 the Supreme Court of New Jersey weighed in, holding that the parents of Karen Ann Quinlan could authorize physicians to remove their comatose adult daughter from a respirator.[10] In an environment of uncertainty over patient rights and autonomy, medical and nursing students were required to add humanities and a new breed of professional ethics courses to their schedules. A wholly new interdisciplinary field, bioethics, was born.

Health care ethics is an enormously complex matter. The American Medical Association (AMA) has promulgated ethical standards for physicians, consisting of nine simple statements of principle.[11] The official interpretations of these principles by the AMA's Council on Ethical and Judicial Affairs serve as vital supplemental guidance. Early in the life of bioethics, philosophers who became involved in teaching medical ethics struggled with the need to simplify the task. Philosophers Tom Beauchamp and James Childress published a legendary treatise seeking to model and discipline ethical reasoning. What are we supposed to think about when we think through an ethical question, they asked? In *Principles of Biomedical Ethics,* they appeal to four general concepts that they refer to as ethical principles: beneficence, nonmaleficence, justice and autonomy.

In considering whether a person in a coma should be removed from life support, Beauchamp and Childress suggested that decision makers think comprehensively about the ethical issues by applying their four principles. Along these lines, perhaps *autonomy* is violated by pulling the plug on someone without his or her informed consent. Perhaps *beneficence* requires allowing such a patient to die with dignity. Perhaps *justice* in the allocation of health care resources warrants discontinuing medical care for hopeless cases. Perhaps concerns for *nonmaleficence* arising with respect to overanxious organ banks or unkind families exploiting comatose kin argues for not permitting them to authorize pulling the plug. The value of a moral reasoning heuristic like Beauchamp and Childress's for people unaccustomed to self-conscious moral analysis can be great. The four principles appear explicitly in the ethical code of the American Academy of Physician Assistants. Still, critics of the "four principles" approach complain that appealing to the four principles becomes rote and mechanical. Moreover, the four principles do not exhaust all of the morally relevant considerations that medical problems raise.

Health care providers need to be taught business as well as medical ethics. The mission of the medical profession is noble, but many physicians and health care concerns are in it for the money, and some take this interest too far. A Union City, New Jersey, ethics scandal involved a local lawmaker and a psychiatrist. Oscar Sandoval was accused in 2002 of paying Nidia Davila-Colon a bribe to secure a contract between his company and Hudson County. Admitting her guilt, Davila-Colon was convicted of bribery and sentenced to three years and a month in jail; Sandoval escaped charges by cooperating with law enforcement authorities.

BUSINESS ETHICS

Business ethics is part of the training and culture of corporate managers, much as medical ethics is part of the training and culture of physicians and nurses. Professor Thomas Donaldson of the Wharton School of Business has adapted methods and principles of social contract theory to pragmatic aims. He uses social contract theory as a framework for conveying professional standards to business audiences. Well aware of the theoretical limits of social contract theory as a comprehensive moral and political philosophy, Donaldson believes asking corporate managers to think of themselves as parties to a social contract of reciprocal benefits and burdens is an effective way to elicit ethical compliance.

At times, the business community is plainly indifferent to reciprocity, cooperation and the common good. Indeed, principal offenders in recent scandals seem to have no sense of a social contract. Former New York Stock Exchange chairman Richard A. Grasso was asked to resign when the public learned that he had accepted a $140 million salary package that looked "wrong" to the layman but "right" to the board that approved it. Former Tyco CEO Dennis Kozlowski was indicted for attempting to evade $1 million in sales tax on the purchase of artwork by pretending to ship paintings purchased in New York to his offices in New Hampshire. Former ImClone CEO Sam Waskal violated insider trading laws to help family avoid major losses on the stock market. Just prior to the Food and Drug Administration's official announcement of plans to deny

The generation of young adults schooled in ethics in the 1970s and 1980s has been noteworthy for its obsession with money, power and celebrity.

========

approval of Erbitux, a cancer drug developed by his firm, members of Waskal's family sold off ImClone shares, as did Waskal's buddy, the domesticity maven Martha Stewart. Stewart sold off her 3,928 ImClone shares, whose price had already fallen to below $60 per share. Federal authorities charged Waskal's father with insider trading, and Stewart and her Merrill Lynch broker Peter Bacanovic with lying to investigators, conspiracy and obstruction of justice. Soon after conviction for lying in March 2004, Stewart resigned her posts as an executive and board member of the company she founded, Martha Stewart Living Omnimedia.

Waskal, Bacanovic and Stewart will never be as notorious as the handful of super-rich men who have come to symbolize ethical compromise in high finance. Marc Rich fled to Switzerland in 1983, escaping prosecution for nearly $50 million in tax evasion, and for violating a ban on trading oil with Iran.[12] Ivan Boesky was convicted of insider trading in 1986 and forced to pay a $100 million fine.[13] Boesky blew the whistle on Michael Milken, the junk bond financier and inside trader whom prosecutors described as "an unreconstructed and unapologetic" felon whose crimes were crimes of "greed, arrogance and betrayal."[14] Milken went to jail and agreed to pay more than $1 billion in fines and penalties. In 1990 Charles Keating was ordered to pay back $40.9 million that he lost in shady deals involving the failed Lincoln Savings and Loan bank. The California bank went under to the tune of $2 billion, even though five U.S. senators, dubbed the "Keating Five," intervened with bank regulators for favorable treatment. One of the senators was former astronaut and clean-cut hero John Glenn.

Commenting in February 2003 on the federal fraud indictment of four former executives of Qwest Communications, Attorney General John Ashcroft implied that the men charged with securities fraud, wire fraud, making false statements and conspiracy in the neighborhood of $33 million, acted "out of sheer greed."[15] Other Qwest officials faced civil fraud charges levied by the SEC for inflating corporate revenues by $144 million in 2000 and 2001. Qwest promised to restate its accounts back to 2000, but delayed doing so for more than a year, maintaining its elite "Q" sticker symbol on the New York Stock Exchange.[16]

LEGAL ETHICS

The 1970s Watergate break-in scandal prompted a more gradual but serious new ethics regime for lawyers. A number of the central players in the Watergate scandal were lawyers. After Nixon's resignation, an embarrassed American Bar Association (ABA) decided it was time to require professional ethics courses in all ABA-accredited law schools. The requirement was implemented, and I myself have taught the course. States now require new lawyers to pass a standardized legal ethics examination and some, like Pennsylvania, require members of the bar to take a couple of hours of continuing ethics education annually.

The American Bar Association Model Rules of Professional Conduct is a book-length set of rules for practicing lawyers spelling out how they may and may not handle a range of situations. (Several states, including New York, still follow versions of an earlier ABA statement of ethics, the Canons of Ethics.) The Rules state how attorneys must safeguard client funds, protect client information, obtain and get rid of clients and communicate fees. The ABA strictures have become binding requirements whose violation may count as evidence of malpractice or misconduct for which a lawyer can be reprimanded or disbarred.

In the past, lawyers were ethically required to keep client misconduct a secret, though a lawyer could quietly withdraw from representation of an unethical client. Official ethics rules of the legal profession placed client interest before the public interest. Lawyers owed confidentiality to all clients equally, even those engaged in fraud. Under rules of ethics drafted by the American Bar Association and adopted by the state of New York and other states, a lawyer whose client refused to rectify a fraud could reveal the fraud to a third party, but only if he or she could do so without violating the obligation to maintain client confidentiality.[17] An attorney could withdraw from representation in disgust, but was not permitted to notify authorities of misconduct revealed in confidence. Suppose, for example, a company hired "Abe," an honest lawyer. Abe met in private with the officers of the company. The officers reveal that their company seriously inflated revenue in order to keep stock prices artificially high. What could Abe do? Abe could advise the client to come clean with the public, but he was not supposed to reveal the secret wrongdoing to anyone else, since he learned about it in a confidential conversation with his client. In the wake of Enron, the American Bar Association House of Delegates voted to change the Model Rules of Professional Conduct so that lawyers can ethically disclose crime or fraud that threatens financial harm to the public.[18]

Good ethics may no longer require lawyers to function as partners in crime, but lawyers and judges can be dishonest in their own rights. In January 2002 Justice Victor Barron of the New York State Supreme Court in Brooklyn was arrested for demanding a $100,000 bribe from a lawyer. He pled guilty and was sentenced to jail for three to nine years. Strict ethical standards require that judges avoid even the appearance of impropriety. But in major cities in the Northeast, there is a feeling afoot that some state judges are crooked and that judgeships are for sale. In Brooklyn, New York, prosecutors investigating the judicial selection process suspect that judgeships in that city have been bought.[19] New York City mayor Michael Bloomberg and other high-ranking city officials have gone on the record as critics of the highly political process of selecting state judges, and of judges who accept meals and cigars from civil litigants who are seeking favoritism. In the town of Mount Kisco, a suburb of New York City, Justice Joseph J. Cerbone was removed from office in 2003 after the New York State Commission on Judicial Conduct found "an apparent inability or unwillingness to learn from his mistakes, to recognize misconduct and to adhere to high ethical standards required of judges."[20] Cerbone dismissed a case against a man accused of assaulting a woman after taking the improper step of telephoning the woman to tout her alleged assailant's character. The woman backed out of the case, not realizing that the justice knew the man's family and had served as its attorney.

A unanimous special ethics court removed from office the chief justice of the Alabama Supreme Court, Roy Moore. Justice Moore disobeyed a federal court order to remove an illegal religious monument of the Ten Commandments he had erected in the state supreme court building. In a strange case of judicial dishonesty, San Jose federal judge James Ware was officially reprimanded by a nine-judge panel for telling a lie in professional settings. For years he told spellbound audiences that as a child growing up in Alabama he had witnessed a racial hate crime perpetrated against his brother. The truth of the matter was that Ware was not the brother of a real Alabaman named Ware whom racists had killed. The attention-seeking judge had no connection to the horrific episode. Ware's lie can be compared to lies told by Edward Daily, who posed as a Korean war veteran ordered by his American commanders to slaughter hundreds of innocent civilians at No Gun Ri. He wrote books about it, organized veterans' groups, and took his fabrication to national television.[21]

DEADLY FORCES

In 1997 a number of Washington, D.C. police officers were suspected in a corruption scandal that led to a grand jury investigation. The chief of police himself resigned over the allegations of financial improprieties. Ethical failure on the police force prompted then Interim Police Chief Sonya Proctor to issue a code of ethics for the Metropolitan Police force, exhorting officers to secure public safety and earn trust by being impartial, fair, moral, decent, professional, stable, effective, efficient, honest and faithful. Ethics guidelines for police officers are important, but this code was a broadly worded list of general virtues that did not spell out the chief's expectations. "Today, I am publishing a Code of Ethics which will communicate unequivocally to our employees the standards I believe the community has a right to expect from its public servants," she announced in a December 15, 1997 statement.[22] The high-toned code seemed to be too little, too late.

After Roger Wertheimer got his Harvard Ph.D. in philosophy in the 1970s, he became a police officer in Oregon—not a typical career path. As his first big assignment, he was permitted to devise ethical standards for the use of deadly force. His proposed standards were shelved. Judging by the amount of attention given to police ethics today, however, Wertheimer may have been ahead of his time. Large police departments today are governed by professional ethical rules pertaining to relations with the community, constitutional rights and the use of deadly force. The Institute for

Criminal Justice Ethics stands as evidence of heightened public concern about police use of force and surveillance. A couple of years ago, Wertheimer's interest in applied ethics and the uniformed services took him to the United States Naval Academy, where he served a term as the Distinguished Chair in Ethics. Housed above the base museum, the United States Naval Academy hosts a Center for the Study of Professional Military Ethics, staffed by military and civilian ethicists.

All of the military academies emphasize ethical leadership. The U.S. Military Academy at West Point includes ethics in its curriculum, as does the U.S. Air Force Academy. Leaders at the Naval Academy believe military officers need a firm ethical foundation that includes knowledge of Western ethical traditions and the specific moral requirements of combat. So the academy begins with the eighteen-year-olds placed in its care.[23] Naval Academy students study moral reasoning and leadership. There are specific priorities—a constitutional paradigm—drilled into naval officers. The ship comes first; shipmates come second; and the self last.

Retired Admiral Henry "Hank" Chiles sat with me in his office at the U.S. Naval Academy in Annapolis, Maryland, to talk about ethics. He is a modest man, so I had to learn from others about how he earned his four stars. Before his retirement from active duty, the admiral was Commander in Chief, U.S. Strategic Command. Trained in submarine and nuclear warfare, he spent many years at sea, on ships and commanding submarines. He commanded the U.S. Atlantic Submarine Fleet and held a major NATO post, Commander Submarines Allied Command Atlantic. Chiles managed to take some time during his military career to attend Oxford University for a master's degree in politics, philosophy and economics. After a long span of active duty, it would have been perfectly respectable for Chiles to retire to Miami with a view of the beach. Instead, he took a position teaching military ethics to midshipmen at the U.S. Naval Academy. Chiles could have rested on his laurels. However, he chose to do something that no one could do better.

When I met Chiles in December 2001 he was near the end of his stint at Annapolis. He unfurled a seasoned perspective on ethical leadership, reducing the ethical requirements of military leadership to a few key points—"bumper stickers," he called them. The first was an unexpected question: "Can we be trusted?" With regard to the military, Chiles asked, how else do we convince mothers and fathers to turn their young, impressionable children over to us to make them into professional killers? Chiles's second bumper sticker was related to the first: "We have to train leaders who can be trusted with power." We place terrifyingly destructive military power in the hands of a few fallible young people—like twenty-three-year-old pilots—who, for all we know, could have their own agendas, Chiles said. His third point was another starkly phrased observation: "We are not going to be the Nazis of the twenty-first century." The fourth bumper sticker was this: "You cannot expect fellow fighters to risk their lives for you if you are a liar and a cheater." For Chiles, this means military officers need to be ethical through and through, in their personal lives as well as in their professions. "Guys who cheat on their wives raise suspicions that they have been ethically sloppy in other ways. Officers cannot fall off the track." And there is for Chiles a broader importance to honesty as well: "Ethical behavior is a requirement of gaining international trust. Personal trust facilitates international efficacy."

We all have an idea of what ethical commitment is like for parents, teachers and politicians, even if we have not performed those roles. Even though the United States invests heavily in its military and we depend vitally on the nation's military might, typical Americans do not closely identify with the military and do not have a good sense of the ethical dimensions of the military's lethal responsibilities. In countries like Italy and Israel, where military service is mandatory, the particular form that ethical commitment takes in the lives of military officers may be more readily appreciable. I grew up as an army brat surrounded by active duty military personnel, but my trip to Annapolis was necessary to remind me of the overt role moral engagement often plays in military life and training.

I was surprised by Chiles's utter directness about the killing mission of the military. It may be fairly easy, though, to be direct when you endorse tempering America's might with individual integrity and virtue. But Chiles was also direct in his endorsement of military secrecy. He spoke of some civilian and military leaders as being "designated liars" in the national interest. Aspects of weapon-making, bio-terrorism, nuclear weaponry—these require secrecy; some information has to be classified. We did not talk about the Middle East, and Chiles was not eager to criticize fellow officers by name for the errors of Vietnam. He did say, however, that the military reacted strongly to the way the Vietnam war was conducted and "we need to take our oaths more seriously. We learned from that experience." I was impressed, but Admiral Chiles was unassuming. "You know, the man you should really try to talk to about ethical military leadership is Colin Powell," he suggested.

THE INSTITUTIONALIZATION OF ETHICS

Americans are fortunate. We have a pervasively just rule of law. People who live under the sway of oppressive governments may be taught the oppressor's values but not how to reason independently about ideals of their own values. People who live in fear or want are easily won over by perverse ideologies of the sort that led to the Holocaust, ethnic cleansing in the former Yugoslavia and Rwandan genocide. Groups allowed to view themselves as morally superior may commit the error of our Founding Fathers: promote the right abstract moral ideals but apply them inconsistently and intolerantly to "inferior" blacks, indigenous tribes or new immigrants. However, the constitution they enacted has slowly allowed the American people to bring moral ideals closer together with political realities.

As we have seen, the proud ideals of the American people are reflected in the very numerous moral education efforts currently under way in schools, colleges, universities and government. Our ideals are also reflected in the work of nonprofit foundations, institutes and centers that have sprouted up since 1980, such as the Josephson Institute of Ethics and the John Templeton Foundation, which have had a major role in the production of values, promoting character education for children and adults. The work of other organizations merit recognition. For example, based in Gulfport, Mississippi, the National Institute of Ethics certifies ethics instructors and provides programs designed to improve the ethics of employees, law enforcement officers and children. It describes itself as "the nation's largest provider of training that helps prevent employee misconduct and enhances integrity."[24] The board of the Institute includes Preston Covey, a police firearms trainer and full-time ethics professor at Carnegie Mellon University in Pittsburgh.

Other ethics organizations have international focus and ambition. With close ties to Canada and Great Britain, the Institute for Global Ethics in Washington, D.C., has as its program areas business ethics, children's ethics and public policy advocacy. Prominent ethicist Sissela Bok and Harvard Law Professor Martha Minow, both my former mentors, sit on its advisory board. A final example, the Washington, D.C.–based Ethics Resource Center (ERC) has a hefty $3 million operating budget. The ERC describes itself as "a nonprofit, nonpartisan educational organization whose vision is an ethical world."[25] According to the ERC mission statement, the organization seeks to foster ethical practices in individuals and institutions, by "inspiring individuals to act ethically toward one another, institutions to act ethically, recognizing their role as transmitters of values, and individuals and institutions to join together in fostering ethical communities." The ERC's four "shared values" are honesty, trust, respect and excellence. The emphasis at ERC is on character development rather than tough ethics laws. Indeed, in response to the idea that ethics rules can clean up corporate corruption, an ERC press release asserts that "fixing the rules and doubling the penalties is not fixing the problem." According to ERC spokesperson Stephen Potts, "the real issue we should be examining is personal and organizational integrity." Perhaps we could use tough laws in addition to a better personal ethic of professional responsibility.

RE-EDUCATING SOCIETY FOR GOOD

It is comforting to learn that Americans are pouring heart, head and money into the job of educating character. I have made point here of mentioning a great many programs, organizations and institutions by name to drive home that we are a society very rich in diverse ethical resources. But there are three reasons to avoid self-congratulation. First, although ethics education has been an academic emphasis within higher education for three decades and in sectors of elementary and secondary education for at least ten years, the results are ambiguous. The generation of young adults schooled in ethics in the 1970s and 1980s has been noteworthy for its obsession with money, power and celebrity. Whether our efforts with ethics education since 1990 will result in a generation of citizens with better ethical tendencies remains to be seen. Second, the number and variety of currently available resources for ethics education is impressive; yet it is too early to know whether the resources are adequate to the tasks ahead. If we are lucky, educators will soon turn government and private dollars into the curricula our children's ethical growth requires. Third, the domain of moral education is full of dilemmas no amount of money and innovation can help us resolve. Partisanship and political battles fought on the horns of these dilemmas do our children no good. Our responsibilities, not our politics, should guide the stands we take concerning competing theories of moral development, competing processes and substantive approaches to curricula, and competing options of religion and patriotism-free or -rich approaches to moral schooling.

CHAPTER 5

AN ETHIC OF WORK

One of the values Americans still expect moral education to produce is a basic work ethic, applicable to people in every role in the economy, from the sanitation worker and the construction foreman to the small business owner and the corporate executive. A century ago the German sociologist Max Weber published a classic assessment of western work values. *The Protestant Ethic and the Spirit of Capitalism* (1904) described a tendency within Protestant, capitalist societies for rich and poor alike to work for work's sake. Under the Protestant work ethic, Weber explained, the highest good is to combine "the earning of more and more money" with "the strict avoidance of all spontaneous enjoyment of life."[1] Weber depicted the perpetually industrious Benjamin Franklin as an American embodiment of the Protestant ethic: "A penny saved is a penny earned." Instead of working to live, the Franklins of the capitalist world live to work. Work is a context for the display of moral and practical virtues.

Yet there is nothing uniquely Protestant about valuing work. Americans of many backgrounds view hard work well performed as a moral imperative. We embrace careers and professions as proving grounds. Success at meaningful, hard work establishes mettle. A work ethic shared by executives and hourly wage earners alike asks that those who labor find personal meaning in the tasks and responsibilities of the workplace, too.

HARD AT WORK

We are certainly putting in the hours. Government statistics report that the manufacturing work week was 40.9 hours in September 2002; the work week for nonsupervisory workers on private nonfarm payrolls was 34.3 hours. The number of hours salaried professionals work appears to be on the rise. Having the ability to work at home and on the road has increased the number of hours professionals work. With a laptop and a cell phone, there is literally no place on earth where business cannot be conducted. The Bureau of Labor Statistics of the U.S. Department of Labor reported in May 2001 that 19.8 million people performed work at home at least once a week for their main employers, half on an unpaid basis. While Europeans famously enjoy paid vacations of a month or more each year, Americans are lucky to have two weeks off with pay each year.

Many women now grow up expecting to combine traditional female domestic roles with traditional male career roles. A woman in my community has seven children between the ages of three and fifteen and a thriving practice as an eye surgeon. Carol is exceptional both in her commitment to a large family and in her professional achievements; but having kids and a full-time job or profession is very common. Whereas only 31 percent of women with infants worked outside the home in 1976, by 1998 most did. U.S. Census Bureau data from 1998 indicated that 59 percent of women with infants under the age of one worked outside the home, and 78 percent without infants under one were in the workforce. Teenagers work, and so do seniors. The number of workers over the age of sixty-five has increased dramatically and is expected to rise, both because federal law now prohibits age discrimination in employment and because many seniors need to work to meet their expenses.

The American work ethic is so strong that we tend to look down on people without jobs or businesses. In 2002, the unemployment rate for blacks was twice that for whites—about 5 percent for whites and 10 percent for blacks. The Hispanic rate was 7 percent. The teen unemployment rate was 17 percent. People on public assistance are stereotyped as lazy and lacking a work ethic, even if they are busy caring for small children.

But the stigma is rarely warranted. A 1996 Census Bureau report indicated that only 7.7 percent of unemployed adults between twenty and sixty-four years old give a lack of interest in work as the reason for not working. For the rest, the reasons are illness, injury, child care, inability to find work, school attendance, pregnancy or retirement.

WORKPLACE ETHICS

It is important now to speak not simply of the work ethic, but more broadly of an ethic of the workplace. There is an especially important role in contemporary society for an ethic of workplace that includes the best of what the old work ethic was about but that goes beyond it. Workplace ethics require diligence, excellence, pride of accomplishment, and integrity. The kind of integrity required begins with honesty, respect for the person and property of others, and self-control.

An ethic of the workplace so conceived is a useful framework within which to interpret the current ethical crisis in American business. Ethical failure in corporate America reflects a breakdown in the workplace ethics of corporate managers. These busy, proud, ambitious men and women have gotten some things right: they diligently work long hours and achieve excellence in technical knowledge and skills. But they lack moral integrity. Important forms of self-control are missing. They disregard the interests of others affected by their greed.

The workplace ethic is also a useful frame within which to interpret the expectations of employers and coworkers that employees erect judicious firewalls between their personal and professional lives. One thing many employers expect employees to do is to keep their home lives in check during business hours. This can be hard. Women with young children and elderly parents know perhaps better than any other category of worker that caregiving cannot be squeezed into the lunch hour. A society cannot ignore business practices that make it impossible for workers to be active caretakers. Nor can society ignore the emergence of business practices that run roughshod over employee privacy and autonomy. A related expectation of employers and federal law is that workers cabin their sexuality. Home is supposed to stay home; sex belongs outside the workplace, too. Commentators complain about depersonalized, uptight workplaces arising out of the insistence on firewalls, but there is a lot to be said for them.

WORK/HOME FIRE WALLS

D on Winthrop and his wife, Maggie, own a jewelry store in downtown Philadelphia. Don's sister Marge is a part owner of the store. Don's father, Samuel Winthrop, started the business more than eighty years ago. I visited the store to talk to Maggie about restringing some pearls. When I arrived, Don was in the back working on a piece of jewelry and Marge was helping another customer. Don and Maggie's eleven-year-old son, Zach, brought a friend into the store while I was there. Zach stepped behind one of the glass display cases with pride. For the benefit of his overawed chum, he pointed out his favorite items of merchandise, accurately identifying the precious stones and metals from which they were crafted.

The Winthrop family is lucky. Their personal lives are fully integrated into their work lives. Running a small business is no picnic. There is financial pressure and personal strain. But more than most American workers, Don and Maggie are at liberty to do what might be termed "mixing business with pleasure." For them, work is like home. Don and Maggie actually live in a house a mile or so away, yet the time they spend in the store in many respects resembles the time they spend at home.

No workplace supervisor holds Don or Maggie accountable for their interpersonal conduct. No corporate manager subjects Don and Maggie to an employee code of conduct governing what workers can say to one another. For Don and Maggie, no topic of conversation is off limits. Pat and Maggie have the freedom, if and when they are so inclined, to tell tasteless jokes, gossip and goof off. They do not have to worry about a boss monitoring their e-mail, listening in on phone conversations or making unwelcome sexual advances. If their son, Zach, gets the flu and cannot go to school, Don and Maggie can bring him in to work or stay home with him, no questions asked.

The Winthrops are atypical. More typical Americans earn a living at jobs in which they are expected to set boundaries between personal and professional realms. For large business concerns, the firewall expectation is embedded in corporate culture and policy. Business managers know from experience that workers who habitually bring their personal lives into the office or plant may be less productive. Conducting personal business on company time is to some extent unavoidable; medical appointments have to be made; calls from a child's school have to be returned; vital plumbing repairs have to be scheduled; grieving friends and relatives have to be consoled. Still, in typical workplaces in business and industry, conducting personal business at work is frowned upon.

Workers are expected to erect a firewall between their work lives and their home lives, but I once worked with a man who simply could not do it. For a year or so before I went to law school, I had a position at a government agency. I was about twenty-six. A well-meaning, Ivy League–educated man whom I will call Jack had a position there, too. I liked Jack. He was a sentimental romantic in his midthirties, utterly preoccupied with his personal life. His job at the agency meant little to him. He was married and had children. He also had a lover. Since Jack could not safely communicate with her from his home, he spent hours on the phone with his lover each week at the office. Lunchtimes and coffee breaks with Jack were long discussions of the trials and tribulations of his romantic life. But Jack also cornered people in their offices to update them on the latest turn of events in his tiresome saga. I heard about every tryst with the lover and every fight with his wife. Jack had no sense of boundaries. Although I had never invited him to my home, he once asked if he could use my apartment for an afternoon with his friend. I reluctantly handed over my keys. I valued Jack's friendship, but I came to believe he was undermining my ability to work and my reputation as a professional.

Some workers succeed where Jack failed; they manage to keep their home lives out of the workplace. But workers will typically face additional expectations. To create an atmosphere of professionalism, company rules may disallow the comfortable garments, hairstyles and body ornamentation workers most prefer. Furthermore, workplace rules may seek to keep interpersonal relations among employees strictly professional. Company rules commonly discourage, and may even prohibit, the formation of intimate sexual relationships among employees. Such rules have multiple goals: they aim to keep workers focused on the employer's bottom line, and to reduce the perception of favoritism and sexual harassment. The supervisor who fondles subordinates has an ethical integrity problem, much like the clerical worker who steals postage. He or she also harms another; there is a victim. Since sexually inappropriate behavior is potentially discriminatory, distracted and distracting, ethical concerns are raised by a worker unable to curb sexual impulses in the office. Both the supervisor and the employee may also be breaking the law.

Because of the double firewall expectation of a work/home divide and a professional self/real self divide, workers risk getting fired if they place too many personal phone calls, send too many personal e-mails or surf salacious Web sites. Telling tasteless jokes jeopardizes jobs, too. Racial humor, sex-related humor, humor that pokes fun at a coworker's religion or culture is exceedingly common but officially unwelcome in larger companies. Teasing, flirting and dating among employees is increasingly prohibited by cautious employers seeking to avoid sexual harassment claims. Openly discussing and practicing one's religion at work may be disfavored as unprofessional, even by large employers who must accommodate religious minorities to avoid charges of discrimination.

As a practical matter, wage earners and professional employees must exercise caution in bringing the spirit of personality and play into the performance of their job responsibilities. The caution required of professionals and executive-level employees is a special challenge since they are often *required* to mix business with social pleasures. The ubiquitous business lunch mixes work with the sensual pleasure of food and the warmth of casual conversation, but out of respect for the professional/personal firewall, the pleasure must conform to certain norms of moderation. For example, a business meal should be nice but not opportunistically extravagant. It is fine to have cocktails but never to the point of intoxication. The company retreat is a common occurrence nowadays, a ritual merger of work and play. A weekend retreat might be designed to combine, for example, strategic planning exercises with recreational sports. In these faux informal settings, it would probably be a mistake to take the coworker with whom you just enjoyed a game of tennis to bed. Doing so might even violate explicit company policies.

In the increasingly diverse business world, norms of moderation are not the only ones governing official social interactions. Cultural sensitivity norms apply, too. In the name of graciously mixing business with pleasure, members of the white collar set can make serious mistakes. One common category of error is to assume that what you regard as pleasurable will be pleasurable to the client or employee you are supposed to be entertaining, even though their opposite sex or different ethnoracial group or religion would signal otherwise. A golf game at your private club with a potential customer innocently mixes business with pleasure. But the mix becomes less innocent if the customer is a woman and the course restricts women players. One summer when I was a law student I worked in a prominent New York law firm that had repressive rules of decorum—no loud conversations, no coffee cups in the hallways, strictly business attire. A senior partner at the firm took me to lunch at a private Wall Street eating club that would not have admitted me as a member. This lunch in a distinguished club was supposed to be a treat, but there was more insult than pleasure for me in such a place.

Jewelers Don and Maggie Winthrop are immune from daily worries about insulted summer interns, risque e-mails, wine at lunch and employee dating policies. But there is one sort of worry from which self-employed small business owners like the Winthrops are not immune. Like the rest of us, they have to be mindful of their work ethic. They have to work hard, well, and in a sufficiently professional manner to earn the confidence of customers, suppliers and financial institutions. Too much leisure, sloppy record keeping and slack standards of workmanship would quickly destroy their business. A strong workplace ethic has enabled the Winthrops to weather tough times.

We hear a lot about companies that reach into employees' personal lives with bans on smoking and drug use after hours. We hear about firms that ban coworker dating outright or that require coworkers to formally report their intent to date to superiors, in an effort to fend off sexual harassment complaints. We hear about companies that access employee e-mail without specific cause. One company even appropriated its employees' DNA in an attempt to determine which employees might be more likely to develop carpal tunnel syndrome. In 2001 it came to light that the Burlington Northern Santa Fe Railroad Company had secretly performed DNA tests on workers who gave blood for other purposes. The company subsequently settled a lawsuit filed under the Americans with Disabilities Act of 1990 on behalf of its workers nationwide by the Equal Employment Opportunity Commission. The company agreed to discontinue DNA testing and to pay workers monetary damages.

The need to keep a critical perspective on employer domination of the workforce is undeniable. The work ethic can be used as a tool to persuade workers to accept what are in fact intrusive and unreasonable demands motivated by the desire for profitability. In addition, the work ethic tells employees in dull, repetitive, low-paying jobs that they should find meaning and excellence in the work they do. Few jobs are as inherently unsatisfying as working in a fast-food chain dishing up hamburgers, nuggets and fries, day after day. I knew this even before my life as a starving student forced me to briefly take a job at Burger King.

With his obsessive talk about his marriage and sex life at work, Jack was an example of the worker who does not respect an ethic of the workplace. Jack did not find the work he was supposed to do intrinsically rewarding, interesting or challenging. He did not even seem to believe excellence in his job was worth pursuing as a means to an end. Workers like Jack pose a problem for their coworkers. Work was not the proving ground for Jack that it was for me. I wanted to do a good job at what was my first professional position outside a university. I had been hired as the result of an aggressive affirmative action effort to secure qualified minority professional staff, and I did not want to disappoint the people who had gone out of their way to bring me in. I wanted to produce excellent work. I found aspects of my job very interesting. I was also ambitious for myself. It is alarming to look back and see how much I allowed Jack's time-consuming social expectations to impair my ability to do my job well.

Part of Jack's problem was that he was brilliant and underemployed. I have had plenty of low-paying, low-prestige jobs in the past at which I did not excel. During college summers I worked bussing tables in a restaurant, only the minimum wage paycheck kept me moving. I did what I had to do, but I was careless and sullen because I found the work humiliating. If asked to pitch in to help the dishwashers or janitors, I resisted, malingered, slowed down. Willingness to pitch in at work is a sign of being cooperative, but it is hard to be cooperative in settings where the work is dirty, dangerous and low-prestige.

Poorly motivated workers are a big problem for workplace managers. Uncommitted workers may not stick around very long. The investment in their hiring and training is wasted. Lack of motivation undermines productivity and the quality of the work product. Unmotivated workers may be more likely to fake illness to exploit company leave policies or lie about the number of hours worked. They may be more likely to claim a business purpose for personal phone calls and travel. Bored workers may be more tempted to enliven the work day with ethically dubious office hanky-panky.

SEXY AT WORK

One of the domains in which most everyone can potentially excel is the domain of work. "Find work you like, and do well at it" is the advice I give anyone. Excellence in work has intrinsic and extrinsic rewards. The extrinsic rewards can include the praise, admiration and gratitude of others. It can also include material gain. Good workers may be rewarded with promotions, plum assignments, pleasant offices, higher salaries and leadership.

Suppose that instead of obsessing about his personal problems with his wife, Jack had devoted a similar amount of time at work to hitting on the women in the office. Jack the ambivalent husband and Jack the sexual harasser challenge the quest for worker excellence. Title VII of the Civil Rights Act of 1964 prohibits discrimination in the terms and conditions of employment on the basis of a long list of traits that include, sex, race and religion. One of the primary purposes of the rules against sexual harassment implemented under Title VII has been to improve economic opportunities for women by making employers and employees more accountable for discriminatory, sex-related speech and conduct in the workplace. The injuries termed "sexual harassment" are a problem because they are offensive and appropriate earnings and opportunities. But I am emphasizing another problem with sexual harassment that goes directly to the work ethic: it impairs the ability of distracted, demoralized workers to achieve excellence and be rewarded for excellence.

A number of prominent legal scholars are critical of the firewall expectations that ask workers to keep the home out of the office and their real selves at bay. After all, these critics say, we are caring, feeling, sexual beings; our essential humanity cannot and should not be suppressed. George Washington University law professor and journalist Jeffrey Rosen has argued that sexuality should not be banned from the workplace. We work hard and spend much of our day at work. We need to be able to let our hair down at work and to be free of intrusive scrutiny and penalty. Yale University law professor Vicki Schultz is a noted critic of sexual harassment laws. In her opinion, the laws threaten to penalize nondiscriminatory sexual self-expression in the workplace. Schultz contends that efforts to ban sexuality and sex talk from the workplace are misguided. She doubts that there is any connection between being productive and profitable and allowing people to be who they really are at work. She points to work settings, such as adult entertainment–oriented businesses, where sexual openness among coworkers positively enhances the work experience and the work product.

I part company with these sentiments out of concern for the fate of the work ethic and the just, egalitarian workplace. Limits on workplace sociality protect workers' and employers' vital interests. Sociality can undermine the work ethic, and compromise female and minority workers in traditionally white male employment settings. The case for firewall limitations is especially strong in larger, ethnoracially diverse workplaces in which men and women work side by side and in competition for scarce rewards. The political equality that has allowed women and minorities to enter the workplace and the professions is potentially undermined by sexualized work settings. Stereotypes of incompetence and hypersexuality plague African American and Hispanic workers. First-generation workers from families bereft of privilege and a history of past success may feel special economic pressures to do their jobs well, and the distractions of uninhibited sociality can undermine such workers.

Most people who oppose employers' efforts to limit personal relationships in the workplace on privacy and free speech grounds nevertheless accept the legitimacy of ethical rules against personal relationships between professionals and their clients. In the United States it is considered a very serious breach of ethics when a physician, psychiatrist or lawyer has a sexual affair with a client. Licenses are at stake for violation of clearly promulgated ethical codes and conventions; at root is a concern for the vulnerability of clients and patients who are vitally dependent upon objective advice. We do not refrain from ethically sanctioning professionals on the grounds that they are sexual beings and their clients and patients are autonomous consenting adults. We know that introducing intimacy into the relationships inherently marked by unequal power and authority can be detrimental.

Power and authority come in many forms. Jack and I, for example, were nominal peers. We earned the same salary and had very similar responsibilities. But he had a kind of authority and power over me nonetheless. He was white; he was a man; he was older; he was married and had children; he came from an affluent family; he owned a house. Reasonable minds can disagree about the ethics of sexual relationships with coworkers, subordinates, clients, students and others encountered professionally in the course of one's business or employment. But the case against it is especially strong when the people involved are in any respect unequal.

The temptation to yield to sexual attraction at work is understandably great—a worker's well-groomed, dynamic, involved, efficacious persona is often potentially sexy. Someone who might not seem attractive pushing a grocery cart or reading a newspaper on a park bench might seem enormously attractive hard at work displaying talent or resourcefulness.

When I ask people how they met their spouse or partner, the answer is often, "we met at work." Although work is by no means the only place intimate partners become acquainted, many people do meet their future

When certain sexual lines are crossed, even among consenting adults, accusations or impropriety, abuse of power and unfairness are inevitable.

spouses and partners through their jobs, proving that mixing business with intimacy is commonplace.

The DuPont Company is a Fortune 50 corporation headquartered in Wilmington, Delaware. It is a conservative old firm with a staid personality. Like most large firms, it has found it necessary to formulate a policy about workplace intimacy. In 2002, spokesperson Irv Lipp released a statement of the company's policy on "office romance" to a Wilmington newspaper. The policy, which did not mention the word "sex," reflected a desire to avoid the arrogance of dictating a professional self/real self firewall for mature adults, while plainly discouraging what it terms "romantic" involvements, especially between superiors and subordinates. It begins with the statement, "The personal life of employees is their business" and continues: "DuPont does not take a position on an employee's personal involvement with coworkers, customers or vendors."[2] The company encourages its employees to examine any romantic involvement to determine if it "(1) negatively reflects on the employee or the company; (2) affects the employee's feelings on business decisions; or (3) is likely to be disruptive to the effectiveness of the organization." Interestingly, DuPont does not prohibit relationships between supervisors and subordinates, but labels them "inappropriate and of particular concern." Where "personal involvement becomes incompatible with appropriate professional practices and has the potential for compromising the individual's or Company's professional integrity, the Company must take measures to adjust the work environment." Reading between the lines, office romance might lead to anything from reassignment within the company to termination.

The DuPont policy reflects what I think has become a pervasive view. Under the right circumstances, quietly dating a coworker on one's own dime and time poses no practical problem, but deeply mixing work and sexual intimacy is tricky. A blunt sexual overture can be a disastrous discourtesy—there are so many ways to exploit and be exploited, intrude and be invaded, offend and be offended. It is for this reason that ethical caution is called for when considering a work-related sexual liaison.

The precise reasons for ethical caution with respect to sex in business and work relations will vary with circumstance. When I was an attorney practicing at Cravath, Swaine & Moore in New York, a senior partner took me to assist him in conducting a deposition. Someone passed a handwritten note to me that read: "You are very pretty and I bet you are a good lawyer, too." I was not certain who wrote the note; there were a lot of dark suits in the room. If opposing counsels' client had written the note without the attorneys' knowledge, it was a minor impropriety about which I could do little. However, if an opposing counsel had himself written the note or approved its delivery, it was a serious professional impropriety implicating the American Bar Association's rules of professional conduct and the rules of civil procedure, about which I could complain. In order to show my toughness, though, I tossed the disturbing note into the trash. I did not want to make an issue of what was clearly an issue anyway: my being the only black and only female lawyer in the room. The man who sent me that note may not have appreciated the spot he put me in. He may have created turmoil trying to be nice. And that is precisely why keeping things on a strictly professional basis is often the most ethical course. You can create unimagined discomfort, even be unethical, just trying to be nice.

SLEEPING IN CLASS

The amount of sexual activity in the academy gives lie to the stereotype of academics as asexual nerds. John Stuart Mill once suggested that if you want to know which of two things is better, you should ask someone who has experienced both. For more than twenty years I have operated on the belief that academicians have an ethical obligation to refrain from sexual relationships with students and colleagues. I have managed to meet that standard, and vastly prefer life with the firewall to life without it. I also know that life without the firewall is a mixed proposition.

When I was a young professor in the 1970s, I dated a colleague in my department who was also my immediate supervisor. I also dated unmarried young professors when I was a student. My conscious intent was never to seek advantage through sex, but perhaps conscious intent in such situations is not all that matters. Certainly my dates' stature as professors was related to my willingness to befriend them, yet I believed their main attractions were intelligence, wit, sensitivity and, compared to my fellow students, maturity. Although those relationships were genuine and led to lasting friendships, I have come to regret them.

A student who dates professors pay a price: the student's successes may be wrongly attributed to the lover/mentor and their failures wrongly blamed on the distractions of romance or vain expectations of having the wheels greased. Peers may isolate and harass students who date professors. The professors who date students pay a price, too. They may be accused of favoritism in awarding grades, fellowships and prizes. The need, at some schools, to worry about secrecy and detection will demand time and energy that the professor could otherwise spend on work. The disapproval or envy of senior colleagues could have an impact on decisions about a junior professor's promotion and tenure.

When certain sexual lines are crossed, even among consenting adults, accusations of impropriety, abuse of power and unfairness are inevitable. I have heard of professors watching X-rated videos with their students for fun. A few years ago a professor friend told me that she was having an affair with a student at her school who was fifteen years her junior. She confessed to necking in empty classrooms and in her office. Once I walked into a male colleague's office and noticed a condom on the floor. A married professor I know had a stormy extramarital affair with a graduate student, which included a loud, ugly fight in the corridors of the university. I was disturbed by the conduct of these people. Their failure to erect a firewall had a very significant adverse affect on institutional morale. This is the sort of disruption "to the effectiveness of the organization" I am sure Dupont officials had in mind when they discouraged the romantic liaisons they did not forbid.

WORKING WOMEN CHOOSE

Compare two women who have embraced different visions of professional/personal boundaries. Fifty-year-old Marian has built a very high wall. Twenty-seven-year-old Tracey maintains a low wall.

Marian is a business executive in full command of the ethics of work and the work ethic. In her position as a senior vice president for a large publicly traded company, she is squeaky clean. No insider trading, no padded expense accounts. She puts in very long days and shows no signs of letting up. Marian's work ethic is a product of experience and breeding. She learned from watching friends combine intimacy and work just how costly it can be, and as the daughter of Dutch-, Scottish-, and English-ancestry parents, she is the fully legitimate heir of the Protestant work ethic.

Marian has worked for twenty years now at a series of banking, management and pharmaceutical firms, where the norms of upper management dictate long hours—especially, she believes, for women. Marian believes top female executives have to be smarter than average and willing to put in more hours. "In my old company," she said, referring to an international pharmaceutical firm where she served as a vice president for human resources, "there were six vice presidents in the main office, three male and three female. The guys delegated and went home at six." The women had smaller staffs and stayed until eight at night. Marian dislikes the "work hard, play hard" management culture of young, high-flying companies like Enron used to be. She laments, though, that executives at older companies preach balance but model overwork. "It's a kind of macho thing. You know you should work less. You applaud the firm policies that allow flexible family leaves and generous vacations. But because you want to get ahead, be excellent and meet expectations, you keep working extra hard, and everyone around you does, too."

For a number of years Marian was single and spent nearly all her time at work. Dating someone she met at work would have been natural since she had little life outside of her work, but she has not done it. She is adamant about maintaining a professional/personal firewall. "I am extreme," she admits: "I have a firm rule for myself against sex or romance of any sort with my coworkers. I have never wanted anyone at work to think about me in sexual terms, never wanted the gossip, never wanted the conflicts of interest." Marian is a very attractive woman. She is fashion-model tall, stylish, trim-figured and blond. She is interesting, well traveled and a good conversationalist. Still, she says, no one has ever propositioned her. "I think I must send a signal that I am not going to respond to any overture or familiarity, and so men leave me alone." Marian believes her unwillingness to mix work with pleasure has contributed to her smooth success in the corporate world. As for romance, she has achieved success there, too, with a man she met outside of work and married a year later.

I would guess that few women in the coming years will take Marian's absolute stance against workplace romance. Younger women may come to understand the career risks of interoffice dating, but have not grown up with the same sense of the difficulty of making it in a "man's" world. Tracey is a good example.

Tracey plans to be a lawyer. She grew up in New England and describes herself as "an affluent WASP." Tracey attended a conservative private college in the south that she disparages as "money-oriented." It is remarkable that someone so young has already accomplished so much. Before entering an Ivy League law school Tracey interned for two United States senators on Capitol Hill, and spent time in Africa with the Peace Corps.

After college, Tracey briefly waited tables in a pizza parlor. She soon landed a professional job analyzing legislation for a small, for-profit health policy research firm. She was one of thirty employees. The office was friendly; the staff went out once a week for drinks. Three of the men from the office were housemates, including Ned, a man with whom Tracey began a romance. Ned and Tracey were both unattached and about the same age. Although Ned was not her supervisor, he was a supervisor on another team in the office. The firm had no explicit policies on dating.

Tracey says her relationship with Ned initially had a positive impact on her work. It "made going to work more fun." It added "an incentive for leaving the house each day." Ned's office cubicle was three down from Tracey's, so they saw a lot of each other during business hours. Yet there was very little flirting. The two exchanged few personal e-mails or phone calls. Once Ned tried to discuss a personal problem in their relationship, but Tracey insisted that the discussion would have to wait until they left the office. "I could tell from his wanting to do that that maybe the relationship wasn't going to work," she said.

The couple kept things fairly low-key, but the romance was not a secret. It was impossible for Ned to conceal the affair from his housemates, so everyone in the office knew about the relationship, except for the president of the company. Tracey is not sure who in the office finally notified the president, but she thinks it might have been "a woman who was never friendly to me." The president was furious, and angrier still that she was the last to know. She wanted to fire Ned and Tracey. She agreed to let them stay only after other employees assured her that Ned and Tracey had not behaved inappropriately in the office and that the relationship had not affected anyone's work. Ned soon left the company anyway. Within five months of its inception the relationship was over.

Tracey says she had no sense of caution when she started dating Ned. As a general matter, office romances seemed okay. When she worked as a waitress in the pizza parlor, she had dated a fellow employee, this one her supervisor, without incident. Tracey explains that she was living in "a young city" in which people commonly met their lovers at work. People spent a lot of time at work. Tracey argues that "work is a safe place to meet someone to date, compared to, say, a bar. You know the person you meet at work has a job and a decent background. They have been prescreened. You know who they are."

Tracey anticipates that she will approach future workplace relationships with caution. She was treated with civility by male and female coworkers before, during and after the affair with Ned. No one looked at her differently. No one assumed that she, a petite blond, was a bimbo. No one sexually harassed her. But there was one problem: people talked about her behind her back. She was an object of special scrutiny and controversy. She discovered that it can be uncomfortable to know that others in an office "are discussing you and fighting about you behind your back." Moreover, she now believes she was only willing to have the affair because "I was not invested in the job." She knew she was bound for the Peace Corps and law school. The job was "not a step toward my ultimate career; it was something on the way that didn't count that much toward it." In a situation in which the job matters, Tracey says she will be more concerned about "having mentors in the office and making it on my own merit." In the old days of Yankee business when her father was young, she explained, "it was all about who you know. You got a job by knowing people. It isn't like that anymore. Merit matters. Office romances can mess that up." If having objective mentors and supervisors is important to advancement on merits, it would be dangerous to have a workplace romance, she concluded. "It's about self-esteem, too. You want to know you got where you got because you deserved it, not because you slept with someone or had friends in the office." Tracey views her future legal career as a proving ground, much in the way that Marian has viewed her career in the corporate world. With that in mind, I expect her new, more cautious ethic will serve her and future coworkers well.

CHAPTER 6

REAL ETHICS FOR BUSINESS

I attended a dinner symposium for business and professional women hosted by the Women's Athenaeum in New York City—elegant surroundings, a view of the water, good wine. The topic for the evening was financial accountability. Speaking in the wake of Enron, WorldCom, and the Sarbanes-Oxley Act, a dynamic CEO offered frank but dangerous advice about corporate ethics.

A RESPONSE TO SCANDAL

The Enron corporation once boasted investors and 21,000 employees worldwide. With the help of the Wall Street banking community and accounting firm Arthur Andersen, Enron executives unscrupulously erected a facade of profitability from its energy commodities, telecommunications, broadband and other businesses. In anticipation of a federal investigation, Arthur Andersen destroyed potentially incriminating documents—a crime of obstructing justice, for which the firm was found guilty in June 2002. Enron's bankers also faced charges. The Securities and Exchange Commission and the Manhattan District Attorney accused J. P. Morgan Chase and Citigroup of helping Enron to cheat the investing public. Authorities say the bankers, keen on profiting from interest payments, knowingly cloaked billions in loans to enable Enron to conceal the extent of its debt. Although the bankers admitted no wrongdoing, Chase agreed to pay $135 million and Citigroup agreed to pay $120 million.[1]

J. P. Morgan Chase Vice Chairman Marc J. Shapiro told New York District Attorney Robert Morgenthau that "Our view, historically, was that our clients and their accountants were responsible for clients' proper accounting and disclosure of the transactions."[2] Shapiro's remark was a transparent rationalization by a pragmatist seeking to justify sidestepping the ethical point of view because following the profit motive was irresistible. Federal prosecutors reduced the complex Enron transactions to simple terms. It "boils down to lying, cheating, and stealing."[3] The gargantuan WorldCom corporation collapse was a product of the same triad of moral vices that brought down Enron. The firm misled the public by overstating its income by $11 billion, and the resulting scandal led to a $200 billion loss to shareholders.

President George W. Bush signed the Sarbanes-Oxley financial responsibility and disclosure statute into law on July 30, 2002. To fight corporate corruption of the sort witnessed at Enron, the act requires that the Securities and Exchange Commission (SEC) appoint a knowledgeable, five-member Public Company Accounting Oversight Board, empowered to register accounting firms and to set standards, including ethics standards, for auditors. The act addresses some of the numerous ethics abuses that came to light during the Enron affair, specifically requiring accounting firms to maintain, for seven years, audit work papers pertaining to clients who are publicly traded companies, for example. Enron officials and their bankers concealed the company's unviable financial condition from the investing public. In response, Sarbanes-Oxley requires prompt disclosure of material changes in a firm's financial condition. To curb self-dealing, the act prohibits companies from issuing special loans for company insiders. CEOs and CFOs are required to certify the lawfulness and veracity of company financial statements. Companies must disclose whether they have ethics codes for their officers, too. The act provides for multimillion-dollar fines and long prison terms for chief executive officers and financial officers found guilty of wrongdoing. To make it easier for shareholders to sue, the act extends to five years the statute of limitation for investor suits for civil fraud. To make it more likely regulators will learn about fraud, the act requires securities lawyers to report evidence of material violations of law within a corporation up the ladder to corporate officers, and if necessary, to the board of directors, and encourages whistle-blowing by giving employees who reveal corporate misconduct an enhanced right to sue for damages if they face retaliation.

"IT'S ONLY ETHICS, NOT MORALS!"

The CEO who spoke to us at the Women's Athenaeum reacted to the new legal environment created by Sarbanes-Oxley with a bit of semantic philosophy: she drew a distinction between "ethics" and "morals" and turned her distinction into a call to action in an over-regulated economy. The Sarbanes-Oxley rules are only ethics, not morals, she began. Morality, she continued, is personal; ethics, on the other hand, is public. A person's morality consists of the personal values he or she has come to hold, under the influence of family, religion and community. Ethics, she continued, are the rules laid down by society to regulate business and the professions. She advised that ethical rules should be viewed pragmatically, like other potential barriers to getting what you want for your company. She explained ethics rules as products of politics, and that executives should therefore feel free to bend, stretch and lobby their way around them. Her message for the ethics-conscious post-Enron world: If you want to be successful, do not be dominated by ethics to the detriment of the bottom line.

Ethics vs. Morals

The CEO made too much of her distinction between ethics and morals. In the parlance of everyday English, the words "moral" and "ethical" are used interchangeably in judgments about right and wrong, good and bad, virtue and vice and justice and injustice. Lying, promise breaking and cheating are variously condemned as "immoral" and "unethical." Around universities in the English-speaking world, philosophers use "ethics" and "moral philosophy" as synonyms for the study of right and wrong. I have adopted this practice myself throughout this book. The words "ethics" and "morality" have no essences or etymologies that demand strict, distinct usage. Some linguists would even tell you that both words derive from ancient Greek and Latin roots with overlapping meanings.

In certain contexts "unethical" and "immoral" do carry distinctively different connotations. "Ethics" often connotes shared standards that have become publicly applicable, official or legal; or standards of responsibility that pertain to specific social roles or professions. Special ethical standards are said to apply, for example, to teachers, doctors, public officials, lawyers, journalists, athletes, corporate officers and accountants. Professionals acting in their professional capacities are bound by ethical principles devised by industry associations or built into employment policies and laws.

"Morality" often connotes, by contrast, personal or group standards that may be deeply cultural or religious. "Morality" is easier on the ears when referring to the dominant traditions present in a society. "The morality of the United States and the morality of Singapore differ," someone might say. In business and the professions, the popular practice is to refer to ethics or professional ethics rather than to morality. We could speak of the morality of a doctor or lawyer, but it is most common, when speaking about the obligations of a professional in his or her professional capacity to speak of ethics.

A well-known rule of professional responsibility established by the American Bar Association prohibits attorneys from commingling client funds with their own. An attorney holding money for a client is supposed to place the money in a separate bank account set up for that purpose. If the attorney commingled funds, she would be branded unethical and subject to official reprimand and loss of license. Were the attorney to commit adultery with a neighbor, those who felt compelled to judge her could condemn her as unethical, but would probably use the term "immoral." This is just the way we talk.

Gaming Sarbanes-Oxley

My pragmatic CEO is not alone in dismissing ethics rules as something to game. In fact, despite bipartisan support for Sarbanes-Oxley in Congress, after the passage of the act, law firms, accounting groups and trade associations quickly began intensely lobbying authorities to weaken the rules. By January 2003, barely six months after the passage of Sarbanes-Oxley, SEC staff members were complaining that the agency had moved toward adopting watered-down versions of the rules everyone thought Sarbanes-Oxley mandated. Complaints continued after the ethically embattled Harvey Pitt handed over the helm of the SEC to William H. Donaldson. On the first birthday of the Act, the *New York Times* reported that "a number of companies and Wall Street institutions have complained that the new rules imposed over the last year have been too strict and have quietly begun to lobby Congress and the Commission to roll them back."[4]

It is true, of course, that ethical rules governing the professions are products of political institutions; law is born of politics. Legal rules come about through the actions of legislatures, regulatory agencies and professional associations. Public comments, industry lobbying and horse-trading impact the ethical rules that flow out of Washington and state capitals. The Sarbanes-Oxley Act contemplates a close relationship between the Oversight Board and the industries it regulates; at the same time, the act retains authority for the board to embrace or reject standards proposed by partisans, as it deems appropriate.

Many of the standards that regulate the business and professional world as a result of political processes will deserve the same respect that is given to the standards of personal life that come to us through upbringing and cultural traditions. Why? They are based on the same principles of honesty and fair play. The accountant at work should not help a company steal from its investors; the accountant at home should not help a friend steal from her mother. Ethical standards adopted by lawmakers, business and professional associations are often specialized applications of general moral standards.

Law Floats on a Sea of Ethics

Moral standards merit respect when formalized into legal or operational guidelines. "In civilized life, law floats on a sea of ethics," Chief Justice Earl Warren once remarked.[5] I have quoted the justice before, and do so again to underscore that the value foundation of politically created ethical rules is sometimes the same as that of culturally grounded moral rules. Admittedly, this is not always so. Yet ethics rules that seem arbitrary can have a deeper purpose. The Pennsylvania rule that lawyers must take two hours of continuing legal education instruction in ethics from an approved provider is arbitrary. The number could be one or three, and why not? But beneath the arbitrary rule for lawyers is a very important concern. The concern is that lawyers understand their responsibilities for their clients' welfare and property. Lawyers ought to keep informed about what the courts, laws and professional associations say.

"UNETHICAL, BUT NOT FROM A BUSINESS POINT OF VIEW"

Boasting $18.5 billion in sales in 2002, the Weyerhaeuser Company describes itself as "one of the world's largest integrated forest product companies" and a company with "high ethical standards."[6] Critics say the century-old company has a shameful history of land-grabbing, monopoly and deforestation.[7] In September 2003 Weyerhaeuser announced plans to pay $68 million to settle two class-action lawsuits pending in federal district court in eastern Pennsylvania. The suits complained that Weyerhaeuser and other major-container board and packaging producers had conspired to fix or manipulate the prices of linerboard used to make corrugated boxes. Weyerhaeuser's vice president and general counsel Robert Dowdy dismissed the suits as "without merit," and the company admitted no wrongdoing.[8]

The massive Columbia/HCA Healthcare Corporation was exposed for billing fraud in the 1990s. In 2001, New York U.S. Attorney Mary Jo White delivered the bad news that "Health care fraud is a big and booming business."[9] She was announcing a 100-count indictment against Westchester County chiropractor Andrew Orlander, convicted of joining forces with a physician in a scheme to bill $10 million in fake and inflated insurance claims.

In 2003, Richard M. Scrushy, the founder of HealthSouth, the country's largest rehabilitation hospital, diagnostic imaging and outpatient surgery centers concern, was accused by the federal Securities and Exchange Commission of fraudulently inflating the firm's earnings by $1.4 billion. A few days after the SEC began investigating the firm, a container of what appeared to be incriminating shredded e-mails was found near the files of former company executives. The government has charged more than a dozen HealthSouth executives with fraud for inflating the company's finances, all of whom have agreed to plead guilty. In Southern California, Tenet HealthSystems Inc., Alvarado Hospital and hospital executive Barry Weinbaum were indicted on charges of illegally compensating physicians in the millions for referring patients to Alvarado. In 2003, a U.S. Senate committee began investigating unnecessary heart surgeries and other improper procedures attributed to Tenet's Redding, California hospital. Tenet may be "ethically and morally bankrupt, the committee concluded."[10] Tenet stated that it would fully cooperate with the investigators.

To the detriment of the public, businessmen and -women sometimes reject the moral point of view; or, equally disturbing, embrace their own self-serving business ethic. Sometimes they do so proudly. In 2003 the New York State Ethics Commission charged seven officials of the Nassau County Medical Center with accepting prohibited gifts from vendors seeking to do business with the hospital. The violations came to light after an anonymous whistle-blower notified the Commission. The State of New York Public Officers Law, Sections 73(5) and 74, frowns on accepting gifts on the job. The law authorizes the state Ethics Commission to issue advisory opinions interpreting its prohibitions. Advisory opinion No. 94-16 of the Commission is black-and-white. Neither public officials nor public employees are permitted to accept anything of value in excess of $75, if the gift is intended or could be expected to influence a decision. The $75 amount is in one sense arbitrary. Why not $100 or $50? And why not an exception for gifts from vendors who offer better deals to the state after wining and dining state employees?

Richard B. Turan, president of the public agency that runs Nassau County's system of hospitals, nursing homes and medical centers serving the poor, seemed to think the ethics rules were too arbitrary to command his allegiance. Turan was charged with three violations of the rules for accepting about $700 worth of food, travel and entertainment. Turan said he reimbursed the party who gave him tickets to a hockey game but admitted the other violations. Some men in his position would have been contrite, but not Turan. He was unrepentant. He described his violations as "technical" and as not personally benefitting him and other officials treated to free plane tickets, limos and expensive meals. He argued that the gratuities he accepted served a good purpose: they saved the public a lot of money. By accepting vendors' illegal gifts he was able to negotiate goods and services for the hospital at lower prices than expected. Turan also made an interesting argument that the violation of state ethics rules did not violate genuine business ethics. By "business ethics" he seemed to have meant the rational businessperson's sense of what is a significant crossing of the lines: "We're very confident that what we did was legally and ethically correct from a business ethics point of view."[11]

In making excuses for himself and fellow officials, Turan gave incomplete consideration to the equities of the matter. His effort to out-think ethics fell flat. He ignored the issue of fairness to the vendors who obeyed their side of the ethics law and made no effort to offer hospital officials illegal gifts. He ignored the possibility that such a vendor might have offered an even lower price than the briber. Turan overlooked matters of responsible leadership, too. Turan set a poor example for others in public employment. His actions implied that any state employee may break the ethics rules if he or she personally believes it is the economically smart thing to do for the government. He implied that the public should not be concerned about corruption when officials flout ethics but reap only small private gain. Ironically, Turan has been criticized for being a poor financial manager all around. He gave controversial raises to two staff members, undertook expensive hospital renovations, and left his agency millions in debt in 2002. Turan cannot be personally blamed for everything, but under his watch, state and county comptrollers reported that his agency's cash on hand plummeted from $56 million to $28 million in less than eight months in 2003, and that midway through 2003 his agency was already running a $9 million deficit.

The business sector runs amok, ethically speaking, when it supplants law and common morality with individuals' or industries' ad hoc, self-serving ideas about business ethics and smart business moves. Men and women like the two I have described here cultivate contagious disrespect for official ethics rules on the ground that the rules are technical and political. We must fix our attention to ethics laws' concrete potential to protect the economy. Ethics has a practical point. Put to work against enmity, injustice, want and pain, our shared ethical capacity is grounds for pride, as great as the pride that flows from the savvy business move. Communal caretaking, not individual profiteering, is the essential end cherished ethical values commend.

THE WISDOM OF SELF-REGULATION

The amount of costly ethical vice in the world of business and the professions has made the idea of industry self-regulation instantly suspect. It would be hard to completely trust corporate accountants, stock analysts, and mutual fund dealers to write their own rules after revelations of self-dealing such as we have seen in recent years.[12] Legal rules like the Sarbanes-Oxley regulations seem necessary to tell professionals what they may and may not do and create incentives for compliance. Other legal rules seem necessary, too, like rules that dictate requirements of membership in a chosen profession and rules establishing mandatory ethics training.

One pervasive device of self-regulation for business and the professions is the adoption of a written ethical code. Industries and professional associations commonly adopt ethical codes. The Center for the Study of Ethics in the Professions housed at the Illinois Institute of Technology received a grant from the National Science Foundation to make its collec-

Ethics codes can function as public relations, "moral cover" for a profession in need of respect from the general public.

tion of 850 codes of ethics available on the Web. The codes the Center archives range from a few sentences long to book-length.

However, not every industry or professional code is designed as serious ethical guidance for people in the field. Some have other primary purposes. Ethics codes can function as public relations, "moral cover" for a profession in need of respect from the general public. A code can signal that the group or business sector is ethically self-aware and committed to serving the public's needs.

I recently noticed a "code of ethics" for pharmacists posted on the wall of a retail drugstore. The code consisted of a few pithy service standards. A code of this sort is primarily designed to publicize a commitment to customer needs. The Society of Professional Journalists has promulgated a code of ethics that sets out standards for news gathering and reporting. This code is detailed enough both to serve as guidance for journalists concerned about the nature or the scope of their responsibilities, and to function as a signal to the general public that Society members have the welfare of the public in mind in the work they do. Reporters are empowered by the First Amendment to gather news and information of value to the public, but the Society's code sets ideal limits for journalists who might neglect reasonable expectations of civility and privacy. The code has no teeth, though, because no material penalties attach to disregarding it.

Professional realtors have both an ethics code and an ethics education requirement. As of January 1, 2002, members of the National Association of Realtors are required to take a three-hour course on their code of ethics. When I first heard about the NAR code, I was surprised to learn that real estate professionals took themselves so seriously and was impressed by their stated ideals. The preamble to the NAR code works hard to elevate the stature of the profession. It asserts that the survival and growth of a free civilization depend upon the "highest and best use of the land and the widest distribution of land ownership."[13] Realtors must devote themselves to "fulfilling their grave responsibility and patriotic duty to zealously maintain and improve the standards of their calling."[14]

Not all responses to ethical scandal are merely symbolic moral cover. Major ethics scandals can prompt serious new ethics regimes with the force of law. The Enron corporate accounting scandal led in short order to a new corporate ethics regime; the hard-hitting Sarbanes-Oxley Act of 2002 mandated tough rules of enhanced accountability for auditors and corporate managers, backed by long prison terms and hefty fines.

THE ETHICS REGULATION STAVE-OFF STRATEGY

Self-regulatory professional codes can also serve as part of what I call an "ethics regulation stave-off strategy." Since public criticism can lead to government regulation, preemptively adopting voluntary ethics rules is one way industries and professional groups can sometimes avoid unwanted government intervention. Industries commonly complain that the rules and regulations laid down by state and federal authorities are unwarranted and onerous. Firms resist regulation they believe will cut into corporate profits, lower salaries and harm consumers. To stave off more burdensome government regulation, some industries adopt voluntary schemes of self-regulation that include ethical safeguards. These politically and economically motivated ethics standards may be strategic, yet even ethical standards adopted as a result of the stave-off strategy may be better than preexisting standards or no standards at all. The new ABA fraud disclosure rules are an example of moral cover and the regulation stave-off strategy, to the extent that in adopting the rules the "ABA was knuckling under out of fear that government regulators might step in to require more cooperation from lawyers if they failed to change the way they do business."[15]

Fair Information Practices by Online Businesses
Another example of what I mean by the stave-off strategy is the adoption of fair information practices by online businesses. For most of the 1990s there was considerable momentum for federal laws regulating Internet privacy and trade practices. Consumers who engaged in online business transactions were poorly informed and deliberately misled. Firms concealed their intent to market consumer data they collected online. Firms broke promises to keep consumer data acquired in online transactions

confidential. Young children were targeted by marketers to disclose personal information about themselves and their families. Congress enacted the Children's Online Privacy Protection Act, which went into effect in 2000 to deal with children's online privacy, but adults' privacy was left unguarded.

Under Chairman Robert Pitofsky, a Democrat appointee, the Federal Trade Commission studied the problem and recommended federal regulation of Internet privacy. To stave off government regulation, industry began to adopt stricter self-regulation including voluntary privacy notices and voluntary limits on the disclosure of confidential information to third parties. One form of self-regulation firms initiated was to seek the certification of TRUSTe, an industry-affiliated organization set up to certify that companies have adopted a standardized set of fair information practices. The fair information practices seek to balance consumers' interests in controlling personal information with Web business operators' interest in using personal information to design and sell products or services. In the space of a couple of years, voluntarily posted privacy policies went from rare to typical.

In this case, industry self-regulation helped to stave off government regulation. In a sudden about-face, on October 4, 2001, the Federal Trade Commission announced that it would not seek federal internet privacy legislation, a victory for proponents of a policy preference for self-regulation by the online business community. In a speech before the Privacy 2001 Conference in Ohio, FTC appointee Chairman Timothy J. Muris, a Rebublican appointee, stated that he would continue to aggressively enforce existing Internet and consumer privacy laws adopted during the Clinton years, including the Gramm-Leach-Bliley financial privacy rules whose efficacy he doubted. But he said he would not seek a federal statute requiring firms doing business over the Internet to adopt fair information practices: "We need to develop better information about how such legislation would work and the costs and benefits it would generate.... [L]egislating broad-based, privacy protections is extraordinarily difficult."[16] Responding to the about-face on privacy, Sarah Andrews, formerly of the proprivacy Electronic Privacy Information Center expressed surprise: "It kind of smacks of ideology."[17] Republican Dick Armey of Texas perceived welcome humility in Muris's announcement: "the chairman rightly recognizes Congress is often unable to keep up with the fast changing online world."[18] The consolation for the general public is that this time self-regulation has proven to be better than no regulation at all.

Conflicts of Interest on Wall Street

In a second example of the stave-off strategy of industry producing ethical rules to avert unwanted government regulation, the government embraced the rules of industry and made them law. In the 1980s, stock analysts developed an uncomfortably close relationship with investment banks responsible for mergers and initial public offerings of stock. In the 1990s, analysts advised clients to purchase stock in which analysts themselves had a professional interest or stake. They also publicly trumpeted stocks they privately derided. These practices eventually came to light. Seemingly fearful of draconian government regulation, the Association of Securities Dealers and the New York Stock Exchange devised ethics rules for stock analysts. Research directors at fourteen Wall Street firms spent six months negotiating new voluntary rules among themselves. The rules were formulated in the wake of a storm of political controversy about who to blame for analysts' previously unchecked conflicts of interest. Marc E. Lackritz, president of the Securities Industry Association, announced the new rules, stating that "the concerns have been that research recommendations are biased, analyst conflicts undisclosed, their language confusing and their compensation skewed to investment banking. These best practice standards call for clear disclosure and will preserve the independence and objective judgment of Wall Street research."[19] The Securities and Exchange Commission approved the stock analyst rules drawn up by industry groups on May 8, 2002, with only minor changes.

The short-lived SEC chairman Harvey Pitt, himself under attack for conflicts of interest, was promptly criticized for failing to insist on tougher rules than the Commission approved under his watch. As reported by the *New York Times*, "some Democrats, institutional investors and consumer groups complained that the rules were both tardy and tepid and were intended by industry cheerleaders to head off more stringent proposals for a ban on allowing analysts to work on merger and underwriting business for clients of their investment banks."[20] The inadequacy of the rules was suggested when just short of a year later the SEC announced a $1.4 billion settlement of fraud charges against Salomon Smith Barney, Credit Suisse First Boston, Merrill Lynch, Goldman Sachs Group and Morgan Stanley.[21] One of the terms of the settlement was that stock analysts would be segregated from firms underwriting business to avoid conflicts of interest creeping into their recommendations.

I do not consider the ethical rules of the Sarbanes-Oxley Act as part of a stave-off strategy. They are not an example of industry self-regulation masquerading as government ethics rules. As previously detailed, the Sarbanes-Oxley Act was signed into law by President Bush in July 2002. The corporate accounting accountability measure was described by some as a sweeping, quick and appropriate response to corporate and accountant wrongdoing. John T. Dillion, chairman of the Business Roundtable, praised the law as "the right bill at the right time." However, some members of Congress, including Congressman John Boehner and Senator Phil Gramm, argue that the law overreaches. Boehner was quoted in the *New York Times* complaining that the law represents a "stampede by members to get something done, regardless of what it is, to cover them politically."[22]

ETHICAL CONSULTANTS

Self-regulation through the adoption of ethical codes, rules and policies is one kind of moral cover. Another type is reliance upon professional ethics advisors and consultants, whose affiliation with one's business or industry bespeaks a serious investment in addressing ethics concerns.

I served as an ethics consultant for a couple of Internet start-up companies concerned that their products or business methods might run afoul of the public's laws and ethical expectations. I was an unpaid consultant for a company whose business plan contemplated use of marketing data on individuals that raised information privacy concerns. A second company paid me $50,000 for a year's worth of ethics advice and public relations about a business plan for an Internet portal that would link children's homes and schools, and include some commercial advertising.

Ethics consultants have to take special care that they do not allow themselves to function as moral cover for unethical conduct. I do not think it is inherently wrong to accept money for giving ethics advice, any more than it is wrong to accept money for psychological advice. In fact there are now philosophers in New York who have hung out shingles and dispense "clinical" philosophy for an hourly fee. However, to be paid to give knowingly unethical ethics assurances is to stoop very low indeed. I have had to decline working with companies who clearly only wanted to use my name or only wanted me to rubber-stamp their enterprises. At the same time, I have found making judgments about what companies really want from their ethics' consultants difficult. A firm once tried to sign me up on the basis of a single letter and a phone call. Some ethicists have accepted advisory roles, only to later resign when it became clear that their advice had been ignored or improperly solicited. Bioethicist Glenn McGee resigned from the ethics advisory board of Advanced Cell Technology, Inc., after learning that the company had begun cloning animal and human embryos for stem cell research without consulting its ethics advisors.[23]

The public sector is highly dependent upon ethics consultants but is generally unable or unwilling to pay them. The judicial system depends upon ethicists to serve as expert witnesses in lawsuits requiring evidence of ethical standards of care in medicine, law and business accounting. Expert witnesses tend to be paid by the parties who hire them to testify. The role of a hired gun ethicist is a delicate role that one is obligated to perform well. The ethicists with the most integrity testify only when doing so is consistent with their well-considered values and beliefs.

A lot of ethics consulting relating to health and medical research goes on for free. Bioethicists are professors, physicians, lawyers or clergy with knowledge of ethical issues relating to the care and treatment of the human body. They commonly advise patients, families, health care providers, researchers and drug companies. Hospitals rely heavily on bioethicists and formal ethics committees to weigh the ethical implications of courses of care either recommended by physicians or administrators or sought by patients and their families. Hospital ethics committees may include doctors, nurses, social workers, psychologists, members of the lay community, academics and clergy. Institutional Review Boards (IRBs) that include ethicists and other professionals and laypersons oversee human subject research and examine ethical questions of privacy, autonomy and safety raised by government-funded research. Federal regulations require IRBs for federally funded research on human subjects. I currently serve on an IRB for a health care–related nonprofit organization, the Family Planning Council of Philadelphia.

Ethics consultants assist government agencies and officials, generally without compensation beyond reimbursement for expenses. A National Bioethics Advisory Commission or Council on Bioethics appointed by the president of the United States has been in place for several years. The National Aeronautics and Space Administration (NASA) has retained Paul Root Wolpe, a colleague of mine at the University of Pennsylvania, as its own bioethicist. Following the explosion of the space shuttle *Columbia* in February 2003, Wolpe defended the concept of manned spaced flight, explaining that direct involvement with NASA had allowed him to better appreciate the agency's mission.

During the initial years of the human genome project, the National Institutes of Health and the Department of Energy convened a working group on the Ethical, Legal and Social Implications (ELSI) of the Human Genome Research. Congress mandated that 5 percent of its appropriations for human genome research go to ethics. I served without pay on the ELSI working group with other lawyers and social scientists. A subcommittee of the National Advisory Board for Human Genome Research, on which I also served, the ELSI working group focused attention on issues of privacy, autonomy and fairness raised by approaches to gene research and its future clinical applications. Some of the outside consultants with whom I worked questioned the willingness of NIH administrators to take on the very toughest and most politically sensitive ethical issues. For example, some of my colleagues on the ELSI working group felt more attention should go to the objective evaluation of controversial behavioral genetics and IQ research. Shortly after I left the NIH to devote more time to my expanding family, ELSI was disbanded.

Whether working for individuals, business or for government, ethics consultants can be a genuine resource for informed ethical decision making, or they can devolve into mere agents of moral cover. People who rely on ethicists have to be on their guard against truly bad advice. Emory University ethicist John Banja was quoted in the *Atlanta Journal Constitution* on January 7, 2003, offering some cruel advice for his hometown Atlanta Falcons regarding how they should treat Donovan McNabb, a player on an opposing team returning to play after his broken ankle had just healed: "Go for his ankle, go for his spine, try to break his neck. McNabb certainly knows people are going to do that."[22]

PRODUCING PROUD VALUES

As this chapter and the three preceding chapters reveal, the production of moral and ethical values is decentralized and multifaceted. The mechanisms and sites of moral education are plentiful. The production of values happens at home, at school and at work. It is a matter of conversation, encouragement, modeling, regulation and sanction. The political dimension of the production of values and ethics regulation must not be overlooked either, for politics has the potential to undermine the possibility of implementing truly effective measures.

Gaining control over the production of values is an impossibility. The focus must be on constructive input at key junctions. It is plain that we must establish the stage of life and the settings in which moral education can effectively take place. We must also ask which of the mechanisms of moral education—religion, law, institutional rule, role modeling—make sense for what sorts of misconduct. For the ethical violations that take place in the world of high finance, I believe the heavy hand of the law to create specific guidelines may be essential.

The part of ethical living that is supposed to be easy—namely, following simple, familiar rules—turns out not to be so straightforward. Indeed, good choices of any kind are not easy, but we can improve the picture with well-designed moral education, disciplined workplace ethics and more effectively regulated businesses, professions and industries.

PART III

CHOOSING WELL
ON NOVEL GROUND

CHAPTER 7

THE CHILD I ALWAYS
DREAMT ABOUT

Innovation in medicine and biotechnology is importing "drastic changes into cherished and admired ways of life."[1] The nature of our bodies, our offspring and our environment are increasingly up to us. Along with opportunities to design the character, quality and length of life, scientific innovation has brought ethical questions of arresting modernity to our horizons. Some innovations of ethical significance—like stem cell research and gene therapy—vex us with their looming moral ambiguities and uncertainties. While they excite passionate public policy debates from the lab to the White House, other innovations, such as elective cosmetic surgery, have unappreciated ethical significance.

To contend with the ethics of innovation, we have to elevate moral self-education to the status of a central imperative of our times. Conscience needs assistance. We need to take time to think, talk and read about the promises of science before embracing them. We will not necessarily feel completely certain about what to do, once we have taken time to understand and assess our options, and once we have recognized the moral dimensions of new possibilities. But our choices will be better informed and, to that extent, more responsible. Indeed, the end of rashly embraced innovation is the beginning of moral responsibility in a major region of the new ethical landscape.

I wanted a backyard garden. I hired a landscaper named Jim. There was a *certain* garden I longed to have. I did not say to Jim, "Please build me a garden." I said to him, "Please build me *this* garden." I showed him pictures I had clipped from magazines and sketches I had made. I wanted a row of boxwood in front of a wall of climbing hydrangeas. I wanted a hillside of shade-loving perennials. I wanted an oval of thick, green grass. I wanted a foot path of Pennsylvania gray slate stepping stones. I wanted natural wood fencing high enough to keep out the deer. I wanted cedar benches for seating. I wanted to train honeysuckle on the east side of an iron arbor and clematis with tiny white flowers on the west.

Human beings are designers. We design gardens, kitchens and jewelry. We design lives. I had a general plan for my life, developed while I was a young adult. I would get a Ph.D., publish a book that would sit on the shelves of the Library of Congress and have children, in that order. I stuck to the plan as best I could. I managed to get the Ph.D. and publish books without undue difficulty. But because of an illness, it turned out that I could not bear children, so I had to modify the plan. We adopted Adam in 1991 and Ophelia in 1996. They are beautiful, lively children, named for my husband's father and my great-great-grandmother.

Life is full of setbacks and surprises; plans have to change. Expectations have to be adjusted. It can happen to anyone at any stage of life. It happened to my in-laws. After they had carefully planned for their retirement years in advance, Adam and Josephine were going to spend winters in Florida and summers in New York. They bought a house in Florida and a condominium in New York. But all too soon after retirement Adam developed a host of health problems. Commuting up and down the East Coast quickly became impractical with Adam's failing eyesight, Parkinson's disease, heart trouble, and cancer, so "Nana" and "Pop-Pop" sold the house in Florida and became full-year residents of New York. Adam passed away all too soon.

Since we design our lives, we are impelled to design our children. We often have very specific ideas about how we would like our offspring or adopted children to fit into the overall design of our lives. To the extent that we can have a say in what our children are like, we will understandably want a say. This is not to suggest that children are mere enhancements for their parents' fixed agendas. Unselfish motives for parenting can dominate. Still, even altruistic parenting takes place within the framework of planned lives. In order to fit into the preexisting picture, a child will need to have some characteristics and not others. People tend to care deeply about the physical, emotional and intellectual traits of the children who will share their lives.

Just as a gardener-to-be contemplates a *certain* garden, the parent-to-be contemplates a *certain* child. Parents want children to whom they have given birth, for example. Or they want adopted children of their same ethnoracial ancestry. Some people want children with physical beauty. A social worker at a Lutheran social services agency told me of a man looking to adopt who rejected a normal, healthy infant on the ground that he felt the child's eyes were too far apart. At least one Internet Web site purports to auction off the eggs of beautiful models.[2] Some people want especially intelligent children. Now that it is possible for women to have children with the help of egg donors, prospective parents have openly advertised in campus newspapers at Ivy League colleges for tall, fair, Caucasian egg donors with high SAT scores. (There is a demand for the sperm of healthy male geniuses, too.) The ad that got us all talking appeared in 1999 in campus newspapers at Harvard, Princeton, Stanford, Penn, and Yale. A couple that described itself as loving and caring offered $50,000 for an egg donor. To qualify the donor had to be "intelligent, athletic, blond, at least 5'10", have a 1400+ SAT score, and possess no major family medical issues."[3]

That *certain* child for whom some people long is not necessarily a generic bright beauty, though. She is the daughter with the family's distinctive nose or unruly hair. He is the son with his father's quirky smile and hereditary short stature. Gay or straight sexual orientation can be a parental preference, too. Asked by a reporter what kind of baby she wanted, the then childless pop star Madonna replied that she wanted a gay boy.

In a sense, designing our children is not merely an option, it is a high ethical responsibility. To parent is to respond to needs, but also to cultivate traits and dispositions. Parents are responsible for pressing the stamp of enlightened civilization on their young charges. When it comes to the basics of health, hygiene, literacy and morality, children should not be left on their own. They should be tended, taught and tethered. They have to be turned into cooperative, caring adults capable of surviving and contributing. We really should "design" our children sufficient to those paramount objectives.

Most parents, though, have even larger design objectives for their children. They want *certain* children and they know some of the ways to get them. If a man wants Jewish children, he knows to go after a Jewish mate who wants to raise her children as Jews. If a man badly wants blond kids, he knows not to gamble on a Japanese or West African mate, all of whose ancestors have had black hair. If a woman wants a healthy child, she knows she should stay away from alcohol during pregnancy, rule out cocaine use and get prompt, appropriate treatment for syphilis, gonorrhea and AIDS. If parents want happy, well-adjusted children, they know they need to rear them in loving, abuse-free homes and communities. Parents know to provide healthy food, exercise and encouragement. Parents who want talented, high-achieving children know to invest time and money in extra educational, cultural and athletic opportunities. Yet these venerable approaches to producing great kids are not foolproof; they leave a lot to chance. For those parents looking for greater certainty in the design of their children, genetics may prove to be the key to getting them the children they really want.

GENETIC ARTISTRY

Contemporary genetics is the study of the molecular basis of biology. Gene science is science on a mission, thanks in large measure to the Human Genome Project, a successful international research initiative that was heavily funded for more than a decade by the U.S. government. Completed in April 2003, its goal, as explained by the National Institutes of Health, was to determine "the DNA sequence of the human genome." The eventual goal is to "read nature's complete genetic blueprint for building a human being," which means learning the locations of the genes through which inherited traits are transmitted.[4] Blueprint in hand, the science of genetics offers the hope of new drugs and new therapies to treat illness and disease. An unprecedented number of patent applications are flooding the U.S. Patent Office, as corporate and academic researchers clamor for the right to exploit genetic technologies and discoveries in lucrative new commercial ventures.

The nucleus of a human cell normally contains forty-six chromosomes, each consisting of DNA (deoxyribonucleic acid) molecules. Additional DNA is found outside the cell nucleus in structures called mitochondria. The genes found in DNA control heredity. The forty-six chromosomes are really twenty-three pairs, including the unique pair that determines sex. Women normally carry the pair of sex-determining chromosomes designated as XX; and men, the pair designated XY.

Nobel Prize winners Francis Crick and James Watson advanced scientific understanding of genetics in the 1950s by uncovering the double helix structure of DNA, often illustrated as a spiraling or twisting ladder. Molecules of DNA are constructed of four chemical bases, pairs of which join together to form the "rungs" of the ladders. Genes are segments of DNA of varying lengths. The human genome consists of 30,000 to 40,000 genes. Genes are coded for specific proteins. Each gene contains the instructions needed to orchestrate the synthesis of one or more of the 100,000 proteins that are components of cells, tissues and enzymes responsible for sustaining life.

The sequence of genes along strands of DNA explains the variability of inherited human traits. Alleles, or variations of a single gene, result in the varieties of normal health and appearance. Blue eyes and brown eyes are the result of normal but distinct alleles of the genes responsible for eye color, whereas a defective ("mutated") gene can mean that a person is at risk for an atypical appearance or disease. Aside from identical twins, everyone's DNA is a little different (which is why DNA can be used as a tool of forensic identification). The genes people carry within them provide important clues about their unique future health and capacities. For example, a woman with the genetic mutations known as *BRCA1* or *BRCA2* is at an increased risk of breast cancer. In some instances, genes carry more than clues. They flat-out determine whether a person in whom they reside will have a specific trait. An infant who inherits two copies of *DELTA F508,* the cystic fibrosis gene, will have cystic fibrosis. If an infant only inherits one copy of the gene, she would be a "carrier" and have no symptoms of the disease.

Were parents able to exercise greater control over the genetic traits of their children, they could insure both that their children matched their fantasies and that they were otherwise healthy and fit. With the help of science and biomedical technology, quite a bit can already be done to insure that our children will turn out to be the people we imagine.

To reduce the risks of unhealthy children, some couples anticipating pregnancy undergo genetic testing for hundreds of disorders, such as sickle cell anemia, cystic fibrosis and Huntington's disease. Couples are also turning to what is called "preimplantation genetic diagnosis" (PGD). A very new and emerging practice, PGD entails extracting DNA from two- to three-day-old embryos created by in vitro fertilization. After screening for genetic disorders, doctors then can select one or more healthy embryos for implantation into the mother's womb for an otherwise normal pregnancy. In addition to PGD, sonograms, fetoscopy, amniocenteses, chorionic villi sampling and other prenatal procedures can detect more than five hundred conditions. Tay-Sachs disease, a progressive, fatal inherited disease in which sufferers lacking a vital enzyme begin in infancy to lose major mental and physical capacities, is one of these. Some genetic testing is invasive. Amniocenteses require extracting fluid from the amniotic sac in which fetuses develop inside a woman's uterus. Chorionic villi sampling requires extracting tissue surrounding the fetus. Both procedures are reasonably safe but carry a heightened risk of miscarriage.

Most of the conditions for which current prenatal testing has been developed have no cure, and some have no effective treatments. There is no cure for Tay-Sachs. Nor is there a cure for Down's syndrome. Less commonly known as Trisomy 21, Down's syndrome is a chromosomal disorder associated with mental retardation, heart abnormalities, and distinctive facial features. Women over thirty-five are statistically more likely to give birth to children affected with Down's defining genetic profile, an extra copy of chromosome 21. Older pregnant women routinely undergo amniocenteses to determine whether they are carrying a normal fetus. The maternal serum alpha-fetoprotein test, originally developed to uncover neural tube defects, is used to test for Down's. What women do in response to a positive Down's test is left up to them, of course. The basic options are to rear a child with abnormalities and potential health problems, abort the fetus or pursue adoption. Adoption is not a realistic option, since it is nearly impossible to place a mentally retarded child for adoption. Families seeking to adopt are rarely willing to take on a child with anything other than mild, treatable abnormalities. Taking advantage of widely available prenatal testing and abortion, if a woman wanted a daughter with a high IQ, she could abort viable fetuses with Down's syndrome in her quest to get one.

It is an open question just how much control over the fate of children society should entrust to parents and doctors. Indeed, one of the most important public policy questions our society faces is whether to entrust parents with greater say about the design of children. If public policies encourage the new and emerging high-tech design strategies, they place additional power in the hands of individual consumers of genetic services. In fact some lawyers are claiming that Americans have a constitutional right to use any reproductive technology that becomes available, including cloning. They rely on the Fourteenth Amendment guarantee of liberty for their argument in favor of unchecked access to high-tech reproduction. (The right of research scientists to develop reproductive technologies has been defended as a First Amendment right of speech and expression.) The Clonaid company, founded by the leader of an off-beat religious organization called the Raelian Movement, has announced an aggressive cloning research agenda. Procloning fertility researcher Panayiotis "Panos" Zavos argues that the constitutional right to privacy entails a constitutional right to clone. He has testified in defense of cloning before Congress and has joined forces with Italian researchers seeking to quickly produce cloned children.

I do not believe that the Constitution requires state and federal governments to permit reproductive cloning. It is true, though, that the U.S. Supreme Court has repeatedly held that Americans have a near sacred right to choose whether to have children: the right to bear and rear children is a constitutional right, and so is the right not to. Normally, the law does not permit a man to be sterilized against his will, nor can a woman be denied access to birth control and abortion. Procreation is a domain of choice.

Everyone knows about *Roe v. Wade* (1973), the case that established the right to abortion as a fundamental right of privacy protected by the Fourteenth Amendment.[5] In *Roe,* the Supreme Court held that states may not enact laws that criminalize providing and obtaining medically safe abortions. Less well known is *Skinner v. Oklahoma* (1942), an earlier case that established the right to bear children.[6] In this case a man named Jack T. Skinner had been convicted of stealing chickens and armed robbery. Under the Oklahoma Habitual Offender Sterilization Act, persons convicted twice of felonies involving "moral turpitude" could be sterilized. Through sterilizing felons, the state hoped to improve society by preventing the transmission of inborn traits responsible for criminality to new generations. When Skinner was declared eligible for sterilization under Oklahoma law, he brought suit against the state. Finding in Skinner's favor on equal protection grounds, the Supreme Court held that "We are dealing here with legislation that involves one of the basic civil rights of man. Marriage and procreation are fundamental to the very existence and survival of the race. The power to sterilize, if exercised, may have subtle, far reaching and devastating effects. In evil or reckless hands it can cause races or types which are inimical to the dominant group to wither and disappear."[7] Cases before and after *Roe v. Wade* repeated the holding of *Skinner* that the right to procreate is inviolable. The principle of reproductive freedom was affirmed in the Court's decision upholding *Roe v. Wade,* *Planned Parenthood v. Casey,* (1992): Government may not unduly burden the right to procreate with prohibitive restrictions and regulations.[8]

In a sense, designing our children is not merely an option;
it is a high ethical responsibility.

As a group, the reproductive rights decisions of the Supreme Court entail wide powers of choice over bearing children—but not complete choice. Some methods of having children have been discouraged and even prohibited by state courts and federal policy makers. For example, New Jersey has refused to enforce surrogate mother contracts. In the infamous 1988 *Baby M* case, William Stern was a physician who badly wanted a biologically related child.[9] He had lost family in the Holocaust and was especially anxious for blood kin. Stern's wife, Elizabeth, also a physician, feared pregnancy would exacerbate her mild multiple sclerosis, so William Stern contracted with Mary Beth Whitehead to bear his child. Whitehead was to be artificially inseminated with Stern's sperm, become pregnant, deliver the child, and relinquish her maternal rights so that Elizabeth Stern could legally adopt the child. However, when a baby girl was born, Whitehead changed her mind. A nationally publicized dispute erupted over who were the lawful parents of the anonymously designated child, Baby M. Against the argument that the *Skinner* and *Roe* cases entail a right to procreate even by artificial and surrogate-assisted means, the New Jersey Supreme Court invalidated the surrogacy contract as baby selling contrary to humane public policy. The Court then determined that Stern was the child's legal father and Whitehead was the child's legal mother, with rights of custody to be determined by reference to the best interests of the child.

In theory, human cloning is another technique through which a man in William Stern's situation could ensure genetically related children. Indeed, once cloning is possible, someone like Stern will be able to produce a son who is, genetically speaking, virtually his identical twin. The technique that might be used is called somatic cell nuclear transfer, in which a person's DNA is inserted into a donated egg and the egg is stimulated to divide. The resulting embryo is implanted in a woman's womb and grows into a baby that is the twin of the adult who provided the nuclear DNA. In Stern's case, cloning might work like this. First, Stern's wife (or another fertile woman) would donate one of her eggs, and Stern would donate a cell from his body (not a sperm cell). Next, a technician would remove the DNA-filled nuclei of both the egg and the somatic cell, discarding the egg's nuclear DNA. The DNA from Stern's somatic cell would then be transferred to the egg using micro ejection or electro fusion. The egg would form a blastocyst, which would be implanted into a willing woman's womb and mature into a baby. Because the baby would have the same DNA as Stern, it would be genetically his twin. If the egg were taken from Stern's wife, the mitochondrial DNA existing outside her egg's nucleus would be passed on to her husband's clone, giving her something of a biological and genetic tie to the child, too.

Human cloning is wildly controversial in the United States, and several states, including California, Michigan and Virginia have already outlawed it. In 1997 Dolly the sheep was cloned in the United Kingdom using somatic cell nuclear transfer, and the uproar began. Other sheep, cattle and mice have been successfully cloned amidst a din of controversy, too. New science relating to human life has been a particular interest, even target, of the White House. In August 2001 President Bush announced limits on human embryonic stem cell research that some scientists feared would impede medical research. In its report of July 11, 2002, the President's Council on Bioethics recommended a complete ban on human cloning and a four-year moratorium on biomedical cloning research.[10] The Bush White House later announced its position on cloning: "The administration unequivocally is opposed to the cloning of human beings either for reproduction or for research. The moral and ethical issues posed by human cloning are profound and cannot be ignored in the quest for scientific discovery."[11] The Food and Drug Administration has asserted jurisdiction over human cloning and has erected prohibitive barriers to cloning as an alternative form of human reproduction, citing safety concerns. In 2003, the United States House of Representatives passed a total ban on human cloning.[12] The bill calls for a $1 million fine and a ten-year jail sentence for violations. Major bills to prevent human cloning have been introduced into the Senate, though none had passed as of the start of 2004. Italian researchers are openly conducting research on human cloning. Rumors of women pregnant with clones produced by Clonaid or Italian scientists have been widely circulated since the fall of 2001.

Cloned human infants will likely be a reality soon and ethical judgments about the technology will grow more urgent. The number and varieties of techniques for exercising greater control of the traits of children are likely to expand. We are a permissive society, and money can be made from providing options to families, some of whose quests for their own perfect children know no bounds. However, no matter how permissive society's laws and policies, individuals retain an ethical obligation to evaluate for themselves whether to embrace or eschew the genetic hyperdesign of children. Society's choice need not be the individual's choice. The next generations of young adults must confront for themselves the ethical question of how aggressively to take advantage of the options presented to them by biomedical science.

It is troubling to hear reports of people lining up for cloning in advance of any knowledge of its efficacy or safety, and cloning will have an ethical cloud around it so long as the safety of clones cannot be strongly assured. Some of the fears surrounding cloning are admittedly silly. There is no reason to think that clones would be inherently soulless or inferior to other human beings.

One appeal of reproductive cloning is that children can be deliberately cloned using the cells of persons who are known to be free of genetic diseases. By selecting whose cells to clone, parents of the future can thoroughly and easily design their children. It will be no trouble at all to have a child that looks like Dad, or a supermodel. Of course the clone will have to be raised and educated. The environment in which a clone is reared will have as much or more to do with his or her future prospects as his or her genes. Parents who bank on genes could face big disappointments.

There are several other situations in which cloning might be useful. Suppose a married heterosexual couple want a son genetically related to the husband, but the husband cannot produce sperm. Cloning might permit a cell in the man's body other than a sperm to be the source of DNA for the creation of an embryo that could be implanted in the wife's uterus and born into the world as the couple's child. Suppose a lesbian couple wanted a female child genetically related to one of them, but carried by the other. Cloning could make this happen. One woman could be the source of the genetic material, and the other could be the gestator. The journal *Nature* reported in 2004 that Dr. Tomohiro Kono and colleagues in Japan created a healthy mouse named Kaguya with no father and two genetic mothers, suggesting a future of dual-mother reproductions for humans. Gay men could produce cloned children of their own, too, with the help of a surrogate gestator.

I believe the scientific and medical risks of cloning will be ironed out sufficiently to make the clone as safe and healthy as the formerly feared "test tube" baby. Cloning may come to be seen as just another way of having a baby—not of producing a subservient race or a master race, but simply of having a baby. Yet social objections to cloning may prove to be its downfall. One objection relates to the possibility that cloning living and dead family members will create added psychological risks for the people involved. Clones may face familial and societal expectations that they be like the person whose DNA they share. We know that identical twins generally thrive and do well; they do not have a host of special problems simply because they are not genetically unique. But we do not know what it might be like to be the "twin" of the father with whom one lives or the dead sibling missed by your parents. Complex interpersonal dynamics in clone-inclusive families could make people miserable. It may make Grandma unhappy to know that her grandson is a clone of her good-for-nothing dead husband. She knew he was a violent wife beater but never told anyone. It could make a child sad to know he was cloned only because his parents needed to harvest a kidney or bone marrow to save an ailing sister.

Parents have already begun to produce children who will serve as sibling donors, a practice that excites ethical controversy. In the best known case, six-year-old Molly Nash was gravely ill with Fanconi anemia. The child's chances of surviving her bone marrow disorder would substantially increase if she could be treated with a transplant from a sibling with a matching human leucocyte antigen. Molly had no such sibling, but her parents Jack and Lisa Nash decided to create one. Using in vitro fertilization and preimplanation genetic diagnosis (PGD), after several tries an embryo with the desired antigen was created and implanted in its mother's uterus. Newborn Adam Nash's placenta and umbilical cord blood provided stem cells which were transferred to his sister to save her life. Faced with ethical criticism, Lisa Nash said the decision to bring Adam into the world to save Molly was "what we had to do for us." Lisa hopes "that people who felt this was inappropriate for them . . . not judge me unless they've been there."[13] University of Minnesota bioethicist Susan M. Wolf has examined the ethics of using PGD to create donors and her greatest concern is that sibling donors will be called upon, even exploited, for donations throughout their lives.[14]

Returning to cloning, a further problem is that of unauthorized clones. Given the ease with which genetic materials can be obtained, famous people, attractive people and objects of obsession may wake up to discover they have been cloned. Anyone who got their hands on Brad Pitt's dirty Kleenex could have his baby. Dead people who would never have consented could be cloned. Dead men are already having children produced from their frozen sperm. Legal protections against nonconsensual cloning could be enacted and might go a distance to alleviating the problem; cloning facilities could require informed consent of living donors. But there would be abuses. This possibility was brought home when billionaire Steve Bing had his trash raided by a private investigator hired by a man seeking to prove that Bing was the father of his wife's child. The company that performed a paternity test on blood taken from Bing's dental floss supposedly had an informed-consent policy in place. They either ignored their own policy or got duped.

Finally, states may seek to ban cloning, and Congress may preemptively ban it permanently, too. Against the claim that the right to privacy entails the right to clone, legal bioethicist Lori Andrews has argued that cloning is different from other modes of reproduction. Cloning is a process of genetic mix, rather than genetic duplication.[15] Different social, environmental and generational influences of duplication versus mixing means courts have a rational basis for treating normal and cloning reproduction differently. Government may even have an arguably compelling interest in curbing cloning. Concerns about biodiversity, for example, get raised by the possibility that a society of people with common tastes and values will all want to have children with the same few characteristics. Human variety keeps the species more robust and resistant to disease and disability. Moreover, cloning could become a form of private eugenics. Social pressures might lead families to conclude that they had to clone their children to produce children of a certain stock. George Annas makes a loftier claim against cloning that could sway the courts. Cloning is a change in kind in human production; it "threatens human dignity and potentially devalues human life."[16]

Being ethical parents means approaching children with an orientation of care. Children are vulnerable because their knowledge is limited and their powers of independent judgment are immature. Parents therefore have a heightened responsibility to vigilantly discern and meet children's needs. Children need and deserve something from their parents, that their parents above all others ought willingly to give: loving acceptance. The attitude of care marked by loving acceptance can easily clash with the attitude of design. When I built my garden I chopped down more than a dozen perfectly healthy pine trees just because they did not fit into my plan. Parents with a design for life should not take the same chop-down view of children that I took of the pine trees. Children have to be left standing.

PICKY PARENTS

David and Stephanie Harnicher wanted a child, and they went to the University of Utah Medical Center Fertility Clinic for help. They did not say to the fertility doctors, "Please help us conceive a child." They said, "Please help us conceive a child who will resemble David." There was a certain child they dreamed of having. It would have David's curly dark hair and brown eyes. David and Stephanie wanted a child who was David's biological offspring or who would appear to the world as such. With these desires in mind, the Harnichers agreed to the following procedure: A quantity of Stephanie's eggs ("ova") was removed from her ovaries and placed in a petri dish. Microscopic holes were drilled into the sides of the ova to allow a mixture of David's sperm and the sperm of an anonymous donor to easily enter and fertilize. After fertilization, the ova were implanted into the walls of Stephanie's uterus, with the hope that she would become pregnant with one or more fetuses.

Stephanie did become pregnant, and gave birth to healthy triplets. Some infertile couples would have viewed this as an exceedingly happy ending. But the Harnichers were not happy. One of the triplets had red hair. David and Stephanie felt wronged. They sued the University of Utah Medical Center for malpractice and negligent infliction of emotion distress. They alleged that the fertility clinic used sperm from an anonymous donor with straight, light-colored hair, whom they had not approved, rather than from an approved anonymous donor with David's coloring. The Harnichers said that, because of the actions of the fertility clinic, they "suffered severe anxiety, depression, grief and other mental and emotional suffering and distress which has affected their relationships with the children and each other."[17]

Stephanie and David Harnicher were undone by the rigid expectation of a complement of brown-haired children. They wanted that. They paid for that. However, one of their three healthy children had red hair. They lost their lawsuit against the fertility clinic and a subsequent appeal. The Utah state court would not even let them go through with a trial. The judge who wrote the opinion in the Harnichers' appeal, *Harnicher v. University of Utah Medical Center* (1998), hinted that some parental disappointments might give rise to a legitimate basis for complaint, such as if one of the triplets had been "unhealthy, deformed, or deficient" or if there had been a "racial or ethnic mismatch." But in a case of hair color mismatch, the judge said a reasonable person of normal constitution should be able to "adequately cope." The Harnicher suit is striking evidence of just how invested some contemporary American parents-to-be can become in the design of family portraits.

Many parents want kids of their own who look like them and who exhibit a stock set of virtues and accomplishments. These are the children to whom thoroughgoing loving acceptance most easily goes. My racially mixed adopted children did not look like me when they were babies—a fact that, I must confess, caused me some trouble. They were light-skinned and had blue eyes. My husband suspected I might be in for a bit of discomfort. The day we saw infant Adam at the adoption agency for the first time, he asked "Is this baby too light for you?" After we took

Adam home, the "whose baby is that?" question was asked many times by people noting a disparity in skin tone and hair color in the family. I was often taken to be Adam's and Ophelia's nanny. Both my children's skin and eyes have darkened to the point that we look like a biologically "natural" family. But I can relate to some of the reasons Stephanie and David Harnicher were upset about having a kid with red hair in an otherwise brown-haired family. The busybody questions will seem endless.

Any parent, biological or adoptive, can make the mistake of prioritizing design, though. I became a new parent with distinct ideas about how to feed, clothe and, most important, educate my children. I had the same design expectations I know I would have had for my biological children. I went to Harvard, and they would go to Harvard, too. The focus on providing a formulaic set of beneficial educational opportunities for my son resulted in a degree of neglect of his actual needs. When Adam turned four, the quest for admission to the best private kindergartens began in earnest. It scarcely occurred to me that the neighborhood public school might be better for him than one of the elite private schools.

Admission to private school required that Adam be tested by a licensed educational psychologist. I had no regrets about the $1,000 fee, because the psychologist said things I wanted to hear: "he speaks as well as a nine-year-old," "he separates easily from his mother," and "agility unsurpassed in a child his age." My every proud suspicion of greatness was confirmed. I made a list of the schools that should be honored to admit my bright, friendly, handsome, athletic son, starting with Sidwell Friends, the school attended by Chelsea Clinton, daughter of the president of the United States. I went to open houses at Georgetown Day School, Maret School and Beauvoir School. I took Adam in for interviews at these schools and a few others equally exclusive. My husband and I did our best to write answers to pretentious admissions screening questions like, "With what musical instrument would you compare your child and why?" Believing my son deserved the best, I pulled every string—I even took Adam to meet the wife of a board member of one school so that she could write a letter of recommendation on his behalf in good conscience.

It did not work; he was wait-listed. In the end, he was admitted into an elite day school, and I took a sigh of relief. Set for life!

But he was not set for life in that school. The school was a complete mismatch. It conformed to my abstract educational philosophy of learning and my aspirations, yet it could not accommodate my child's learning style. He was unhappy and uncooperative for the first time in his little life. We pulled him out after a year and put him into our neighborhood public school. He loved first grade there and performed well.

When it was time to enroll my daughter in school, five years later, my design impulses had been tamed a bit. I knew that I should not assume I was doing best by her to get her admitted to a famous school. I tried to figure out who she was as best I could, and to put her needs ahead of my ideal designs.

Science offers the lure of certainty. Yet science does not always give you what you want. Science is a human enterprise, and the techniques for designing children are not foolproof. Errors can happen, and parents must be prepared for the response of loving acceptance that they hoped they would not be called upon to muster.

Laureen and John Doolan's first child, Samantha, was born with cystic fibrosis (CF). Persons affected with cystic fibrosis suffer severe respiratory problems and may also have digestive difficulties. About half of CF sufferers do not live past thirty. The Doolans wanted a second child, but understandably, not a second child with CF. Since Laureen and John were both carriers of the CF gene, there was a 25 percent chance that any child they conceived would also have CF. Hoping to insure a second, healthy child, Laureen and John turned to the science of *in vitro* fertilization and preimplantation genetic testing. They would forgo natural conception. They would have their potential children screened for CF *prior* to pregnancy.

This is how they did it: Eggs were harvested from Laureen's ovaries and fertilized with her husband's sperm outside her body in a laboratory vessel. Ten fertilized eggs were sent to the Genzyme Corporation for genetic testing. Genzyme was to determine which fertilized eggs were free of the *DELTA F508* cystic fibrosis mutation. Something went wrong. A fertilized ovum mistakenly designated CF-free was implanted in Laureen's womb. Laureen gave birth to Thomas, a second child with cystic fibrosis.

Having gone to so much trouble to produce a child without CF, Laureen, John and their son Thomas brought a lawsuit for wrongful life and loss of consortium. "Loss of consortium" is a category of injury courts allow when a person is deprived of intimacy with a spouse or child. They lost the suit, *Doolan v. IVF American (MA), Inc* (2002).[18] Thomas's claim for wrongful life was rejected by the Massachusetts Superior Court on the ground that being brought into the world as a result of negligence is not an injury recognized in the courts of Massachusetts. There is no legal right to be born as a healthy person who meets his parents' expectations, or not at all. The court also rejected Laureen and John's claim of loss of the "society and companionship" of a healthy child. Justice John C. Cratsley interpreted the Doolans' claim as a claim to the loss of the society and companionship of a purely hypothetical child who existed only in a world of fantasy and intention, puzzling over how anyone could claim to have a loss of consortium with a hypothetical person. That child might have been emotionally unavailable or short-lived for other reasons. The Doolans might have had a poor quality relationship with the hypothetical CF-free second child. The hypothetical son without CF could have "been afflicted with another type of birth defect or long term illness," Cratsley reasoned on behalf of the court.[19] The Doolans wanted a life that included a relationship with a healthy child. They had a very good reason for seeking a healthy child; they already had a sick child. They got a second sick child, and are called upon by the law to cope, not sue.

We cannot turn to science for certainties. Lab technicians make mistakes; physicians make mistakes; genetic counselors make mistakes. In the future, we may be required by the laws of our society to accept many of the emotional and the financial burdens of erroneous, unwanted life that owes its existence to our voluntary collaborations with science. Parents who play God get no special pass.

STRONGER THAN YOU THINK

What happens when children are born who do not fit the plan? Although the Doolans brought a lawsuit complaining of the birth of a child affected by CF, I do not doubt that they ultimately approached Thomas's care with loving acceptance. I know several families with children who are mentally ill or severely autistic. In my experience, most parents do a good job of readjusting their expectations and providing appropriately loving homes. They do not fall to pieces. They are resourceful, even though emotional, medical and educational means may be barely adequate. When children do not fit the preexisting design, parents redesign around the reality, the way the gardener redesigns around an underground spring or the boulder that cannot be moved after all.

Phil and Rachel are busy lawyers whose first child, Seth, was born with severe autism. Other boys his age play video games, read Harry Potter books, and compete in team sports. Seth cannot speak, read, write or control his feelings. Phil and Rachel rose to the challenge of combining the need for two incomes with parenting a special-needs child. They became aggressive advocates for their son to insure an appropriate education. Phil gave up ambitions to run for elected office, but he and Rachel have maintained high-powered careers. For a time Rachel worked four days a week, though. Parents like Phil and Rachel love their disabled children just as they are, letting go of fantasies of rearing "perfect" kids. Special rewards can accompany the special burdens of rearing children with extraordinary needs. This couple has had the confidence to have two other children, both typical little girls, doing fine.

Because I have seen a number of families successfully shift their life plans in response to an unanticipated disability, I have come to think potential parents should be advised to invest a lot less in efforts to produce perfect children. Life can be very good without the children of our fantasies. Be secure, I want to say, in your ability to love and care for actual children. I have to keep telling myself this, too. It is not a message any parent can hear once and believe continuously, forever. Try to convince the gardener not to care about the color of her tulips or where the poison ivy might begin to creep.

CHAPTER 8

CONSUMPTION ETHICS

I s it anyone else's business if you eat a hamburger for lunch or take drugs to relieve depression? Moralizing about food and drugs cuts deeply into the very idea of a private life. What next! However, food and drugs do raise many important ethical issues. The choices we make about what we consume can harm other people, both people we know and people we do not know. Voluntary use of food and drugs makes us morally complicit in the harms linked both to our acts of consumption and to the methods through which substances we consume are produced and sold.

It is unrealistic to suppose that we should all master chemistry, biology, nutrition, agriculture and labor economics before our next meals; yet, overcoming the cluelessness that impairs ethical engagement often leads us to understand that seemingly private acts have public consequences. Just to get by, the next generation will need to know more science than the previous ten put together. We already need a careful understanding of the natural and social sciences to live well and live right in the world remade by science and technology. We may eat, drink and be merry, but we should ideally aim to do so in ways that reflect educated moral concern for humanity and its habitat.

GETTING OFF DOPE

Americans heartily consume drugs and spend a pretty penny for the right to do it. By some estimates, Americans spend $154 billion a year on prescription drugs, $18 billion on over-the-counter drugs, and another $67 billion a year on illegal drugs.[1] We seem to love our drugs, and yet an ethical cloud surrounds the drug use landscape.

The use of illegal drugs certainly violates laws enacted with public health and safety in mind. Brutal crime, vice and excessive risk accompany lucrative illegal drug markets. Addiction threatens the lives of chronic cocaine and heroin users and their families. Millions of people are merely occasional users of addictive drugs. However, chronic users of cocaine in the United States number an astounding 3 million; chronic users of heroin number a whopping .9 to 1.1 million. Cocaine, heroin, methamphetamine, and marijuana are the four most popular illegal drugs. Addiction and criminality are their predicates.[2] Undaunted by the risks, eager users spend almost $36 billion a year on cocaine (including crack cocaine), $11 billion on marijuana, $10 billion on heroin, and $5.5 billion on methamphetamines.[3] Billions more go to other controlled substances. People over fifty recall the hallucinogens favored by their generation; LSD, mescaline, peyote and "magic mushrooms" are still around. More popular with young adults and teenagers are "party," "club," "rave" and "trance" drugs, which include Ecstasy, PCP, Rohypnol, GHB, Ketamine, and Demerol. Rohypnol has been a drug of choice for date rape.

Illegal uses are made of medicines approved by the Food and Drug Administration as prescription antidepressants, stimulants, tranquilizers, sedatives and analgesics. I have heard of people injecting Ritalin, an oral medication commonly used to treat hyperactivity, directly into their veins for a cocaine-style high. Pain medications also have a long-standing reputation for abuse. OxyContin, an opiate used to treat severe pain in cancer patients, has been subjected to well-publicized abuse by young adults and teenagers. Radio show host Rush Limbaugh admitted to addiction to prescription painkillers in the fall of 2003. A former housekeeper said Limbaugh sent her out to score large quantities of OxyContin and other drugs from illegal dealers and that he consumed dozens of pills a day.

Florida college student Matthew Kaminer died after ingesting one of 124 OxyContin pills stolen by a twenty-year-old friend who worked in a drug store. Products sold over the counter, such as codeine-containing cold medicines and diet pills, also have histories of abuse, along with alcohol, tobacco and inhalants not intended for human consumption at all.

Georgetown University is a Catholic institution in the Jesuit intellectual tradition. Ethics are freely and rigorously debated at Georgetown, home to the prominent Kennedy Institute of Ethics. Founded in 1971, the Kennedy Institute was one of the very first centers for bioethics research in the world. Georgetown also boasts a fine undergraduate college and strong graduate and professional schools, including a world-class law school.

One afternoon I was about to present a paper about the ethics of illegal drugs, "Against Recreational Drug Use," to a group of Georgetown University law professors. I was especially nervous that day. It was the mid-1990s, the "Age of Crack." Drug crime and drug policy made the front pages of the *Washington Post* nearly every day. I knew most of the people in the audience pretty well but had not yet revealed to them that I was closely involved in the life of my sister, a recovering crack addict. I guessed that most of the people in the room thought of drug use as morally innocuous, whereas I had come to view drug use as seriously unhealthy and wrong. I felt like someone who had come to throw cold water on a party. Yet I did not want to come across as a self-righteous "Just say no!" moralist, or the scolding church lady caricatured on *Saturday Night Live*. I do not think there is anything inherently and invariably wrong with the altered states of consciousness brought on by marijuana or a glass of wine. Formerly uninformed about the potential for harm, experience had led me to overlook moral dimensions of drug use. My experience with someone close to me becoming an unlikely addict led me to a radical change of perspective.

A dozen years ago my sister, a well-employed civil servant, wife and mother became a crack addict. "Gwen" is not my sister's real name; with her permission, I am going to use a pseudonym. Gwen was thirty-five. She found a new circle of friends. She began spending nights in seedy urban crack houses. She began showing up at work late and in skimpy evening-wear. She began asking family members and friends for large sums of money. She began to neglect her son and fight with her husband. At first, no one knew the cause of her problems. Eventually the family began to suspect drugs. Before the nightmare was over, Gwen had faced arrest, lost her marriage, spent a month in a hospital, lost her job, spent her savings, gone on and off welfare, and repeatedly disappointed her child and family. To cope with my frustration over the mess illegal drugs had made of *our* lives (because family and friends suffered, too), I began to rethink my pre-viously libertarian stance on the use of recreational drugs. I used to think that if people want to use drugs, we should let them. It's their body; it's their business! I learned the hard way that the impact of illegal drug use is less contained. It is not just a matter of ingesting a substance into a body.

A problem of justice and public health for society, the use of recre-ational drugs is also an ethical problem for individuals. Reflective drug users do not think of themselves as unethical or immoral. They feel they are exercising liberties to which they are entitled. Medical uses of illegal drugs by cancer and AIDS patients presents a special set of ethical con-cerns, as do sacramental or religious uses of narcotics. The Supreme Court has been kind neither to sacramental nor medical drug users. A decision a decade ago declined to extend the First Amendment to sacra-mental peyote users, and a decision in 2001 held that medical use of mari-juana is not exempted from the federal drug laws, no matter what state law-makers and voters might prefer.[4] Philosopher Douglas N. Husak, a knowl-edgeable critic of U.S. drug policies defends what he terms the "moral right of adults to use drugs for recreational purposes."[5] Husak asserts that the criminalization of drugs as benign as marijuana may be one of the greatest injustices in American history. With defenders like Husak to back them up, drug users can feel harmless and blameless. Maybe a little naughty, but certainly not bad. The drugs they consume go only into their own bodies and do not hurt others. Drug use breaks the law, but the law is moralistic, harsh and unfair to minorities, emphasize drug users. Drug law does not merit moral respect, they conclude. I offered two lines of argu-ment against the popular claim that street and party drug use is harmless and blameless: first, drug use is more harmful to users and others than one might think; and second, drug use makes users morally complicit for drug violence, disease and community breakdown.

First, as I argued that day at Georgetown, drug use plainly affects other people. Drug use that involves smoking affects unintended users exposed to secondhand smoke, including children who may be nearby. Pregnant women who ingest drugs deliver them to their fetuses. Babies can be born sick and cocaine-addicted. Alcohol use by pregnant women can lead to infants born with birth defects and developmental delays. Drug use imperils pregnancy itself and may result in the birth of babies at risk for longer-term health and cognitive problems. Needle sharing among injection drug users transmits blood-borne diseases like HIV, hepatitis B and hepatitis C. Drug use, much like gambling and the lottery, channels the income of the poor away from necessities. Chronic daily cocaine and heroin users spend on average about $300 a week on the drugs. Methamphetamine users spend about $100 a week. Pot smokers spend about $100 per week.[6] The risk of addiction to cocaine, heroin and similarly powerful drugs will materialize in a percentage of cases. Addiction is not limited to any single social class or race. No one can be sure if he or she will be the one to fall prey to addiction. You could be one of the lucky ones who uses without getting addicted. But your involvement in drugs could seduce friends and family members who are more vulnerable than you into drug use and addiction. It may start with an extramarital affair with a drug user, a party with neighbors, an experiment with your cousin, a rite of passage with your son, but drug use is social and therefore contagious. Addiction is, too.

Addiction impairs reason and moral capacity. My sister Gwen has recovered physically and spiritually, but I believe she required nearly five years to regain complete rational clarity. Moreover, she had to unlearn the evasiveness, deception and distrust that had become a way of life. When addiction happens, the addict imposes burdens of care on family, friends and employers moved by concern to intervene. Someone else winds up paying the addict's rent and taking care of their children and sick parents. Hospitalization and rehabilitation are expensive. A month in a drug recovery facility can easily cost $3,600–$6,000. In the fall of 2002, the Addiction Recovery Institute in New Jersey Center quoted a price of $5,600 for a twenty-four-hour detox service for addicts. The Institute's seven-day outpatient detox service went for $2,300. For all these reasons of harm, risk and expense, I conclude that it is wrong in a moral sense to knowingly introduce recreational drug use into one's life.

Secondly, there is the problem of complicity. Comfortable middle class and affluent drug users are morally complicit in the brutal world of drug trafficking. That world seems far removed from our living rooms, even after a trip through a bad section of town to "score," but as we sit in our living room using drugs in front of the big-screen TV, young people are getting killed and going to prison in record numbers. Like gun-wielding dealers on the street and invisible kingpins who control them, drug users are complicit in the violence, disease and family breakdown associated with drugs. Unless they are the tiny minority that grows or manufactures its own drugs, drug users are morally complicit in the urban American and international violence associated with the particular drugs they use. Marijuana users frequently assume that there is little violence associated with the market in grass. In May 2001, the *New York Times* published a story exploding the myth that those who deal in marijuana are not subjected to the street crime and violence associated with crack and heroin. On the contrary, marijuana dealers are also killing and being killed in shocking numbers.[7]

After my talk, I invited my colleagues in the Georgetown audience to ask questions. I remember two questioners vividly. You always remember the people who have made you squirm. The first was Professor Larry Gostin, a prominent civil libertarian and public health lawyer. He sounded perturbed. "Aren't you turning what is really a health problem into a moral problem?" he asked. "Doesn't moralizing about drug use make it harder for people to get the help they need? Isn't it blaming the victim? Don't studies show that alcohol is a greater social problem than drugs?" This was an excellent series of questions, important challenges.

My intent in "moralizing" about drugs is to get people who have a choice about drug use to be more circumspect. Not everyone can make a meaningful choice about drug use: they may be already addicted, or someone more powerful forces them to smoke, swallow, snort, inhale or shoot

The choices we make about what we consume can harm other people, both people we know and people we do not know.

═══════════════

up. My intent is to make clueless people with choices socially aware and self-aware, and the already aware people think twice. I have a similar view of "moralizing" about alcohol and alcohol addiction, which I believe also pose major social, health and ethical problems. I see no point in shaking fingers of blame at the alcoholics or drug addicts one is about to drive to the hospital for treatment. They need medical care, jobs and insurance like everyone else. Yet I do believe the moral dimensions of drug and alcohol use merit a place in discussions of responsible lives. There is a point to telling your children that heavy drinking or drug use is morally wrong for the harm it does. And a friend on the brink of excessive drug or alcohol use is potentially helped by a moral reminder of the care and concern they owe themselves and the people around them.

Ascribing moral fault to recreational drug users does not necessarily mean moving away from public health initiatives or criminal justice reforms favored by liberals. Even if using drugs is morally undesirable behavior, needle exchange programs might still be a good idea on public health grounds. Legal reform may still be called for, too. Indeed, I believe some illegal drugs perhaps ought to be controlled only, not criminalized. The case for decriminalizing marijuana is arguable, especially in light of mounting evidence of beneficial, straightforwardly medical uses. More important, if drugs are going to remain illegal, justice clearly requires changes in criminal law and criminal procedures. We need to firmly establish comparable criminal penalties for comparable drugs, and comparable law enforcement and punishment for members of all races and both sexes. An African American in possession of crack and a Caucasian in possession of crack face radically different chances of going to jail, which is clearly wrong. The standard sentence for crack cocaine sales has been higher by years than the standard sentence for powdered cocaine sales. The 1986 U.S. Congress enacted a mandatory minimum sentence for cocaine and crack trafficking. The sentence for the sale of 50 grams of crack and 5000 grams of powder cocaine was the same: 10 years in federal prison. Since crack is preferred by poorer users, many of whom are members of ethnoracial minority groups, the disparity has an adverse class and race impact. A report of the U.S. Sentencing Commission throughout the 1990s found that "over 88 percent of those sentenced for crack offenses are black, while only 4.1 percent of those sentenced for that offense are white. Most of those who use crack, however, are white (52 percent of reported crack users are white, 38 percent are black)."[8]

The second memorable questioner at Georgetown was Professor Louis Michael Seidman, an expert on constitutional law. Mike is a really smart, very nice man who always prefaces his penetrating responses with "That was a terrific paper!" He usually then uncovers a major flaw. He has sent me back to the drawing board more than once. Mike posed this question in response to my paper. He said, "You recognize that while some use drugs for fun or sociality, many people use so-called recreational drugs to self-medicate for depression, anxiety or pain. Aren't they entitled to medication? How can there be anything wrong with using illegal drugs when half the people we know, heck, half the people in this room are on Prozac?" Mike had a point. Experts say much illegal drug use has precisely the same purpose as the legal drugs prescribed by doctors. Can we blame self-medicators for medicating? Are they to be faulted because their drug of choice happens to be illegal? Since people get addicted to prescription drugs and alcohol all the time, the potential for addiction cannot be the basis of a distinction. So why condemn one and not the other?

My answer is the complicity factor. Neither Prozac users nor Wellbutrin users are complicit in a murderous black market, whereas cocaine and pot users often are. Suppose the government tomorrow arbitrarily declared Premarin, the commonly prescribed hormone replacement drug, illegal. Unable to purchase the drug from reputable pharmacists, a market in illegal Premarin brand estrogen would develop, marked by violence and cruelty. In this hypothetical world, it would be immoral to use street Premarin. The injustice of the law might not suffice to excuse noncompliance, and it certainly would not suffice to justify indirectly contributing to violence.

GETTING ON MEDS

An ethical cloud surrounds the use of legal drugs, too. Psychiatric drugs have aroused special controversy. A report of the United

States Surgeon General issued in 2000 declared that one out of five Americans suffers from a mental health problem. In a preface to the report, Surgeon General Dr. David Satcher wrote that "Tragic and devastating disorders such as schizophrenia, depression and bipolar disorder, Alzheimer's disease, the mental and behavioral disorders suffered by children, and a range of other mental disorders affect nearly one in five Americans in any year, yet continue too frequently to be spoken of in whispers and shame."[9] Americans encouraged to seek mental health care have sometimes heeded the advice. Many have been prescribed medications to relieve their symptoms. Many have achieved the elusive goal of recovery, now put forward by policymakers as the objective for national mental health policy.

Beneficial when used with care, psychiatric medications bear the burden of ethical concerns about overprescription, misprescription, and abuse. "Do no harm" is the first ethical duty of physicians. Critics worry that physicians too freely prescribe psychiatric medications to adult patients. Another concern is that psychiatrists, parents and schools have joined forces to overmedicate children with behavioral problems and minor attention deficits. Boys are no longer boys. They are psychiatric patients with treatable disorders. Ritalin, a stimulant used to treat attention deficit disorders, has come (unfairly in my view) to symbolize the controversy over when to cope, when to drug, and when to rely on other clinical and therapeutic resources.

Throughout American society a climate of skepticism exists about both childhood and adult mental illness. The spate of recent books tell a cautionary tale of psychiatry and its tools. The titles of a few are revealing of the general tenor: *Bitter Pills: Inside the Hazardous World of Legal Drugs, They Say You're Crazy: How the World's Most Powerful Psychiatrists Decide Who's Normal, Of Two Minds: The Growing Disorder in American Psychiatry*, and *Out of Its Mind: Psychiatry in Crisis, a Call for Reform*.[10] A degree of skepticism is certainly called for by our history of abuses. Years ago merely socially deviant people could easily be classified as mentally ill and shut away. Seriously ill and dangerous mentally ill people have languished without effective treatment, and have been victimized by crackpot clinicians. Overall, persons deemed mentally incompetent have been shut away against their wills, straitjacketed, drugged, loboto-mized, electrically shocked, psychoanalyzed by unqualified practitioners, lost, ignored and shamed. Psychiatry is more humane today than it was a hundred years ago; however, the recent shift to a predominantly pharmaco-logical approach to mental health, pushing psychotherapy to the margins, is a cause for legitimate concern. Some people with mental illness only see their psychiatrists when they need a medication adjustment or a refill.

I met a stranger on an airplane one day when I was worked up about the problem of childhood mental illness. What should a parent do, I asked him, if her child is angry, suicidal and sad? He listened very empatheti-cally, then asked if perhaps a puppy would not help a disturbed boy or girl. His kindhearted suggestion was troubling. Laypeople whose families have not been touched with childhood mental illness often cannot imagine that warm loving kindness is not enough to soothe some children. Because they cannot imagine a mentally ill child, they naturally doubt the value of administering strong psychoactive drugs to children.

We give our children the full complement of childhood immuniza-tions against measles, mumps, polio, tetanus and so forth as recommended by their pediatricians and required by law for school. For ear infections and bouts of strep throat we give them Amoxicillin. For pain, over-the-counter drugs like Tylenol and Motrin; Robitussin for coughs and colds; dabs of Neosporin on minor cuts and bruises. Parents rarely give a second thought to treating children with medicines like these, but more powerful and controversial medications are required when children begin to learn with severe difficulty, become irritable and profoundly sad, or are prone to slap, spit on and swear at their teachers.

One gets a rare glimpse into the complexity of contemporary appli-cations of psychopharmacology in a lawsuit filed in federal court in New York in 2002.[11] Patricia Weathers of Millbrook, New York, brought the lawsuit on behalf of her son, Michael Mozer. Ms. Weathers alleges that Michael was medicated with Ritalin for attention deficit disorder at the insistence of the public school he attended for first grade, on the basis of evaluations by school psychologists. Thereafter Michael's problems esca-lated from a mild attention problem in school to severe worrying, tics, rage attacks and hallucinations. Miseducation, misdiagnosis, overmedication, and mismedication on Ritalin, Dexedrine and Paxil, all caused her son years of severe neurological, emotional and behavioral disturbances, Weathers contends in the suit. If Michael did have bipolar disorder as one of the professionals who evaluated him eventually concluded, Ritalin and Dexedrine were probably not the right medications. Stimulants have the capacity to activate mania—including rage attacks—in bipolar children. There may indeed have been a connection between Michael's worsening symptoms and the medications he took. In any case, Weathers lost control of her son as school administrators, teachers, physicians and psychologists ran the show. Weather's suit on behalf of Michael is styled as an indictment of Ritalin and Paxil by her attorney, Alan Milstein. To me, it is not at all clear who or what is the real culprit in Michael Mozer's case. I do believe the case underscores the need for parents to have—or be prepared to acquire—a sophisticated knowledge of medical science in order to retain authority, agency and dignity in their lives.

I am inclined to admire parents who resist medication that they feel is inappropriate, dangerous and ineffective. However, it would be wrong to assume, after hearing about a medication history like Michael Mozer's, that educators and physicians are incompetent or that the purpose of medicating children is simply to make it easier for adults to control them. Children act up, they don't go crazy, skeptics seem to assume. But children do go crazy. Even children who are not abused and neglected develop mental illness. Failure to administer appropriate medication can lead to needless injuries, violence and suicides. Without medication, bouts of mania, hallucination and depression can worsen. Without medication, it would be impossible for some children affected by mental illness to live with their parents and siblings, because they would be too dangerous. Children requiring physical restraint are at risk of inadvertent injury by well-meaning adult caregivers. Without medication, some children become academic failures. By this, I do not mean that they get C and D grades. I mean they barely learn to read or fall two to three grade levels behind in reading and math. Medicating young children with mental illness can make it possible for them to learn to read, write and develop self-esteem. For this reason, I respect the tenor of the American Academy of Child and Adolescent Psychiatry's policy statement against "Restrictions on the Prescribing Practices of Child and Adolescent Psychiatrists by Managed Care Formularies."[12]

However, parents whose children need medication are not happy to learn that most medications prescribed for children with mental illnesses are not tested on children prior to their approval by the Food and Drug Administration. (But what parent would volunteer their children for a toxicity study of a new drug, anyway?) For example, child psychiatrists have often prescribed the drug Effexor, a product that earned $2.1 billion for Wyeth worldwide in 2002. In 2003, Wyeth announced doubt that the medication was of benefit to young children, ages six to seventeen, suffering from depression or anxiety. The company issued a letter to physicians warning that recent clinical studies suggest an increase in hostility, aggression and suicidal risk in a small percentage of children. In the absence of specific warnings like this one, pediatric psychiatrists rely on trial and error to determine effective dosages of Effexor and other psychoactive drugs, cautiously guided by their own and colleagues' clinical successes and failures.

Parents of children with mental illness are not alone in having to make tough choices about health care. Imagine having to decide whether to separate conjoined twins, one of whom is likely to die in surgery. When I was a little girl, my mother once treated my ear pain with my own warm urine, a folk remedy. Legitimate medical remedies may seem equally preposterous. Doctors at Johns Hopkins pioneered a surgical procedure that between 1968 and 1996 cured twenty-nine out of fifty-four children of disabling epileptic seizures. In this procedure, called hemispherectomy, nearly half the child's brain is removed.[13] According to Dr. John M. Freeman, who heads the Hopkins Pediatric Epilepsy Center, "Half a brain that works well is better than a whole brain that is seizing constantly."[14] Even parents with desperately ill children might balk at something that sounds so barbaric. It is hard to believe that a child with half a brain may actually be seizure free and more intelligent, but it appears perfectly true.

EATING RIGHT

Perhaps it should not be surprising that an ethical cloud surrounds drug use. An ethical cloud surrounds everything we put into our bodies, including food. Indeed, the line of demarcation between food and drug has been blurred by the "nutriceuticals" phenomenon that Stewart Truelson says is big in the future of agriculture. Writing for the American Farm Bureau Association, Truelson notes the convergence of pharmaceuticals and food into "functional" food products designed to supply the health benefits of traditional drugs, while supplying the aesthetic and nutritional benefits of ordinary wholesome foods.[15]

We have to eat, and Americans spend $700 billion a year on food. Is eating a moral act? According to the National Catholic Rural Life Conference (ANCRLC) it is: "We can oppose the industrialization of agriculture, animal factories, and policies that depopulate the countryside, give us food insecurity, gamble with food safety and food production, and make serfs of family farmers, and despoil the environment."[16] In short, we should eat with respect for the dignity of the people who produce our food, particularly the family farmer. Broader conceptions of the ethics of eating are also being voiced.

In an article for the *National Catholic Reporter Online,* Rich Heffern outlined a comprehensive agenda for an ethic of eating, arguing that "concerns about the food system seem to cluster around six areas, with considerable overlap."[17] Before sitting down with their next hamburger, Heffern would have consumers concerned about eating with ethical integrity consider a mouthful of consequences of their diet. The six classes of consequences are: (1) *environmental effects* such as genetic engineering, biodiversity, energy consumption, air pollution and groundwater pollution from animal waste, disinfectants, antibiotics, pesticides, herbicides and chemical fertilizers; (2) *food quality and taste,* lest we deaden the senses and destroy our aesthetic appreciation of foods, (3) *food safety,* in the face of food processing techniques that expose humans to e-coli, salmonella, carcinogenic chemicals and radiation, (4) *social justice* for laborers who "receive few benefits and work daily in an environment saturated with harmful pesticides, fungicides and other chemicals," (5) *cruelty to animals* deprived of exercise and the opportunity to meet behavioral and biological needs; and finally (6) *agribusiness food monopolies* resulting from an increasingly small number of food processors and suppliers who crowd out small farmers and even sue critics for "food disparagement."[18]

Oprah Winfrey was sued by the beef industry for doing little more than expressing a preference for not eating red meat. Heffern does not include vegetarianism as a clear mandate of an ethic of eating. However, some of the groups and individuals most open to recognizing eating as a moral act are vegetarians and vegans. In his 1998 book *Vegan: The New Ethics of Eating,* Erik Marcus explored the health, environmental and animal cruelty arguments for the meatless diet. Vegans eat no animal products whatsoever, including milk, eggs or butter. When one of my brothers was a strict vegan I had to prepare some inventive Thanksgiving dinners to work around his diet.

After nearly two decades of chicken and fish, Americans are once again relishing red meat. Fine dining establishments unashamedly offer up towers of rare beef. This is happening, though, at a time when it seems that nearly every teenage girl is a vegetarian, when mad cow and hoof and mouth diseases have called into question the safety and humanity of consuming farm animals; and when the corporate agricultural sector is suddenly touting the superior virtues of soy products for combating osteoporosis and heart disease. What should we eat?

Moral concerns about the food we eat mirror concerns about the drugs we take. An ethic of consumption pertains to both. We are obligated, in a moral sense, to consume with an eye toward healthy and responsible lives. We should therefore avoid food and drugs that harm our bodies. But there is more. We should avoid food and drugs that come to us with a price tag of suffering or cruelty. We should not harm to consume, nor be complicit in harm to consume. We should consume in light of the best evidence, about safety, nutrition, environmental impact and harm.

Trying to eat in accordance with an ethics of consumption requires consideration of how the food we eat gets to us. Food that reaches us as a result of discrimination, unfair wages or inhumane working conditions also runs afoul of the ethic. It is wrong for consumers with choices to eat foods grown, produced or packaged in ways that seriously harm people or degrade the human environment. For years it was not politically correct to eat lettuce and grapes from California out of solidarity with agricultural workers pressuring for better wages and working conditions. I got with the program. Today, I confess, as a busy working mother, I spend less time than I should keeping abreast of where my food comes from. My kids get their Happy Meals. My friend Kara smokes marijuana, but would not buy food from McDonald's out of concern for the treatment of its low-paid, nonunion workers. We all have different priorities.

For many people, the ethical demand that we consume without harm means paying careful attention to the suffering of the animals we consume. I was raised on Southern African American soul food. My children and husband recoil when I tell them of the neck bones, pigs' ears, liver and canned meat I scarfed down as a child. I grew to be more selective about my diet later on. For several years I did not eat veal because I was persuaded that the way calves were reared to produce veal was distinctly cruel. My concerns about cruelty to animals eventually led me to become a vegetarian for a number of years. However, about the time I became a busy lawyer, the concerns faded and I resumed life as a carnivore. No more pigs' ears, though.

Eating meat is controversial because of evidence that (1) meat-eating is an avoidable, less healthy alternative to vegetarianism; (2) animals experience pain and suffering, and large mammals may be cognitively or emotionally similar to human beings; (3) meat production is inefficient and harmful to the environment, due to the costs of feeding farm animals and animal waste contamination of the water supply. There are other reasons for not eating meat. In some countries, meat eating has extended to killing and eating endangered mammal species, the so-called "bush meat" consumption problem. This international concern is not much of an issue in the United States. Religious reasons for avoiding meat consumption are recognized by Jews, Muslims and Hindus.

The use of animals to test and manufacture drugs and other products also has ethical consequences. The ethical treatment of animals may mean that we do not eat them, wear them or use them casually or cruelly in research. Sally is a vegetarian who does not wear clothing or shoes made from animal products. Her children eat fake soy-meat and she avoids buying them the leather sneakers other children in the neighborhood wear. By contrast, I wear leather without serious guilt. I even own a fur coat that I inherited from my mother-in-law and another that I picked up at a thrift shop for $100. I had no idea that my purchase was anything more exotic than nutria (a rodent, sometimes spelled nutrea). I took the "rat" coat to be cleaned and the furrier let me know that I had "lucked" upon a $5,000 vintage baby seal and mink jacket. Bill (who is not a vegetarian) chided me for wearing the coat to work one day, arguing that wearing the coat would send a message of indifference to the plight of endangered species.

Animals are deliberately exposed to hazards, traumatized and diseased in hopes of reducing human injury and suffering. Is this justified? That worms and fruit flies are used in research is not of much interest. Rodents are a particularly important class of research animals whose treatment, along with that of domestic and farm animals is controversial. Genetics research is greatly indebted to the lowly mouse for its services as a model organism. Monkeys and apes are Man's closest relatives in the animal world. Research on them has been exceedingly controversial, leading animal rights' activists to raid labs. In an infamous case of research using primates, University of Pennsylvania scientists who had engaged in trauma studies using monkeys were condemned for cruelty after the broadcast of a videotape showing them deliberately crushing the animals' skulls. The point of the arguably important research was to measure the damage that results from various degrees of force, but the tape revealed callous researchers joking around as they went about their gruesome tasks.[19] Members of People for the Ethical Treatment of Animals (PETA) took the tapes from Penn's labs and made them public. Many state and federal laws mandate humane treatment of research animals. Unsatisfied radical opponents of animal research argue that, by definition, intentionally exposing sentient creatures to major illness and injury is profoundly inhumane.

In my judgment, any animal rights' activists more concerned about chickens than the demoralized laborers employed in chicken processing plants have got it wrong. However, cruelty to animals *is* a genuine ethical concern for human beings. Cruelty to animals is a sign that something is wrong with a human being. It can be a sign of emotional disturbance. It can be a sign of carelessness and indifference to suffering. We ought to use animals for food, clothing and research, if at all, in ways that minimize suffering. We are morally called upon to reduce animal product consumption and to pay higher prices for animal products as needed to meet the demands of just, humane and environmentally safe animal management.

Science has brought us irradiated foods and genetically altered foods. Should we eat them? One school of thought says we should embrace irradiated meats for the same reason we embraced the pasteurization of milk. Both are ways of heating foods to kill harmful bacteria. This, it seems, is basically a safety issue. The only reason not to eat irradiated foods that are otherwise ethical to eat would be that the process of irradiation introduces additional hazards. For some people the issue of genetically altered foods goes beyond safety to the morality of eating food whose genetic makeup has been tampered with by profit-seeking researchers. The broader issue is whether to support mankind's manipulation of plant life, if doing so could have serious, and perhaps unforeseen negative consequences on the food supply or the natural environment. Recent reports suggest that it has become futile for average consumers to attempt to avoid genetically altered foods, because so much of the available produce has been altered. The general problem here is just how much it takes for consumers to master the science needed to know what is best. We need to get our heads out of the sand on important issues relating to food and the treatment of animals. Like others, I am not anxious to be persuaded that I should not wear leather and that I should go back to being a vegetarian. Yet we all need to make a good-faith effort to confront the potential for harm.

CHAPTER 9

LIVING BEAUTIFULLY

You have a pleasant face, but a sleeker nose would make you down-right gorgeous. You can afford cosmetic surgery, so should you do it? "Why hesitate?" whisper the tastefully designed World Wide Web pages and advertisements in local newspapers around the country. "You deserve to feel good about yourself." We do deserve to feel good about ourselves. But we also deserve a better appreciation of the ethical dimensions of widely available aesthetic procedures. Beauty is now a consumer good, to be bought and sold. Feel-good cosmetic surgery makeovers are the stuff of reality television programs. The market has dimmed our view of the ethical dimensions of the unbounded quest for good looks.

The family of my husband, Paul, is Italian. His mother's ancestors, the Potenzas and Gattolis, came to the United States a hundred years ago. The Castellittos, his father's ancestors, came to the United States about the same time from the town of Campobasso. Neither side of my husband's family is known for dainty noses. You may have seen the Castellitto nose in the movies. The Italian actor Sergio Castellitto, also of Campobasso ancestry, does it proud. My husband has a version of the nose and his niece Liz was born with it, too. We used to joke that Liz looked a lot like Paul, in drag. She had my husband's slender build, thick brown hair and the kind of arched, bumpy nose that has made rhinoplasty a household word. During Christmas break of her sophomore year Liz had a $6,000 nose job. When she returned to college after the holidays, she was modeling a perky, cover girl profile.

Young women like Liz are not the only ones who care about the shape of their noses. Men also care. Hanging in the Uffizi Gallery in Florence, Italy, Piero Della Francesca's portrait of the Duke of Urbino depicts every profile-conscious man's worst nightmare. The unfortunate duke had a nose you could hang a towel on. Not to be mistaken for a clothes hook, many a young man has had rhinoplasty, too.

Italians are not the only people with distinctive noses. My father's ancestors were mainly African and Cherokee. Many members of his family inherited a narrow-bridged, wide-bottomed organ that we affectionately call the "Benton Nose." Prominent African Americans Otis Graham and Faye Wattleton are both known for refined, elegant looks, and both have spoken publicly about submitting to the surgeon's knife. Their formerly broad noses were whittled away to meet a cosmetic ideal. Noses seem to matter. A Jewish scholar I know is so good humored and brainy, you would not think he wanted for anything. Faced with a balding head, ample gut and thick glasses, he decided to begin his middle-age makeover with a nose job.

In the United States and all over the world, personal appearance has entered the arena of choice. We can now choose how we look. A hundred years ago, with the availability of anesthesia and antiseptics needed to make facial surgery a tolerable risk, the New York physician Dr. John Orlando Roe helped the "pug-nosed" Irish look English. Techniques and technologies available today have made a miraculous variety of fully elective aesthetic surgeries routine. According to Beverly Hills physician Dr. Ryan A. Stanton, "The way you look is your choice."[1] Like Dr. Stanton, Dr. Robert Gutstein promises that "nearly every contour of the human body can be enhanced through plastic surgery."[2] Physicians offer their patients a menu of options aimed at improving the appearance of the face, chest, breasts, arms, abdomen, thighs and calves. The menu even lists enhancements of the penis and vulva. Any part of the anatomy can be made bigger, smaller, smoother, sleeker, fuller or flatter.

Sometimes plastic surgery is needed to help cure a congenital deformity, surgical wound or injury. Darla is a thirty-something, charming, bright corporate manager who suffered from debilitating headaches and back pain for many years. The cause of her suffering, physicians explained, was her breasts. They were huge. Darla's husband was worried about a surgical solution, but she went for breast reduction surgery to relieve her pain, and it worked. Her pain disappeared completely, and she is no longer the butt of jokes. Plastic surgery is clearly an important medical resource for people like Darla. But individuals who look and feel perfectly normal use plastic surgery all the time simply to look and feel better.

Natural endowments are no longer the name of the game, even in premier beauty contests. Juliana Borges, the stunning twenty-two-year-old Brazilian entry in a recent Miss Universe pageant, admitted to nineteen surgical procedures en route to the crown. "The surgery is just to give you a little polish," Borges explained.[3] Ms. Borges had a Pygmalion. Evandro Rossi, a professional manager of beauty contestants in Rio de Janeiro took her on as a "rough gem that hasn't been worked."[4] To polish his gem into an international beauty, surgeons pinned back her "Dumbo" ears and streamlined a fleshy midsection with liposuction. They inserted chin and cheek implants. They inflated her thin lips and augmented her small breasts. "And why not? "Why shouldn't I make use of these scientific advances?" Borges queried.[5]

Unfortunately, mainstream social and economic rewards have sometimes been directed on a preferential basis to people who do not look "ethnic." The beautiful and sexy have an advantage, but so, it seems, does anyone who looks less ethnic—whether it be less Irish, less Italian, less Chinese, less Jewish or less African. The troubled singer Michael Jackson, who would have been a fabulously wealthy pop star in any case, went too far in his attempt to mute his race, and entertainers outside the mainstream make similarly grotesque elections. It is unfortunate that workers in the adult entertainment industry have responded to incentives to undergo painful and expensive augmentation of the breasts and genitals. Strippers, erotic dancers and sex workers exaggerate their sexuality with breast implants hoping to attract opportunity and additional customers.

ADORNMENT

For people who cannot afford (or stomach) the fruits of medical science, there are plenty of other ways to enhance physical beauty. Diet, exercise and cosmetics work wonders on receptive, younger bodies. Americans spend billions each year at cosmetic counters seeking to look, feel and smell better. Billions more are spent in hair salons. You can get cut, colored, curled, uncurled, braided and locked. Like makeup and hairstyles, fashionable clothing and jewelry are familiar beauty electives. The body-piercing phenomenon has created a demand for jewelry that barely existed twenty years ago: eyelid rings, nipple rings, navel rings and tongue studs. Permanent and temporary tattoos are enjoying an era of popularity, too. My niece Liz seeks beauty in every medium with gusto, a true child of her time: diet-thin, colored hair, bold makeup, a new nose, navel ring, multiple ear piercings and a tattoo at the base of her spine.

Beauty is an art form, the body a canvas. It is sobering, though, to be reminded that our aesthetic standards are seldom original. They are shared, cultural. In the United States aesthetic standards are heavily influenced, even manipulated, by the cosmetic, fashion and entertainment industries. The more content we are with the way we look, the fewer profits the beauty industries earn. Beauty-related industries do more than influence our standards of beauty. I began wearing lipstick and business suits when I was a law student seeking a job in corporate law. I continue to wear them, not only because I think they make me look better dressed, but also because of the connotations of glamour, hygiene and youthful vibrancy that surround the affordable products of Clinique and Saks Fifth Avenue.

Beauty for beauty's sake is not the whole story of why people decorate their bodies. A primary motivation is the desire to be acceptable to others. Both men and women try to conform to prevailing standards of good looks within the groups and subgroups to which they wish to belong, so that they will be attractive to others in those groups. John Travolta's performance in the film *Saturday Night Fever* was a memorable, sympathetic portrayal of the vulnerability of masculine vanity among working-class ethnic Italians in New York. We got to see a man preen himself on camera. Thirty-five years ago radical feminists injected discomfort into the desire to attract mates through girly fashion choices. Feminists rejected makeup, bras, skirts, and high heels as inauthentic pandering to the preferences of a male-dominated culture. Today the willingness to bear the discomforts of high heels and the expense of nylon hose is not generally interpreted as a sign of brainwashing. Women running major companies in heels know that they are much more than ornaments.

Bodily adornment is not generally a big moral or ethical issue; however, it can be. Some minority groups within American society situate bodily adornment squarely in the realm of the moral. On Sundays the Amish families of Lancaster County, Pennsylvania, can be observed meandering along in their horse-drawn buggies or relaxing on their porches, in plain, nineteenth-century attire. It would be a moral issue for an Amish woman to suddenly abandon drab colors and adopt the fashion look of a Jennifer Lopez or Hillary Clinton. On neighborhood streets in Philadelphia and New York, black Muslim men go about their business in dark suits and bow ties. Muslim women cover their heads, arms and legs. Conservative interpretations of Islamic traditions call for dark, drab colors, but I recently saw a Muslim woman draped in bright pinks and oranges. Her clothing preserved her modesty but was, I thought with a smile, dangerously appealing. There is a moral dimension to the dress codes of Catholic schools. The uniform, simple style of clothing is supposed to encourage decorum and civility conducive to learning and piety. And of course the traditional modest garb of Catholic nuns and priests has religious and moral significance.

A style of adornment can have moral implications outside of the specific context of religion. Styles of adornment can be offensive to the legitimate feelings and sensibilities of others. They can shock the conscience and show disrespect for valued institutions and cultures. Students of constitutional law read about a man who sported FUCK THE DRAFT on the back of his jacket as he walked into a courthouse back in the 1960s. The man was criticized on moral grounds but defended by civil libertarians as having First Amendment rights of free expression. His strong language was offensive to some and his implicit criticism was considered disrespectful to a nation whose young men were dying on foreign soil. On the other hand, the Vietnam war was politically controversial in the extreme, and political speech merits protection in a free society.

People who decorate their bodies with symbols like swastikas and confederate flags that are assaultive to minority groups get criticized for moral insensitivity. This area of moral criticism is tricky. One person's fighting words are another's cultural symbols. People who wear eccentric or "ethnic" hairdos in the workplace or to school are criticized for inappropriate conduct. Administrators at my high school regarded long kinky hair as dangerously subversive. In an abundance of caution, the school banned the "Afro pick" comb for its potential as a weapon. Ethnically specific adornment can be seen as politically provocative or distracting. In the 1990s, an African American attorney was chided for wearing a colorful West African style kente cloth draped over his business suit in a Washington, D.C., courtroom. The lawyer explained his adornment as an expression of his minority cultural identity. African Americans are in the majority in Washington, yet the judge interpreted the black lawyer's choice of clothing as disrespectful to the court and threatened sanctions.

Mainstream popular culture represents bodily adornment as a realm of individual choice and taste. As such, it is not supposed to be a realm for ethical hesitation. You want braids, get braids. You want a tattoo, get a tattoo. You want a ring through your navel, get a ring through your navel. You want big breasts, get big breasts. Fitness is also a mattter of choice. You want to lose a few pounds, it is okay to diet and work out.

Yet bodily adornment is a realm for ethical engagement. Obsessing about looks can fuel serious eating disorders like anorexia and bulimia. Moreover, obsessing about your looks can develop into a character flaw. Prioritizing beauty can be not only shallow but wrong. It would be irresponsible to consider making a nail salon appointment as more important than voting in a national election. It would be even worse to routinely spend money that your children need for nutritious food on expensive fashions for yourself, or for them. It can be wrong to give no consideration to how your cosmetics are brought to market. Should you wear lipstick that was tested on human subjects who happened to be incarcerated "volunteers" desperate to earn a few extra dollars as human guinea pigs, or on actual guinea pigs handled with cruelty?

It would be foolish to argue as a general matter that lipstick, a Botox injection or a standard nose job is a significant ethical problem. However, there are two neglected ethical questions connected to cosmetic procedures that I would like to highlight. When is it ethical for an individual to take on a medical risk? Should perfectly normal and healthy people assume the unnecessary medical risk of aesthetic surgery? And what level of self-acceptance is due as a condition of self-respect and group pride? There is an ethical dimension to allowing oneself to despise physical traits that are normal but "too ethnic."

Surgical beauty seeking is potentially troubling in a way that most adornment with clothing, jewelry and hairstyles is not. The trouble is partly a matter of the risks involved relative to the benefits received. Liposuction costs a lot of money and can kill you. Lipstick is cheap and ridiculously safe—even in shades with names like Devil Red and Hell Fire. Reparative and restorative surgery has risks, but the benefits are generally exceedingly high. I have no morally tinged criticism to make of the people who visit the orthodontist for braces to improve their smiles, and my heart goes out to people who seek cosmetically curative surgical remedies for massive birth defects, accidental maiming or cancer. I certainly see the point of postmastectomy reconstructive breast surgery. A person born with a misshapen skull or whose jaw is crushed in an automobile accident is not the sort of person whose elective cosmetic surgery troubles. I am troubled, though, by people with normal, whole bodies who resort to surgery as a way of seeking to realize ideals of beauty.

BOTCHED JOBS

G ale wanted to do something to get herself out of a funk. A mother of three school-aged children, she had just been dumped by her boyfriend. Then, within the space of a few months she survived an automobile crash, a rape that left her pregnant, and a cancer scare. One day Gale met a great-looking woman who had recently had a breast job. Gale decided she would get one too. A naturally trim thirty-five-year-old, Gale achieved the figure of a Barbie doll after saline breast augmentation. But today, she is angry. Following surgery, Gale began to lose her hair and was diagnosed with an autoimmune disorder. Her augmented breasts are unnaturally hard, pocked and misshapen. She showed them to me when I interviewed her in her home for this book, and I was sad for her. She blames her surgeon, a man who misrepresented his qualifications for performing the operation and now blames her for not properly caring for her breasts after surgery as he had prescribed. She is suing mad because she believes she did everything she was told. Her plastic surgeon has offered to try and correct his mistake for a sum of thousands of dollars which the single mom cannot afford to pay.

Medical science has made it possible for us to look and feel better, and sometimes we yield to our insecurities. We leap at novel approaches to "perfect" our bodies. The bra size 34A could be increased to 36D. We are eager and trusting. Some recent options have proven highly disappointing. Others can threaten lives, unexpectedly.

One afternoon the phone rang. It was a nurse from the intensive care unit at a hospital near Baltimore. "I am calling about your brother Michael. There has been a complication from his surgery. He was losing a lot of blood here in the ICU so we had to rush him back to the operating room." Her call came as a complete surprise. I am especially close to my brother Michael. We have spent a lot of time together as adults. He is a handsome, unmarried, well-built lawyer, famous for his semivegan diet and for taking dates to see Disney movies. He has a lot of friends and is well liked. At the time of the call he was practicing law in Washington and training to bike in a marathon—to benefit AIDS research—which was only three weeks away. He had not said anything to me about having a health problem. As far as I knew, he was as healthy as a horse. It turned out that Michael was indeed as healthy as a horse. The surgery that nearly killed him was elective.

In the days after Michael almost bled to death alone in a Baltimore hospital room, I discovered that he had always been self-conscious about what he thought of as excessive perspiration. The purpose of the elective surgery was to make him sweat less. I had no idea that Michael had a significant perspiration problem or that he thought he did. Michael said he tried to hide the problem. In the summertime, he changed shirts several times a day. He avoided shaking hands. He did not like to hold hands with his girlfriends because he felt his palms were clammy. He felt self-conscious in business meetings, where he feared perspiring would be interpreted as nervousness. All of this from a man who seemed perfectly self-confident and impeccably groomed.

A couple of months before surgery, Michael discovered on the Internet that excessive sweating has a medical name, *hyperhidrosis*. One currently available treatment for hyperhidrosis is Botox (botulinum toxin) injections. The injections are expensive and generally have to be repeated to maintain efficacy. An alternative remedy is a surgical procedure, upper thoracic sympathectomy. This older, permanent remedy works by turning off the upper body's thermostat. Sympathectomy is described by experts at the Columbia University Department of Surgery's Center for Hyperhidrosis as "the gold standard of treatment for this disease, by which all other treatments must be judged."[6] The procedure is thought to be safe. The Center for Hyperhidrosis reports that "The success rate is in excess of 98 percent, with very few side effects or serious complications." The procedure is performed under general anesthesia. The surgeon makes a small incision inside the armpit, near the chest. Next, the surgeon locates and severs certain sections of the sympathetic nerves that govern the upper body's temperature control functions. The procedure used at Columbia University involves endoscopic identification of the second through fourth ganglia. "The branches to the main sympathetic chain at each level are identified and divided, then the main chain is removed," doctors say. Patients are advised that after the operation, they will no longer perspire from the armpits, brow or hands. However, to compensate, their bodies are likely to perspire more below the waist. The thermostat for that region is left undisturbed.

Michael's primary care doctor tried to discourage him from having surgery, but at his insistence she referred him to a Baltimore specialist. Michael's desire for dry shirts and hands led him to put himself under the

When is it ethical for an individual to take on a medical risk?

knife and almost cost him, and those of us who love him, his life. His near bleed-out occurred because his surgeon had failed to adequately cauterize severed blood vessels. Before surgery, the jovial specialist had assured Michael that he would be out of the hospital the day after surgery and that he would be able to bike the charity marathon in a few weeks as planned. Indeed patients are generally home within twenty-four hours. Instead, Michael wound up on a morphine drip, in great pain, with foot-long surgical wounds stapled shut, and a weak, emaciated body that took months to heal. He did sweat less, though.

We take on medical headaches like Michael's and Gale's with inadequate attention to what can go wrong. It pays to talk to a variety of people who have undergone medical procedures like the one you are contemplating to hear their experiences. Just based on how Gale looks in a sweater and the right bra, a casual observer gets a favorable impression of breast implants. All covered up, Gale has a figure to envy and emulate. But listen to Gale's story and you get a different picture. She will tell you that her election was a product of insecurity and depression. She would tell you that she is too embarrassed to pursue an intimate relationship with a man. Now that he has healed, Michael's views about his experience are more mixed. He has scars and does not have the strength for marathons anymore, but he enjoys intimacy more than ever. He thinks he might be willing to go through his nightmare all over again.

We need to do more than to listen physicians' lists of strictly medical risks. We need to understand that the availability of a procedure does not mean that it is perfectly safe. Good doctors performing approved procedures in standard ways can still hurt you. And not all medical accidents and mistakes of judgment are considered malpractice for which you can be compensated. One should consider how the expected and unexpected hardships of cosmetic surgery will impact lives and families. Anyone with a web of responsibilities and commitments to others must think hard about whether the risks of illness, injury and death associated with elective surgery are worth the benefits. The standard approach to getting a patient's informed consent for surgery neither bars nor much facilitates such thinking.

Michael expected to be back at work the Monday following his surgery, and that none of his friends and family would ever know about his hyperhidrosis. He put my name down on the hospital admission form as next of kin and notified his best friend that he was going in for "routine tests." Michael was acting privately, autonomously and independently, as grown men are allowed. But his surgery made him dependent. Friends and family drove great distances to visit him in the hospital. He had to be nursed by family for ten days after his release from the hospital. His family and friends had to juggle schedules, child care responsibilities, and the like. We were anxious to do things, of course. When you love people deeply, you want to help in these ways. But by the same token, when you love people deeply, you do not want to have to help in these ways. Care and concern for others should make each of us cautious about unnecessary major medical procedures. That concern extends to employers. Michael's coworkers and supervisors were inconvenienced by his long absence from the office, but gracious about it.

There is, though, a tough question about when medical procedures are "necessary." There is an argument to be made that Michael's surgery was not purely elective at all. He had a condition with a medical name attached to it. The fact that no one was bothered by it but him and perhaps his most intimate partners may be irrelevant. Gale's breast augmentation surgery was purely elective. Depression following trauma is a medical problem, but cosmetic breast surgery is a costly, ineffective way to address that problem. Lucy, another friend, changed her sex from male to female. Were Lucy's carefully considered sex change operations "elective" or medically indicated? The mental health professionals with whom she worked for years deemed it a medically appropriate procedure to cure gender identity disorder. Yet there was nothing imperfect-looking about Lucy's male body; in fact, she was an unusually handsome man. Is it ethical to take on low medical risk to change your sex, but not to change the shape of your breasts?

Another ground for ethical concern about beauty seeking is what it says about self-acceptance and pride. Gale wanted to look sexier. Some African Americans want to have more European-looking noses and lips.

Biracial blacks like my kids used to get treated as extra cute just because their African features are less pronounced: their skin, hair and eyes are lighter, noses and lips thinner. I am unnerved by the spectre of people of color allocating their newly found economic resources to changing their bodies to resemble the bodies of certain idealized European Americans. We need to accept ourselves as capable of being beautiful. We need to accept the beauty we already possess.

Members of some ethnoracial minorities have religious reasons to avoid plastic surgery. Some religions, including Islam, deemphasize and discourage physical vanity. Members of some Christian sects, including Seventh Day Adventists and Christian Scientists, disapprove of even certain life-saving medical procedures, like blood transfusions. A minority of American Jews believes that cosmetic surgery runs afoul of the Jewish law against gratuitous wounding. But where religion is not a barrier, minority group members may find the lure of the knife irresistible. Blacks and Asians here and in other parts of the world are tempted to try to look as Caucasian or "all-American" as possible. In Thailand, many women have come to admire the idealized slim Western woman. But Thai women often have proportionately thicker calves than European American women of otherwise similar build. Calf-reduction surgery performed in Thailand has virtually crippled some of the women who have undergone it. Meanwhile, here in the United States, surgery to increase calf-size is sought-after enough to appear on plastic surgeons' lists of services.[7]

ETHICAL LONGEVITY

Even if you do not care how you look, you probably do care about how long you are going to be around. Living longer is not inherently better than living well, yet you do not have to search hard to find good reasons for living past eighty. Fear of the finality of death is reason enough for most people. But we should value long lives for other reasons, too. First, long lives make possible the profoundly deep interpersonal and intergenerational relationships that by their very nature benefit from long duration. Second, we need long lives to have the time to make good on our potential for proficiency in our endeavors. The promising young musician killed in an auto accident brings on the lament of lost chance.

Although there is ample reason to want a long life, the case is less clear for extending average human longevity to, say, 150 years. Someday it may be possible to live longer by choosing to undergo a simple procedure or take a medication. Perhaps we will someday be able to elect gene therapy for ourselves and children that will enable longer lives. But if you could live to be 150, would you do it? And how would you wish to spend all that extra time? What if you could live to be 150, but for the last 75 years you would have to live with the panoply of health concerns and bodily deterioration associated with old age today. Would it be worth it? We may run into serious social and economic problems if biomedical innovation extends our lives much beyond current natural limitations.

More than two dozen genes associated with longevity in yeast organisms have been discovered, two of which have human gene analogues. Scientists have already discovered that minor manipulations of the DNA of fruit flies (*drosophila melanogaster*) and roundworms (*caenorhabditis elegans*) can more than double their life spans. Mice are biologically closer kin to humans than yeast, worms or fruit flies. Aging research on mice has uncovered some of the mechanisms of aging resistance. According to an article published in *Nature* in November 2001, a specific gene mutation of the Ames mouse called "*prop-1*" appears to be strongly associated with increased longevity. In principle, some scientists are now guessing, the human life span could be significantly expanded. Should we go for it?

Longevity is a matter for ethical engagement. Living a long life is a worthy and understandable aspiration, but some thought must be given to the kinds of longer lives that are worth living and changes in the social and economic infrastructure that would be needed to accommodate substantially longer-lived populations. We would need to rethink the life cycle, clearly. We might conclude that people should spend more years in school and perhaps that the number of years of mandatory schooling should be increased. Planning to have multiple careers and marriages might seem like a good idea if the normal life span were 150 years rather than 80 years. We might conclude that longer-lived people should periodically change their identities in order to get more out of life and experience more of life's possibilities. Plastic surgery could play a routine role in helping very long-lived people revamp their appearances.

The desirability of longer lives might depend upon which phase of life was extended. It is one thing to spend a hundred extra years as robust as a forty-year-old, and something else again to spend forty extra years as a hundred-year-old. Slowing down or eliminating the aging processes that begin after thirty is the real fantasy of longevity, not just living longer in one's declining years. For women, longevity on the youthful end of things raises the prospect of having childbearing years extended. While children are a joy, I suspect few women would welcome eighty years of menses, contraception, pregnancies and diapers to change. Of course, biological sciences sophisticated enough to help us to double our life spans could also easily address the problem of unwanted fertility. Indeed, one of the genetic techniques for extending the longevity of fruit flies also, for some reason, makes the flies sterile.

Longer-lived people will need employment. Our current economic system is based on the expectation that a certain number of us die and retire, making room for new generations of workers. There could get to be a serious surplus labor problem in a world in which people lived much longer. On the other hand, the added demand for food, housing, clothing and entertainment could result in ample jobs. We could experience a crisis in caretaking, though, if people began living longer but with declining health. Dependency demands could add to the already mounting caretaking pressures faced by middle-aged women, and to a lesser degree, men. My older sister Cynthia's caretaking pressures are good examples of the kind of responsibilities midlife already can bring. In her mid-fifties, she has the usual grandmotherly caretaking roles. Her son, daughter-in-law and their five small children live a few miles away. She also shares responsibility for our aging father. Until our Aunt Anne recently died at sixty-two of multiple sclerosis, she sometimes sought out Cynthia's help getting around. Anne had no spouse or child of her own to care for her. Cynthia assumed complete responsibility for another childless, unmarried aunt, Lillie Ruth, until her 2004 cancer death at eighty. Longevity at the far end of life will add names to the list of kin that loving men and women like Cynthia will spend their middle years assisting. All other things being equal, Cynthia would prefer to have more time for her hobbies—traveling and bowling—and her grandchildren.

The willingness to buy longevity has to depend upon whether we conclude, after examining the facts and reflecting on their significance, that living longer is more kind than cruel. This important judgment will hinge on more than the motives of the people seeking longevity. It will also depend upon whether well-meaning private choices can be backed up with adequate public and private resources.

Finally, longevity options will raise serious questions of autonomy. I can imagine a world in which the option of longevity comes to be mandatory: life is good, so everyone should live as long as possible. Wishing to live a normal life span of 80 years rather than a new supernormal life span of 150 would be viewed as suicidal. The choice of a shorter life would be discounted the way we discount the choice to put a gun to one's head.

Some contemplated modes of increasing longevity will require that our parents make decisions on our behalf. Parents will decide whether they want their offspring to have the particular genetic trait required for longevity, which will give one generation the power to decide the longevity of the next. The man or woman who would have chosen a shorter life, for example, is compelled to have a longer one. Longevity also raises questions of fairness. Suppose the price tag on longevity medications or therapy is high and there is no government subsidy. Anyone who can afford the age cure gets to live longer, but everyone else dies after a now normal life span. We could wind up with a society in which the rich lived not just a few years more than the poor, as they currently do, but decades more. Bill Gates might become the grandfather of us all. We could let it happen.

The longevity questions I have raised so far relate primarily to a world of the future, but there is considerable ethical novelty tied to longevity already afoot in the existing world. Imagine that you are a man of fifty-two. You have a wife, grandchildren and a community of friends. You are glad to be alive. Now imagine that you develop health problems. You get exhausted walking across a room. It is hard to breathe lying down. One day stunning news comes from the cardiologist: your heart is failing and you have only six months to live. Chances are you would regard such news as a horrible catastrophe. Your life expectancy was seventy-two not fifty-two! You want to make an effort to stay alive, but how far should you go to extend your life?

A BROKEN HEART

This exact question was presented to Philadelphian James "Butch" Quinn.[8] A baker by trade, at fifty-two Quinn was diagnosed with congestive heart failure. Standard treatments would be of no avail. Drugs could not help him, and it was too late for a human heart transplant. Quinn's doctor thought he might have as many as six months to live, and put him in touch with Dr. Louis E. Samuels, Associate Professor at MCP Hahnemann University Hospital and Surgical Director of the Cardiac Transplant Team. In October 2001, Dr. Samuels delivered Mr. Quinn an even gloomier prognosis. He said Quinn's death was imminent. He would probably die within fourteen to thirty days.

But Dr. Samuels also offered Quinn a kind of hope. Dr. Samuels was geared to conduct clinical trials of an experimental artificial heart manufactured by Abiomed, Inc. He offered to enroll Quinn in AbioCor artificial heart transplant trial studies. According to a November 6, 2001 Abiomed press release about the trials, "The first two procedures were performed at Jewish Hospital in Louisville, Kentucky, on July 2 and September 13. The third implant took place at Texas Heart Institute and St. Luke's Episcopal Hospital in Houston, Texas, on September 26. A fourth implant was performed at UCLA Medical Center on October 17."[9] The AbioCor trials were approved in advance by the federal Food and Drug Administration.

Research on human subjects is tricky business, governed by a thicket of ethical and legal requirements. The most basic requirement of private sector and government-funded research is that the subject of an experimental study consent in writing after being fully informed. The subject must be told the purpose and nature of experimental procedures in non-technical language. The likely costs and benefits of experimental study must be plainly revealed. In the early stages of medical product development, researchers do not anticipate benefits to the subjects; volunteers are sought on the basis that their participation may help others in the future. Experienced researchers know that care must be taken when describing the benefits of research. Even after researchers ask volunteer subjects in a clinical trial to sign an informed consent document clearly stating that they will not benefit from experimental research, optimistic subjects may continue to expect a direct benefit.

Mr. Quinn believed the battery-powered, computerized implantable heart would extend his life and he assumed a longer life would be a benefit to him and his family. As a result of Mr. Quinn's mechanical heart, he did live longer than physicians predicted. Instead of living two weeks, a month or six months after the ten-hour operation in which he became the fifth person to receive the AbioCor mechanical heart, he lived ten months. In a lawsuit filed after Quinn's death, his widow alleged that researchers "represented to the Quinns that, as a result of the operation, Mr. Quinn stood to have a good quality of life." But, according to his wife, Irene, Mr. Quinn did not have a good quality of life after the surgery. He had a wretched, wrongful life.

The problems began right away. The day after surgery, doctors announced that the AbioCor was operating flawlessly but that the patient— Mr. Quinn's identity was kept secret for some time—was "experiencing pulmonary distress requiring external oxygenation support." On New Year's Eve, less than two months after his November 5, 2001 surgery, Mr. Quinn suffered a stroke. The stroke blurred his vision and slurred his speech. It weakened the entire left side of his body. A month later, he developed breathing problems, accompanied by severe pain in his back and chest. On March 6, 2002, Mr. Quinn was placed on a ventilator. The Quinns grew desperately unhappy with the medical and nursing care Mr. Quinn received. They balked at the mounting financial costs of participating in the study. After a second massive stroke, Quinn's condition quickly deteriorated. On August 25, physicians declared him brain-dead.

On behalf of herself and her husband's estate, Irene Quinn sued the manufacturer of the AbioCor heart. She also sued her husband's patient advocate, Dr. David Cassarett, M.D., Tenet Healthcare Corp., Drexel University and Hahnemann University Hospital. Mrs. Quinn's lawsuit claimed injustices, including malpractice, lack of informed consent, infliction of emotional distress, misrepresentation, defective product liability, and the claim that most interests me, wrongfully extended life. He lived too long. Most of these claims were eventually dropped, but Mrs. Quinn eventually received a small settlement from Abiomed.[10] Life is good. However, a longer life is not necessarily a gift. When you wish for longevity, be careful what you wish for.

James Quinn was a biotech hero. He submitted to months of what he came to regard as torture motivated, in part, by a desire to help others. Whether his participation in the Abiomed study was uniquely valuable to future heart patients remains to be seen. But it is not clear, with the benefit of hindsight, that he made the best choice for himself and his family. His decision to live longer was a source of protracted misery for the people to whom he had the most distinct and immediate obligations of care and concern; himself, his wife, children and his grandchildren, and his friends. For so many Americans tempted by the promises of biomedical innovation, the lure of living longer undermines the surer bet of dying well.

CHAPTER 10

THE BEST WAY TO DIE

"You won't die until the Good Lord is ready," my mother used to say to allay our fears about dying. (It did not work with me.) Although she was a Southern Baptist and a believer, Carrie Mae Cloud Allen was not above backing up an article of faith with hard empirical proof. "One time they tried to electrocute a man. They put him in the chair, turned on the power, and he just sat there. They couldn't kill him. It wasn't his time. Lord wasn't ready." For many years I assumed the story of the man who escaped electrocution was just a folk tale, but my mother was a teenager living in Georgia when the infamous Willie Francis incident took place in nearby Louisiana.

Willie Francis was a seventeen-year-old African American convicted of murder and sentenced to die in the Louisiana electric chair on May 3, 1946, between noon and three o'clock.[1] The day and time arrived. Officials strapped Willie in the electric chair and placed a hood over his eyes. The executioner checked the power gauges and finally flipped the switch. According to eyewitness Reverend Maurice L. Rousseve, the prison chaplain, at the moment the electricity was applied, "Willie Francis' lips puffed out and his body squirmed and tensed and he jumped so that the chair rocked on the floor. Then the condemned man said: 'Take it off. Let me breath.' (*sic*) Then the switch was turned off. Then some of the men left and a few minutes after the Sheriff of St. Martin Parish, Mr. E. L. Resweber, came in and announced that the governor had granted the condemned man a reprieve."[2] The teenager returned to his prison cell, unharmed.

Louisiana state officials took the position that a latent defect in the equipment caused it to malfunction. There had been insufficient juice to stop Willie's heart from beating. So, they argued, they were entitled to fix Mr. Thomas Edison's invention and try again. However, Willie's lawyers protested that the State was not entitled to a second electrocution after botching the first one. To have a second try would be a form of double jeopardy. Moreover, it would be unconstitutionally cruel and unusual punishment to force a man who had made the psychological preparations for death once to repeat them all over again. The Eighth Amendment does not permit torture.

The Supreme Court of Louisiana disagreed. Willie Francis had one last hope, the U.S. Supreme Court. He petitioned the High Court. His unique case, *Louisiana ex rel. Francis v. Resweber* (1947),[3] was argued by a fine lawyer, James Skelly Wright, who later became a federal judge. Still, the High Court turned Willie down. Louisiana had a second go of it after the Court's ruling, and Willie Francis died in Old Sparky, as thousands would after him.

It is reassuring, in a way, to think that there is a plan for human life. When I was three, I swallowed a bottle of aspirin, thinking it was candy. I could easily have died, but doctors pumped my stomach and I survived. The science of pharmacology almost killed me, but the science of emergency toxicology intervened, according to the plan. When I was a passenger in a Ford Explorer that flipped over in a low-speed collision with a Cadillac on Los Angeles's Mulholland Drive, I could easily have died, along with my whole family. The rented Explorer was totaled, but we occupants walked away with barely a scratch. The police officers who came to the accident scene said they expected to find only dead bodies in the wreckage. Instead they found my children, my husband and me shaken up but needing little more than a few Band-Aids and a taxi back to our Santa Monica hotel. "If it is not your time," Carrie Mae Cloud Allen's ghost seemed to whisper in my ear as I stood in awe of a miracle on Mulholland Drive, "an SUV can't kill you." The Good Lord has a plan.

But where is the reassurance in all this for the person who does not believe in a God of plans and miracles? Or any God? And what if a person is a believer, but concludes on his or her own that the time for death has come? Sometimes people want to hasten death because they are very old, very sick or tired of suffering. Sometimes young, otherwise healthy people are so depressed and unhappy they want to die "before their time." For such people it can seem that God and man conspire to keep the poor in spirit on earth for their own mysterious purposes.

I want to emphasize the extent to which death is subject to the ethical control of the individual these days. However, I must first acknowledge the degree to which it surely is not. We have a good chance at long lives. Medical standards are high and aided by technology. Sophisticated pharmaceutical remedies are plentiful. Public health and safety are communal priorities. Still, people die suddenly and tragically every day while engaged in ordinary, unavoidable activities. Car accidents are a major cause of fatalities. Even sober people wearing their seat belts can get killed. People die in accidents at work, in house fires, and from unprovoked violence. There is simply no way to shield oneself from untimely death.

Our friend Steve was thirty-five. He had a great job in a Beverly Hills law firm. He and his wife lived in a charming little house in Laurel Canyon with an Italian garden that backed up to a steep hill. Suddenly Steve began losing weight and looking remarkably thin for a man who had always been something of a teddy bear. At first, Steve's doctors were not concerned, but when they eventually ran tests, they found incurable pancreatic cancer. Steve was given six months to live. He lived about six months to the day, weak and emaciated at the end.

Aunt Naomi Allen was sitting in her living room one afternoon, when the phone rang. On hearing that one of her favorite cousins had just died, Naomi, who suffered from severe hypertension, collapsed and died, too. A lively woman in late middle age, a minister at her church, a mother of six, and a grandmother, she dropped dead of shock and grief.

Cousin Lee Eric Young was headed for the Ivy League. Everyone was proud of him. He had had a rough childhood of sexual abuse by neighborhood bullies to overcome. Lee Eric arrived at Cornell University, eager for

Planning for our own deaths—sudden or lingering—is the last act of kindness we can show the world.

his freshman year to begin, but returned home the following spring for good. He took a job in a bank and tried to join the army. His army physical revealed that he was HIV positive. About the time he was to have graduated from Cornell, he was back in his parents' home, dying of AIDS. He passed away.

PLANNING FOR THE INEVITABLE

Planning for our own deaths—sudden or lingering—is the last act of kindness we can show the world. We humans have no control over when we are born, but we have some control over when we die and what happens to our remains. Few of us exercise this power. We avoid responsibility for death, and we live in a society that encourages us to avoid that responsibility. We could easily take practical responsibility for the disposition of our remains, yet many of us play no role in the selection of a cemetery, burial plot, casket, crematory or mortician. We know family and friends will want a memorial service, funeral or obituary, but we play no role in planning them.

Some of us are thoughtful about planning for death, though. Planning for death may be an emerging trend. (Talking about planning for death is certainly a trend.) Some Americans are buying burial plots in advance and choosing caskets. Americans commonly now prepare "living wills," "durable powers of attorney" and "advance directives" concerning medical care. We also prepare traditional wills dictating the distribution of wealth and possessions. Many of us are psychologically and emotionally better prepared for our own deaths and the deaths of family members these days, a readiness fostered by hospice workers and clergy.

Planning for death is an act of kindness, though a qualified kindness. The people who love you may prefer not to hear you speak of your death. They may prefer to believe that you believe you are not soon to die. We are deeply wedded to the practice of feigned optimism in the face of inevitable death. When you muster enough realism to make plans, loved ones may be hurt by the plans you make. They prefer burial; you, cremation. You want secular, but they want religious. You want Rabbi Gold, but they want Rabbi Silver. You want the family plot in Massachusetts, but they want your grave close by in Arizona. Taking responsibility may mean a certain amount of painful negotiation with friends and kin. It is ultimately best—more caring—to have those difficult negotiations take place while you are alive. It is less caring to leave everything to others for when you are gone. The practical need to figure out what to do to respect law, religion, your wishes, and their own needs, all in the hours and days immediately after you are gone may undercut loved ones' ability to mourn and, as some traditions do, celebrate your passing.

Admittedly, some of the plans people make for their deaths get ignored. The ill and elderly are widely encouraged to exercise living wills and advance directives to insure that they will not be kept alive "on a machine" and that they can "die with dignity," but it is unclear how often physicians and hospitals rely on living wills. The language of living wills is typically too vague to specifically guide caretakers, not to mention that, in the case of sudden illness or accident, the fact that a person has a living will may be completely unknown to hospital staff. Some doctors will ignore even a well-drafted, available living will. If your preference to die (expressed in a living will) is in conflict with the preference that you live (expressed by an attentive parent, spouse or child at your bedside), your physician will usually side with your family in order to avoid a lawsuit. Your doctor is likely to listen to your next of kin if you are in a coma or on death's door, not to a piece of paper in your chart or safe deposit box.

What does a planned death look like? We can follow the model of aviation hero Charles "Lucky" Lindbergh, who died in 1974 of lymphoma, after planning his demise in excruciating detail, but for me there are humbler examples, close to home. Affected by multiple sclerosis, my Aunt Anne's health was declining. She was only sixty-two when she was found dead on her bathroom floor, but we discovered that Anne had prepared for her death. Her personal papers were neatly arranged in readily found files. She had executed a will and paid for a cemetery plot. She had updated the beneficiaries on her insurance policies and investment accounts. More remarkably, she had written her obituary and planned her funeral. She had selected the church, the pastor, and the people to give the eulogies. She had selected the songs to be sung by the congregation and a designated soloist. She had planned so well that the family was left to squabble about trivia, like the color of the dress in which her corpse would be laid out at the wake.

Planning the fine details of death is still unusual enough to catch the eye of the media. Ms. Dale O'Reilley was the fifty-four-year-old New Jersey writer and magazine editor who carefully chose the precise date and manner of her death in June 2001. O'Reilley suffered from amyotrophic lateral sclerosis, Lou Gehrig's disease, and had become dependent upon a ventilator to help her breathe. She had lost the ability to move any part of her body other than a few facial muscles. Before the date she selected for dying she said good-bye to friends and family, planned her cremation, booked a site for her memorial service, and donated her brain to science. She executed an advance directive instructing her physician on the chosen date to sedate her and turn off her ventilator.

Under New Jersey law, doctors must heed patients' instructions to end "artificial" life support, such as O'Reilley's ventilation. *In re Quinlan* (1976) settled the matter. This case was a landmark battle over the fate of Karen Quinlan, a twenty-two-year-old who had overdosed on alcohol and tranquilizers in 1975. The New Jersey Supreme Court held that a competent person, or the guardians of an incompetent one, have a right to terminate artificial ventilation of a hopelessly ill patient. The court described the Quinlan case as a "matter of transcendent importance, involving questions related to the definition and existence of death; the prolongation of life through artificial means developed by medical technology undreamed of in past generations of the practice of the healing arts."[4] It found that Karen had a constitutional right of privacy to make an independent decision about the use of a ventilator; and that because she was incompetent to make that decision for herself, her legal guardian could do so on her behalf.

Karen Quinlan lay in bed at Saint Claire's Hospital in Denville, New Jersey, in a vegetative coma with no apparent chance of restored mental capacity. Acting on behalf of his daughter, Quinlan's father Joseph went to court so that Karen could be allowed to die. A practicing Catholic, Joseph Quinn consulted with his parish priest and the Catholic chaplain of Saint Claire's Hospital. He testified that he would not "have sought termination if that act were to be morally wrong or in conflict with the tenets of the religion he so profoundly respects."⁵ The Quinlan court ruled that at the request of a legal guardian, the use of life support to assist the breathing of a person in a vegetative coma may be terminated if both the attending physician and a Hospital Ethics Committee agree that the comatose patient has no hope of recovering "a cognitive, sapient state."⁶ Joseph Quinlan won the right to have Karen's body freed from the burden of mechanical ventilation, although when the machine was disconnected, Karen did not die. She lived on for more than eight years in her vegetative state, until June 11, 1985.

FALSE ALLURE OF SUICIDE

My dear friend Carl came to the United States from Europe as a child, speaking no English. He was slow to adjust to life in a public housing project. He was taunted for looking and sounding different from other children in the neighborhood. His family was anything but a haven. One of Carl's parents had a serious eating disorder. The other was a schizophrenic who verbally and sexually abused his children. Carl tried to commit suicide and remained under the care of a psychiatrist throughout his childhood. By the time I met Carl he was in his mid-twenties, living on his own, but struggling mightily with inner demons. He had talent enough to achieve wealth and fame, yet when he was depressed he self-medicated with too much alcohol and cocaine; and when he was not depressed, he undermined himself with undeserved shame, anxiety and suppressed rage. Carl's friends lived in fear of something terrible happening.

Carl called me one night when he was about thirty-five to say that he was sitting on the edge of the bathtub about to kill himself. I was hundreds of miles away and could do nothing but call the police in his hometown, who arrived in time to rescue him. Then I lost track of Carl for about twenty years. He finally got back in touch after being released from a long hospitalization following another suicide attempt. Carl had flung himself through a window.

Suicide is rarely part of a sound plan for the end of life. My call for taking a greater responsibility for death should not be read as an implicit endorsement of suicide. I do not advocate it, and if, like me, you have ever had to rescue someone from slitting their wrists in a bathtub, pull someone out of an open window, or take a butcher's knife away from someone's throat, you understand why. The desire to commit suicide is commonly linked to situational setbacks or mental illness, and these are not circumstances in which people should end their lives. Thoughts of suicide can stem from the feeling that one is helpless to solve financial and emotional problems, or from the depressive phase of bipolar illness. For sufferers in these categories, relief can come in the form of therapy, medication or the passage of time. Carl was not properly medicated for his mental illness until he was nearly fifty-five.

Accident victims facing painful medical treatments, arduous rehabilitation, disability and disfigurement sometimes express the death wish. Bioethicists debate the now famous case of Dax Cowart, a man who was severely burned and blinded in a gas explosion in the 1970s. While in the hospital, Mr. Cowart expressed a desire to be allowed to go home and die. He presented his case in a logical and rational manner. *Please Let Me Die,* a widely circulated film made of an interview between Mr. Cowart and a Texas psychiatrist, shows Cowart at an emotional low point; yet from his torched, decimated body comes a strong voice clearly articulating reasons for wanting to discontinue medical treatment and being allowed to die. A formerly handsome, independent and active individual who enjoyed flying and horses, Cowart could not look forward to life as, in his words, "a cripple." Moreover, the chemical bath treatments for the burns that covered most of his body were excruciatingly painful. Cowart believed he would suffer additional pain learning to walk again and from the multiple surgeries that would be required to restore the use of his hands. Psychiatrists who evaluated Cowart determined him to be mentally competent, but Dax was kept alive against his will. His mother, his lawyer, his brother and his doctors wanted him alive. There was also one medical reason to overlook his death wish. Wishing to die, the medical experts said, is a typical phase in the progress of recovery from massive burn injuries. The pain medications Cowart received assured that he was not likely to remember the ordeal of the chemical baths or suffer unduly from physical pain.

I first heard of Dax Cowart and saw him on film when I was a teaching assistant in a medical humanities course at Michigan. My job required that I watch *Please Let Me Die,* over and over again and discuss it with group after group of medical students. No matter how many times I saw the film, I never got used to its graphic agonies. At that time, Dax Cowart convinced me that the desire to end one's life could be rational and right. But a few years later, Dax convinced me that there is more to consider when deciding the ethics of whether to heed a request to die than whether the person making the request can articulate a rational argument.

Dax Cowart far exceeded his own expectations of recovery, and made a longer, follow-up video about his case. In this film he is not in a hospital bed or chemical bath, helpless and wounded. He is a prosperous professional, standing tall, narrating the events of his misfortune. He is blind, but he can walk and use his hands. Cowart recovered nicely. Cowart got married (and divorced), went to law school, and became an attorney. He also became a "right to die" advocate, and continues to believe he ought to have been allowed to die. I watched *Please Let Me Die* again a couple of years ago when I was teaching bioethics at Yale Law School. Viewing the tape this time, I was less struck by Cowart's impressive rationality than by the overall context of pain and loss that would lead any clearly sane and reasonable person to feel miserable and trapped.

Despite congenital cerebral palsy and quadriplegia, Elizabeth Bouvia went to college and married. When her husband left her, she wound up in a public hospital. She did not want to eat; she wanted to die. She filed suit in a California court to win the right to refuse nasogastric force-feeding. Ironically, after an exhaustive, successful court battle, Bouvia decided that she no longer wanted to die. She and Dax Cowart are symbols of "rational" seekers of death who eventually decide to continue life. Some bioethicsts who have studied Bouvia's case say her desire to die seemed to have had as much to do with the lack of intimate companionship as with the inherent difficulties of living without the use of arms or legs. In the initial stages of recovery, Dax had a combative relationship with his mother and lacked an intimate partner to help him through the survivors' guilt of losing his father in the same automobile explosion that maimed him.

KIND UNTIL THE END

If I am correct in my lay judgment that most suicides are products of intense situational helplessness or chronic mental illness, it makes little sense to reason about the ethics of suicide with anyone likely to do it. They need to be given some help—therapy, medication, love. Blaming these victims is unfair. It is worth noting, though, that suicide imposes a terrible burden on the individuals who are left behind. Killing oneself in an unselfish manner is not as easy as some people might think. Forcing people to watch you starve yourself to death is cruel. Floors, walls, and furniture splattered with a gunshot victim's blood are more than a mess. Sane, kind people who want to end their lives do not want to fling themselves through windows in the presence of their families or leave their corpse hanging from a rope in the family home. These are simply not ethical options. The grotesque and bloody consequences for others can make suffering on seem like the ethically better course.

Americans are fond of saying they want to die with dignity, but what does dignity require? The form of dignity many terminally ill patients want is not yet available on a reliable basis in the United States. They want to be free of technologies that prolong life while having access to technologies that end life. Many terminally ill patients believe that a death whose place, time and manner they and their physicians choose is dignified and self-determining. They believe that the unplanned, impersonal hospital death that involves high-tech life support and drugs is not dignified and self-determining.

The vast majority of American jurisdictions do not permit physicians to heed competent patients' requests for delivery of a lethal drug to end life. Dr. Jack Kevorkian, "Dr. Death," has been unsuccessful in escaping criminal prosecution for building "suicide machines" and administering lethal injections. Now in his seventies, Kevorkian is serving ten to twenty-five years in a Michigan correctional facility for the second-degree murder of Thomas

Youk, a man he directly injected with a lethal drug. An actual videotape of the killing was aired on national television at Kevorkian's instigation.

Oregon is the only state to have passed a law permitting assisted death. The right to die advocacy group Compassion in Dying has been a major force behind the law that Oregon voters approved in 1994 and 1997 ballot initiatives. However, the fate of the Oregon law is uncertain. U.S. Attorney General John Ashcroft cautioned Oregon physicians that they would face prosecution by the Federal Drug Enforcement Agency under the Controlled Substances Act if they proceeded to prescribe lethal doses of controlled drugs for dying patients. While traditional medical uses of controlled substances do not violate the law, the Justice Department has argued that assisted suicide is not a bona fide medical procedure.

A ruling by the Supreme Court that federal drug laws can rule out physician-assisted suicide would be another major loss for the Compassion in Dying movement in that all-important forum. In 1997, in a pair of "assisted suicide" cases, the U.S. Supreme Court decided that the Constitution allows states to prohibit physicians from helping terminally ill, competent adults hasten their deaths to relieve suffering. In *Vacco v. Quill* (1997), the Court upheld statutes enacted by New York lawmakers outlawing assisting suicides.[7] Plaintiffs argued that it violated equal protection of law for the state to permit refusing and withdrawing life support, but to ban assisting suicide. Both are ways people without hope can bring an end to their lives. Why should a competent person with end-stage pancreatic cancer or AIDS linger on, but someone like Nancy Cruzan, an automobile accident victim in a vegetative coma, be allowed to die? In *Cruzan v. Director, Missouri Department of Health* (1990), the Court held that patients in a vegetative coma have a strong liberty interest in being allowed to refuse life support if there is clear and convincing evidence that refusal would be their wish.[8] The Court reasoned that it is one thing when a patient terminates life-sustaining medical treatment and "dies from an underlying fatal disease or pathology" and it is something else when "a patient ingests a lethal medication prescribed by a physician" and is killed by that medication. Cruzan's father (her legal guardian) eventually won the right to order that her feeding tubes be removed, when acquaintances came forward with stories of conversations with Nancy in which she had said she would not wish to live comatose and dependent on life support.

The Cruzan case precedent casts a shadow of unconstitutionality over the law passed by the Florida legislature in the fall of 2003 to prevent the death of Terri Schiavo, a woman in a persistent vegetative state. Schiavo's husband insisted his wife had a right to die because she expressed a desire never to live in a vegetative state, kept alive through artificial means. Supported by Florida's governor, legislature and right-to-life groups, Schiavo's parents believed their daughter continued to have the capacity to respond to their affection and wanted her fed.

A group of philosophers affiliated with NYU, Harvard and MIT—Ronald Dworkin, Thomas Nagel, Robert Nozick, John Rawls, Thomas Scanlon, and Judith Jarvis Thomson—submitted a brief to the Supreme Court critical of state laws striking down physician-assisted suicide. This unusual, so-called Philosophers' Brief filed in connection with the 1997 assisted-suicide cases was deeply critical of the distinction between allowing someone to refuse life-sustaining treatment, causing someone to die, and hastening death by lethal injection. On the other hand, most Western moral traditions—secular and religious—oppose suicide. The Enlightenment philosopher Immanuel Kant described suicide as self-murder, an ethical wrong for rationally autonomous persons. For one "to dispose of one's life for some fancied end, is to degrade the humanity subsisting in his person and intrusted to him to the end that he might uphold and preserve it."[9] Bioethicist Dr. Sherwin Nuland, whose book *How We Die: Reflections on Life's Final Hour* (1995) was a best seller, has argued against the major premise of the right-to-die movement that dying with dignity has to do with escaping unavoidable pain. Dying with dignity, he suggests, may have more to do with living as well as one can.

State lawmakers in New York have voiced the fear that if doctors were allowed to engage openly in voluntary active euthanasia for the terminally ill, society would begin a descent down a slippery slope toward compulsory euthanasia of the poor and unwanted. Moreover, healthy people suffering from temporary setbacks or depression could come to see suicide as an acceptable option. Much the same worries led Washington lawmakers to ban assisted suicide. In *Washington v. Glucksberg* (1997) the Court held that "substantive due-process" liberties of private choice do not prevent states from banning assisted suicide.[10] Assisting suicide has been banned for 700 years in the common law. It is a feature of our nation's history and traditions.

Supporters of assisted death frequently point out that the Netherlands has permitted physician-assisted suicide for many years without a deterioration in respect for life. Through some European eyes, however, the mere fact that people are dying at the hands of physicians is evidence of a "culture of death," a term of condemnation used by German Catholic leader Cardinal Karl Lehmann. Nonetheless, the concern that some 3,500 Dutch men and women a year are euthanized upon request is qualitatively different from the genocide-motivated Nazi Holocaust that Cardinal Lehmann compares it to. Aware that the eyes of the world are upon it, the Netherlands has moved to exact stronger laws regulating assisted death. One law that went into effect in April 2001 embodied guidelines developed by the Royal Dutch Medical Association, limiting suicide to consenting adults with conditions of unbearable and unrelievable suffering. Two physicians must certify that a candidate for assisted suicide meets the medical criteria. Typically, death takes place at the patient's home, where a physician administers a powerful sedative, followed by a second drug to stop breathing. In December 2001, Dr. Phillip Sutorius was convicted for violating the law in 1998 when he administered a lethal injection to a former senator, Edward Brongersma, who had complained only of being dizzy, immobile and tired of life.

When I hear that someone has committed suicide, I always feel as though a jewel has been thrown away into the ocean, a tiny jewel or a large one, but a jewel all the same. I felt that way when I learned in the fall of 2003 that Carolyn Heilbrun, the feminist, novelist and scholar, had ended her life. She was getting on in years and had always planned to die by her own hand. Family, friends and admirers were saddened by the loss of a great woman whose philosophy of dying had been no secret.

It seems you ought to have a very good reason to impose your death on others, and to rob yourself of life and the potential for recovery. Generally speaking, you owe yourself and others a better reason than "I am tired of living." But suppose the diagnosis is pancreatic cancer, and you are given six months to live. Death within six months is a certainty. You do not like the thought of friends and family hovering over your bed as you start to waste away. You are averse to the side effects of palliative chemotherapy and the prospect of pain. You have enough sleeping pills to end your life before you have to tell your friends and family about your illness. Should you die now, by your own hand? Now might be an ethically acceptable time in this case, but only if you have done your best to make humane practical arrangements for your death and said proper good-byes to all the people who love you and will be closely affected by your end. And only if you have listened in earnest to others' reasons for why you should remain among the living, with them, in their protective care, a bit longer.

PART IV

JUST LIVING TOGETHER

CHAPTER 11

BEYOND YOUR OWN KIND

The dividing line between Philadelphia's Mainline suburbs and the city of Philadelphia is clearly marked. Drive east on Lancaster Avenue, past single-family homes, a seminary, a hospital, with trees everywhere. A block after you reach the sign that says WELCOME TO PHILADELPHIA, the trees disappear, giving way to warehouses, abandoned fast-food restaurants, storefront churches, row houses and litter—lots and lots of litter. I have always been struck by how suddenly the trees disappear, as if giving up hope.

For two years I drove my daughter, Ophelia, into Philadelphia on Saturday mornings for ballet lessons. Our usual route took us east along Lancaster Avenue. Once, when Ophelia was about five, we had just crossed the city line when she said, "This place should not be called Philadelphia." I asked her what it should be called instead. I fully expected her to say "Filthydelphia," an unfortunate nickname favored by children, but her actual response caught me off guard. "It should be called Brown Town, because all the people are brown." I had been struck by how suddenly the trees ended. She was struck by how suddenly the white people ended.

Ethics demand that we expand concern from an inner circle of self, family and friends to a broader circle of classmates, coworkers and clients, and then on to an even broader circle that includes strangers, community and nation. It is to that third realm of concern that I turn, mindful that some readers of this chapter and the next will conclude that I have extended morality's mission too far. Yet, in my judgment, if we are to live in harmony as equal citizens in a democratic society, we need one another's trust—despite differences—and participation in civic involvements that redound to the common good. We cannot live insulated and complacent and yet also live fairly and responsively. There are many preconditions of mutual trust and many civic involvements I might emphasize, but the two that I have chosen, ethnoracial integration and voting, reflect my identity as a citizen whose parents grew up under compulsion of law in the racially segregated communities of the Old South, without meaningful political voices. I worry that we still share a nation we do not fully coinhabit.

NEO-SEGREGATION

Philadelphia is not exclusively brown, and its western suburbs are not exclusively white. After all, my brown children and I live in the suburbs. Yet Americans do live apart in brown towns and white towns. Decades after Congress enacted civil rights legislation and the Supreme Court struck down the laws that separated the races, American segregation is more complex than the pervasive black/white racial divide. We are segregated by income as well as by race, color, ethnicity, religion, language, sexual orientation and national origin. We have Hasidic neighborhoods and Hmong neighborhoods. There are Native American "reservations" and Amish farming communities. We have Puerto Rican blocks in New York City and Irish blocks in Boston. In large cities there are gay neighborhoods and straight ones.

In the middle of the last century "restricted" was the polite term for schools, clubs, neighborhoods and firms reserved mainly for whites and non-Jews. "Segregated" was the polite term most often used for the divided way of life that separated blacks from the immediate society of whites. Segregation was mandated by overtly racist Jim Crow laws in the South and enforced by traditional norms in the North. School systems were segregated by race, along with municipal swimming pools, retail businesses, restrooms, water fountains and residential neighborhoods.

Until World War II, the United States military segregated service members into all-black units and all-white units, but the war ended most segregation in the army. For African Americans who grew up in the South in the 1940s, the army was a refuge from segregation. That, according to my father, is the main reason he joined up, at age seventeen, and stayed in the army for twenty-five years. Yet, even in the 1960s, the integrated army routinely transported the children of its African American service members to segregated black schools. As a consequence, when my father was stationed at Fort McClellan, Alabama, I was bussed to a Jim Crow kindergarten in nearby Anniston. When he was later stationed at Fort Benning, Georgia, I attended the integrated base middle school, while my older sister was bussed against her parents' will to a civilian Jim Crow high school for blacks in nearby Columbus.

Official segregation is over, and the term "segregation" has gone out of daily use, but it is still applicable. We used to be a society in which people tended to stick to their own kind, and we still are. Segregation stubbornly persists despite major public policy initiatives aimed at desegregation. Workplaces and public accommodations (hotels, restaurants, movie theaters, trains and the like) are often racially integrated; however, many industries and business sectors are still dominated by whites or another specific group, and in some areas of the country residential and school segregation is as extensive as it was prior to the Civil Rights Act of 1964.

Segregation is a popular preference. It is also a morally dubious one. According to a 1997 Gallup poll survey of white Americans with school-age children, 41 percent would object to sending their children to a school in which more than half the children were black.[1] Overall, blacks of all social classes (poor, middle-class and affluent) tend to live in segregated, virtually all-black communities. Housing segregation by race is not wholly voluntary. Economic factors, fear of racially motivated violence and the desire for acceptance and community constrain choice and mobility. Religious institutions and certain businesses (for example, hair salons and funeral parlors) are often segregated by race, too. By choice, I take my son to skilled black barbers in brown town, and my daughter and I visit a black stylist in brown town for our hair.

In the United States, segregation is neither officially sanctioned nor the strict cultural rule. We are permitted to form intimate bonds with people of other backgrounds, and we do it all the time. No one would be all that surprised to learn that a white businesswoman with roots in rural south Georgia had befriended a fellow black businesswoman from the posh Buckhead section of Atlanta. Today, friendships and marriages between people of different ethnoracial and regional backgrounds are common. Intermarriage has been lawful for so long that young people can scarcely believe that state laws used to prohibit marriages between white people and Africans, Asians and Native Americans. The year I went to high school was the same year the Supreme Court in *Loving v. Virginia* struck down laws banning interracial marriages.[2]

The rate of intermarriage is up since then. However, intermarriage is not equally popular with all groups and remains somewhat morally controversial. Until very recently students at Bob Jones University were only permitted to date members of their own race, presumably to discourage "immoral" interracial intimacy and marriage. Census data show that about 98 percent of married black women are married to black men, down only slightly from about 99 percent in 1960. Some African Americans view marriage between blacks and whites as disloyal, harmful to families and self-hating, but still there has been an increase in the number of blacks who marry whites.

My husband, Paul, and I have strikingly different backgrounds. He grew up in the Northeast; I grew up in the Pacific Northwest, Pacific and the South. He is Italian American, I am African American. He was raised a Catholic and attended parochial schools. I was raised a Protestant and attended military and public schools. At dessert time, he looks for cannoli, while I head for the sweet potato pie. Our two mixed-race children are not alone in their schools. On the contrary, children of blended parentage are common in suburban classrooms. Seven-year-old Reeta in our township is an apt example. Reeta's mother, Nancy, is Mexican American and her father, Mahesh, is originally from Nepal. Nancy and Mahesh met in a dormitory at Stanford University, and they are both physicians.

Notwithstanding families like Reeta's and my own, ethnoracial seg-regation is still the rule in the United States. Many Americans seem to believe that interracial or interethnic intimacy should be legal and rare. My children live in a multicultural household, but they inhabit an overwhelm-ingly affluent white, Jewish and Christian world, until recently wary of the poorer, grittier "brown towns" they traverse. We are a multicultural soci-ety, but our many subcultures mingle superficially, uneasily and for lim-ited, largely utilitarian, purposes.

IMMIGRATION TO SEGREGATION

Chevy Chase, Maryland, is an old community, made up of a cluster of residential villages, each with its own name. For many years I worked in Washington, D.C., and lived in Chevy Chase. We were drawn to our vil-lage by its narrow tree-lined streets, its older homes and its proximity to the biking trails of Rock Creek Park. Soon after moving into the Village of Martin's Addition, I began looking for someone to help me care for my son. I wanted to return to work full-time, even though I was ambivalent about turning over the baby to a stranger. Although I was offering an above-average wage, the job required intimate association with me and my nonstandard family: African American mom, Italian dad, mixed-race son. I wondered who would feel comfortable in my home.

Carol said she would. Carol was young, pretty, white and experi-enced in child care. She had spent some time in college. She seemed promising—until she asked for an advance on her salary so that she could rent an apartment, and then suddenly left town. She never worked a day. A more mature West Indian almost got the job, but at the last minute she could not produce the required green card. As lawyers, my husband and I felt a special obligation to avoid the Zoë Baird problem of hiring an undoc-umented worker and not paying the required nanny taxes. Through an employment agency I eventually hired a woman about my age who was a native of the Philippines. Her name was Normita. As a child care provider, "Normi" was a dream come true. She was energetic, loving, social and reliable. Adam thrived under her care, as did Ophelia. Normi was with us as a "live-out" nanny for more than six years.

Normi's was a remarkable story. You had to admire her. When the youngest of her three sons was an infant she left her children in the hands of her husband and came to the United States alone, seeking a better economic future for them all. She had been an office worker in the Philippines, but to escape the dire economy of her homeland, she was willing to take advantage of the insatiable U.S. demand for Philippine babysitters. After working as a live-in nanny for an American family for five years, she had earned the right to apply for the status of a permanent resident. Green card in hand, she was able to bring her immediate family to the United States. When I met her, her husband and three sons had only recently arrived. Five years later, she and her husband would become naturalized U.S. citizens.

When Normi had worked for us for about a year, I decided to invite her family over for a sit-down dinner. They accepted the invitation. There were some awkward moments. My guests spoke simple, halting English. There were lulls in the conversation. The meal I prepared was not much to the liking of Normi's polite children, since I had not anticipated how alien the food I served would seem to them. Still, it was a warm occasion. Afterward, Normi thanked me and revealed that she had been very nervous about coming to dinner, even though she was accustomed to spending hours a day at my house with the members of my family. She had lived in the United States for a half dozen years at that point, but mine was the first social invitation to an American home she had received. Although she lived in a thriving ethnically diverse suburb of the nation's capital, her social universe outside of work was 100 percent immigrant Filipino.

STICKING TO YOUR OWN KIND

There are positive dimensions of sticking to your own kind, and they warrant emphasis. Sticking with your own kind signifies an alliance, an acceptance of a common history, identity and mutual dependability. It signifies approval of the group. If a man of Korean ancestry marries a woman of Korean ancestry, the union says to the world, I believe women in my group are attractive partners. If a Korean American does business with a Korean American grocer or jeweler or lawyer, she says to the world, I believe my group is intelligent, honest and industrious. "I like and trust my own kind" is a powerful message of self-respect and solidarity.

Marrying within your own group signals the intent to perpetuate *your* people through childbearing and child rearing. Sticking to your own kind can further the goal of family unity, too. Families more readily accept intimate partners who fit in. Same-kind partners often appear to fit in more readily than outside selections. The presumption that a same-kind partner will fit in may facilitate the blending of extended families following a marriage or the commencement of a long-term relationship. In a society in which government presupposes the existence of family networks to provide child care, sick care, and elder care, family members can need one another badly. Intergroup intimacy risks introducing the political and social divisions present elsewhere in the society into the home and family. A less cohesive family will do a poorer job of responding to the demands of illness and misfortune.

Intimacy with people of other religious and cultural groups can also lead to a watering down of ritual and to more self-conscious modes of self-expression. I believe concerns about family harmony, ritual and self-expression explain why Americans of all backgrounds and persuasions actively and routinely struggle with questions about the morality of out-marriage, interracial dating, transracial adoption, and other forms of integrated lifestyles. People worry about losing themselves, too. A Puerto Rican college student came to me in tears after she attended a sample law school class in which she heard fluent legalese spoken by expert practitioners for the first time. "If I become a lawyer, how can I go back home to my family talking like that?" she cried. The loss of self through association with an alien culture can be terrifying.

My interracial marriage has not been without costs. My father went all-out to help celebrate my brief first marriage to an African American, but he did not attend my second wedding to an Italian. He said he was too busy at work to take the day off. My mother half-seriously referred to my biracial son as a "half-breed," and my mother-in-law expressed concerns that an adopted mixed-race child might be "too dark." My husband is unable to understand what my older relatives say when they speak to one another in their Southern black dialect, much as I had trouble understanding some of the Italian I heard spoken in his home when we first met in the 1970s. My family plays bid whist, dances and sings when it gets together; his family kisses and then eats and eats and eats.

ISLAND NATION

So, sticking to your own kind has a point. There is much blameless comfort in choosing to stick to your own kind: the easy conversation; the inside jokes; the familiar rituals, the sense of positive contribution to a group of people with whom you closely identify. However, it is a special challenge, a moral challenge, to live virtuously under American-style segregation today. Anyone who wants to be fair-minded and to respect others as equals will have a hard time with it. Sticking to your own kind and expecting others to do the same can have poor motives and consequences.

A positive effect of Jim Crow segregation was the evolution of vital ethnic neighborhoods and unique cultural forms. Yet, segregation slows the dissolution of old animosities between the races. As a child, I thought prejudice and stereotyping were products of limited intelligence. Get an education and free the mind from the chains of bigotry! I thought bigots were just stupid big mouths who had managed to grab a little power. But I learned the hard way that otherwise very intelligent people can foster barely credible forms of prejudice. Segregation sustains prejudice and stereotyping.

To earn money when I was a law student I worked as a teaching assistant in moral reasoning courses at Harvard College. All Harvard freshmen were required to take these courses, so there was plenty of work for instructors. One day in my class we were debating the justice of affirmative action policies. With utter confidence in the truth of her claim, one of my students stated that there were no intelligent black people in her home state of Oklahoma. None. She came to this conclusion because the *one* black woman she thought she knew well and admired had proven to be an ineffective leader on a local school board.

Comfortable, segregated lifestyles foster pernicious stereotyping. Fair-minded people must work extra hard to discourage and avoid generalizations about character and ability based on a person's demographic profile. Those who live segregated lives must take care not to disparage and exclude others who should be respected and included. There is an obvious relationship between stereotyping and wrongful discrimination in education, employment and business opportunities. Moreover, as empirical research by Stanford psychologist Claude M. Steele suggests, awareness of negative stereotypes about one's group actually impairs one's ability to perform.[3] Old people stereotyped as having poor memories, remember less. Like white men stereotyped as less gifted than Asian men, and like white women stereotyped as less gifted than white men, black test takers stereotyped as less intelligent than whites score less well than they otherwise would on tests they believe measure their intellectual abilities. Steele speculates that when faced with difficult tasks, people typically want to perform well. Just about everyone is made anxious by fear of corroborating the negative performance stereotypes of which they are mindful. Anxiety works to undermine the ability to meet challenges, and awareness of negative stereotypes about one's group creates additional anxieties that make performing difficult intellectual tasks more difficult.

In segregated societies you have to work extra hard to acquire basic knowledge of the interests, values and practices of other groups. Without such knowledge, one is bound to be less effective in leadership roles that entail responsibilities for a diverse population. But multicultural competence is not just for teachers, work supervisors and politicians. Effective democratic self-government presupposes an ability of all citizens to understand competing points of view—a competence that segregation clearly impairs. Segregation even impairs knowledge of biological similarities. My parents told me stories of German civilians who welcomed black and white American soldiers with joy after the defeat of the Nazis, but were surprised to learn that blacks did not really have tails. And, unable to comprehend why blacks and whites were not permitted to mingle in the South, my older sister concluded as a child that it must be because whites did not have to urinate or defecate.

Finally, in the United States some groups have been in historical possession of more social, economic and political power than others. Some of the envy, enmity and distrust between various ethnoracial groups relates to material disparities and competition for economic resources. Sticking to your own privileged group can be a way of unfairly monopolizing advantages to which other groups have a claim. Sadly, members of excluded, disadvantaged groups may feel that they have to turn their backs on their own group's culture, customs and practices, the price of assimilation into dominant groups. Ironically, segregation simultaneously pushes members of subordinate groups toward and away from one another, necessitating and penalizing group-based loyalty.

WORKING FOR AN ITALIAN

Her name was Josephine Marguerita Maria Potenza. Her mother Ofelia's Tuscan ancestors were from the Isle of Elba. Her father's family came from a small town near Naples. During World War II Josephine worked as a secretary for the owner of the Lup-o-matic Machine Company in Bronx, New York. The company was owned by a Mr. Lupo, a fellow Italian American anxious for the success of his wartime industry. The tumblers of Mr. Lupo's "Lup-o-matic" machines converted rough pieces of plastic into smooth ones for use in the construction of airplanes. Josephine earned $18 a week, decent pay in those days, though by no means top dollar, to work full-time answering the main company telephone. She also took dictation at the lightning speed of 116 words per minute from a man so hyperactive that his personal physician came by the office to administer tranquilizers.

There was one curious requirement of Josephine's job at Lup-o-matic. She was not allowed to use her real name. Mr. Lupo wanted his company to make a good impression on the outside world. He decided that since "Potenza" means "power" in Italian, Josephine Potenza would become Jo Powers, the all-American working girl whose forebearers might have come over on the *Mayflower*. When the phone rang, Josephine answered, "Miss Powers speaking," in melodic tones calculated to insure that no one would be put off from doing business with the Lup-o-matic company by their negative stereotypes of ethnic Italians.

One day Genung's Department Store in Manhattan offered Josephine $25 a week to work as secretary to an Irish American advertising executive. She accepted. Lupo tried to lure her back. Josephine did not return, but briefly considered going back on the condition that she be allowed to use her own name.

My mother-in-law was Mr. Lupo's sunny "Jo Powers." Hers is a quintessentially American story about a familiar American moral dilemma: To stick to one's own kind or not. If you identify as an Italian, it can mean something special to have a fellow Italian as a boss and to contribute to his business success. Likewise it can mean something special to have an Italian stenographer and to contribute to her welfare. Yet sticking with your own ethnic kind has costs; it can be self-limiting, impractical and financially unsound. If Mr. Lupo had stuck to his own kind, he believed he would have had no chance for success in his chosen line of business. To secure customers, he thought he had to reach out to other groups. Eager for success at a time when many Americans snubbed the Irish and the Italians, Lupo hired his own but burdened the most visible with a false WASP identity. Ironically, getting a job "down in the city" with a company that was not run by Italians was a way for Josephine to fully reclaim her Italian identity. To earn a higher wage and recover her pride, she was willing to break ranks with the Italian community and add thirty minutes to her commute. If Josephine had stuck to her own kind, she would have squandered talent in a high-stress, low-paying job that required her to pass as something she was not.

Weighing costs and benefits is part of what is involved in resolving dilemmas of personal association. But there is more to it than making prudent calculations. Josephine reckoned that low self-esteem and small paychecks were too high a price for same-kind association and loyalty. Since she took care of her mother, she needed all the honest money she could earn. Lupo reckoned that the cost of asking Italian employees to settle for less pay and don WASP masks was worth the benefit of a more robust business. I think Josephine made a good decision and do not blame her for approaching it pragmatically.

Just as there are more and less practical ways to handle sticky dilemmas, there are more and less ethical ways to do so, too. We can do wrong by failing to heed the demands of concern for our own cultural or ethnoracial group. This was Mr. Lupo's error. It was unfair of him to ask Josephine to change her name while retaining a recognizably Italian name himself. That he could do business as an Italian suggests that his concern about the damage an Italian secretary would do his firm was greatly exaggerated. Genung's readily hired Josephine and had no problem with the name "Potenza." Lupo had little to lose by a higher degree of ethnic loyalty and understanding. Sometimes people impose false identities to save lives; you can understand why a Jew in Nazi Germany, even a person of great character, would pass his children off as Christian. But it is harder to excuse forcing an employee to pass as a WASP when the stakes are low, as they were for Mr. Lupo.

Lupo did wrong while trying to protect himself from wrongful discrimination. Immoral prejudice against Italians led to immoral prejudice by an Italian. It is wrong for majority or powerful groups to exclude. This kind of conduct can be defended as loyalty, community, or identity, but behind the invocation of those ideals can lurk something morally sinister: exclusion, segregation and cultural parochialism.

YOU STICK, THEREFORE I STICK

Josephine Marguerita Maria Potenza married Adam Castellitto, an Italian American war veteran whose ancestors also hailed from Tuscany. Adam was among the air corps members who prepared the *Enola Gay* for its controversial war-ending atomic mission over Japan. Adam died several years ago, but a collage of photographs and newspaper clippings documenting his extraordinary duties hangs on the wall of my mother-in-law's foyer. Josephine and Adam raised two sons—Richard and my husband, Paul—in Westchester County, New York, and sent them to Catholic schools. They are good people.

My husband once remarked that he did not know a single person growing up who was not an Irish or Italian Catholic. When pressed on this point, he could recall only four exceptions: his pediatrician, a comic book salesman, an aunt by marriage, and the friend of an uncle. His strikingly insular experience took place decades ago; but as Normi's immigrant family's experience illustrates, growing up with ethnic, racial and class segregation is still a possibility for Americans.

Insularity is not, however, limited to the children of immigrants. Most of my law students over the years have come from middle-class or affluent nonimmigrant families (former assistant U.S. Attorney General Viet Dinh was a noteworthy exception). They have been top graduates of elite colleges and universities. They have traveled to other countries and speak foreign languages. Yet several times I have invited classes to my home only to have one student remark that he or she has never before been inside the home of an African American. A faculty-student gathering entailed novelty of a different sort for one young man. For a time I lived in a two-bedroom condominium on Connecticut Avenue in Washington, D.C., a beautiful apartment in an elegant prewar building that I was proud to call home. I invited my students for a party, and "Joel" was among those who came. Joel, who had grown up in Florida and graduated with honors from the University of Miami, expressed amazement that an apartment could be a successful professional's primary and exclusive home.

ODD, POROUS BOUNDARIES

Our neighborhoods are segregated. Our public schools are segregated. Our religious institutions are segregated. Our fraternities and sororities are segregated. Our hair salons are segregated. When you think about it, we do very little together.[4] A few of us play and sleep together, but mostly we work and shop together, returning in the evenings to segregated realms. There are walls between us, but the walls are permeable. There is movement between and among us, but genuine intergroup intimacy is remarkably ambivalent and bounded.

William Shakespeare depicted the complex nature of these artificial divides. *Romeo and Juliet* is a tragedy of boundary crossing. *The Merchant of Venice* is as well. In *The Merchant of Venice,* a businessman named Antonio needs ready cash to help a friend. He hates Jews, but in a pinch he is willing to borrow money from the Jewish moneylender Shylock. And while Shylock hates Christians, he is willing to do business with Antonio, although he refuses a dinner invitation. "I will not smell pork," he declares.

Like the characters in Shakespeare's play, we live among others but scarcely with them. Living apart provides us room to disparage others. Not so long ago, in Italian families in the Northeast, going to a Chinese restaurant might be termed "going to Chinks"; large American cars were called "Jew-mobiles" and African Americans termed "eggplants." In African American families in the South, whites were labeled "crackers" and "trash." As a verb, "Jew" was sometimes used as a synonym for "cheat." Living apart creates both incentives and pressures to disparage. It is easy to gloss over the fact that a tune by a popular rap artist describes squinted eyes as "chinky" if none of your friends are Chinese. One of the ways people evidence group membership and group loyalty is to walk the walk and talk the talk. It takes a great deal of moral character to refrain from casual racism and ethnic slurs when others do it freely; and real courage to call others on it.

A lot of people are understandably reluctant to take on the risks of intimacy outside their own groups for fear of being perceived as traitors. Another reason is a lack of trust in the Other. They are afraid of cruel and thoughtless barbs. They are not sure intimacy with people of other groups can ultimately nourish and sustain their particular ethnoracial identities. They lack basic trust in people of other backgrounds. A Jewish acquaintance told me she could never marry a non-Jew because she feared that a moment of anger could awaken a sleeping serpent of anti-Semitism in her spouse. A black woman I know said she would be insulted if a white man asked her out on a date: he should know better. An Asian ancestry medical student at Yale told me of a hospital patient who explicitly refused to be cared for by her because he could not trust a physician of her race. A sophisticated African American lawyer admits that he cannot bear the thought of having his corpse handled by a white mortician. As we look across racial and ethnic divides, we Americans are not enemies, but we are not exactly friends. Ambivalence and distrust in relationships with people of other ethnoracial groups is the unfortunate fact of the matter. It is not as bad as it once was, but it is not over.

Indeed, some seeming evidence of improvement dissolves on closer inspection. It is misleading to assume that the men and women one observes going about in mixed relationships are without ethnoracial ambivalence. It is possible to regret some of the implications of whom you love. In this respect, we do not get the whole story about the state of race relations from looking at census data reporting the rising number of people in interracial marriages or the number of people identified as mixed race. The seemingly happy interracial couple may be afraid to have children. Pam, a self-aware European American lamented that were she to have a child by her African American husband, she would feel that the child belonged to black society more than to hers.

At a recent reunion of my father's side of the family in Atlanta, four of the children present had one black biological parent and one white biological parent. Taken in isolation this fact could have been interpreted as evidence of successfully congenial race relations south of the Mason-Dixon Line. At last! Yet, in every single case, the mixed-race child's white parent had felt ill-suited to rear her son or daughter and had given the child away to be reared by its black parent or a black adoptive mother. Both the white mothers and the white fathers had made this choice.

UN-NEIGHBORLY NEIGHBORS

A few years ago in a Connecticut courtroom, Wilfred and Michelle Chaisson pled no contest to charges that they had harassed a mixed-race family next door, with whom they shared a driveway.[5] Disputes over the use of the driveway escalated into racial slurs, threats and intimidation. A superior court judge placed the Chaissons, who had erected a confederate flag in front of their New England home, on probation and ordered them to undergo cultural diversity training.

If you are wondering whether you ought to make an effort to include people of other backgrounds into your circle of friends, your condominium association, your church, your children's school, or your workplace, stop wondering and just do it.

――――――――――――

Last year an affluent white businessman who lives in my neighborhood and who has three young children of his own noticed my son and another twelve-year-old getting off the school bus. He nearly ran the children off the road with his car and then verbally assaulted my son, threatening to "fuck" him up if he ever "fucked" with him. "And you too!" he said to my son's female companion. The alarmed children immediately called home on their cell phones and their fathers called the police.

This was not the first time my neighbor had done something like this; the trouble began five years ago after our seven-year-old boys, best friends at the time, were involved in a street hockey accident for which the neighbor faulted my son. His son had not been wearing a face guard. In my neighbor's mind, my son was an aggressive bully who deliberately knocked out his son's front teeth with a hockey stick. No other version of the facts would do. "There are no such things as accidents," he told me, condemning us all as an unfeeling family unwelcome in his community.

The police arrived swiftly, but they were not anxious to charge the man with a crime. Although something other than racial prejudice could have explained the attack on the children, the initial reluctance of the police to act transported me back in time to the Old South, when whites could get away with trying to keep African Americans in their place with threats of violence. I believed that if an African American man had done to white children what the white man had done to my mixed-race son and his half-Jewish female friend, there would have been no hesitation about pressing charges. Eventually the ugly character of the attack sunk in with the police: an adult had assaulted two children getting off a school bus with an automobile, and threatened to physically injure them. The police charged the man with disorderly conduct. The sensation of being transported back in the Old South resurfaced in the courtroom a few months ago when a character witness called by the defense cheerfully described my son's attacker as a "loving father" and "devoted friend." The attacker's lawyer defended his client by characterizing him as an angry father "acting, as any father would, out of concern for the safety of his children." The judge did not buy the outlandish defense and fined the unneighborly neighbor $300. But in the end the man achieved his aim: terror. The only black mother in an upscale white neighborhood, I live in constant fear for my children's emotional welfare and safety.

One of the attractions of sticking to your own kind is that you do not have to worry so much about doing something stupid to offend others. Yet sticking to our own kind also makes errors of cultural misunderstanding more likely. Segregation breeds ignorance of other cultures, which in turn breeds inadvertent offense. I discovered this firsthand.

As undergraduates, my husband, Paul, and I spent a semester in West Germany. We even lived for a month in Cologne with an elderly German couple, Frau and "Opa" Schreiffer. The Berlin Wall was still up, and we did not bother trying to get to East Berlin; but in 1995, more than twenty years after our initial visit to Germany, we decided to pay a visit to the capital of the newly reunified republic. We had an active four-year-old son to contend with, so we planned our trip with care. We selected a hotel with a pool near the city zoo and the Tiergarten. We marked the public parks near the important sites on the tourist map. We brought along a comically oversized stroller and took turns pushing Adam from place to place as we traversed every quarter of the huge metropolis on foot. Like everyone else who visited Berlin in the mid-1990s we marveled at the large number of construction projects on the magnificent city's east side. We, too, endlessly speculated about the exact causes of the still visible disparities between the dowdy east and the fashionable west.

Our visit happened to coincide with the opening of the rebuilt Neue ("New") Synagogue on Oranienburgerstrasse in the Scheunenviertel Jewish district, a building on our list of places to visit. The Neue Synagogue stands on the site of an earlier, nineteenth-century synagogue that was smashed and looted by the Nazis on the evening of November 9 and the morning of November 10, 1938, the infamous Kristallnacht. Visiting the Neue Synagogue was a powerful, emotional experience for me. This was no mere tourist attraction. It was a holy place, and a memorial to the Holocaust. We went through a thorough, airport-style security check to get inside. There were metal detectors and questions; every bag and camera was carefully examined. Even the silly stroller was inspected as though suspect. After visiting the lovely space and taking in moving exhibits and architecture, I felt an identification with European Jewry for which I was unprepared. Slavery, the Holocaust; the Holocaust, slavery. I was tearful, overawed.

After an hour, my encounter with history was interrupted by the persistent tugs of a boy no longer able to remain quiet and sit still; Adam needed to run around. So we three left the Neue Synagogue in search of a playground. Berlin has fabulous public playgrounds and we had plotted one nearby, but just around the corner we came upon an understated cemetery marked by a plaque. We took out *Fodors* and learned that the small plot had been the main cemetery for the Jewish Quarter. As we walked into the cemetery, Adam noticed little piles of stones here and there. We allowed him to run freely about the cemetery dismantling the piles and rearranging them. We adults strolled, imagining aloud, with chills running down our spines, what it must have been like to live in Scheunenviertel— the Stable Quarter—as the deportation of Jews to the concentration camps began. When it was time for us to go, I allowed Adam to take a few stones for his pockets as souvenirs of his visit.

Weeks later I was telling the story of my vacation to a Jewish friend. I mentioned the afternoon in the old Jewish Quarter and what my son had done with simple stones to amuse himself as I pondered history. It was then that I learned: placing stones on a grave is a way many Jews symbolically erect a tombstone to show honor for the dead. My moment of empathy and identification had also been a moment of thoughtless desecration. You cannot give others the respect they are due when social isolation prevents you from knowing what counts as respect.

EXTREME BIAS: WE CAN DO BETTER

The point of legally mandated racial segregation was to force people to stick to their own kind. It was unjust and morally wrong, yet we are expected to turn a blind eye to ethnoracial segregation today merely because it is no longer directly imposed by law. It is just what people prefer. My claim is that segregation does not lose its taint simply because it is what people making individual private choices want. In many situations of privilege and prejudice, sticking to your own kind can be a moral wrong. It is not wrong to stick to your own kind to avoid getting lynched or locked up in jail, but American apartheid is over. Violence and punishment are no longer common responses to interethnic, interrace relationships. The costs of mingling outside your own group have lowered. There is still intragroup accountability and social pressure; however, the individual and societal benefits of integrated lifestyles are considerable and ought to be reaped.

The United States is morally compromised by its voluntary segregation. This is my view and I know that it is not widely shared. I know people who think I have it backwards. Sticking to your own kind is praiseworthy, not condemnable. Indeed, not sticking to your own kind is sometimes experienced as an aggressive or thoughtless imposition on others. You should not go where you are not wanted. If you do, you deserve the glares, the groans, the sudden excuses, the hostility. Lorraine Hansberry captured this troubling attitude in her play *A Raisin in the Sun*. A black family scrapes up the money to buy a house, but their prospective neighbors are whites who do not want the neighborhood integrated. In the film version of the play, a representative of the white neighborhood association offers the family cash in exchange for a promise to move elsewhere.[6] When they refuse, he takes umbrage at the fact they would persist in going where they were not welcome. How unreasonable of them!

Going where you are not wanted is certainly a failure of etiquette in some limited contexts. You should not wander into the hosts' bedroom during a dinner party or try to sell candy at a home where people are gathered to mourn a death. By contrast, moving into a new neighborhood to raise your family is not inconsiderate, unjust or immoral.

Homosexuals are among the few groups left that many Americans feel they have a right to overtly and categorically exclude from their society. A 2003 Supreme Court decision decriminalized gay sodomy, yet, recent legal efforts to ban gay marriage and recent First Amendment decisions of the Supreme Court potentially reinforce antigay bigotry. In a 2001 case, the Supreme Court permitted the Boy Scouts of America to exclude a gay scout, ruling against a gay man who sued after his scout membership was taken away because he revealed his homosexuality.[7] Five years earlier, the Court ruled that the organizers of the traditional Saint Patrick's Day parade in New York City could prevent gay and lesbian Irish Americans from marching.[8]

I am not making a case here for neutralizing cultural differences or abandoning race—not that we even could. Amplifying one's cultural heritage is a legitimate strategy for finding meaning, especially given the homogenizing and alienating potential of large-scale democracy. We should address that potential by embracing diversity and identity, not by jettisoning broad, open conceptions of human commonality. If you are wondering whether you ought to make an effort to include people of other backgrounds into your circle of friends, your condominium association, your church, your children's school, or your workplace, stop wondering and just do it. You are hearing the faint voice of a better self speaking above the conventional chatter.

CHAPTER 12

LEAVE HOME
ON ELECTION DAY

The infamous 2000 election contest put Republican George W. Bush in the White House and ended Democrat Albert Gore's career in national politics. Many things went wrong in Florida, whose governor at the time happened to be the Republican candidate's loyal brother. Registered voters in some districts said they were turned away at the polls. The design layout of paper ballots confused many voters, who later complained that they had accidentally cast a vote for the wrong person. A lack of uniform standards for issuing absentee ballots came to light. And when thousands of paper ballots had to be recounted by hand, near comic disagreements erupted over how to count ballots cast with partly detached chads. An eleventh-hour decision by the United States Supreme Court in *Bush v. Gore* (2000), settled the procedures that would decide the election.[1] Many welcomed the Court's intervention, while many others were appalled by the determinative role the Court was willing to play. There was predictable chest thumping by disappointed partisan Democrats, but reflective worry as well. In a dissenting opinion in *Bush v. Gore* that Justices Ginsburg and Breyer joined, Justice Stevens wrote that the real loser in the election of 2000 was not Vice President Gore, but "the Nation's confidence in the judge as the impartial guardian of the rule of law."[2]

The Saturday after the historic election, long before the Supreme Court stepped in, I ran into a neighbor in the doorway of our daughters' dance school. "Francine" is an aggressively stylish businesswoman with expensive tastes and conservative values. Her like-minded husband is a prominent surgeon. I had not seen Francine in a while, so I started to chat. "Isn't this amazing? Five days after the election and we still don't know who the next president will be." Francine readily agreed. She gave me her take on the situation, revealing a Republican bias, whereas my response announced the opposite tilt of a Democrat. The entrance to a tiny tapper's dance studio on a weekend morning is not an apt setting for political debate, so I shifted the conversation to an election-related topic about which Republicans and Democrats in my township agree: our polling places are terrific.

Five minutes from home, I vote in a magnificent stone church surrounded by an ancient cemetery and mature trees. No traffic, long lines or broken machines. No lost registration records or punch cards with hanging chads. I took my fourth grader to the polls with me for a hands-on civics lesson. As we arrived, friendly faces greeted us. Republican grandmothers offered homemade cookies. A volunteer easily found my name in her neat-looking book of registered voters. Adam and I stepped into a voting booth, closed the curtain and faced the simple, state-of-the-art electronic voting apparatus. I told Adam which party I wanted to vote for. He pressed a single button and cast my votes exactly as I intended. "Tomorrow," I had assured him as part of the lesson, "we will have a new president." The joke was on me, though. The next day we had only a legalistic and partisan squabble about which candidate was entitled to Florida's electoral votes. Our Norman Rockwell of a voting experience morphed into a weird Salvador Dalí.

Francine smiled warmly as I told her my story. I inquired about her own surely pleasant experience at the polls. "How did it go for you?" I asked. "Any problems?" Francine looked a little embarrassed. She had not voted. She explained that she had been away on business on Election

Tuesday and that she had not arranged for an absentee ballot. According
to Federal Election Commission figures, since 1984 women have voted at
a higher rate than men in federal elections. Francine is the sort of woman
you would expect to vote. She is well-educated. She runs her own business. She has control over when and where she schedules meetings. She
has a child at home, but she also has a maid, a nanny, a secretary and a husband to help out. My educated, hardworking, affluent, law-abiding neighbor neglected what ought to have been a moral priority.

Voting in national elections appears to be a low priority for most
people, not just Francine. Neither men nor women vote in impressive
numbers. Between 1984 and 1996 only between 45.3 percent and 60.8
percent of eligible registered voters went to the polls.[3] In 2000, Federal
Election Commission estimates placed the voting rate for eligible registered voters at 67.5 percent, but for the total voting age population, at only
51.3 percent. Not voting in November 2000 meant that nonvoters were
left out of the fun of poll-experience anecdote-swapping around town. But
there are larger consequences to consider. Although we seldom talk about
voting in purely ethical terms, I believe voting in major elections should
count as one of the minimal moral obligations of citizenship.

The basic civics lesson on the rights of citizens is clear. The government owes us liberty and equality. Everyone has the same rights of free
speech, free religion, free association, immunity from arbitrary search and
the right to be punished without cruelty. The Bill of Rights guarantees as
much. Our equal rights also include the right to travel, the right to marry
and the rights to have and educate children. Neither state nor federal government is supposed to infringe these rights.

The basic civics lesson on the responsibilities of citizenship is a
murkier business. We think we know what our government owes us, but
we are less sure we know what we owe our government. One responsibility
of citizenship is straightforward enough: obey the civil and criminal law.
We are not required by law to vote in the United States. No criminal or
civil penalties are attached to sitting out elections. Yet voting strikes me as
a responsibility of citizens in a democratic society. Voting is legally
optional, but I suggest that it is morally obligatory.

A REASON TO VOTE

One reason to vote goes to the symbolism of voting. We ought to vote to honor our commitment to the ideals of self-government. Although most registered voters vote, fewer than half of the people who are eligible to vote actually do so in typical elections. Voting is a way of signaling approval of a democratic form of government that understands citizens as participants who share sovereignty. Another symbolic reason for voting is that it can be seen as payback. In exchange for all of the benefits of citizenship, the voter pays a debt of gratitude in the form of citizen involvement.

But voting is more than a symbolic gesture. The best reasons to vote point to the central place of elections in determining who will lead and hold power. We are a self-governing nation. Our system is democratic. Officials are supposed to be elected, and if diminishing numbers elect them, the system of elections loses legitimacy and risks falling apart. If only a few participate in electoral politics, it may make for a cheaper, more focused, less factious process; however, our democracy will no longer be truly representative. Every adult who can vote, should, in recognition of our mutual dependence upon the meaningful functioning of a highly successful democratic form of government. Voting is an expression of concern for the welfare of the community. It matters in whose hands we entrust the power to protect and provide.

Even in demographically homogeneous communities there will be differences in opinion, and voting can be a way of helping leaders determine the preferences of the majority. Voting is thus a requirement and an exercise of majoritarian government. When one votes Republican or Libertarian or Green or Socialist or Democratic or Independent, one is both choosing a representative and sending a message to fellow citizens and leaders about what is wanted and expected. Voting as a way of communicating preferences is especially effective in states that make use of ballot initiatives and referenda regarding specific issues. Vote is voice with respect to crucial decisions that affect our lives. Robert A. Dahl is surely correct when he states that the "scale of crucial decisions has expanded beyond the nation state to transnational systems of influence and power."[4]

But many decisions about matters closest to home in our "advanced democratic society" are much more local.

Groups like the League of Women Voters make the case for voting all the time. The familiar reasons for voting are persuasive in a general way, but in practice the reasons are not compelling enough to sway people to act. People have other ways to spend their time (on business trips for example). People do not think they get anything out of voting. Individual votes do not matter very much. It is rarely the case that whether or not a particular person votes uniquely changes the outcome of an election. Voting is not smart. As Donald P. Green and Ian Shapiro explain, some rational choice theory concludes that "the chance of casting a decisive vote is absurdly small, probably less than suffering a severe accident en route to the polls."[5]

It matters, though, both as a public symbol of our commitment to a way of government, and, more concretely, as a fair contribution to a process for which one person is equally responsible with others. If everyone had Francine's priorities, everyone would feel justified in skipping the vote. If everyone skipped the vote, we would be in serious trouble. There would be a crisis of legitimacy.

Americans whose civic involvements, enterprises, lifestyles and tax contributions otherwise imply a commitment to our democratic way of life doubt that pulling a lever or pushing a button in a voting booth is a symbolic gesture they need to make. If a woman is president of the parent teacher association at her school and raises money for the poor through her church, is it really so bad that she skips a presidential election or, for that matter, a gubernatorial or mayoral election? In the United States we have a strong tradition of civic engagement outside the voting booth. Harvard professor Theda Skocpol has carefully studied the history of civic engagement in the United States. She and coauthor Morris P. Fiorina point out that: "From the very beginning of the American nation, democratic governmental and political institutions encouraged the proliferation of voluntary groups linked to regional or national social movements.... Moral reform movements, farmers' and workers' associations, fraternal brotherhoods and sisterhoods, independent women's associations, veter-

ans' groups, and many ethnic and African American associations all con-
verged on this quintessentially American form of voluntary membership
association."[6]

Nonvoters free ride on the system by leaving voting to others. To free
ride occasionally is a moral misdemeanor. Someone whose views on major
issues are similar to her fellow townspeople's may feel comfortable free
riding on their participation. Since her townspeople's voices are like her
voice, their vote is effectively her voice, too; she gets the same outcome for
less effort. Voters in homogeneous districts cannot easily imagine that they
are hurting themselves or their communities by skipping an election. But
for an adult to persistently free ride on other voters is seriously unfair, a
morally indefensible form of citizenship. The free rider problem contributes to low voter turnout, which leaves our leaders with uncertain
accountability, mandate and authority. "My vote does not matter" is a
thought that can lead to problems of the sort analyzed by Mancur Olson.[7]
People want the benefits of collective action in the form of government or a
labor union or income taxation, but they commonly do not want to participate in voting, union meetings or tax payments. If few enough people
actively participate in the collective institutions and practices they believe
beneficial to all, those institutions and practices collapse.

We ought to participate in the business of government and politics in
other appropriate ways, too. Since precisely what level of participation is
actually required to sustain our mode of government is difficult to tell, the
best practice is to remain reasonably well informed and to participate in
electoral politics as much as one reasonably can.

DISENFRANCHISEMENT

The conversation about voter responsibility must include a discussion
about disenfranchisement. A great many Americans have lost the right
to vote. They try to vote but cannot. Some registered voters go to their
polling places and find that the lines are too long or that their names are
not on the list of properly registered voters or that the voting machines
have not been set up or do not work properly. This is a kind of disenfran-

chisement, especially if the reason the voting process has broken down in a given district has to do with race discrimination or party-affiliation discrimination. Civil rights advocates who scrutinized the Florida presidential election of 2000 believe they found strong evidence that qualified and registered African Americans were turned away from the polls. Angry about the situation in Florida, Columbia University Professor Manning Marable summed things up this way:

> In Florida's Palm Beach County, 19,000 ballots were thrown out. In Duval County, 27,000 ballots were declared void. Over 12,000 of these discounted votes came from only four districts that have over 90 percent African American voters. In some majority black precincts, over 30 percent of all votes were actually thrown out! Thousands of African Americans who had registered and were legally qualified to vote were not permitted to do so, because they were erroneously listed as having been convicted of a felony. There were dozens of documented cases of blacks going to the polls who were stopped or harassed by local cops.[8]

Floridians of all races complained of disenfranchisement because the paper ballots they cast were not counted or were disqualified. Disenfranchisement can also occur when the ballots are so poorly designed that intelligent people cannot tell what to do with them. My husband and I voted in the 2002 midterm elections in Pennsylvania. Afterward I asked him whether he had voted on a referendum to allocate additional state monies to fire and police departments. I mentioned that I had almost failed to notice the referendum on the crowded computer screen. "What referendum?" was his reply. He had completely missed it.

Disenfranchisement by administrative glitch is one stubborn problem, and disenfranchisement by discrimination at the polls is another—and perhaps the most troubling. A third problem is disenfranchisement by legal mandate. Several states permanently bar voting by persons ever convicted of a felony. All but a few suspend the right of prisoners and probationers to vote. A community center heavily used by African Americans in Ardmore, Pennsylvania, stocks an ample supply of voter registration forms—fill it out and mail it in. But the application prominently lists four qualifications for voting: (1) be a citizen for at least a month before the next election; (2) be a resident of the state for at least a month to vote in local elections; (3) be eighteen; and (4) "not have been confined in a penal institution for a conviction of a felony within the last five years." The Human Rights Watch Sentencing Project projects that in a few years more than four million people and up to 40 percent of black men will have lost the right to vote.[9] African American men are overrepresented in prisons and are an increasingly disenfranchised minority. Again, Professor Marable on the situation in Florida:

> Over thirty percent of all African American adult males in Florida are disenfranchised for life, because of the antidemocratic restrictions against ex-felons. Most Florida Republicans would like to restrict the voting rights of the other 70 percent as well. In fact, Florida State House Speaker Tom Feeney, who had insisted that the Republican-controlled legislature should select a Bush slate of Electors no matter who actually won the state's popular vote, also suggested the reinstatement of "literacy tests," the legal tool of segregationists. Feeney stated to reporters: "Voter confusion is not a reason for whining or crying or having a revote. It may be a reason to require literacy tests."[10]

The importance of the vote is implicit in the legislative act of taking it away from law breakers. If the vote is so grave a responsibility that we think serious law breakers should not be allowed to participate in a government "of, for, and by the people" then surely law-abiding citizens should make voting a priority. To do otherwise is a kind of hypocrisy.

The lost right to vote is an individual problem for the men and women caught up in the criminal justice system, but it is also a communal problem for the population groups to which affected persons belong. For most of our national history, African American men and, of course, women were denied a right to vote. When blacks technically got the vote after slavery ended in the final third of the nineteenth-century, intimidation and discriminatory eligibility and registration procedures kept most blacks from voting. The rate of black voter registration and turnout is still lower than the rate for whites. This is significant because polling data suggests that, as groups, blacks and whites do not see eye to eye on a range of issues, including poverty policies, affirmative action and criminal justice. Assuming viewpoint disparity is real, it is particularly important that the eligible voices within the 12 percent black minority be heard in the democratic process. Vote is voice.

Suppose my friend Francine had been Nick, an African American man contemplating whether to go to the polls or get on an airplane on election day. Ideally, he would have exercised his absentee ballot option or would have rescheduled the meeting in advance. Barring that, Nick should have gone to the polls first thing election morning and taken a later flight. That would have been my advice to him and to Francine. Yet Nick has something to consider that Francine, a European American, does not. Nick should think about whether the polity can do without his minority voice in light of current patterns of minority disenfranchisement. Nick has a special reason for making voting in local, state and federal elections a priority.

Black men do not all think alike. It would be absurd to suggest that they do. African Americans argue with one another about public policy all the time. I am suggesting, though, that there may be overall commonalities in the way black men (and other discernible population groups for that matter) view certain issues. If there are, African American men have a special reason to go to the polls. Black men can amplify their collective voices through voting and other forms of political participation.

Making the extra effort to get to the polls is not the only thing a citizen like Nick can do in response to the problem of disenfranchisement. He can support legal reform efforts aimed against the harsh and discriminatory public policies that land so many blacks in jail and terminate their franchise in the first place. Drug laws and enforcement practices cry out for reform, in as much as black male drug users are far more likely than white users of the same drug to be convicted of a felony and spend time in jail.

EMBRACING CIVIC DUTIES

Voting is the second great responsibility of citizenship after obeying the law. Voting is the least we can do; yet civic responsibility does not end there. There are tertiary responsibilities of citizenship. In local politics the dedicated participation of single individuals can make a big difference to a community's commitment to education, the environment, business enterprise and law enforcement. A vocal member of the school board or an aggressive city council member matters. The tertiary responsibilities of citizenship vary widely with talent and opportunity. For example, there is a responsibility to assume positions of leadership, if and only if you have the right skills and personality. The personal costs of elected office holding are enormous. The money it takes to get elected; the loss of privacy; the risks of life and limb; the time. Not everyone has what it takes for political leadership. Not everyone can sit on a citizens' council. Not everyone is temperamentally suited for getting into the thicket of running things. And some people just do not have the time. A physician whose speciality is urban emergency medicine would have little time to also serve on his or her local school board. Exhausted young parents and dog-tired seasonal farm workers may have to settle for obeying the law and voting in major elections.

And yet there are many activities short of running things that people can do in the name of civic responsibility. One of them is affiliating with the civic groups so beloved by the republican tradition. Another is donating money or goods to charity. A third is hands-on volunteerism. I am no extraordinary patriot. I vote and do little else that would count as direct involvement in political decision making. However, I have devoted a great deal of time to serving on government committees and the boards of not-for-profit charities and public-interest advocacy groups. I suspect Francine has done some of this work, too.

One highly demanding mode of civic responsibility is military service. The draft is required of all young men in some European and Asian countries. We have no mandatory military service in the United States at the moment. For those who volunteer for service, the military is seen as a way to give and to get. You give a tour of duty and you get a signing bonus, a job, an education, discipline and leadership skills. A generation ago military service was emphasized as a requirement of high national political office. Today, few middle- and upper-income Americans view military service as a personal duty or serious option for themselves and their close kin. Now that baby boomers and women without veteran status are ascending to power, it is unlikely that a candidate's military service record will loom large on the list of virtues for Congress or the White House in the future. Still, John Kerry's Vietnam service record appears to have helped him outpace other Democrats in the 2004 presidential election.

SPEAKING FOR YOURSELF

I hate to admit the number of times I have gone into a polling booth and confronted a referendum for the first time or pulled the lever for a candidate I knew nothing about. It is interesting that a nation of supposed patriots takes so little interest in the routine responsibilities of democratic self-government. That we do not vote and may not even know the names of our representatives in Congress is sometimes interpreted as evidence of political disgust or apathy. Apathy could be expected since, as David Riesman pointed out a half century ago, "The complexity of society, its segmentation, the difficulty of comprehending it, the consistent failure to have it act the way people say they would like it to act—all of these factors induce political apathy."[11] But perhaps that is not it at all. Perhaps some nonparticipation is a measure of the level of comfort, security and trust we ultimately feel in our nation's institutions. If people thought the ship of state was at risk of sinking, they would want to know more about the captain and what was planned for our rescue. They would want to make sure their voices were heard. (We know how to march, riot and terrorize when we are really mad.) If people think the ship of state is sound, they might just stretch out in a chaise longue and take a long nap. The people who do not vote and do not follow politics could be cynical or indifferent, or they might just be persuaded that all the likely winners are bound to do a decent job.

Some public opinion experts contend that political discontentment and procedural problems, rather than contentment, explain why the voters' turnout rate in national elections has dropped 30 percent in forty years. People do not vote because they are busy, lack transportation to the polls, have not registered or do not believe the candidates constitute a good or meaningful choice. They do not vote because they are sick of negative campaign ads, because they feel the issues have become too complex to master; or because they do not know anyone who votes. I heard a young woman interviewed on the radio explain that she was not voting in the 2002 midterm elections because "I couldn't care less." Younger citizens, eighteen to twenty-four years of age, are especially absent from the polls. They are free riders on the people they assume will take care of things, namely their parents' and grandparents' generations.

I was not always a voter. I began voting regularly only after I was thirty. The turning point may have been a particular federal election, the results of which literally sent me to bed with a sick headache. How could that have happened, I wondered? Well, I let it happen. I let my fellow citizens chart the course. Their candidate, a man I did not think had a prayer of winning, was elected and promptly dismantled policies that I deemed vital.

AN AGENDA
FOR BETTER ETHICS

Stand back from the ethical landscape you have journeyed with me and imagine it as a grand scene depicted in an oil painting hanging on a museum wall. The world of ethics makes for a crowded canvas, a busy Brueghel. You may need time to absorb the full picture: our patterns of ethical failure in the midst of plentiful moral resources; the challenge of novel, high-impact choice and opportunity; our social insularity and political complacency. But soon you will be ready to do to the ethics scene what the museum visitor would never do to an art treasure—*change it*. We can all join in efforts where we work and live to repaint the ethical landscape. All we need to get started is a renewed commitment to the ethical enterprise and practical strategies like the baker's dozen offered here—some time-honored, others freshly conceived for our time and place.

HOW TO FIGHT ETHICAL FAILURE

Take Yourself More Seriously. Begin by recognizing what you are—a sentient creature with a short time on earth, equipped with the capacity for making responsible judgments and acting on them. What you choose to do and how you choose to do it are measures of character. Love, work, public service and citizenship are proving grounds. Do not squander your gifts. Give your family, friends, employers, communities and country the benefit of your best. And do not forget the rest of the world.

Repeated ethical failures—such as fraud, infidelity and cheating—point to the conclusion that humankind is destined to waste its unique capacity for good. Yet plentiful evidence to the contrary can also be found. Many people merit praise for the way they conduct their lives. They work hard and well for worthy ends. They give others their due and approach the world with what is increasingly recognized as a distinct virtue: care.

Firefighters, police officers and emergency medical personnel endure rigorous training, go without sleep and sometimes put their lives on the line. Volunteers return time and time again to bleak shelters to read to homeless children. Foster parents take troubled youths into their own homes, bearing the daily strain of cradling society's most vulnerable and displaced. Men and women in our midst, in full possession of strong characters, are accomplishing good that often goes uncelebrated.

Of some generous people we say that he or she has a "heart of gold"—a pure, solid, moral core, easy to treasure. But most of us do not have hearts of gold and never will. Our ethical cores are fallible chambers full of conflicting thoughts and feelings. For most of us, doing the right thing is a process marked by self-conscious effort rather than a seeming instinct. Heroes of character include people whose ethical acts come with a struggle.

Resist Temptation. Ethical temptation can be as obvious as that last truffle on the dessert tray and as difficult to avoid. A goodly percentage of our ethically engaged moments consist of mustering the strength to fight the temptation to do what we believe we should not. It is usually obvious when and why you should not lie, break your promises or cheat the public. Doing the wrong things in personal and professional life happens often, not because the rules are uncertain or the situation gray, but because people lack the willpower to do the plainly right things. To fight temptation, know your weaknesses and steer clear of them. This is common sense. If you do not want to go on a drinking binge, empty the liquor cabinet and stay away from the liquor store. Consider constructive alternatives that make unethical conduct avoidable. If walking into a casino means your children's school tuition will not get paid, vacation in Ocean City rather than Atlantic City. When you feel the dizziness of temptation coming on, take immediate action. Walk away; close the door; call a cab. In addition, focus on the harm you will cause if you make the unethical choice. Take steps to minimize harm. If you do not think you can avoid extramarital sex but know it would be disastrous to get pregnant, use birth control.

Accept Blame. Our ethical culture is rightly tolerant and compassionate. Our ethos is responsive to exceptions, excuses and justifications. As a result, we have become clever at concocting imagined grounds for exoneration. Some people seem to believe somewhere out there lies a good excuse that can redeem them. We run from blame, even when the choices we have made are clearly wrong. That bad habit is threatening to turn America into a culture of cheaters. We must shake the habit of overreliance on exceptions, excuses and justifications.

Ethical behavior is not simply a matter of "fessing up" after you get caught. It was good of U.S. Naval Academy history professor Brian Van-DeMark to accept responsibility for careless errors when reviewers discovered more than fifty unattributed passages from other works in his book *Pandora's Keepers: Nine Men and the Atomic Bomb*.[1] Diana Brooks, former chief executive officer of Sotheby's, the elite auction house, also accepted responsibility when she was convicted of collusive price-fixing with rival Christie's. Brooks told the judge who sentenced her to probation that she would "forever bear the burden of what I have done, " and apologized to "all the people I've hurt."[2] It is certainly admirable to take the blame after getting caught, but it is even better not to cave in to the rationalizations that lead to unethical conduct in the first place.

Learn from Mistakes. We must not only accept the pervasiveness of ethical failure but also seek to learn from our mistakes. Many people are profound ethical failures. You and I are ethical failures from time to time. Still, our value as creatures endowed with the capacity to judge and act responsibly endures. We can do better. This is a basis for hope.

One of the lessons I have learned is that most of the personal mistakes I made as a young person could have been avoided at a low cost, even though it did not seem that way at the time. At twenty-two, it seemed too hard to pass up sex with my pal Lennie, even though he was dating my best friend. How could I turn *him* down? (It was easy to turn down the complete stranger who offered sex the day he met me in front of Saint Peter's Cathedral, when I was a frightened nineteen-year-old touring Rome alone.) I can still recall the keen disappointment my graduate school friends and I felt before we decided to cut in front of hundreds who had arrived earlier to see the King Tut exhibit. We just had to cut the line. We had come so far. And, finally how I yearned as a teenager to hear my name announced over the intercom as top scholar. I needed that, despite the fact that I had just been skipped a grade and had already established a reputation for being bright.

What is striking to me now is that had I not made these mistakes, my life would have been entirely fine, and perhaps better. I did not need sexual intimacy with Lennie. There were other men in my life. The affair with Lennie was short-lived, and once he got married our close friendship evaporated. In many instances, ex-lovers are not as welcome as other old friends. Had Lennie and I remained just friends, I am sure I would be closer both to his family and to Amy's today. As for the King Tut exhibit, it is true that I would not have gotten in on the first try had I not cut line, but the Field Museum became more efficient about issuing tickets. My friends and I could have returned another day. As much as we enjoyed the exhibit, we probably would have enjoyed it even more without the stress of having been up all night. The top scholar stunt was the most unnecessary of all. I still have the badly mimeographed three-line form letter my parents received notifying them that for one grading period I was top scholar. My mother returned it to me along with all my old report cards years ago. The honor which meant so much to me did not affect my parents' level of pride in me; did not affect my class rank; did not get me voted "Most Intellectual" senior year; it did not enhance my college admissions or anything else of lasting importance in my life. After the initial thrill wore off, which did not take long, the ruse was just a source of shame.

Be a Cleaner Competitor. Cheating and related forms of dishonesty are costly to society and hurtful to the individuals they victimize. Noncheaters should examine whether they engage in behaviors, like conspicuous consumption and belittling competitors, that encourage others to cheat. The rest of us can acknowledge our vulnerability to cheating and take measures to strengthen our resolve against it. One way to curb the impulse to cheat is to take oneself out of competition with others. While it is imperative that firms compete with one another for customers or clients, it does not follow that the individuals who work in firms need to think of themselves deep down as competitors. The rhetoric of capitalism does not have to become the rhetoric of the soul.

Cheating in sports, business and politics is sometimes prompted by a keen desire to conquer a specific competitor. The foe in question could be someone in one's own field or sport whom one needs to defeat in order to achieve the top accolades or exact revenge for a prior defeat. To remain heavyweight champion of the world, it is said that Sonny Liston went into the ring with liniment on his glove hoping to prevail over Muhammad Ali. The foe need not be one's own personal rival: Tonya Harding's friends struck down figure skater Nancy Kerrigan hoping for a national championship and an Olympic gold medal for Harding, not for themselves. The foe need not even be in one's field. Imagine a brother and sister, both professional school students, one in law, the other in medicine, competing still for parental approval. The law student's cheating in law school may be prompted by the felt need to outshine his sister's success in the medical field. Comparisons are inevitable. To compare is human and sometimes there is a specific foe that must be defeated—that is what the job entails. Strive for excellence without focusing unduly on where you stand in relation to others. Hardworking adults in the business and professional worlds will get the things they need even if they are not on the top of the heap. People who enjoy what they do and want to do it well often turn out to be winners without overcompetitive dispositions.

Do Not Try to Outthink Ethics. It is hard to comply with ethical rules that stand in your way. The material rewards of ethical violation often seem to overwhelm the rewards that religious and philosophical traditions promise as virtue's prize. Many religions provide that what we call ethics is also godly right conduct with a spiritual payoff. Religions may point to the potential for self-realization through good works; but many people think all they need to realize themselves is more money.

Ethics is a practical good, more valuable in the long run than trying to make a fortune. Common ethical values comprise a practical scheme of social cooperation that makes for a less uncertain, fearful world. But you have to want to cooperate. If money, success or your love of art become your priority, you may find yourself choosing to suspend your ethics for a while and pursue "smart" unethical means to your ends. Yet the "smart" thing is sometimes the wrong thing by any standard. Individuals sometimes get away with flouting professional ethics and giving lip service only to common morality. They can make a lot of money that way. But the ever present danger is that what looks like a "smart" move to wrongdoers often enough turns out to be unethical and easily detected criminality.

Good-looking and well-employed, Glen DaSilva, Derrick Davis and Chris Harn were friends in their late twenties. They had met at Drexel University in the 1990s, where they had belonged to Tau Kappa Epsilon fraternity. All three decided to strike out on their own before getting a college degree. They went their separate ways, but reunited in 2002 to make some quick, easy money on a fraudulent off-track betting scheme.[3]

Chris Harn worked for Autotote Systems, a Newark, Delaware software firm that processes wagers on horse races. Autotote had only recently worked on upgrading the OTB system that Harn and his friends allegedly conspired to cheat. The three men planned to place bets on the Breeders' Cup World Thoroughbred Championship after the winners had been determined, and then to exploit Chris Harn's access at work to the computers that controlled telephone wagering to make it appear that their bets had been placed before the races.

Chris Harn showed up at work on a day he was not supposed to be there and used his password to log into the computer system that recorded bets made at the Catskills Off-Track Betting in Poughkeepsie, where Davis and DaSilva had accounts. Davis had only recently opened his account, just in time to turn a $1,152 wager into a miraculous $3 million win. But telephone records smacked of conspiracy, revealing that the three friends had called one another as the races were being run. According to the *Philadelphia Inquirer*, Davis and DaSilva tested positive for cocaine at the time of their arrests. All three men were convicted of crimes and sent to jail.

Nurture Caring, Fair-minded Youth. Our society needs men and women of strong character to do its work. Participate in the production of values in ways called for by your roles as parent, teacher, coworker, professional, business leader and citizen. At home, at school and in professional training, encourage understanding of the demands of honesty, fairness and concern for others. Special attention must be paid to shaping the values of the young. Ethically engaged parents will model a beneficent and just spirit for their children, but nurturing ethical capacity in others is not only a role for good parents. It is also a role assumed by others directly responsible for guiding youth.

Ethical misconduct by young people raises the sad possibility that the adult world is falling down on the job. Formal programs of moral education for school children are under way all over the country. Support these programs and resist allowing their implementation to become political battlegrounds. Modify existing programs that do not help young people make sense of the complex values of the geopolitical world around them and that fail to convey ethical know-how as well as ethical knowledge.

Heavy drinking, reckless driving, illegal drugs and sexual promiscuity are troubling behaviors whose correction is an understandable priority. However, the "good kids"—the academic stars who steer clear of substance abuse and unsafe sex—can easily lack vital elements of character, too. For example, the Internet has been an attractive nuisance for teenage geniuses. Teens hack into other people's computers and spread vicious computer viruses. Precocious teens have also exploited the anonymity of the Internet to manipulate the stock market. Fifteen-year-old Marcus Arnold had never attended law school or passed the bar, but he offered popular legal advice on the AskMe.com Web site from his home in Perris, California.

Like deception and fraud, acts of sheer selfishness are disturbing in gifted adolescents and speak badly of their moral educations. Moorestown, New Jersey high school seniors Blair Hornstine and Kenneth Mirkin got into an ugly fight over which of the two of them should be designated the school's valedictorian. Hornstine had achieved the highest grade point average. She had earned it in a curriculum designed to meet her special needs. A disabled student suffering from an immune deficiency, she had completed many of her studies at home on her own. School administrators wanted Hornstine to share the valedictorian honor with Kenneth Mirkin. He was a close second and had earned his high marks in a standard curriculum. Like Hornstine, who had a 4.6 GPA and a near perfect 1570 SAT score, Mirkin had won entry to college at Harvard for the fall of 2003.

But Blair Hornstine was dead set against sharing the spotlight with her exceptional classmate. Daughter of a Camden superior court judge, Hornstine sued the school district for discrimination. Public reaction to Hornstine's tactics was so negative that her lawyer complained that she was being harassed. In response to Hornstine's suit, Mirkin retained his own lawyer, who argued that Hornstine did not deserve sole honors, since unlike Mirkin, Hornstine had been given extra time to take tests, had had personal attention, and had been exempted from physical education classes weighted less heavily in calculating the GPA. Federal judge Freda Wolfson nonetheless ruled in the girl's favor, condemning what she termed "strange and relentless" efforts by school officials to rob Hornstine of her hard-won achievement.[4] Moorestown High School heeded the judge and named Hornstine sole valedictorian. In the end, though, Hornstine's selfishness backfired. Journalists covering the widely publicized fracas discovered that Blair Hornstine had plagiarized columns she wrote as a student for a local newspaper. Harvard withdrew its offer of admission, and Mirkin alone carried the Moorestown banner to the Ivy League pinnacle.

We should cultivate the capacity for sharing the spotlight and finding joy in the success of others. We need to learn to appreciate the merits of others that may place them ahead of us and on top. If it brought you genuine pleasure to know that skilled competitors have done their best and prevailed, it could make your disappointing losses easier to swallow. Beaming

Olympic athletes with no chance of winning a medal honestly tell interviewers, "I am just glad to be here on the same field with these great competitors!" Joy may be harder to arouse when you are not marching into an Olympic stadium, and others' victories seem to entail your humiliating losses.

My friend Richard played competitive Scrabble with his son. They played for years, until finally, shortly before his bar mitzvah, the boy finally beat his father. Richard was delighted in defeat. Not envious or angry, but overjoyed. The reason parents delight when their children better them in fair competition is that the parent identifies with the child in such a way that the child's victory is important to him as a sign of flourishing. Fathers want sons to flourish. A son's victory is a father's victory, too. The reason a relief pitcher can be overjoyed when his teammate pitches a perfect game is that they both belong to the same team. They are both Braves or Dodgers or Twins. One way to cultivate joy in the success of others is to enlarge one's sense of kinship. It's a race, but it's a human race.

Advice of this sort sounds lovely. And it has to be right. But it is easier to offer idealism than to pursue it. You cannot in the blink of an eye go from being a ruthless competitor, willing to leave the gate ahead of the gun if you could get away with it, to a gracious loser, delighting in a rival's decisive victory. The jerk in the office who just got your promotion is not your son! The opponent in the final round of the big chess tournament is not your teammate! And while you might learn to graciously lose to a fellow Italian, you feel differently about losing to the Irish competitor or the Mexican one. I suspect there are still men who would do anything to avoid being beaten by a woman. Enlargement of a sense of kinship is simply unthinkable for some people. Clearly, another large goal for moral education must be to encourage broader capacities of identification with other races, ethnic groups and the opposite sex.

Enforce Ethical Standards. An anticheating ethic has arisen because cheating can hurt cheaters, the people and organizations they care about and their communities. An educational emphasis on building stronger individual and institutional character is vital but insufficient. We should also work toward forms of life that make pernicious cheating less likely. We can make it less likely that people will be tempted to cheat by adopting more effective institutional approaches to deterrence.

No single one-size-fits-all scheme of deterrence crafted from the armchair will be of any use. Deterring cheating in sports is not the same as deterring cheating in business or higher education. In sports, coaches and athletes will probably have the best insights for guiding the design of strategies for deterrence. In education, students, teachers and administrators—the people most familiar with the context—will have the best ideas. One sensitive educator's suggestion is that faculty view students as not having fixed morals, but as developing a morality that can be affected by discussion and experience in the classroom.[5] In other words, teach students the anticheating ethic, do not just preach it or assume they already have it. Other made-for-education deterrence measures include the consistent use of advertised detection technologies and methods. Computers can catch cheaters who plagiarize, using programs like Turnitin (Turnitin.com). Glatt Plagiarism Services employs the "cloze procedure" for determining authorship of scholarly writing. The investigator takes the text a suspected plagiarist claims to have written, removes every fifth word and asks the suspect to replace the missing words. A plagiarist will fail the task, whereas a genuine author will not.

In one of many business ethics scandals that made the news in 2002, federal authorities charged that the assets of the Adelphia Communications Corporation had been plundered by former executives and members of the John Rigas family at a cost to investors of billions. John Rigas, the company founder, and his sons Timothy, Michael and James, allegedly borrowed $2.5 billion dollars for personal use and sent the company that prosecutors say they used as their personal piggy bank into bankruptcy.[6] To counter the wave of ethical failure in business, foster personal values and workplace ethics, and support the use of the law as an indirect tool of adult moral education and discipline.

The political will to enact and enforce sufficiently tough laws for some forms of wrongdoing does not always exist. White collar criminals have enjoyed preferential treatment when compared to street criminals. Probusiness regulators like the former Securities and Exchange Commissioner Harvey Pitt may be reluctant to create sanctions unpopular with industry. A sentence of life in prison might deter insider trading; but it is doubtful that Congress could ever be persuaded to give insider traders the same criminal treatment as first degree murderers and drug lords. A society cannot afford to shoot itself in the foot: if the legal penalties for insider trading were to become too tough, potential investors might shy away from stock ownership or adopt suboptimally timid approaches to buying and selling securities.

If threat of sanction does not work to deter misconduct, law enforcement and whistle-blowing may bring it to light. We can encourage whistle-blowing to deter unethical conduct through fear of detection and sanction. On the other hand, employees protective of their careers fear that the "whistle-blower" label will set them back professionally; students in need of recommendations to graduate or professional school and employment may be unwilling to call their teachers' research or pedagogic irregularities to the attention of authorities. The federal Sarbanes-Oxley Act (2002), labor laws and state and federal whistle-blower protection acts afford some protection against corporate retaliation for exposing unethical conduct. The Enron accounting scandal came to light in part due to one woman's whistle-blowing efforts. Sherron Watkins wrote a memorandum to former Enron chief Kenneth Lay setting out her concerns. She later broke ranks completely and spoke publically against company executives to government authorities. Kim Emigh, former financial analyst for WorldCom, said he complained to his superiors about financial irregularities two years before the company's troubles came to light with the help of whistle-blower Cynthia Cooper. Emigh lost his job just weeks after suggesting that newly implemented procedures were fraudulent and illegal. Sometimes it is the wrongdoers who lose their jobs. Whistle-blowing by their own students led to job loss for the Montgomery County, Maryland teachers who gave students advance copies of the questions that were to appear on a standardized achievement test.

Societies must impose sanctions against cheating. The law can be no friend of cheating, since fear of negative sanction—especially fear of legal punishment—contributes to the prevention and deterrence of cheating. In the United States, cheating in business and commerce triggers criminal and civil penalties too numerous to state. Stealing business secrets, interfering with contracts, deceptive trade practices, consumer fraud, insider trading—these are just a few examples of advantage taking in business addressed by civil and criminal law. Where cheating itself is not clearly illegal, the kinds of things people might do in furtherance of a scheme to cheat are often illegal. For example, even if interfering with the outcome of an amateur figure skating event is not a crime, deliberating maiming a person is criminal battery—and a tort, too.

Tough laws and administrative regulations can deter some wrongdoing, but sometimes tougher penalties are not the best way to combat cheating. The poor may be motivated to cheat because they do not have the resources at hand needed to prevail in fair play. Imagine a woman who commits welfare fraud to get an extra thirty dollars a month to put healthy food on the table for her children. She has genuine, unmet needs and no resources she can honestly marshal. She is no moral monster. Access to jobs, education and birth control may be the humane way an economically just society responds to small-scale welfare fraud.

HOW TO MAKE NOVEL CHOICES WELL

Search for Hidden Ethical Issues. Just about everyone puzzles from time to time about where ethics begins and where taste, etiquette and prudence leave off. Is tardiness an ethical issue or a matter of manners? What about eating McDonald's hamburgers or getting a nose job—matters of ethics, or taste? How about dating a coworker or marrying a person of a different race? Defining ethics precisely is not a simple task, even for great philosophers. "The boundaries of the study called ethics are variously and often vaguely conceived," wrote Henry Sidgwick in the opening pages of his influential treatise, *The Methods of Ethics.*[7]

We need to know what counts as ethics. Not all important choices qualify as ethical. Some choices are merely aesthetic, such as whether to purchase a blue car or a red one. Discerning the domain of the ethical is a concern for everyone, but is especially pointed for anyone responsible for moral guidance. People charged with the vital task of moral education are expected to know the parameters of their mission. People refereeing ethical disagreement commonly yearn for a general definition of the category of concerns that count as ethical, but on the new ethical landscape we need to keep our moral radar on all the time. There are harms to self and others that are not obvious. Our lives are interdependent and mutually accountable. Our complicity in harms seemingly caused by others is always something to look out for.

"Should I cheat?" and "Should I buy a kidney on the black market?" are obvious ethical questions. But what about "Should I donate a lobe of my lung to my friend?" and "Should I stick to my own kind?" The latter pair of questions concerns matters that are not always understood as implicating morality or ethics. And yet a bit of digging around uncovers ways in which they connect to ethical ideals.

As we have seen, voting is an act of citizenship, a way of participating in the institutions of self-government. In ancient philosophy, participation in democratic self-government was a realm of ethical virtue, but it is less commonly understood in distinctly moral or ethical terms today. The dimensions of citizenship need to be uncovered and rearticulated for people in the present generation—beneficiaries of legal reforms in the last half century that offer women and minority groups unprecedented opportunities to influence local and national politics.

If what we did had no impact on others, ethics would be unnecessary. But we lead interconnected lives. Notwithstanding the vast body of institutionalized ethics in the United States, our understanding of the ethical responsibilities that flow from unavoidable human interconnection has lagged behind the rapid pace of science and politics. It is time to catch up.

Self-educate. Because we have so many new options presented to us in daily life, the core ethical mandate of our time may be continuing moral self-education. The facts of the matter do matter. It takes some fact-finding, as well as some ethical mining on the part of the responsible moral agent, to figure out whether to pursue choices made possible by science. There are things we need to know before we sign on for research, elect surgery, try a new reproductive technology or take the latest drug.

A couple of years ago the dean of admissions at the University of Pennsylvania Law School donated a kidney to her brother. Janice Austin's act was unquestionably one of care, courage and generosity. I placed her on a pedestal for it, and when I learned the whole story of her private moral struggle, I placed her on an even higher pedestal. Janice's brother was gravely ill with hepatitis and kidney failure. He needed an urgent transplant, but was at the bottom of a long waiting list. Suffering from liver disease made him a poor candidate for a kidney donation in any case, but his physicians were willing to go forward if a suitable donor could be found. Janice stepped up to the plate to save her brother's life, but not without moral deliberation and uncertainty.

A number of people Janice spoke to urged her not to donate. "He's only your half-brother," some friends pointed out, as if that were a sufficient reason to check familial generosity toward a man with whom she'd grown up. "You need to keep your body whole," urged others, believing spiritual integrity requires a body that goes to the grave intact. Once Janice decided to donate a kidney, she had to then decide between two surgical procedures; an innovative laproscopic surgery, in which the kidney is cut away with tiny instruments through tiny incisions and then pulled through a small incision with the surgeon's own hand, and the traditional surgery in which the kidney is excised and lifted through a very large transverse upper abdominal incision. The risk of damage to the kidney she wished to donate was greatest with the innovative procedure; but the traditional procedure would leave her with a substantially larger surgical wound and scar, and would require a longer time for recovery. Some people advised Janice to minimize risk to her own health by opting for the innovative procedure, but others said commitment to donation meant she should do it in the way that maximized the likelihood of her brother's receiving an undamaged transplant organ.

Although kidney transplants have become safe and routine from a medical point of view, undergoing major surgery to benefit another is never routine from a moral point of view. It is an act of heroic self-sacrifice. Janice Austin does not regret her decision, though she believes it affected her metabolism and immune system in ways she wished she'd known about beforehand. "I used to feel robust, now I feel like crap," she says frankly but without self-pity.

As previously mentioned, removing half of the brain has proven to be an effective cure for severe seizure disorders in young children. The first parents to authorize hemispherectomy on a child were in a more difficult position ethically than those who followed. The burden of giving ethically informed consent was very high. The first children to receive any new, experimental procedures are indeed human guinea pigs. Nonetheless, Erica McNeil of Massachusetts was anxious for her son, Alex Malo, to undergo a procedure—tested only on pigs—to lengthen his abnormally short lower intestine. She readily gave her consent, because Alex's life was on the line. Serial transverse enteroplasty, a unique new surgery developed by Dr. Heung Bae Kim, saved the boy.

We need to dig deeply to uncover all the ethical dimensions of the choices we make. Religion, moral education, conduct codes and laws are in place to guide us. Critical familiarity with existing ethical resources is but a starting point. We need to research our options because we are making choices whose risks and impacts are not well understood, in a social and political context unlike any other. Information to educate and inform our ethical choices has never been easier to gather. We have television and newspapers, and we have public libraries and the Internet to boot. Common access to libraries, the Internet and a college diploma turn out to be mandates of moral justice.

Smoking cigarettes carries a risk to smokers, though I would not say that it is necessarily immoral or unethical. But once you are aware of secondhand smoke injuries, you have to think twice before lighting up in the car on the way to the beach with other people. You might hurt them. Are you obligated to know that secondhand smoke is a factor in lung disease? The obligation of continuing self-education requires an open mind with respect to emerging evidence about the harmfulness of comfortable old practices like smoking in poorly ventilated spaces.

HOW TO BUILD BETTER COMMUNITIES

Acknowledge Interdependence. You are not an island, and you cannot afford to be complacent. We are social animals who live interdependent lives. Expand your realm of moral concern to embrace strangers, as well as kin and friends, of all backgrounds. Make choices mindful both of your obligations to others and of your need for others. Your good choices can provide material resources as well as serve as a source of pride for the people close to you. By the same token, your bad choices will have serious implications for intimates left to pick up the pieces when your life falls apart. And your intimate family and friends are not the only ones affected by what you do. When you use illegal drugs or consume produce harvested by mistreated farm workers, others are affected—adversely affected—by what you do. Expand your field of vision to the broader consequences of choice. Make choices mindful of the possibility that you are complicit in remote injury and injustice to strangers.

Traditional African American culture is characterized by thick and extensive kinship ties, which is doubtless true of many other American ethnic groups as well. We give and take. When I needed someone I could trust to help me care for my newly adopted infant son until I was ready to hire a nanny, my brother Michael stepped up. He was a law student at the time, but made room in his schedule to act as his nephew's babysitter. Several years later, I came to Michael's aid when he nearly lost his life in elective surgery. He moved in with me while he recovered.

I have sometimes been called upon to help kin less close than Michael. Years ago I got a phone call out of the blue from a pregnant thirteen-year-old whom I had never met, but whose mother told her to call me for moral advice. This tragically placed teen turned out to be a distant cousin, living in poverty with her mother and younger siblings in a trailer park. The girl's Southern drawl was articulate and sweet. She did not want to have a baby, she said. She wanted to stay in school. Her young boyfriend was in denial, but her estranged father said she ought to keep the baby. I spoke to the girl for a long time, and it became clearer as we spoke that she and her overwhelmed mother did not just want my advice, they wanted me to help terminate the pregnancy.

I wound up referring them to a Planned Parenthood clinic in a nearby city, and paying for the services they elected to receive there.

The extraordinarily caring way some people go about building and sustaining relationships is proof of ample character, even if their choices are ones we ourselves can scarcely fathom. At the end of a seminar I taught on privacy, one of my students followed me back to the office. Good-looking, I thought to myself. Luke was 6 foot 2 inches tall with a slender build, nicely chiseled European features, and shoulder-length brown hair. Fabio was hot at the time, and I reckoned Luke to be a clone—still surprising, though, in a law student with a high-pitched Midwestern accent. Luke explained why he had come by. "I wanted you to know that during the course of the semester I am going to begin a transformation from male to female, and I would very much like to be called Lucy." I cannot recall what I said, only how I felt: hysterical. After Luke left me, I dashed to the office of the dean of students. How can I teach my class if a twenty-eight-year-old man comes in wearing skirts and lipstick? How can I prevent the other students from acting up? What am I supposed to do? The dean had no good advice for me, so I turned to my friends. Adrian provided the solution. "Relate to Lucy as Lucy," she advised, "just as you relate to me as me. You know you do not have to look African American to be African American. You do not have to look female to be female, either."

So Luke was a woman with a man's phenotype. I got it. The next time I sat down with Luke, she fully emerged as Lucy. We had a conversation in which I self-consciously related to my pupil as a younger woman in need of a mentor. Over time I became very comfortable with Lucy. She was kind, earnest and direct. She told me about her dog, her parents, and her wife—she was legally married to a beautiful woman whom "Luke" had wed at age twenty-two. As our bond grew, Lucy filled me in on the details of the psychotherapy, counseling, hair removal, medications and surgery for which she was in store.

Advances in surgery and pharmacology have made sex reassignment an appealing option for people like Lucy, whose physical bodies do not match their gender identities. At the same time, changes in law and society have made it somewhat easier for transsexuals to avoid blatant discrimination. For example, Lucy secured a good job with a religious institution after she began her transformation. Yet neither the possibility of viable surgery nor the existence of laws against discrimination served as motivation for my student to shed her identity as Luke to become Lucy. Her choice was driven by her own internal needs, and she moved ahead to resolve her uninvited dilemma cautiously.

In years of counseling and therapy, Lucy reflected deeply upon the impact that her becoming a woman would have on others, especially her wife and parents. A medical diagnosis of "gender identity disorder" was not justification enough, in her view, to rush forward to achieve her controversial aim. She included friends, family and the people she worked for in every step of her decision making. She invited their opinions and understandable concerns. Lucy was reared by her mother, a schoolteacher, and a stepfather who is an attorney. She had a brother and a wife. Lucy wanted to preserve her ties to all the people she cared about: "It made no sense to me not to try to preserve the past." She attributed her desire to preserve intimate relationships while firmly resolving to be true to herself to two major influences: her mother modeled kindness combined with honesty and steady resolve; and Lucy's involvement with feminist theory, with its emphasis on equality and care, seasoned her values as well.

Lucy's years of effort paid off. Her mother, who had raised and loved a handsome and intelligent son Luke, accepted Lucy fully, as did her brother. Lucy's stepfather showed his continued love by paying for Lucy's sex reassignment surgery. As for Lucy's wife, they ended their marriage, although they did so on good terms.

Value but Improve Traditions. Three days after we buried my mother, it was my father, Grover Cleveland Allen, Sr., who lay on the brink of death in a hospital. My mother had been ill with lung cancer, so we had not expected her to live a long life. But my father had been perfectly healthy when he contracted the same vicious pneumonia that had just killed his wife of forty years. The doctors who treated him gave the family little hope. They sat down with us in the waiting room and quoted dire statistics, showing us X-rays of lungs completely white with infection. When I left the hospital for the night, I recited the Twenty-third Psalm over and over again. The next day my father was sent by helicopter to a larger hospital, where he made a full recovery.

The ancient vintage of religious ethics does not make it irrelevant. We have not entirely outgrown our traditions. You could get a better job if you lied about prior work experience, but you allow the opportunity for profitable deception to pass. Where did the moral resolve come from? It was learned in Sunday school, or Hebrew school or from Buddhist grandmothers. The wisdom of the ages serves the vital need of our times for guidance and comfort.

Yet we must maintain a clear-eyed, realistic stance toward existing ethical resources and traditions. Communities are defined, in part, by their traditions. But traditions are not beyond reproach. Recognize the origins of existing ethical resources and traditions in venerated ancient religions and philosophy, but do not assume that the ways of the past should be copied exactly. Indeed, established religious groups are actively reexamining the traditions of hierarchy and secrecy that contributed to sexual abuse by the clergy. The Roman Catholic Church has slowly made changes to adjust to a world that is less accepting of patriarchy and sectarian loyalties. Our legal and business traditions demand the same critical fidelity. Long-standing ethics laws and business practices are open to question, much as new ones are, since both can be less than optimal. We sometimes have to prune our roots to achieve good.

A FINAL WORD

The pessimist thinks, "What is the point?" But ethics do have a point. The point is a more peaceful, just world in which individuals secure more of what they want and need because they and others live cooperatively. Pessimism leads to caring less or caring not at all. Pessimism undermines much needed ethical faith, the belief that acting in accord with common moral rules bestows long-term benefits on individuals and on our communities.

Americans enjoy many blessings. A national commitment to legal reform, science and technology initiated in the last century has transformed our society in many desirable ways. Compared to fifty years ago, diverse groups of Americans have more medical options, more economic options and more political voice. As in the past, ethical living requires coping well with the lives Fate has dealt. Increasingly, though, our lives routinely demand that we choose well from among myriad options for shaping our common destinies. We have every reason to give ethics our best shot.

I believe ethical living as conceived here importantly contributes to the amelioration of want, indignity and terrifying evil. Being engaged by ethics, alive to ethical capacity, carries a reward. We are enlarged by the magnitude of our responsibilities for shaping the future. Every human life takes on a singular majesty when dedicated to the noble quest for ethical living.

AN AGENDA FOR BETTER ETHICS

1. *Take Yourself More Seriously*
2. *Resist Temptation*
3. *Accept Blame*
4. *Learn from Mistakes*
5. *Be a Cleaner Competitor.*
6. *Do Not Try to Outthink Ethics*
7. *Nurture Caring, Fair-Minded Youth*
8. *Enforce Ethical Standards*
9. *Search for Hidden Ethical Issues*
10. *Self Educate*
11. *Acknowledge Interdependecne*
12. *Value but Improve Traditions*

INTRODUCTION: THE NEW ETHICAL LANDSCAPE

1. David Boies represented the federal government in *U.S. v. Microsoft Corporation,* a complex antitrust case alleging uncompetitive practices, originally filed May 18, 1998 in the District Court for the District of Columbia; he represented Napster in *In Re Napster Inc. Copyright Litigation* in the District Court, Northern District of California; and he represented Vice President Al Gore in *Bush v. Gore,* 531 U.S. 98 (2000).

2. See, for example, Peter Singer, *The President of Good and Evil: The Ethics of George W. Bush* (New York: Dutton, 2004); idem, *How Are We to Live?: Ethics in an Age of Self-Interest* (Amherst, N.Y.: Prometheus Books, 1995). Other ethics books with practical orientations include, Aaron Hass, *Doing the Right Thing: Cultivating Your Moral Intelligence* (New York: Pocket Books, 1998); Bruce Weinstein, *What Should I Do? 4 Simple Steps to Making Better Decisions in Everyday Life* (New York: Perigee/Penguin, 2000); Alan Wolfe, *Moral Freedom: the Search for Virtue in a World of Choice* (New York: W. W. Norton and Co., 2001); and Randy Cohen, *The Good, the Bad, and the Difference: How to Tell Right and Wrong in Everyday Situations* (New York: Random House, 2002).

3. Kurt Baier, *The Moral Point of View: A Rational Basis of Ethics,* 1965 Abridged Edition (New York: Random House, 1965), 1.

4. *Lawrence v. Texas,* 123 S. Ct. 2472 (2003).

5. *State v. Hawaii,* 66 Haw. 616, 671 2d 1351 (1983) (Nakamura, J.). Lauren Mueller was accused of engaging in sexual conduct with another person in return for a fee. She moved to have the charge dismissed because the alleged sex acts

took place in her apartment and were not solicited in a public place. She later unsuccessfully appealed her conviction on privacy grounds.

6. *Barnes v. Glen Theater,* 501 U.S. 560 (1991).

7. See, for example, Mary Midgley, *Can't We Make Moral Judgements?* (New York: St. Martin's Press, 1993).

8. G. E. Moore, *Principia Ethica* (Cambridge: Cambridge University Press, 1971), 1. The book was originally published in 1903.

9. George Bernard Shaw (1856–1950). I have been unable to locate the original source of this oft-quoted remark.

10. Arthur Schopenhauer, "Psychological Observations," in *Essays of Schopenhauer,* trans. T. Bailey Saunders (New York: Wiley Book Company, n.d.), 79.

11. Jane McAlister Pope (Commentary), "Tennessee Murder Symptomatic of Chilly, Deadly Days in Politics," *Charlotte* [N.C.] *Observer,* October 23, 1998.

12. Mr. Traficant addressed the odd remark quoted here to the House Committee on Standards of Official Conduct on July 18, 2002, the day the Committee recommended his expulsion from Congress; the expulsion vote in the full House of Representatives took place a few days later on July 24, 2002. See Sabrina Eaton, "House Set to Vote Today on Giving Traficant the Boot," *Plain Dealer* [Cleveland], July 24, 2002, A14.

13. See Betsy Hart (Commentary), "There's Plenty of Shame to Go Around; It Looks like Everyone in Condit-Levy Scandal Acted Abominably," *Dayton* [Ohio] *Daily News,* July 20, 2002; Rowland Nethaway (Commentary), "Condit Makes 1 Stupid Move After Another; the Congressman Has Done Everything Possible to Appear Suspicious," *Dayton Daily News,* July 26, 2001.

14. Elliot Turiel, *The Culture of Morality: Social Development, Context, and Conflict* (Cambridge: Cambridge University Press, 2002).

15. The Ethics Bowl was the brain-child of philosophy professor Robert F. Ladenson. See Danielle Svetcov, "Ethics Bowls: Where There is No Final Answer," *New York Times,* August 5, 2001, sec. 4A, pg. 10, col. 3. The quoted description of the Ethics Bowl comes from the Web site of the Illinois Institute of Technology, http://www.iit.edu.departments/csep_EB/eb1.html, where Ladenson is a faculty member and director of the Center for the Study of Ethics in the Professions.

16. Cheating occurs at colleges and universities with honor codes, as well as at those without such codes. Bernard Rosen, "Honor and Honor Codes," *Teaching Philosophy* 10:1 (March 1987) 37–48, suggests that interpreting honor code require-

ments and getting students to view them as binding may be harder than we generally imagine.

17. John Moore (Commentary), "Scouts Are Right to Exclude Gays," *Philadelphia Inquirer*, July 15, 2003, A9. According to Mr. Moore, who has been active in the Scouts, the purpose of the Boy Scouts "is to teach young people to make ethical decisions. They believe, as I do that believing in God is key to this purpose. As a Christian, I depend on the Bible to provide the basis for my morals, and a reasonable interpretation of both the Old and the New Testaments indicates that homosexual acts are wrong."

18. The problems taken up here have been of concern to me for some time. I discuss the problem of incomplete integration in "The Half-Life of Integration," in Stephen Macedo, *Reassessing the Sixties: Debating the Political and Cultural Legacy* (New York: W. W. Norton, 1997) 207–27. I explore the need for diversity in education in "Civic Virtue, Cultural Bounty: The Case for Ethnoracial Diversity," in Stephen Macedo and Yael Tamir, eds., *Moral and Political Education Nomos* 43 (New York: NYU Press, 2001) 434–55. I examine the ethics of intimate interracial relationships in *Why Privacy Isn't Everything: Feminist Reflections on Personal Accountability* (Lanham, Md.: Rowman and Littlefield, 2003).

19. G. E. Moore, *Principia Ethica*, 71–72.

20. Alasdair MacIntyre, *After Virtue*, 2nd ed. (Notre Dame: University of Notre Dame Press, 1997).

21. Adam Nossiter, "Baton Rouge Desegregation Case Nears End," Associated Press, August 11, 2003.

22. *Brown v. Board of Education*, 347 U.S. 483 (1954).

CHAPTER 1. RUNNING FROM BLAME

1. R. G. Heise and J. A. Steitz, "Religious Perfectionism Versus Spiritual Growth," *Counseling and Values* 36 (1991): 11–18.

2. Ann Diller, "Pluralisms for Education: An Ethics of Care Perspective." See www.ed.uiuc.edu/EPS/PES-Yearbook/92_docs/DILLER.HTM.

3. Allan Gibbard, *Wise Choices, Apt Feelings: A Theory of Normative Judgment* (Cambridge, Mass.: Harvard University Press, 1992), 255.

4. Peter Bowden, *Caring: Gender Sensitive Ethics* (London: Routledge, 1997), 1.

5. Immanuel Kant, *Foundations of the Metaphysics of Morals, and What Is Enlightenment?* trans. Lewis White Beck (Indianapolis: Bobbs-Merrill Educational Pub-

lishing, 1959), 17. ("Thus the moral worth of an action does not lie in the effect which is expected from it or in any principle of action which has to borrow its motive from this expected effect.")

6. Stephen Toulmin, *An Examination of the Place of Reason in Ethics* (Cambridge: Cambridge University Press, 1970), 219.

7. Kurt Baier, *The Moral Point of View: A Rational Basis of Ethics, abr. ed.* (New York: Random House, 1965), 155.

8. Paul Ricoeur, "The Concept of Fallibility," in Joseph J. Kockelmans, *Contemporary European Ethics: Selected Readings* (Garden City, N.Y.: Anchor Books Doubleday, 1972), 110–129, 121.

9. See the discussion of the dangers of partisanship in Sissela Bok, *A Strategy for Peace: Human Values and the Threat of War* (New York: Vintage Books, 1990), 3–30.

10. Aristotle, *The Nicomachean Ethics,* trans. Sir David Ross (London: Oxford University Press, 1975).

11. Marcus Aurelius, *Meditations and Epictetus, Enchiridion,* trans. Russell Kirk (Chicago: Gateway Editions, 1956), 11.

12. Karen Heller, "Shared Hypocrisy: The Case of William Bennett, Super-Moralist with a Gambling Habit, Points Up the Duality of the Times," *Philadelphia Inquirer,* May 10, 2003, E1.

13. Susan Neiman, *Evil in Modern Thought: An Alternative History of Philosophy* (Princeton: Princeton University Press, 2002).

14. Susan H. Bitensky, "Spare the Rod, Embrace Our Humanity, Toward a New Legal Regime Prohibiting Corporal Punishment of Children," *University of Michigan Journal of Law Reform* 31, No. 2 (1998): 353–474. See also Susan Bitensky, "Spare the Rod, Embrace Our Humanity," at www.childrightseducation.org/english/archives/sparetherod2.html.

15. *Atkins v. Virginia, 536 U.S. 304 (2002).*

16. "'Crazy' Ex-Congressman Accused of Fraud," UPI, *NewsMax.com* wires, www.newsmax.com/archives/articles/2001/7_5/204623.shtml.

17. *Simpson's Contemporary Quotations* (1988) cites the November 12, 1962, *New York Times* as the source of the quote by Chief Justice Earl Warren.

18. Richard B. Brandt, *A Theory of the Good and the Right* (Oxford: Clarendon Press, 1979). Brandt was also known for a book about the ethics of the Hopi Indians.

CHAPTER 2: CHEATING, THE BIG MISTAKE

1. Henry C. Harpending and Jay Sobus, "Sociopathy as an Adaptation," *Ethology and Sociobiology* 8 (1987): 63S–72S.

2. Since lying and envy are often predicates of cheating, Exodus 20:16–17 comes close to a prescription against cheating:

> 16: Thou shalt not bear false witness against thy neighbour.
> 17: Thou shalt not covet thy neighbour's house, thou shalt not covet thy neighbour's wife, nor his manservant, nor his maidservant, nor his ox, nor his ass, nor any thing that is thy neighbour's.

3. Bernard Gert, *Morality: A New Justification of the Moral Rules* (New York: Oxford University Press, 1988), 129.

4. Ibid., 132.

5. Ibid., 130.

6. Gerald Mars, *Cheats at Work: An Anthropology of Workplace Crime* (Brookfield, Vt.: Dartmouth Publishing Co., 1994) 1, 3. Mars cites four self-report studies from the years 1959–1971, and argues that arrangements that allow workers to "rob, cheat, short-change, pilfer and fiddle customers, employers, subordinates and the state" have serious implications. Regular cheating at work "affects the incomes and life styles of so many people that it has to be studied, discussed and understood by anyone trying to set out a description of the economy, to establish a policy for assessing industrial performance, to institute economic, technical, or organizational change."

7. Bao Zonghao, "An Ethical Discussion on the Network Economy," *Business Ethics: a European Review* 10, No. 2 (April 2001): 108–112.

8. Gerald Mars, *Cheats at Work*. An introduction by Mary Douglas to the 1994 edition points out what is truer still in 2004, that "there has been an extensive growth of electronic controls and surveillance at work." These controls may have reduced the prevalence of certain obvious forms of cheating.

9. Nancy Fimbel and Jerome S. Burstein, "Defining the Ethical Standards of the High-technology Industry," *Journal of Business Ethics* 9 (1990): 929–948.

10. James R. Glenn, Jr., "Business Curriculum and Ethics: Student Attitudes and Behavior," *Business and Professional Ethics Journal* 7, Nos. 3–4 (1993): 167–185.

11. Donald L. McCabe, "Classroom Cheating Among Natural Science and Engineering Majors,"*Science and Engineering Ethics* 3, No. 4 (1997): 433–45, 439: "In general, these results are consistent with prior research—higher levels of

cheating are found in the more vocationally oriented majors of business and engineering, with the highest levels found among business majors."

12. Brian K. Burton and Janet Near, "Estimating the Incidence of Wrongdoing and Whistle-blowing: Results of a Study Using Randomized Response Techniques," *Journal of Business Ethics* 14 (1995): 17-30, 17.

13. Tracy L. Spinrad, Sandra H. Losoya, Nancy Eisenberg, et al., "The Relations of Parental Affect and Encouragement to Children's Moral Emotions and Behaviour," *Journal of Moral Education* 28, No. 3 (1999): 323-37. See generally, Bernard E. Whitley, Jr., Amanda Bichlmeir Nelson and Curtis Jones, "Gender Differences in Cheating Attitudes and Classroom Cheating Behavior: a Meta-Analysis," *Sex Roles* 41, Nos. 9-10 (1999): 657-80; Stephen G. Tibbetts, "Gender Differences in Students' Rational Decisions to Cheat," *Deviant Behavior: An Interdisciplinary Journal* 18 (1997): 393-414.

14. Bernard Rosen, "Honor and Honor Codes," *Teaching Philosophy* 10, No. 1 (1987): 37-47.

15. "Cheating at UVA," *The Richmond (Virginia) Times-Dispatch*, May 13, 2001, F6.

16. Brian K. Burton and Janet P. Near, "Estimating the Incidence of Wrongdoing and Whistle-blowing: Results of a Study Using Randomized Response Technique," *Journal of Business Education* 14 (1995): 17-30; and Dean Allmon, Diana Page and Ralph Roberts, "Determinants of Perceptions of Cheating: Ethical Orientation, Personality and Demographics," *Journal of Business Ethics* 23 (2000): 411-22.

17. Patricia Faulkender et al., "The Case of the Stolen Psychology Test: An Analysis of an Actual Cheating Incident," *Ethics and Behavior* 4, No. 3 (1994): 209-17, 215.

18. See Donald L. McCabe, Linda Klebe Trevino and Kenneth Butterfield, "Cheating in Academic Institutions: a Decade of Research," *Ethics and Behavior* 11, No. 3 (2001): 219-32; Deborah F. Crown and M. Shane Spiller, "Faculty Responsibilities in Dealing With Collegiate Cheating: A Student Development Perspective," *Teacher Business Ethics* 1 (1997): 117-130; and Deborah F. Crown and M. Shane Spiller, "Learning from the Literature on Collegiate Cheating: a Review of Empirical Research," *Journal of Business Ethics* 17 (1998): 683-700.

19. Patricia Faulkender et al., "The Case of the Stolen Psychology Test, 214.

20. Patricia Keith-Spiegel, Barbara G. Tabachnick, Bernard E. Whitley, Jr. and Jennifer Washburn, "Why Do Professors Ignore Cheating? Opinions of a National Sample of Psychology Instructors," *Ethics and Behavior* 8, No. 3 (1998): 215-27.

21. Rick Reilly, "Yo, Please Pass the Truth Serum," *Sports Illustrated*, February 1, 1999, 84.

22. Tom Spousta, "An Apologetic O'Leary Receives Another Chance," *New York Times*, December 9, 2003, D2.

23. William C. Rhoden, "Death at 38; Reviewing a Vibrant Life," *New York Times*, September 22, 1998, D9.

24. For news reports of Mr. Keener's widely quoted public statement see, for example, "Quotation of the Day, *New York Times*, September 1, 2001, A2; and espn.go.com/moresports/llws01/s/2001/0831/1246234.html. The Little League motto and the history of the organization will be found on the Little League's official website at www.littleleague.org/media/archive/heroesrelease.htm.

25. Natalie Angier, "The Urge to Punish Cheats: It Isn't Merely Vengeance," *New York Times*, November 1, 2002, F1.

26. Denise Dellarosa Cummins, "How the Social Environment Shaped the Evolution of Mind," *Synthese* 122 (2000): 3–28.

27. Denise Dellarosa Cummins, "Cheater Detection is Modified by Social Rank: The Impact of Dominance on the Evolution of Cognitive Functions," *Evolution and Human Behavior* 20 (1999): 229–48.

28. Daniel Nettle and Robin I. M. Dunbar, "Social Markers and the Evolution of Reciprocal Exchange," *Current Anthropology* 38, No. 1 (1997): 93.

29. Henk de Vos and Evelien Zeggelink, "Reciprocal Altruism in Human Social Evolution: The Viability of Reciprocal Altruism with a Preference for Old Helping Partners," *Evolution and Human Behavior* 18 No. 4 (1997): 261–78.

30. D. Kay Johnston, "Cheating: Limits of Individual Integrity," *Journal of Moral Education* 25, No. 2 (1996): 159–71; idem. "Cheating: Reflections on a Moral Dilemma," *Journal of Moral Education* 20, No 3. (1991): 283–91.

31. Kim Scheppele and Antal Orkeny, "Rules of Law: The Complexity of Legality in Hungary," in Martin Krygier and Adam Czarnota (eds.), *The Rule of Law after Communism: Problems and Prospects in East-Central Europe* (Brookfield, Vt.: Ashgate/Dartmouth Publishing Co., 1999), 55–76.

32. Ernst Fehr and Simon Gachter, "Altruistic Punishment in Humans," *Nature* 415 (January 10, 2002): 137–40.

33. Cheating can create successful champions, cf. Thomas H. Murray, "The Bioengineered Competitor? Steroids, Hormones, and Individual Rights," *Phi Kappa Phi Journal* (Fall 1989): 41–42.

34. The Associated Press, "Baseball Roundup; Fans Shower Sosa With Cheers, Cork," *New York Times,* June 11, 2003, D7.

35. Jonathan Friendly, "Writer Who Fabricated Story Tells of Pressure 'To Be First,'" *New York Times,* January 29, 1982, A18.

36. Stacey Stowe, "Research Lab Falsified Tests of Toxins, Reports Say," *New York Times*, September 6, 2003, B6.

37. The Josephson Institute of Ethics' primer, *Making Ethical Decisions,* contains a longer, overlapping list of common excuses for wrongdoing.

38. Ralph Frammolino, "ID, Recovery of Bodies Likely to Take Months," *Los Angeles Times*, February 21, 2002, A 21.

39. Michael Graetz, *The Decline (and Fall?) of the Income Tax* (New York: W. W. Norton, 1997). See also Michael J. Graetz and Louis L. Wilde, "The Economics of Tax Compliance: Fact and Fantasy," *National Tax Journal* 38, No. 3 (1985): 355–63; and Jeffrey Dubin, Michael Graetz, and Louis Wilde, "Are We a Nation of Tax Cheaters? *New Econometric Evidence on Tax Compliance," AER Papers and Proceedings* 77 (May 1987): 240–45.

40. John D. McKinnon, "IRS Rides the Ups and Downs of Congressional Whim," *Wall Street Journal*, April 8, 2002, A28.

41. Donald L. McCabe, "Classroom Cheating Among Natural Science and Engineering Majors," *Science and Engineering Ethics* 3, (1997): 433–45.

42. See Gordon Reddiford, "Cheating and Self-Deception in Sport," in M. J. McNamee and S. J. Parry, eds., *Ethics and Sport* (London: Routledge, 1998), 225–39.

43. Thomas H. Murray, "The Bioengineered Competitor? Steroids, Hormones, and Individual Rights," *Phi Kappa Phi Journal* (Fall 1989): 41–42.

44. Deborah F. Crown and M. Shane Spiller, "Faculty Responsibilities in Dealing with Collegiate Cheating: A Student Development Perspective," *Teacher Business Ethics* 1 (1997): 117–30. Deborah F. Crown and M. Shane Spiller, "Learning from the Literature on Collegiate Cheating: a Review of Empirical Research," *Journal of Business Ethics* 17 (1998): 683–700.

45. Felicia R. Lee, "Is America in the Midst of a Cheating Epidemic?, *Star Telegram.com*, October 9, 2003, www.dfw.com/mld/dfw/living/6970318. htm, quoting Callahan. See generally, David Callahan, *The Cheating Culture: What More Americans Are Doing Wrong to Get Ahead* (New York: Harcourt Trade Publishers 2004).

46. Thalma E. Lobel and Ilana Levanon, "Self-Esteem, Need for Approval, and Cheating Behavior in Children," *Journal of Educational Psychology* 80, No. 1 (1988): 122-23.

47. Andrew Greeley, "Marital Infidelity," *Society* (May/June 1994): 9-14, 10.

48. Bell and Whaley, xxviii, make a similar point and also recount that they abandoned the title *How to Cheat* as a title for their book when they learned that "one of the largest bookstore chains" would refuse to carry the book, the authors surmise, for fear of "contamination" by cheaters.

49. cf. E. D. Evans and D. Craig, "Teacher and Student Perceptions of Academic Cheating in Middle and Senior High School," *The Journal of Educational Research* 84 (1990): 44-45. This article concluded that "a student's knowledge of what constitutes cheating is probably formed by middle school age." Twenty to twenty-five teachers investigated "exhibited confusions about some aspects of cheating."

CHAPTER 3. THE CHALLENGE OF MORAL EDUCATION

1. G. J. Warnock, *The Object of Morality* (London: Routledge & Kegan Paul, 1971).

2. See generally Larry Nucci, *Education in the Moral Domain* (Cambridge: Cambridge University Press, 2002); Larry Nucci, ed., *Moral Development and Character Education: A Dialogue* (Berkeley: McCutchan, 1989).

3. Moritz Schlick, *Problems of Ethics*, trans. David Rynin (New York: Prentice Hall, 1939), 200, 205.

4. Ibid.

5. Lawrence Kohlberg, "Development of Moral Character and Moral Ideology," in M. L. Hoffman and L. W. Hoffman, eds., *Review of Child Development Research*, vol. 1 (New York: Russell Sage, 1964), 381-431, 383-84.

6. Ibid.

7. Jean Piaget, *Genetic Epistemology*, trans. Eleanor Duckworth (New York: Columbia University Press, 1970). This book is based on Piaget's 1960 lectures at Columbia University.

8. Mary Jeanne Larrabee, ed., *An Ethic of Care: Feminist and Interdisciplinary Perspectives* (New York: Routledge, 1993), 4.

9. Lawrence J. Walker, "Sex Differences in the Development of Moral Reasoning," in Mary Jeanne Larrabee, ed., *An Ethic of Care*, 143-56.

10. Diana Baumrind, "Sex Differences in Moral Reasoning: Response to Walker's (1984) Conclusion That There Are None," in Mary Jeanne Larrabee, *An Ethic of Care*, ed., 157.

11. Carol B. Stack, "The Culture of Gender: Women and Men of Color," in Mary Jeanne Larrabee, ed., *An Ethic of Care*, 108–11, 109.

12. Georg Lind, *Ist Moral Lehrbar? Ergebnisse der Modernen Moralpsychologischen Forschung.* [*Can Morality Be Taught? Research findings from Modern Moral Psychology*], 2nd ed. (Berlin: Logos-Verlag, 2002).

13. See generally James Rest, *Development in Judging Moral Issues* (Minneapolis: University of Minnesota Press, 1979).

14. The Partnerships in Character Education Program is authorized under Title V, Part D (Fund for the Improvement of Education), Subpart 3, Section 5431 of the Elementary and Secondary Education Act of 1965, as amended by the No Child Left Behind Act of 2001.

15. Michael Josephson, "Character Education is Back in Our Schools," *The State Education Standard* (August 2002): 40–45, 43.

16. P. L. 105–244. Sec. 863. Sense of Congress Regarding Good Character. This was a 1998 Amendment to the Higher Education Act of 1965.

17. See U.S. Department of Education Press Release of October 23, 2002, "$16.7 Million in Character Education Grants Go to States and School Districts," Department of Education website, www.ed.gov/news/pressreleases/2002/10/10232002.html.

18. See U.S. Department of Education Press Release of September 29, 2003, "Character Education Grants Awarded," Department of Education website, www.ed.gov/news/pressreleases/2003/09/09292003.html.

19. Thomas Lickona is the author of an influential book, *Educating for Character: How Our Schools Can Teach Respect and Responsibility*, (New York: Bantam Books, 1991).

20. The Bonner Center for Character Education, University of California, Fresno, caracas.soehd.csufresno.edu/bonnercenter/bonner.htm

21. See www.cortland.edu/c4n5rs/history.htm. See also Thomas Lickona, *Educating for Character: How Our Schools Can Teach Respect and Responsibility* (New York: Bantam Books, 1991).

22. Moritz Schlick, "The Future of Philosophy," in Richard Rorty, ed., *The Linguistic Turn: Recent Essays in Philosophical Method* (Chicago: University of Chicago,

1970), 43–53, 48; idem., *Problems of Ethics,* trans. David Rynin, (New York: Prentice Hall,1939), 200, 205. The book was first published in 1930.

23. Gustav Bergman, "Logical Positivism, Language, and the Reconstruction of Metaphysics," in Rorty, *The Linguistic Turn,* 63–71, 63.

24. Rudolf Carnap, "Empiricism Semantics and Ontology," in Rorty, *The Linguistic Turn,* 72–84, 84.

25. William Kilpatrick, *Why Johnny Can't Tell Right from Wrong: And What We Can Do About It* (New York: Touchstone Books, 1992).

26. James Bernard Murphy, "Good Students and Good Citizens," *New York Times,* September 15, 2002, Sec. 4, P. 15; Col. 2.

27. Betsy McAlister Groves, *Children Who See Too Much* (Boston: Beacon Press, 2002).

28. John Shiffman, "Shock Lingers for Those Affected by Foiled Plot," *Philadelphia Inquirer,* February 8, 2004, B1.

CHAPTER 4. ETHICS GO TO COLLEGE

1. See Marjorie Censer, *Daily Princetonian,* "Bradley '65 Champions Integrity," September 22, 2003, www.dailyprincetonian.com/archives/2003/09/22/news/ 8562.shtml. See also Jen Albinson, "Keeping It Honest: the Princeton Honor Code," *Princeton Alumni Weekly,* November 5, 2003, www.princeton.edu/~paw/ columns/on_the_campus/on_the_campus_110503.html.

2. See press release, Office of Communications, Princeton University, September 16, 2003, www.princeton.edu/pr/news/03/q3/0916-integrity.htm.

3. Fred M. Hechinger, "About Education; Studies Examine the Issue of Ethics," *New York Times,* December 30, 1980, C1.

4. P. L. 105–244. Sec. 863. Sense of Congress Regarding Good Character. This was a 1998 Amendment to the Higher Education Act of 1965.

5. College and Character, A National Initiative of the John Templeton Foundation, Initiative Overview, www.collegeandcharacter.org/overview.

6. *Ibid.*

7. *Christopher Allen Powell v. Kappa Alpha Psi Fraternity et al.*, State Court for the County of Fulton, State of Georgia, Civil Action File No. 95-VS-0098247. See Rebecca McCarthy, "UGA Closes Fraternity While Alleged Hazing Investigated," *Atlanta Journal and Constitution,* May 27, 1993, B7. Christopher Allen Powell's injury was cited in a *New York Times* article covering the problem of violent haz-

ing more generally. Peter Applebomb, "Lawsuit Shatters Code of Silence over Hazing at Black Fraternities," *New York Times*, December 21, 1994, B15.

8. Patrick Healy, "L.I. District Is Criticized in Hazing Case: Pennsylvania Prosecutor Calls School Unhelpful," *New York Times*, September 23, 2003, B1.

9. *Roe v. Wade*, 410 U.S. 113 (1993).

10. *In re Quinlan*, 70 N.J. 10; 355 A.2d 647 (1976).

11. The text of the AMA Code, as revised June 2001, reads as follows:

PREAMBLE:

The medical profession has long subscribed to a body of ethical statements developed primarily for the benefit of the patient. As a member of this profession, a physician must recognize responsibility to patients first and foremost, as well as to society, to other health professionals, and to self. The following Principles adopted by the American Medical Association are not laws, but standards of conduct which define the essentials of honorable behavior for the physician.

I. A physician shall be dedicated to providing competent medical care, with compassion and respect for human dignity and rights.

II. A physician shall uphold the standards of professionalism, be honest in all professional interactions, and strive to report physicians deficient in character or competence, or engaging in fraud or deception, to appropriate entities.

III. A physician shall respect the law and also recognize a responsibility to seek changes in those requirements which are contrary to the best interests of the patient.

IV. A physician shall respect the rights of patients, colleagues, and other health professionals, and shall safeguard patient confidences and privacy within the constraints of the law.

V. A physician shall continue to study, apply, and advance scientific knowledge, maintain a commitment to medical education, make relevant information available to patients, colleagues, and the public, obtain consultation, and use the talents of other health professionals when indicated.

VI. A physician shall, in the provision of appropriate patient care, except in emergencies, be free to choose whom to serve, with whom to associate, and the environment in which to provide medical care.

VII. A physician shall recognize a responsibility to participate in activities contributing to the improvement of the community and the betterment of public health.

VIII. A physician shall, while caring for a patient, regard responsibility to the patient as paramount.

IX. A physician shall support access to medical care for all people.

12. President Clinton pardoned Marc Rich on January 20, 2001. The move was widely criticized and touched off what the *Wall Street Journal* termed a "bipartisan firestorm." Rich's ex-wife had donated $1.5 million to Bill and Hillary Clinton and to the Democratic party. See Jerry Seper, "Fugitive's Ex-wife, Clinton Say Clemency Based on Merit," *Wall Street Journal,* January 25, 2001, A4. See also "Fugitive Traded with U.S. Enemies," *Wall Street Journal,* February 23, 2001, A01.

13. Kurt Eichenwald, "The Collapse of Drexel Burnham Lambert," *New York Times,* February 14, 1990, A1.

14. John Riley, "Feds: Throw the Book at Milken; Fed Prosecutors Say He Crossed Them," *Newsday,* September 27, 1990, 7; Associated Press, "Milken to Pay $47M in Civil Case," *Newsday,* February 27, 1998, 4; Jill Dutt and John Riley, "Milken's World; Market Rigging, Sweetheart Deals and Furtive Talks in the Bathroom," *Newsday,* October 28, 1990, 63.

15. In a widely quoted statement announcing the indictments of Grant Graham (chief financial officer for Qwest's Global Business Unit), Thomas Hall (a senior vice president in the Government and Educational Solutions Group within Qwest's Global Business Unit), John Walker (a vice president in the Government and Educational Solutions Group) and Bryan Treadway (an assistant controller at Qwest), Ashcroft said, "As we continue our efforts to battle corporate fraud, our message is clear. We will protect the integrity of our markets by punishing those who falsify financial information out of sheer greed." United States Department of Justice press release, February 25, 2003, /www.usdoj.gov/usao/co/022503 Frame1Source1.htm.

16. Jonathan Weil, "Critics of the NYSE Say It Is Lax on Late Filers," *Wall Street Journal,* September 8, 2003, C1.

17. I am referring to ABA Code Disciplinary Rule 7-102(B), as amended in 1974.

18. Specifically, the House of Delegates voted to amend rule 1.6 of the ABA Model Code of Professional Conduct to allow attorneys to report crimes or fraud by a corporate client utilizing his or her services to cause financial injury to third par-

ties; and to allow lawyers of corporate clients to report wrongdoing to higher authorities within the corporation.

19. Leslie Eaton and Kevin Flynn, "Judicial Politics as Usual in Brooklyn; and Nearly a Brawl," *New York Times,* September 17, 2003, B1.

20. Judge Cerbone was removed from office October 14, 2003, after a determination dated September 19, 2003, that he had engaged in misconduct on the bench, including financial improprieties, and as had used his court as a forum for expressing personal grievances. The official decisions and press releases of the New York State Commission on Judicial Conduct cited here can be found at www.scjc.state.ny.us.

21. Michael Moss, "The Story Behind a Soldier's Story," *New York Times,* May 31, 2002, A1, A22.

22. The statement of Chief Sonya Proctor can be found at www.dcwatch.com/police/ 971215.htm#statement; the full text of the ethics code at www.dcwatch.com/ police/971215.htm. Proctor took over the force when the previous chief was forced out for alleged improprieties and mismanagement; see David Stout, "Under Fire, District's Police Chief Quits," *New York Times,* November 26, 1997, A16.

23. I spoke to Captain Elizabeth K. Holmes, a trained psychologist about the work she does with character education at the Naval Academy, a place she describes as "essentially an engineering college." She has developed a not-for-academic-credit mandatory program for freshman "plebes" that focuses on honor. She uses a film version of *Henry V* to get across her messages. With students in their second year, the "youngster year," she uses the film *A Man for All Seasons* to encourage reflections about the meaning of moral courage. With her third year "second class" students, the focus is on self-assessment and the meaning of commitment. I asked Holmes why the students received no academic credit for this part of their training. Her reply was telling. Not giving credit signals that ethics is "more important than college credit because character is embedded in everything you do." Holmes spoke of four "pillars" of character for naval officers. The officer's four pillars of character are built up of all the virtues that are needed for responsible fulfillment of their roles: leader, servant to nation, member of a time-honored profession, and fighter. "Officers have to be better and so they are better," she said. The navy has had its share of ethics scandals, though, from cheating to sexual harassment. The impetus to be better may explain the past efforts to conceal or minimize harassment and dishonesty. In the military, there is special shame in failure.

24. The activities and mission of the National Institute of Ethics is described in full at www.ethicsinstitute.com.
25. The activities and mission of the Ethics Resource Center is described in full at www.ethics.org.

CHAPTER 5: AN ETHIC OF WORK

1. Max Weber, *The Protestant Ethic and the Spirit of Capitalism,* trans. Talcott Parsons (New York: Charles Scribner's Sons, 1958) 53.
2. In November 2002, Irv Lipp, a DuPont corporation spokesperson, provided a statement concerning the firm's office romance policy to the Wilmington *News Journal.* The paper quoted portions of the statement in a subsequent article, Esteban Parra, "Your Place, My Place or Our Workplace?" *News Journal (Wilmington, De.),* November 11, 2002, 6D. The full statement was this:

> Statement
> The personal life of employees is their own business. DuPont does not take a positon on an employee's personal involvement with co-workers, customers or vendors. However, if an employee becomes romantically involved with a colleague, that employee is encouraged to examine the relationship to determine if it 1) negatively reflects on the employee or the company; 2) affects the employee's feelings on business decisions, and 3) is likely to be disruptive to the effectiveness of the organization.
>
> Relationships between supervisors and subordinates are inappropriate and of particular concern. When personal involvement becomes incompatible with appropriate professional practices and has the potential for compromising the individual's or Company's professional integrity, the Company must take measures to adjust the work environment.
>
> If an employee becomes involved in a personal relationship that could adversely affect the Company's business, the employee is encouraged to inform management and to work with management on ways to alter the work relationship.
>
> In summary, whenever some aspect of DuPont's business could be jeopardized by a personal relationship, the Company should and will become involved in the situation. The interest of DuPont is limited to altering the work relationship—not interfering with the personal relationship.

1. Floyd Norris, "A Warning Shot to Banks in Others Fraud," *New York Times,* July 29, 2003, C1.

2. Ibid. Shapiro vowed the bank would now "hold ourselves to a higher standard."

3. Clifton Leaf, "White-collar Criminals: Enough Is Enough; They Lie, They Cheat, They Steal and They've Been Getting away with It for Too Long," *Fortune*, March 18, 2002, 60.

4. Stephen Labaton, "Praise Runs into Politics at the S.E.C." *New York Times,* July 25, 2003, C1.

5. See www.bartleby.com/63/49/1649.html, citing James B. Simpson, *Simpson's Contemporary Quotations,* (New York, Houghton Mifflin Company: 1988), attributing the statement, "In civilized life, law floats in a sea of ethics," to Earl Warren, Chief Justice, United States Supreme Court, as cited by the *New York Times,* November 12, 1962. See also Fred M. Hechinger, "About Education; Studies Examine the Issue of Ethics," *New York Times*, December 30, 1980, C1.

6. The quotation is taken from the official company Web site at: www.weyer-haeuser.com/careers.

7. George Draff is one such critic. See www.endgame.org/weyerprofile.html. Draff charges that the world's largest producer of lumber and a leader in the production of paper products is a "cut and run" timber owner.

8. Weyerhaeuser Corporation press release, "Weyerhaeuser Settles Containerboard Antitrust Cases, Will Take 7 Cents Per Share Charge in Third Quarter," September 23, 2003,/www.weyerhaeuser.com/mediagateway/news/newsarchive.asp

9. Robert Worth, "The Fraud Charged at Six Clinics in Westchester and Rockland," *New York Times,* January 31, 2001, B6.

10. Rhonda Rundle, "Senate Panel *is* Investigating Tenet," *Wall Street Journal,* September 8, 2003, B10.

11. Elissa Gootman, "Leader of Nassau Hospital Challenges Ethics Charges," *New York Times,* April 25, 2003, B7.

12. See, for example, Gretchen Morgenson, "Mutual Fund Accused of Fraud in Rapid Trading by Managers," *New York Times*, October 29, 2003 A1, reporting just the beginning of investigations that unearthed improprieties in the mutual funds industry.

13. Code of Ethics and Standards of Practice of the National Association of Realtors, effective January 1, 2004, www.realtor.org/mempolweb.nsf/pages/Code?Open Document.

14. Ibid.

15. Anne Gearan, "Lawyers Get New Ethics Rules," *Philadelphia Inquirer,* August 12, 2003, A9.

16. U.S. Federal Trade Commission, Press Release, "FTC Chairman Announces Aggressive, Pro-Consumer Privacy Agenda, Privacy Protection Resources to Increase by 50 Percent; Enforcement to be Enhanced," October 4, 2001, www.ftc.gov/opa/2001/10/privacy.htm.

17. John Schwartz, "F.T.C. Plans To Abandon New Bills On Privacy," *New York Times*, October 3, 2001, C5; quoting Andrews.

18. Ibid.

19. Stephen Labaton, "S.E.C. Adopts New Rules For Analysts," *New York Times*, May 9, 2002, C5.

20. Gretchen Morgenson, "Wall Street Firms Endorse Ethics Standards for Analysts," *New York Times,* June 13, 2001, C8.

21. Matt Krantz, "SEC: Investment Banks Paid Rivals for Research," *USA Today,* April 29, 2003, 1B.

22. Richard A. Oppel Jr., "Corporate Conduct: The Overview; Negotiators Agree on Broad Changes in Business Laws," *New York Times,* July 25, 2002, A1.

23. Andrea Knox, "Ethicist Spurs Debate on Biological Research," *Philadelphia Inquirer,* July 17, 2001, A1.

24. Gayle White, "Pro Football: Take It Easy on McNabb?," *Atlanta Journal-Constitution,* January 7, 2003, 2C. See also Phil Sheridan, "Ethicist Advises Falcons to Go for McNabb's Ankle," *Philadelphia Inquirer,* January 8, 2003, C1.

CHAPTER 7. THE CHILD I ALWAYS DREAMT ABOUT

1. Stuart Hampshire, *Morality and Conflict* (Cambridge, Mass.: Harvard University Press, 1983), xx.

2. Carey Goldberg, "Egg Auction On Internet Is Drawing High Scrutiny," *New York Times*, October 28, 1999, A26.

3. Gina Kolata, "$50,000 Offered to Tall, Smart Egg Donor," *New York Times*, March 3, 1999, A10.

4. See the official Web site of the National Institutes of Health's National Human Genome Research Institute, www.nhgri.nih.gov/10001694 and http://www.nhgri.nih.gov/10001772.

5. *Roe v. Wade*, 410 U.S. 113 (1993).

6. *Skinner v. Oklahoma ex rel. Williamson*, 316 U.S. 535 (1942).

7. *Skinner v. Oklahoma ex rel. Williamson*, 316 U.S. 535, 541 (1942).

8. *Planned Parenthood v. Casey*, 505 U.S. 833 (1992).

9. *In re Baby M*, 537 A.2d 1227, 109 N.J. 396 (1988).

10. Stephen S. Hall, "President's Bioethics Council Delivers: the Deeply Divided Panel Last Week Recommended a Moratorium on All Human Cloning, Yet a Majority of the Members Had Expressed Support in Principle for Cloning for Biomedical Research," *Science*, 297/ No. 5580 (July 19, 2002): 322.

11. The full text of the White House cloning policy statement of February 26, 2003, can be found at www.nrlc.org/Killing_Embryos/HR534HumanCloningProhibi-tionActSAP.pdf.

12. Weldon-Stupak Human Cloning Prohibition Act (H.R. 534), 241-155.

13. Lisa Nash made the quoted statements at a news conference in 2000. See www.cnn.com/2000/HEALTH/10/03/testube.brother.

14. Susan M. Wolf, Jeffrey P. Kahn, and John E. Wagner, "Using Preimplantation Genetic Diagnosis to Create a Stem Cell Donor: Issues, Guidelines & Limits, " *Journal of Law, Medicine and Ethics* 31, No. 3 (Fall 2003): 324–27.

15. See generally Lori B Andrews, *The Clone Age: Adventures in the New World of Reproductive Technology* (New York, Henry Holt and Company, 1999); Lori B. Andrews and Laurie Rosenow, "Cloning Position Paper of the Institute for Science, Law and Technology," www.kentlaw.edu/islt/cloningposition.html; and George J. Annas, Lori B Andrews, and Rosa M. Isasi, "Protecting the Endangered Human: Toward an International Treaty Prohibiting Cloning and Inheritable Alterations," *Journal of Law, Medicine and Ethics* 28 (2002): 151–78.

16. See generally George Annas, "Testimony on Scientific Discoveries and Cloning: Challenges for Public Policy, before the Subcommittee on Labor and Human Relations, United States Senate," March 12, 1997, 8; and George J. Annas & Sherman Elias, "Social Policy Considerations in Noncoital Reproduction," *Journal of the American Medical Association* 255 (1986): 62–68.

17. *Harnicher v. University of Utah Med. Ctr.*, 962 P.2d 67; 349 Utah Adv. Rep. 3 (1998).

18. *Laureen Doolan et al. v. IVF America (MA), Inc.* et al., 12 Mass. L. Rep. 482 (2000).

19. *Ibid.*

CHAPTER 8. CONSUMPTION ETHICS

1. The 2002 National Institute for Health Care Management data placed spending for prescription drugs at $154 billion in 2002, up from $120 billion in 1999. See www.nihcm.org/spending2001.pdf.
2. Estimates of the amount Americans spend on illegal drugs and estimates of the number of American drug users vary. The Office of National Drug Control Policy compiles data, which I rely on here. See www.whitehousedrugpolicy.gov/index.html. A summary of the sources of federal drug data can be found at www.whitehousedrugpolicy.gov/drugfact/sources.html.
3. Ibid.
4. *Employment Division, Department of Human Resources of the State of Oregon, et al. v. Smith*, 485 U.S. 660 (1988). See also *United States v. Oakland Cannabis Buyers' Coop*, 532 U.S. 483 (2001).
5. Douglas N. Husak, *Drugs and Rights* (Cambridge, U.K: Cambridge University Press, 1992), 2.
6. Again, the Office of National Drug Control Policy compiles data on illegal drug spending. See www.whitehousedrugpolicy.gov/publications/drugfact/american_users_spend/appc.html
7. Kevin Flynn, "Violent Crimes Undercut Marijuana's Mellow Image" *New York Times*, May 19, 2001, A1.
8. See U.S. Sentencing Commission, Special Report to the Congress: Cocaine and Federal Sentencing Policy (Washington, D.C.: U.S. Sentencing Commission, April 1997), 8. See also, U.S. Sentencing Commission, Special Report to the Congress, Cocaine and Federal Sentencing Policy, United States Sentencing Commission (Washington, D.C.: U.S. Sentencing Commission, February 1995), www.ussc.gov/crack/exec.htm.
9. The President's New Freedom Commission on Mental Health, *Final Report: Achieving the Promise: Transforming Mental Health Care in America*, DHH 5 Pub. No. SMA-03-3832, Rockville, MD: 2003.
10. Stephen Fried, *Bitter Pills: Inside the Hazardous World of Legal Drugs* (New York: Bantam Books, 1998); Paula J. Caplan, *They Say You're Crazy: How the World's Most Powerful Psychiatrists Decide Who's Normal* (Reading, Mass.: Perseus Publishing, 1995); T. M. Luhrmann, *Of Two Minds: The Growing Disorder in American Psychiatry* (New York: Knopf, 2000); J. Allan Hobson and Jonathan A. Leonard, *Out of Its Mind: Psychiatry in Crisis; A Call for Reform* (Cambridge, Mass.: Perseus Publishing, 2001).

11. *Patricia Weathers v. Millbrook Central School District et al.*, United States District Court for the Southern District of New York, Case No.: 02-CV-7622 (Judge Conner). The complaint filed by Weathers' attorney Alan Milstein on behalf of her son Michael Mozer is available at www.sskrplaw.com/adhd/weathers.html. The defendants in the suit have denied liability on varied procedural and technical grounds, including *res judicata* (a prior settlement agreement with Ms. Weathers) and lack of subject matter jurisdiction. The defendant's motions for summary judgment were denied in July 2003.

12. The policy statement opposing restrictive formularies in an era of pharmaceutical innovation is available at the academy's Web site, www.aacap.org/publications/policy/ps36.htm

13. The surgery is recommended only for a few of the most severe cases of early childhood epilepsy. See www.neuro.jhmi.edu/Epilepsy/surgery.html.

14. The quote comes from a Johns Hopkins press release, July 28, 1997, www.hopkinsmedicine.org/press/1997/july/970707.htm.

15. Stewart Truelson, "Functional Foods are Big in Ag's Future," *Voice of Agriculture News Room*, September 13, 1999, v. 78, No. 33, www.fb.com/news/fbn/99/09_13/html/functional.html.

16. The Ethics of Eating manifesto of the National Catholic Rural Life Conference quoted in part here is available in full at www.ncrlc.com/card02backtext.html.

17. Rich Heffern's article in the *National Catholic Reporter Online*, "The Ethics of Eating," quoted here is available in full at www.natcath.com/NCR_Online/archives/052402/052402a.htm.

18. Ibid.

19. As explained by the University of Pennsylvania:

> [M]embers of People for the Ethical Treatment of Animals (PETA) broke into Penn labs and obtained a tape of head-injury experiments done on primates. The graphic images of animals were powerful propaganda used by PETA to call for an end to the use of animals in test situations. One outcome was that Penn and other institutions halted testing on primates, and the University established a board to oversee all research involving animals. For [the current Penn research director], there is little resemblance between the treatment of laboratory animals then and now. "We maintain the highest standards of animal welfare in all of our studies," he says. The animal models are used only when measuring effects on "living systems"—and only when anesthetized.

For the full article from which this excerpt was taken and an explanation of the aims of the research that proved controversial in the 1980s, see www.upenn.edu/ researchatpenn/article.php?452&hlt.

CHAPTER 9. LIVING BEAUTIFULLY

1. The precise quotation appeared on a Web site previously operated by Dr. Ryan Stanton, but superseded by www.drryanstanton.com/index.htm, which reflects the same philosophy. Dr. Stanton continues to practice plastic and cosmetic surgery in Beverly Hills, California.

2. The precise quotation appeared on a website previously operated jointly by Dr. Ryan Stanton and Dr. Robert Gutsetin. Dr. Gutstein's current California plastic and cosmetic surgery practice is described at www.plasticsurgerycenters.com.

3. See transcript: Diane Sawyer, Charles Gibson, John Quinones, "Designing Women; Juliana Borges, Miss Brazil, Raises Controversy at Miss Universe Pageant Because of Her Body Sculpting," ABC News, Primetime Thursday, May 3, 2001.

4. Toby Moore, "Outrage as Miss Brazil Has 19 Ops; Knives Out For Beauty Queen," *The Express*, May 5, 2001, 34.

5. Juliana Borges' individual choices as a pageant contestant may reflect a regional trend in Latin America. See Sandy M. Fernandez et al., "Bodies A La Carte; Passionate for Pulchritude, Latin American Women are Reshaping their Form through Plastic Surgery," *Time Magazine* (International Edition/Time Latin America), July 9, 2001, 26.

6. The Center for Hyperhidrosis at Columbia University Medical Center, www.hyperhidrosiscumc.com.

7. Dr. Robert Gutstein has performed the calf-size-increasing surgery. Before and after photographs of one of his patients can be viewed on his Web site, http://www.plasticsurgerycenters.com.

8. The story of James "Butch" Quinn recited here is based on a complaint filed in a lawsuit—*Quinn v. Abiomed et al.*, Court of Common Pleas of Philadelphia County, October Term 2002, Civil Action No. 001523 by attorney Alan Milstein. The complaint can be found at www.sskrplaw.com/gene/quinn/quinncomplaint. pdf.

9. See Abiomed.com for the firm's press releases, including the release quoted here. The firm initially declined to reveal the identity of Mr. Quinn, to protect his privacy.

10. Stacey Burling, "Widow of Man Who Received Artificial Heart Settles Lawsuit, *Philadelphia Inquirer*," June 14, 2003, B2.

CHAPTER 10: THE BEST WAY TO DIE

1. Arthur S. Miller and Jeffrey H. Bowman, *Death by Installments: The Ordeal of Willie Francis* (Contributions in Legal Studies) (Westport, Conn.: Greenwood Publishing Group, 1988).

2. The quotation is from the affidavit of official chaplain Reverend Maurice L. Rousseve, dated May 25, 1946, cited in *Louisiana ex rel. Francis v. Resweber*, 329 U.S. 459, 480, n. 2 (1947), Burton J., dissenting.

3. *Louisiana ex rel. Francis v. Resweber, 329 U.S. 459 (1947).* The Louisiana state supreme court decision from which Willie Francis appealed to the Supreme Court is *State ex rel. Francis v. Resweber*, 212 La. 143; 31 So. 2d 697 (1947).

4. *In re Quinlan*, 70 N.J. 10; 355 A.2d 647 (1976).

5. Ibid. at 658.

6. Ibid. at 692.

7. *Vacco v. Quill*, 521 U.S. 793 (1997).

8. *Cruzan v. Director, Missouri Dept. of Health*, 497 U.S. 261 (1997).

9. Immanuel Kant, *Foundations of the Metaphysics of Morals* 39–40, Lewis White Beck trans. (New York: Bobbs-Merrill, 1959) (1785).

10. *Washington v Glucksberg* 521 U.S. 702 (1997).

CHAPTER 11: BEYOND YOUR OWN KIND

1. For a summary of the Gallup poll results see Charlotte Astor, "Gallup Poll: Progress in Black/White Relations, but Race Is Still an Issue," *USIA Electronic Journal*, Vol. 2, No. 3, August 1997, usinfo.state.gov/journals/itsv/0897/ijse/gallup.htm. The poll in question revealed marked improvement in whites' and blacks' willingness to intermingle. Yet evidence of prejudice and xenophobia remained.

2. *Loving v. Virginia*, 388 U.S. 1 (1967).

3. Claude Steele, "A Threat in the Air: How Stereotypes Shape the Intellectual Identities and Performance of Women and African Americans," *American Psychologist*, 52 (1997): 613-629. See also Claude Steele,. "Thin Ice: Stereotype Threat and

Black College Students," *The Atlantic Monthly*, 284(2) (1999, August): 44–47, 50–54.

4. A report on integration and segregation in metropolitan Detroit showed continuing preferences for many forms of segregation by race, "The Cost of Segregation," Detroit News, January 2002, www.detnews.com/specialreports/2002/segregation5. In the meantime the state of University of Michigan fought to retain affirmative action policies designed to create racially integrated, diverse student bodies all the way to the Supreme Court, see *Grutter v. Bollinger*, 539 U.S. ___, 123 S.Ct. 2325 (2003).

5. Tucker McCormack, "Family Sues Over Harassment," *New Haven Register*, December 29, 2001, B1. Police originally charged the Chaissons with felony hate crimes, punishable by jail time. In March 2001, the couple pled no contest to lesser charges. To avoid jail pending trial, the Chaissons agreed to move from their Milford home, where they shared a driveway with Travis and Maria Simms, a couple with two children. They also agreed to remove a confederate flag they had erected outside at their home. Late in 2001, the Simms family filed a civil suit against the Chaissons, seeking monetary damages.

6. *A Raisin in the Sun* (Columbia/ Tri-Star Studios, 1961).

7. *Boy Scouts of America v. Dale,* 530 U.S. 640 (2000).

8. *Harley v. Irish-American Gay, Lesbian and Bi-Sexual Group of Boston, Inc.,* 515 U.S. 557 (1995).

CHAPTER 12. LEAVE HOME ON ELECTION DAY

1. *Bush v. Gore*, 531 U.S. 98 (2000).

2. Ibid. at 128.

3. I rely here on United States Federal Election Commission statistics. See www.fec.gov/elections.html.

4. Robert Dahl, *Democracy and its Critics* (New Haven: Yale University Press, 1989), 215.

5. Donald P Green and Ian Shapiro, *Pathologies of Rational Choice Theory: A Critique of Applications in Political Science* (New Haven: Yale University Press, 1994), 57.

6. Theda Skopocpol and Morris P. Fiorina, Civic Engagement in American Democracy (Washington D.C.: Brookings Institute Press and the Russell Sage Foundation, 1999).

7. Mancur Olson, *The Logic of Collective Action: Public Goods and the Theory of Groups* (Cambridge, Mass.: Harvard University Press, 1965).

8. Professor Marable Manning's January 9, 2001 essay, "Stealing the Election: The Compromises of 1876 and 2000," is available on his Web site www.manningmarable.net/. It was also published in the journal *Standards* 7, No. 2 (Spring/Summer 2001).

9. Human Rights Watch Sentencing Project, "Losing the Vote: the Impact of Disefranchisement Laws in the United States" (1998), www.hrw.org/reports98/vote.

10. Marable Manning, "Stealing the Election: The Compromises Of 1876 and 2000."

11. David Riesman, *The Lonely Crowd* (New Haven: Yale University Press, 1950), 1.

CONCLUSION: AN AGENDA FOR BETTER ETHICS

1. Martin Weil and Nelson Hernandez, "Book on Bomb Withdrawn after Plagiarism Charge," *Washington Post*, June 4, 2003, B05. VanDeMark said he stood by his book as a whole but "I accept responsibility for rectifying my mistakes."

2. Ralph Blumenthal and Carol Vogel, "Ex-Chief of Sotheby's Gets Probation and Fine," *New York Times*, April 30, 2002, B3, col. 1.

3. Joe Drape, "3 Charged as Bumblers Who Rigged Big Bet," *New York Times*, November 13, 2002, A1. See also Frank Fitzpatrick, "Ex-Drexel Frat Brothers Charged in Betting Case," *Philadelphia Inquirer*, November 13, 2002, A1.

4. Julian Coman, "U.S. Pupil Sues for Being Made to Share Top Prize," *Telegraph*, (London) May 11, 2003, 29. See generally, Toni Callas and Joseph A. Gambardello, "Valedictorian, School Settle Suit after Plagiarism Charged, Ranking Pulled," *Philadelphia Inquirer*, August 22, 2003; and Jill P. Capuzzo, "Seeing Crimson," *New York Times*, July 20, 2003, sec. 14; p. 5; col. 2.

5. Deborah F. Crown and M. Shane Spiller, "Faculty Responsibilities in Dealing With Collegiate Cheating: A Student Development Perspective," *Teaching Business Ethics* 1 (1997): 117–30.

6. Roger Lowenstein, "The Company They Kept," *New York Times*, February 1, 2004, sec. 6; p. 27; col. 3; Sunday Magazine.

7. Henry Sidgwick, *The Methods of Ethics,* 7th ed., reissue (Chicago: University of Chicago Press, 1962). The book was originally published in 1874.

Abiomed, Inc., 203–5

Abortion, 25, 96, 155–56, 271–72

Absentee ballots, 244, 246, 252

Abstinence education, 75, 77

Academic dishonesty, 31–34, 48–49, 50

Academic ethics, 90–108

  in business, 98–100

  campus life and, 93–96

  institutionalization of, 106–7

  in law school, 101–3

  in medicine, 96–98

  in military academies, 103–6

  overview and history of, 90–93

Academic mission, 91–93

Accepting blame, 258

Accident victims, 214–15

Accountability, 128–30, 142

Accountants, 129, 131, 132

Addiction, 170–77

Addiction Recovery Institute, 173–74

Adelphi Communications Corporation, 265

Adoption, 151, 155, 164–65

Adornment, 190–93

Adultery, xxii, 45, 47, 55, 56, 105

Advanced Cell Technology, Inc., 143

Aesop, 84

Affirmative action, xxxvi–xxxvii, 116, 230–31

African Americans (African American culture)

  beauty standards and, 192, 198–99

  child rearing and, 16

  hazing and, 94–95

  kinship ties and, 271

  segregation and, xxxvi–xxxvii, 87, 225, 241–42

  sentencing guidelines and, 176–77

  Tuskegee Syphilis Experiment, 96

  voting and, xxxv–xxxvi, 249–52

After Virtue (MacIntyre), xxxiii

"Against Recreational Drug Use" (Allen), 171, 173, 174, 177

Age discrimination, 110

Aging, longevity and, 199–203

Agribusiness food monopolies, 183

AIDS, 172, 210

Air Force Academy, U. S., 31, 104

Akrasia, 10–11, 15

Alabama Supreme Court, 102

Alcohol prohibition, xvi

Alcohol use, 95, 173, 176

Ali, Muhammad, 260

Alleles, 153–54

Allen, Carrie Mae Cloud, 181, 206, 229–30, 231, 273–74

Allen, Grover Cleveland, Sr., 201, 225, 229–30, 273–74

Allen, Michael, 194–98, 271

Allen, Naomi, 208

Almonte, Danny, 36, 41

Alpha-fetoprotein test, 155

Altruism, 39, 65

Alvarado Hospital, 134

Alzheimer's disease, 17–18, 178

Ambrose, Stephen, 43

American Academy of Child and Adolescent Psychiatry, 181

American Academy of Physician Assistants, 97

American Bar Association (ABA), 101
   Model Rules of Professional Conduct, 101–2, 122, 131, 139

American Enterprise Institute, 44

American Farm Bureau Association, 182

American Medical Association (AMA), 97, 288–89*n*

Americans with Disabilities Act of 1990, 40, 116

Amish, the, 16, 191, 224

Amniocenteses, 154

Amoxicillin, 179

Andrews, Lori, 162, 294*n*

Andrews, Sarah, 140–41

Angel, Good and Evil, 10

Angier, Natalie, 37

Anglo-Americans, 4

Animal rights, 25, 183, 184–86

Annas, George, 163, 294*n*

Anorexia, 3, 192

Antigone (Sophocles), 8

Antinori, Severino, xxix

Anti-Semitism, 236

Apathy, political, 254–55

Applied ethics, 92–93

Arab Americans, 89

Arendt, Hannah, 25

Aristotle, xxxii–xxxiii, 11, 84

Armey, Dick, 141

Arming America (Bellesiles), 44

Army, U.S., segregation in, 225

Arnold, Marcus, 262

Arthur Andersen, 128–29

Artificial heart transplant trial studies, 203–5

Artificial life support, 96–97, 212–13, 217–18

Ashcroft, John, 100, 217

Asian Americans, 22, 39, 236

Aspen Declaration on Character Education, 74

Assisted suicide, 216–20

Association for Practical and Professional Ethics, xxiv

Association of Securities Dealers, 141

Atheism, 81

Atkins v. Virginia, 17

Atlanta Falcons, 145

Atlanta Journal Constitution, 145

Attention-deficit disorders, 178, 179–80

Austen, Jane, xxxiii

Austin, Janice, 269–70

Austin, Ray, 94

Authority, work and, 119

Autism, 168

Autonomy, 97

Autotote Systems, 261

Baby M case, 158–59

Bacanovic, Peter, 100

"Bad rule" excuse, 47–49, 50

Baier, Kurt, xv, 6

Baird, Zoë, 227

Baker High School, xxxvi
Ballot initiatives, 247, 254
Banja, John, 145
Bankruptcies, 30
Barnes v. Glen Theater, xvi
Barron, Victor, 102
Baseball, 35–36, 43
Basketball, 34, 35
Baton Rouge, Louisiana, xxxvi–xxxvii
Baumrind, Diana, 69
Bay, Eugene C., 2, 21–22
Beating children, 16–17
Beauchamp, Tom, 97
Beauty. *See* Living beautifully
Beauvoir School (Washington, D.C.), 165
Beef industry, 183
Bellesiles, Michael, 44
Beneficence, 97
Bennett, William, 11–12, 71
Bentham, Jeremy, 7, 25
Benton Nose, 188
Berlin, 240–41
Betrayal, 100
Bias, 68–69, 176–77, 241–43
Bible, the, xxxiii, 2, 16, 21, 84, 281*n*
Bigotry, 230, 242–43
Bill of Rights, 246
Bing, Steve, 162
Biodiversity, 162–63
Bioethicists, 143–44
Bioethics, xxvii–xxix, 96–97, 143–44
Biomedical science, xxvi–xxix, 20. *See also*
    Genetics
Bipolar disorder, 18, 179–80, 214
Birth control, 87, 156
Bitensky, Susan H., 17
Blair, Jayson, 41, 43
Blame, accepting, 258
Blatt, Sidney, 2–3

Bloomberg, Michael, 102
Bloomfield, Lou, 31
Bob Jones University, 226
Body adornment, 190–93
Boehner, John, 142
Boesky, Ivan, 100
Boies, David, xv, 277*n*
Bok, Sissela, 7, 25, 107, 280*n*
Bonner Center for Character Education,
    75–76
Book of the Dead, 21
Book of Virtues (Bennett), 11–12
Borges, Juliana, 189
Boston University Center for the
    Advancement of Ethics and
    Character, 76
Botox, 195
Bouvia, Elizabeth, 215
Boyles, Oscar P., 55
Boy Scouts of America, xxx, 242–43, 279*n*
Bradley, William "Bill," 90
Brady Bunch (TV show), 87
Brain, removal of half, 181, 270
Brandt, Richard, 23–24
BRCA1, 154
BRCA2, 154
Breast augmentation, 189, 193–94, 197–99
Breast cancer, 154
Breast reduction surgery, 189
Breyer, Stephen, 244–45
Bribery, 41, 49, 98, 102, 134–36
Brongersma, Edward, 219
Brooks, Diana, 258
"Brown Town," 223, 224, 225
Brown v. Board of Education, xxxvii
Bryant, Kobe, 35
Bryn Mawr Presbyterian Church, 21–22
Buddhism, 22, 81
Bulimia, 3, 192

Bullfinch's Mythology, 21, 84
Bureau of Labor Statistics, 110
Burger King, 116–17
Burks, Tommy, xxi
Burlington Northern Santa Fe Railroad
    Company, 116
Burton, Brian, 282*n*
Bush, George H. W., 11
Bush, George W., 72, 74, 78, 129, 142, 159,
    244–45, 250, 251
Bush meat, 184
Bush v. Gore, 89, 244–45, 277*n*
Business ethics, 98–100, 128–45
    cheating and, 29–31, 46
    ethical consultants, 142–45
    ethics versus morality, xvii, 130–33
    self-regulation. *See* Self-regulation
    self-serving ideas about, 133–36
    stave-off strategy, 139–42
    work/home firewall and, 111–27
Business Roundtable, 142

Calf-reduction surgery, 199
California State Department of Public
    Instruction, 72
Callahan, David, 54
Campbell, Ben Nighthorse, 35
Campus life, 93–96
Cancer, 172
Candyland, 45
Can Morality Be Taught? (Lind), 69
Capital punishment, 85, 206–7
Car accidents, 207, 208
Care ethics, 5, 68–69
Caregiving (caretaking), 110, 111, 201–2
Caring, as ethical value, 74, 76
Caring School Community Character
    Education Program, 74
Car jackings, 88

Carley, Robert, 29–30
Carnap, Rudolph, 80–81
Carnegie Mellon University, xiv, 33, 107
Carnivorism, 183, 184
Carpal tunnel syndrome, 116
Carroll, James J., 75
Cassarett, David, 205
Castellitto, Adam, 150–51, 164–66, 234–35
Castellitto, Josephine Potenza (Jo Powers),
    150–51, 185, 230, 232–35
Castellitto, Paul, 187–88, 226, 229–30,
    234–35, 240, 250
Castellitto, Richard, 234–35
Castellitto, Sergio, 187
Castellitto family, 187–88
Catholic Church, xxxiii, 12, 191, 274
Caucasians, 69, 151, 199
Cedrone, Mark E., 18
Cell phones, 20–21
Cemetery, in Berlin, 241
Census Bureau, U.S., 110, 111
Center for Academic Integrity, 93
Center for the Advancement of Ethics and
    Character, 76
Center for the Fourth and Fifth Rs, 75
Center for the Study of Ethics in the
    Professions, 93, 136, 138
Center for the Study of Professional Military
    Ethics, 104
Cerbone, Joseph J., 102, 290*n*
Chaisson, Michelle, 237–40, 299*n*
Chaisson, Wilfred, 237–40, 299*n*
Character, 256–57, 262
Character Counts Coalition, 72, 74–75, 78
Character education. *See* Moral education
Character Education Partnership (CEP),
    71–72, 286*n*
Charitable giving, 253
Cheating, 26–27, 28–57, 260, 281*n*

in business, 29–31, 46

calling attention to, 55–57, 264–67

getting caught, 41–45

in higher education, 31–34, 48–49, 50, 53–55

logic of, 55–57

making excuses for, 45–54

race to the top, 54–55

in sports, 34–37

why it's wrong, 37–41

Cherokee Indians, 40, 188

Chevy Chase, Maryland, 227–28

Child care, 110

Child Development, 69

Childers, Thomas, 43

Children

corporal punishment of, 16–17

genetics and designing, 150–68

mental illness and, 178–81

moral development of, 65–70

moral education of, 71–77, 79–86

Children's Online Privacy Protection Act of 2000, 140

Childress, James, 97

Chiles, Henry "Hank," 104–6

Chinese Americans, 189, 236

Choice, xii–xiii, xxvi–xxxii, 267–70

Chorionic villi sampling, 154

Christianity, xiii–xiv, xxxiii, 2, 70–71

Christian Scientists, 199

Christie's, 258

Chromosomes, 153

Chutes and Ladders, 45

Circumcision, 25

Circumspect moralists, 174, 176

Citigroup, 128–29

Citizenship, 74, 77

responsibilities of, 246, 253–54

Civic duties, 253–54

Civic education. *See* Moral education

Civic groups, 253

Civil liberties, xxix–xxx, 81

Civil rights, xxix–xxx, xxxv, 40, 91, 224, 250

Civil Rights Act of 1964, 40, 225

Title VII of, 117–18

Clandestine rule breaking, 45–46

Client misconduct, 101–2

Clinical trials, 203–5

Clinton, Chelsea, 165

Clinton, Hillary, 191

Clinton, William "Bill," xxii, 72, 77–78, 89, 289*n*

Clonaid, 155–56, 159

Cloning, xxviii–xxix, 39, 155–63

Clothing, and adornment, 190–93

Cluelessness, 88, 169

Cocaine, 170–74, 176–77

Codes of ethics, 94, 136–42. *See also* Student honor codes

Cohen, Randy, xxiv

Cold medicines, 171

College and Character Initiative, 93

Colleges

admission to, xxxvi–xxxvii

cheating in, 31–34, 48–49, 50, 53–54

ethics education in. *See* Academic ethics

Columbia, 144

Columbia/HCA Healthcare Corporation, 133–34

Columbia University, 195

Columbine High School, 89

Columbus, Georgia, xxxvi, 87, 225

Comic books, 84

Company retreats, 114–15

Compassion, 26–27

Compassion in Dying, 217

Competitor, being a cleaner, 260

Complacent islands syndrome, xxxii–xxxiv, xxxv, xxxvii–xxxviii
Complicity, in drug use, 174, 177
Comte-Sponville, André, xxxiii–xxxiv
Condit, Gary, xxii, 56
Confederate flags, 192
Confidentiality, 101
Conflict resolution, 76
Conflicts of interest, 141–42
Congressional ethics, xxi–xxii
Conservatives, moral education and, xv, 77–78, 83–84
Constitution, moral laws violating, xv–xvi
Consultants, 142–45
Consumer advocacy, 91
Consumer privacy laws, 139–41
Consumption ethics, 169–86
    diet, 182–86
    drug use, 170–77
    psychiatric drugs, 177–81
Controlled Substances Act, 217
Conventionalism, 67–68
Conventional period of moral development, 66
Cooke, Janet, 43
Cooper, Cynthia, 31, 266
Cooperation, as goal of ethics, 261
Coping well, xxviii–xxxi
Cornell University, 208, 210
    Program on Ethics and Public Life, 92
Corporal punishment, 16–17, 70
Corporate ethics. *See* Business ethics
Corporate scandals, 29–31, 46, 98–100, 128–30, 133–39
Cosmetics, 190, 192–93
Cosmetic surgery, xxvii, xxix, 187–89
    botched jobs, 193–99
Council on Bioethics, 144, 159
Covey, Preston, 107

Cowart, Dax, 214–16
Crack cocaine, 170–74, 176–77
Cratsley, John C., 167
Cravath, Swaine & Moore, xiv–xv, 122
Credit Suisse First Boston, 142
Crick, Francis, 153
Cruelty to animals, 183, 184–86
Cruzan, Nancy, 217–18
Cruzan v. Director, Missouri Department of Health, 217–18
Cuban Missile Crisis (1962), 86
Cultural diversity, 18–19, 83–85
Cultural diversity training, 237
Cultural relativism, 82–83
Cystic fibrosis (CF), 154, 166–68

Dahl, Robert A., 247
Daily, Edward, 103
DaSilva, Glen, 261–62
Dating
    in the academy, 122–23
    at work, 114–22, 123–27
Davila-Colon, Nidia, 98
Davis, Derrick, 261–62
Deadly force, 103–6
Death and dying, 206–20
    assisted suicide, 216–20
    planning for, 210–13
    suicide, 213–16
Death penalty, 85, 206–7
Deception, 51
Decorum, 115, 191
Deforestation, 133
DELTA F508, 154, 166–67
Democracy (democratic society), xxix–xxx, xxxiv–xxxv, 247, 248–49, 254
DePaul University's Institute for Business and Professional Ethics, 93
Desegregation, xxxvi–xxxvii, 87, 225

Designated liars, 105–6
Designing children, 150–62. *See also*
     Cloning
  picky parents, 163–67
Design of life, xii–xiii, xxvi–xxxii
Deterrence, 264–67
Dexedrine, 180
Diet, 182–86
Diet pills, 171
Dignity, dying with, 211, 214–20
Dillion, John T., 142
Dinh, Viet, 235
Disabled children, 167–68
Discipline and Honor Committees, 90–91
Disclosure rules, 129, 139
Discrimination, xxx, 40, 117–18, 231,
     249–52
Disenfranchisement, 249–52
Dishonest economy, 29–31
Diversity, 18–26, 162–63
DNA, 153–54, 158–59, 200
DNA testing, 116, 166–67
Dolly (sheep), 159
Dominican Republic, 36
Donahue, John J., 44
Donaldson, Thomas, 98
Donaldson, William H., 132
Doolan, John, 166–68
Doolan, Laureen, 166–68
Doolan, Samantha, 166–68
Doolan, Thomas, 166–68
Doolan v. IVF America (MA), Inc., 167
Douglas, Mary, 281*n*
Dowdy, Robert, 133
Down's syndrome, 155
Draff, George, 292*n*
Draft, 253–54
Dress codes, 191
Drinking, 95, 173, 176

Drug abuse, 170–77, 295*n*
Drug Enforcement Agency (DEA), 217
Drug laws, 172–73, 176–77, 217–18, 252
Drug rehabilitation, 173–74
Duke University's Kenan Institute for
     Ethics, 93
DuPont Company, 121, 291–92*n*
Duty for duty's sake, 5–6
Dworkin, Ronald, 25, 218
Dying with dignity, 211, 214–20

Eating, ethics of, 182–86
Eating disorders, 3, 192
Eckardt, Shawn, 35
Edelman, Marian Wright, 72
Education, U.S. Department of, 71–72, 74,
     93, 95
Educational Testing Service (ETS), 34
Effexor, 181
Egg donors, 151, 158–59
Eighth Amendment, 207
Elective surgery, 193–99
Electric chair, 206–7
Electronic Privacy Information Center,
     140–41
Embryonic stem cell research, 159
Emigh, Kim, 266
Emory University, 44
Emotivism, 23, 67
Employee privacy, 111–17
Energy, U.S. Department of, 144
Enron, xxv, 15, 30, 31, 56, 128–29, 139, 266
Environmental effects, 182
Environmentalism, 91
Environmental Research Institute, 29–30,
     44–45
Epileptic seizures, 181
Equal Employment Opportunity
     Commission (EEOC), 116

Equality, xxxiv, 40–41
Equal protection clause, 156
Erbitux, 98, 100
Ethical, Legal and Social Implications
    (ELSI), 144
Ethical capacity, xiii, xix, xxi
Ethical choices, xii–xiii, xxvi–xxxii, 267–70
Ethical diversity, 18–26
Ethical engagement, xxvii, 169, 192, 200
Ethical failure, xii, xxi–xxvi, 9
    how to fight, 256–67
Ethical judgment, xvii–xxi
Ethical know-how, xxv, 11, 26–27
Ethical leniency, 16–21, 26
Ethical resources, xxiv–xxvi, 64, 70, 93–94,
    106–7
Ethical standards, xi–xii, 133
    enforcing, 264–67
Ethical temptation, xxv, 2, 6–7, 34, 257–58
Ethical theory, 23–25
Ethics
    morality versus, xvii, 130–33
    out-thinking, 260–62
Ethics Bowl, xxiv, 278*n*
Ethics codes, 94, 136–42. *See also* Student
    honor codes
Ethics consultants, 142–45
Ethics education. *See* Moral education
Ethics instructors, 106–7
Ethics laws, xxvi, 15, 136
Ethics regulation stave-off strategy, 139–42
Ethics Resource Center (ERC), 107
Ethnic look, 189, 192, 193, 198–99
Ethnoracial segregation, 224–43
Etzioni, Amitai, 72
"Everyone else is doing it" excuse, 51–52
Evil, 15
Evil in Modern Thought (Neiman), 15
Exceptions, 17–18, 26, 258

for cheating, 45–54
Excuses, 17–18, 26, 258
    for cheating, 45–54
Experimental clinical trials, 203–5

Fact checking, 43–45
Fair information practices, 139–41
Fairness, xxxiv, 52, 74, 93
    cheating and, 28–29, 36–41, 52
Faith, ethical conduct and, 7
Family design, 150–52
Family Planning Council of Philadelphia,
    144
Fanconi anemia, 161
Fascism, 81
Fast food employment, 116–17
Faustus, 10
Favoritism, 114, 123
Federal Bureau of Investigation (FBI), 31
Federal character education funding, 71–72,
    74–75, 77–78, 79, 93
Federal Election Commission (FEC), 246
Federal Trade Commission (FTC), 140–41
Feminism, 191
Fernandez, Sandy M., 297*n*
Fetal genetic testing, 154–55, 166–67
Fibbing, 55
Field Museum (Chicago), 14, 259
Figure skating, 35, 260
Financial accountability, 128–30, 142
Financial analysts, 141–42
Fiorina, Morris P., 248–49
Firewall, between work and home lives,
    112–27
First Amendment, xvi, 81, 138, 155, 172,
    191–92
Fitzgeralds and the Kennedys, The
    (Goodwin), 43–44
Flirting, at work, 114

Florida, presidential election of 2000, 244–45, 250, 251
Food, ethics of, 182–86
Food and Drug Administration (FDA), 98–99, 159, 170, 181, 203
Football, 35, 145
Forest Park Junior High, xxxvi
Fort Benning (Georgia), 225
Fort McClellan (Alabama), 225
Fourteenth Amendment, xvi, 155, 156
Francis, Willie, 206–7
Frankena, William, 4–5, 7, 23
Franklin, Benjamin, xxxiii, 109
Fraternities, 94–95
Fraternity Conduct Code, 94
Fraud, 133–34
Free expression, 191–92
Freeman, John M., 181
Free riders, 38, 249, 255
Friendliness, xxxiii, 66
Fruit flies, 200, 201
Fund for the Improvement of Postsecondary Education, 93
Funding, for character education, 71–72, 74–75, 77–78, 79, 93
Funerals, 211–12
Fur coats, 185

Gambling, 11–12
Gamers, cheating by, 45–46
Gates, Bill, 202
Gay and lesbian rights, 242–43
Gender differences, xxx, xxxi
    in cheating, 31
    in moral development, 68–69
    in work, 110
General Services Administration (GSA), 30
Genes, 152–54, 200
Genetically altered foods, 186

Genetics, xxvii–xxix, 152–62
Genetic testing, 154–55, 166–67
Genital mutilation, 25
Genocide, xxxvii, 106, 219
Genome, 144, 152–53
Genung's Department Store, 233, 234
Genzyme Corporation, 166–67
Georgetown Day School, 165
Georgetown University, 54, 171, 173, 174, 177
George Washington University, 118
Georgia Institute of Technology, 94
Georgia State University, 94
Gert, Bernard, 28
"Getting ahead," 52–55
Gibbard, Alan, 5
Gifts, illegal, 134–36
Gilligan, Carol, 5, 68–69
Gillooly, Jeff, 35
Gingrich, Newt, xxxvi
Ginsburg, Ruth Bader, 244–45
Giuliani, Rudy, 43
Glass, Stephen, 43
Glatt Plagiarism Services, 265
Glenn, John, 100
Global Ethics Institute, 107
God, xxxiii, 39, 81, 208
Golden Mean, xxxiii
Goldman Sachs Group, 142
Good for goodness' sake, 5–6
"Good purpose" excuse, 49–50
Goodwin, Doris Kearns, 43–44
Gore, Albert, 78, 244–45, 250, 251
Gostin, Larry, 174, 176
Graduate Record Examination (GRE), 34
Graetz, Michael, 47–48
Graham, Grant, 289*n*
Graham, Otis, 188
Gramm, Phil, 142

Gramm-Leach-Bliley Act of 1999, 140
Grasso, Richard A., 98
Great Books, 74, 84–85, 88
Greed, 53, 100
Greeley, Andrew, 55
Green, Donald P., 248
Green cards, 227, 228
Griffith Joyner, Florence, 35
Guilty conscience, 52
Gutstein, Robert, 188, 298n

Hahnemann University Hospital, 203
Hair color, 164–65
Hairstyles, 190, 192, 193
Hall, Thomas, 289n
Hallucinogens, 170
Hansberry, Lorraine, 242
Harding, Tonya, 35, 260
Harn, Chris, 261–62
Harnicher, David, 163–64
Harnicher, Stephanie, 163–64
Harnicher v. University of Utah Medical Center, 164
Harper, Terry, xxiv
Harvard College, 230–31
Harvard School of Education, 68
Hastings Institute of Society, Ethics, and the Life Sciences, 92
Hate speech, 95
Hawaii, xvi, 86
Hazing, 94–95
Health care ethics, 96–98
Health care fraud, 133–34
HealthSouth, 134
Heart transplant trial studies, 203–5
Heath, Amber, xxiv
Heath, Verna, xxiv
Heffern, Rich, 182–83
Heilbrun, Carolyn, 219

Heise, R. G., 279n
Hemispherectomy, 181, 270
Hepatitis B, 173
Hepatitis C, 173
Heroin, 170–71, 173
Higher education
    cheating in, 31–34, 48–49, 50, 53–54
    ethics education in. *See* Academic ethics
Hill, Anita, 31
Hindus, 184
Hispanic Americans, xxxvii, 110
Hitler, Adolf, 66
HIV, 173, 210
Hoag, George, 29
Holloway, Wanda Webb, xxiv
Holmes, Elizabeth K., 290–91n
Holocaust, 65, 106, 219, 240–41
Homelessness, 61
Home/work firewall, 112–27
Homosexuality, 79, 95, 242–43
Honesty, xvii–xviii, 8–9, 93
Honor codes, xxv–xxvi, 31–32, 34, 53–54, 90–91, 278–79n
Hoof and mouth disease, 183
Hopkins Pediatric Epilepsy Center, 181
Hornstine, Blair, 263
Hospital ethics committees, 143–44
House Committee on Standards of Official Conduct, xxi
Housing segregation, 225
How We Die (Nuland), 218
Human cloning, xxviii–xxix, 39, 155–63
Human fallibility, 6–7
Human Genome Project, 144, 152–53
Human Genome Research, 144
Humanistic psychology, 82
Human longevity, 199–203
Human Rights Sentencing Project, 251
Human subject, 144, 192–93, 203–5

Hume, David, 67
Hungary, 41
Huntington's disease, 154
Husak, Douglas, 25, 172
Hyperhidrosis, 194–98

Ice skating, 35, 260
Idealism, xxvi, 199, 264
Identical twins, 153–54, 161
Identity, 233, 273
"I just cheated a little" excuse, 46–47
Illegal drugs, 170–77
Illinois Institute of Technology Center for
    the Study of Ethics in the
    Professions, 93, 136, 138
ImClone, 98, 100
"I'm just taking what I deserve" excuse,
    50–51
Immature moralists, 63–65
Immigration, to segregation, 227–28
Immoral acts, xvii–xviii
"I'm not bad, the rule's bad" excuse, 47–49,
    50
Impulsivity, 10
In a Different Voice (Gilligan), 68–69
Industry self-regulation, xxvi, 136–39
    ethical consultants and, 142–45
    stave-off strategy and, 139–42
Infertility, xxviii–xxix, 163–64
Infidelity, 45, 47, 55, 56, 105
Informed consent, 96, 97, 197, 204–5
Initial public offerings (IPOs), 141–42
Innovation, ethics of, 149–50
In re Quinlan, 212–13
Insider trading, 30, 98–100, 100, 266
Institute for Criminal Justice Ethics, 103–4
Institute for Global Ethics, 107
Institutionalization of ethics, 106–7
Institutional Review Boards (IRBs), 144

Insularity, xiii, xxxii, xxxviii, 235
Integrity, in college, 90–91
Interdependence, 271–73
Intermarriages, 226, 229–30, 237
Internal Revenue Service (IRS), 43, 48
International Olympic Committee (IOC),
    34–35
Internet privacy and trade practices, 139–41
In vitro fertilization, 161, 163–64, 166–67
Irradiated foods, 186
Islam (Muslims), 184, 191, 199
Israel, 105
Italy, 105
"It's for a good purpose" excuse, 49–50
Iverson, Allen, 35

Jackson, Cynthia, 201–2, 231–32
Jackson, Jesse, 12, 56
Jackson, Michael, 189
Janklow, William J. "Bill," xxii
Jesus Christ, 1, 2
Jewish Quarter (Berlin), 240–41
Jews (Judaism), 152, 188, 199, 236, 241
Jim Crow laws, 224, 225, 230
John Templeton Foundation, 93, 95, 106
Jones, Paula, xxii
Jordan, Michael, 35
Josephson, Michael, 72, 74–75, 79–80
Josephson Institute of Ethics, xxxiv, 32, 72,
    74, 106
Journalists, code of ethics for, 138
Joy, 263–64
Joyner, Florence Griffith, 35
J.P. Morgan Chase, 128–29
Judgment, xvii–xxi
Judgmental, 2, 82
Judicial ethics, 102–3, 143
Junk bonds, 100

Justice, xxxii–xxxiv, 97. *See also* Social justice
Justification, 17–18, 26, 258
Just Say No, 171

Kabbalah, 21
Kaguya (mouse), 161
Kaminer, Matthew, 171
Kang, Jianshi, 45
Kant, Immanuel, 5, 38–39, 218
Kappa Alpha Psi, 94–95
Keating, Charles, 100
Keener, Stephen D., 36
Kenan Institute for Ethics, 93
Kennedy Institute of Ethics, 171
Kente cloth, 192
Kerrigan, Nancy, 35, 260
Kerry, John, 254
Kevorkian, Jack, 216–17
Kickbacks, 29
Kidney transplants, 269–70
Kierkegaard, Søren, xiv
Kilpatrick, William K., 83–84
Kim, Heung Bae, 270
King, Martin Luther, Jr., 87, 93
King Tut, 14, 259
Kinship, 264, 271
Kittay, Eva, 25
Kobayashi, George (Po Chieng Ma), 34
Kohlberg, Lawrence, 65–69
Kono, Tomohiro, 160–61
Koran, 21
Kozlowski, Dennis, 98
KPMG, xxii–xxiii
Kristallnacht, 240

Labor, U.S. Department of, 110
Lackritz, Marc E., 141
Ladenson, Robert F., 278*n*

Landers, Ann, xiv
Lariam, 18
Larrabee, Mary Jeanne, 68
Latin America, 41, 189, 297*n*
Law, xxix–xxx, 106
    values and the, 20, 133
Lawrence Berkeley National Laboratories, 44
Lawrence v. Texas, xvi
Lay, Kenneth, 266
Lazy cheating, 50–51
League of Women Voters, 248
Legal ethics, 101–3, 131–33
Legal mandate, disenfranchisement by, 250–51
Lehmann, Karl, 219
Leisure time, 110, 115
Le Moyne College, 32
Lenient ethos, 16–21, 26
Levanon, Ilana, 285*n*
Levy, Chandra, xxii
Lewinsky, Monica, xxii
Liberals, moral education and, xv, 77–78, 83–84
Libertarianism (libertarians), 7, 81
Liberty, xxxiv
Library of Congress, 150
Lickona, Thomas, 72, 75, 79–80
Life skills, 76
Life spans, 200–201
Lifestyle, 21, 22
Limbaugh, Rush, 170–71
Lincoln Savings and Loan, 100
Lind, George, 69
Lindbergh, Charles, 211
Lipp, Irv, 121, 291*n*
Lipstick, 192–93
Liston, Sonny, 260
Literary canon, 84–85

Little League Baseball, 35–36
Liu, Shili, 29–30
Living beautifully, 187–205. *See also*
 Cosmetic surgery
 adornment, 190–93
 clinical trials and, 203–5
 longevity and, 199–203
Living wills, 211
Lobel, Thalma E., 285*n*
Logical positivism, 80–81, 82
Logic of cheating, 55–57
Longevity, 199–203
Looper, Byron, xxi
Lopez, Jennifer, 191
Loss of consortium, 167
Lott, John, 44
Lou Gehrig's disease, 212
Louima, Abner, xxxvii
Louisiana ex rel. Francis v. Resweber, 207
Louisiana Supreme Court, 207
Love, Gregory, 95
Lovett, Matthew, 88
Loving v. Virginia, 226
Loyalty, xxxiii, 25, 233–34
Loyola Marymount's Center for Ethics and
 Business, 93
Lup-o-matic Machine Company, 232–34
Lying, 1, 17

McCabe, Donald L., 30–31
McDonald's, 184
McGee, Glenn, 143
MacIntyre, Alasdair, xxxiii
McNabb, Donovan, 145
McNeil, Erica, 270
Mad cow disease, 183
Madonna, 152
Magazines, romance, xiv
Major League Baseball, 35–36, 43

Makeup, 190, 192–93
Making excuses, 45–54
Malcolm X, 87
Malo, Alex, 270
Malvo, Lee, 88
Mandatory sentencing laws, 176–77
Marable, Manning, 250, 251
Marcus, Erik, 183
Marcus Aurelius, 11
Maret School (Washington, D.C.), 165
Marijuana, 170–74, 176
Marlowe, Christopher, 10
Mars, Gerald, 281*n*
Martha Stewart Living Omnimedia, 100
Massachusetts Superior Court, 167
Mastectomy, 193
Material rewards, cheating for, 52–55
Matthew, Saint, 1
Meat consumption, 183, 184
Media, the, xxiii–xxiv
Medical ethics, 96–98, 143–44
Medical marijuana, 172, 176
Medical necessity, 198
Medical science, xxvi–xxix, 20
Meditations (Marcus Aurelius), 11
Mental health care, 17–18, 177–81
Mepham High School, 95
Merchant of Venice (Shakespeare), 236
Merrill Lynch, 100, 142
Meta-ethics, 23–25
Methamphetamine, 170–71, 173
Methods of Ethics, The (Sidgwick), 267
Mezvinsky, Edward M., 18
Mice, 159, 200
Michigan State University, 16–17
Military Academy, U.S., 31, 104
Military ethics, 92, 104–6
Military secrecy, 105–6
Military service, 253–54

Milken, Michael, 100
Mill, John Stuart, 25, 67, 122
Milstein, Alan, 180, 296*n*
Minimum wage, 116–17
Minow, Martha, 107
Mirkin, Kenneth, 263
Mischief Night, 78
Miss Universe, 189
Mistakes, learning from, 258–59
Mobile phones, 20–21
Model Rules of Professional Conduct,
    101–2, 122
Money laundering, 29
Monkeys, research on, 185
Montgomery County, Maryland, 49, 266
Moore, G. E., xviii, xxxiii, 80
Moore, John, 279*n*
Moore, Roy, 102
Moorestown High School, 263
Moral cover, 138–39, 142–43
Moral development, 65–70
Moral diversity, 18–26
Moral education, xvii, 61–145, 262
    in grade school, 71–77, 79–86, 108
    in higher education, 90–106
    immature moralists, 63–65
    moral development and, 65–70
    partisan ownership of, 77–78, 83–84, 86,
        108
    patriotism and, 85–86
    religion's role in, 70–71
    substance and process, 79–85
    use of term, 77
Moral extremism, 88–89
Moralism, xv–xvi, 16
Morality, ethics versus, xvii, 130–33
Moralizing about drugs, 174, 176
Moral Point of View, The (Baier), xv
Moral relativism, 82–83

Moral self-education, 63, 268–70
Moral superiority, 106
Moral tragedy, 7–9
Morehouse College, 95
Morgan Stanley, 142
Morgenthau, Robert, 129
Moses, 28
Motrin, 179
Mozer, Michael, 179–80, 296*n*
Mueller, Lauren, xvi, 277–78*n*
Muhammad Ali, 260
Multiculturalism, 83–85, 226–27, 231–32
Muris, Timothy J., 140–41
Murphy, James Bernard, 85–86
Murray, Thomas H., 51
Muslims, 184, 191, 199
Mutual fund industry, 30, 136, 292–93*n*
Myrdal, Alva, 25
Myrdal, Gunner, 25

Nagel, Thomas, 218
Nanny taxes, 227
Napster, 277*n*
Nash, Adam, 161–62
Nash, Jack, 161–62
Nash, Lisa, 161–62
Nash, Molly, 161–62
Nassau County Medical Center, 134–36
National Aeronautics and Space
    Administration (NASA), 144
National Association for the Advancement of
    Colored People (NAACP), xxxv
National Association of Realtors (NAR), 138
National Bioethics Advisory Commission,
    144
National Catholic Report Online, 182–83
National Catholic Rural Life Conference
    (ANCRLA), 182
National Character Counts! Week, 72

National Institute of Ethics, 106–7
National Institutes of Health (NIH), 144
National Science Foundation, 136, 138
Nature, 160–61, 200
Naval Academy, U.S., 104–6, 258, 290–91*n*
Nazism, 65, 96, 105, 219, 231, 234, 240–41
Near, Janet, 282*n*
Needle sharing, 173, 176
Neighbors, un-neighborly, 237–40
Neiman, Susan, 15
Neo-segregation, 224–27
Neosporin, 179
Netherlands, 219
Neue Synagogue (Berlin), 240–41
Neulander, Fred, 12
New College (Florida), xxxvi
New Jersey Supreme Court, 158, 212
New Republic, 43
New York City School District 3, 75
New York Police Department (NYPD),
    xxxvii
New York Review of Books, 25
New York State Ethics Commission, 134–36
New York State Supreme Court, 102
New York Stock Exchange, 98, 100, 141
New York Times, 43, 44–45, 132, 141–42,
    174
New York Times Magazine, xxiv
Nicomachean Ethics (Aristotle), 11, 84
Nietzsche, Friedrich, xiv
Nighthorse Campbell, Ben, 35
9/11 terrorist attacks (2001)
    moral education of children and, 88–89
    patriotism and, 85–86
    religion's role in, 21–22
    whistle-blowers after, 31
Ninov, Victor, 44
Nixon, Richard M., 91, 101
No Child Left Behind Act, 79

Noddings, Nel, 5
No Gun Ri, 103
Nonindifference, 63
Non-maleficence, 97
Normative ethics, 23
Nose jobs, 187–88
Notre Dame University, 34
Nozick, Robert, 218
Nudity, xvi
Nuland, Sherwin, 218
Nurturing, 262–64
Nutriceuticals, 182, 186

Oakland Raiders, 35
Object of Morality, The (Warnock), 62
Office romances, 111–27
Off-track betting schemes, 261–62
O'Kelly, Eugene D., xxii–xxiii
Oklahoma City federal building, bombing
    of, 89
Oklahoma Habitual Offender Sterilization
    Act, 156
O'Leary, George, 34
Olson, Mancur, 249
Olympic Games, 34–35, 260
Online businesses, 139–41
Operation Push, 87
Oregon, 217
O'Reilley, Dale, 212
Orkeny, Antal, 283*n*
Orlander, Andrew, 134
Out-thinking ethics, 7, 135
Outward Bound, 64
Over-the-counter drugs, 170, 171, 179
Oxford University, 104
OxyContin, 170–71

Pacifism, 17
Paid vacations, 110

Pain medications, 170–71

Pandora's Keepers (VanDeMark), 258

Partisanship, in moral education, 77–78, 83–84, 86, 108, 280*n*

Partnership in Character Education Program, 71–72, 286*n*

Patent Office, U. S., 153

Paternity testing, 162

Patriotism, 85–86

Paulino, Rolando, 36

Paxil, 180

Peace Corps, 125, 126

Pearson, Gretchen, 32

Peer mediation, 76

Peer review, 43–45

Penn State University, 75

People for the Ethical Treatment of Animals (PETA), 185, 296–97*n*

Perfectionism, 1–3

Performance-enhancing drugs, 35–36, 39, 51

Personal appearance. *See* Living beautifully

Personal work relationships, 114–27

Pessimism, xxi, 274

Peyote, 172

Pharmacists, code of ethics for, 138

Philadelphia, 223, 224

Philadelphia Inquirer, 88, 262

Philanthropic, 39

Philosopher's Brief, 218

Philosophy courses, 92

Physical discipline, 16–17

Physician-assisted suicide, 216–20

Piaget, Jean, 66

Picky parents, 163–67

Piero Della Francesca, 188

Pitofsky, Robert, 140

Pitt, Brad, 162

Pitt, Harvey, xxii–xxiii, 132, 141–42, 265–66

Plagiarism, 31–34, 43–44, 50–51, 53–54, 265

Planned death, 210–13

Planned Parenthood, 156, 272

Planned Parenthood v. Casey, 156

Plastic surgery. *See* Cosmetic surgery

Plato, xxxii–xxxiii

Please Let Me Die (movie), 214–15

Pledge of allegiance, 81

Police ethics, 103–6

Political apathy, 254–55

Political extremism, 88–89

Political Liberalism (Rawls), xxxiv

Polling places, 245–46

Polygamy, 18–19

Poor judgment, xxi–xxiii

Positivism, 80–81, 82

Postconventional period of moral development, 66–67

Postsecondary moral education. *See* Academic ethics

Potts, Stephen, 107

Poverty programs, 91

Powell, Christopher Allen, 94

Powell, Colin, 106

Power, work and, 119

Practical ethics, xii

Prayer, 81

Preconventional period of moral development, 66

Pregnant women, drug use and, 173

Preimplantation genetic diagnosis (PGD), 154–55, 161–62, 166–67

Prejudice, 230–31, 232–34, 236–40

Premarin, 177

Prenatal testing, 154–55, 166–67

Presbyterians, 2

Prescription drugs, 170, 177–81
Presidential election of 2000, xxxv, 244–45,
  250, 251
Price, Aaron, 95
Price fixing, 133, 258
Pride, xxxiii
Primate research, 185
Princeton University, 90–91
  Center for Human Values, 92
Principles of Biomedical Ethics (Beauchamp
  and Childress), 97
Priorities, 21, 22–23, 184
Privacy, right to, 96–97, 155–56, 162
Private school admissions, 165–66
Privileged groups, 230–32
Problems of Ethics (Schlick), 65
Proctor, Sonya, 103
Production of values, 145
Professional ethics advisors and consultants,
  142–45
Professional ethics codes, 136–42
Professional ethics courses, 92–93, 101
Professional/personal boundaries, 114–27
Professional sports, cheating in, xxi, 34–37
Professors, sex with, 122–23
Project LEGAL, 75
Prostitution, xvi
Protestant Ethic and the Spirit of Capitalism
  (Weber), 109
Protestant work ethic, 109
Prozac, 177
Psychiatric drugs, 177–81
Public Company Accounting Oversight
  Board, 129
Public policy advocacy, 107
Pulitzer Prize, 43
Punishment, 16–17, 70

Quinlan, Joseph, 212–13

Quinlan, Karen Ann, 96–97, 212–13
Quinn, Irene, 204–5
Quinn, James "Butch," 203–5, 298*n*
Qwest Communications, 100

Racism (racial bias), xxxv, xxxviii, 176–77,
  241–43
Racketeering, 29
Raelian Movement, 155–56
Raisin in the Sun, A (Hansberry), 242
Rand, Ayn, 7
Rape, xxxvii, 8, 170
Rational choice theory, 248
Rawls, John, xxxiv, 218
Reagan, Ronald, 11, 71, 77
Realtors, code of ethics for, 138
Reciprocity, 38, 98
Recreational drug use, 170–77
Red meat, 183, 184
Referendums, 247, 254
Regulation stave-off strategy, 139–42
Relativism, 82–83
Religion
  9/11 terrorist attacks and, 21–22
  beauty and, 199
  bodily adornment and, 191–92
  character education and, 70–71, 81
  death and dying and, 207–8
  out-thinking ethics and, 261
Reproductive technologies, 155–63. *See also*
  Cloning
Research
  on animals, 184–85
  on human subjects, 192–93, 203–5
  on stem cells, 159
Respect, 74, 75, 93
Responsibility, 74, 75, 93
Rest, James, 69
Restricted, use of term, 224

Resweber, E. L., 206–7
Retirement, 19–20, 201
Retributive cheating, 51
Rhinoplasty, 187–88
Rich, Marc, 100, 289*n*
Ricoeur, Paul, 6–7
Riesman, David, 254
Rigas, John, 265
Right to die, 96, 97, 212–13, 214–20
Right to privacy, 96–97, 155–56, 162
Ritalin, 178, 179–80
Robitussin, 179
Rodin, Judith, 96
Roe, John Orlando, 188
Roe v. Wade, 96, 156, 158
Rogers, Carl, 76, 82
Role models, 88
Romeo and Juliet (Shakespeare), 236
Rose, Pete, 34
Rosen, Jeffrey, 118
Rossi, Evandro, 189
Roundworms, 200
Rousseve, Maurice L., 206, 298*n*
Rowley, Coleen, 31
Royal Dutch Medical Association, 219
Russell, Bertrand, xiv, 25, 80
Rwanda, 106
Ryan, Kevin, 76–77

Saint Bonaventure University, 34
Saint Claire's Hospital (Denville), 212–13
St. Luke's Episcopal Hospital (Houston), 203
Saint Patrick's Cathedral (New York City), 22
Saint Patrick's Day Parade (New York City), 243
Salomon Smith Barney, 142
Salt Lake Olympic Games (2002), 34–35

Samuels, Louis E., 203
Sanctions, 119, 266–67
Sandoval, Oscar, 98
San Francisco Unified School District, 74
Sarasota-Bradenton Airport, xxxvi
Sarbanes-Oxley Act of 2002, xxiii, 129–30, 132, 136, 139, 142, 266
Sartre, Jean-Paul, xiv, 25
Satcher, David, 178
Saturday Night Fever (movie), 190–91
Scanlon, Thomas, 218
Scheppele, Kim, 283*n*
Schiavo, Terri, 218
Schlick, Moritz, 65, 80
Scholastic Aptitude Test (SAT), xxiv, 151
School prayer, 81
Schools
    cheating in, 31–34, 48–49, 50, 53–54
    moral education in, 71–77, 79–85, 108
School segregation, 235
School uniforms, 191
Schopenhauer, Arthur, xix
Schreiffer, Frau, 240
Schreiffer, Opa, 240
Schultz, Vicki, 118
Science, xxvi–xxix, 20. *See also* Genetics
Scott, Randy, xxii
Scrabble, 264
Scrushy, Richard M., 134
Sears, Roebuck and Company, xxiv
Seasonale, xxvii
Secondhand smoke, 173, 270
Securities analysts, 141–42
Securities and Exchange Commission (SEC), xxii–xxiii, 43, 100, 128, 129, 134, 141–42
Securities Industry Association, 141
Segregation, xxxv–xxxviii, 87, 224–27, 235–43

immigration to, 227–28
island nation, 230–35
Seidman, Louis Michael, 177
Self-acceptance, 198–99
Self-assessment, xviii–xxi
Self-education, 63, 268–70
Self-employment, 112, 115
Self-esteem, 55, 127, 233
Self-interest, xxv, 7, 12, 14, 15, 24, 263
  cheating and, 38, 40–41
Self-regulation, xxvi, 136–39
  ethical consultants and, 142–45
  stave-off strategy and, 139–42
Self-sacrifice, 7, 269–70
Sentencing Commission, U.S., 176–77
September 11 terrorist attack (2001). *See*
  9/11 terrorist attacks
Seriousness, 256–57
Sermon on the Mount, 1, 2
Seventh Day Adventists, 199
Sex bias, 68–69
Sex differences, 153
Sex education, 75, 77
Sex reassignment, 198, 272–73
Sex talk, 114, 118
Sexual harassment, 114–22
Sexual relationships
  in the academy, 122–23
  at work, 114–22, 123–27
Shakespeare, William, 236
Shapiro, Ian, 248
Shapiro, Marc J., 129
Shaw, George Bernard, xviii
Sibling donors, 161–62
Sickle cell anemia, 154
Sidgwick, Henry, 267
Sidwell Friends School (Washington, D.C.),
  165
Silly String, 78

Silvester, Paul J., 29
Singer, Peter, 25
Single mothers, 110
Situational ethics, 24
Six Pillars of Character, 74, 79
Skinner, Jack T., 156
Skinner v. Oklahoma, 156, 158
Skocpol, Theda, 248–49
Slavery, 241
Sloth, 51
Small businesses, 112, 115
Small Treatise on the Great Virtues, A
  (Comte-Sponville), xxxiii–xxxiv
Smart cheating, 38, 52, 56
Smoking, 173, 270
Snipers, in Washington, D.C., 88
Social contract theory, 98
Sociality, in the workplace, 118–19
Social justice, xxx, xxxii–xxxiii
  ethics of eating and, 182–83, 184
Society of Professional Journalists, 138
Sodomy, xvi, 242–43
Somatic cell nuclear transfer, 158–59
Sophocles, 8
Sorensen, Annette, 19
Sosa, Sammy, 43
Sotheby's, 258
Soy products, 183, 185
Spanking, 16–17
Sports, cheating in, xxi, 34–37
Sports Illustrated, 34
Sprint, 30
Stack, Carol, 69
Stages, of moral development, 66–67
Stalin, Joseph, 66
Standardized tests, cheating on, 34, 49, 50
Standard of living, in the United States, 53
Standards of fair play, 264–65
  cheating and, 28–29, 38, **39–40**

Stanford Encyclopedia of Philosophy, 10

Stanford University, 226

Stanton, Ryan A., 188, 297*n*

State Education Standard, 80

State University of New York (Cortland), 75

Stauts, Craig, 88

Stave-off strategy, 139–42

Steele, Claude M., 231

Steitz, J. A., 279*n*

Stem cell research, 159

Stereotypes, 230–31

Sterilization, of felons, 156

Stern, Elizabeth, 158

Stern, William, 158–59

Steroids, 35–36, 39, 51

Stevens, John Paul, 244–45

Stevens, Ted, 35

Stevenson, Charles, 23

Stewart, Martha, 100

Sticking, to own kind, 228–30

Stock analysts, 141–42

Strategy for Peace, A (Bok), 7

Student cheating, 31–34, 48–49, 50, 53–54

Student honor codes, xxv–xxvi, 31–32, 34,
    53–54, 90–91, 278–79*n*

Subjectivism, 82–83

Sugar Bowl Parade, 87

Suicide, 213–16

    assisted, 216–20

Sunday school, 71, 274

Supreme Court, U.S., 156, 158. *See also spe-
    cific decisions*

Surgeon General, U.S., 177–78

Surgical beauty. *See* Cosmetic surgery

Surrogacy, 158–59

Sutorius, Phillip, 219

Swastikas, 192

Sweatshops, 96

Sympathectomy, 195, 197

Syracuse University, 75

Tattoos, 190

Tau Kappa Epsilon, 261

Tax cheating, 39, 41, 47–48, 98, 100

Tay-Sachs disease, 154–55

Technology, xxvi–xxix

Teenage girls, perfectionism in, 3

Telecommuting, 110

Teleios, 2

Temptation, xxv, 2, 6–7, 34, 257–58

Ten Commandments, 28, 102

Tenet HealthSystems Inc., 134

Terrorism, xxxvii, 85–86. *See also* 9/11 ter-
    rorist attacks

Texas Heart Institute, 203

Thailand, 199

Theory of Justice (Rawls), xxxiv

Thomas, Clarence, xxx, 31

Thomson, Judith Jarvis, 218

Tilghman, Shirley M., 90

Tillich, Paul, xiv

Title VII of Civil Right Act of 1964, 117–18

Tolerance (toleration), 16, 82

Top scholar, 54–55, 259

Torture, xxxvii, 207

Totalitarianism, 81, 106

Toulmin, Stephen, 6

Traditions, 273–74

Traficant, James, xxi, 278*n*

Tragedy, 7–9

Transsexuals, 198, 272–73

Travolta, John, 190–91

Treadway, Bryan, 289*n*

Trisomy 21, 155

Tri-State Crematory (Georgia), 46

Truelson, Stewart, 182

Trust (trustworthiness), xi, 74, 93

TRUSTe, 140

Turan, Richard B., 135–36
Turiel, Elliot, 67–68
Turnitin, 265
Tuskegee Syphilis Experiment, 96
Tyco, 98
Tylenol, 179

Uffizi Gallery (Florence), 188
Uncertainty, 7–9
Undergraduate Student Government, 91
Underwood, Harry, 17
Unemployment, 110–11
Unethical ethicists, 11–12
United Methodist Church, xiii–xiv
Universities
    cheating in, 31–34, 48–49, 50, 53–54
    ethics education in. *See* Academic ethics
University of Arkansas, 94
University of California, 75
University of Connecticut Environmental
    Research Institute, 29–30, 44–45
University of Georgia, 94
University of Maryland Institute for
    Philosophy and Public Policy, 92
University of Michigan, xiv, 4, 12, 14, 23, 92
University of Pennsylvania, 95–96, 185
    Department of Bioethics, 92–93
    Law School, 53, 269
University of Pittsburgh, 6
University of San Diego's Values Institute,
    92
University of Utah Medical Center Fertility
    Clinic, 163–64
University of Virginia, 31
U.S. v. Microsoft Corporation, 277*n*
Utilitarianism, 7, 23–24, 67

Vacation Bible School, 64
Vacco v. Quill, 217

Values, xxi–xxvi
    law versus, 20, 133
    production of, 145
Values clarification, 76, 77, 79
    relativism and, 82–83
VanDeMark, Brian, 258
Vegan: The New Ethics of Eating (Marcus),
    183
Vegetarianism, 22, 183, 184–85
Vice, xxi, xxxiii–xxxiv
Vienna Circle, 65, 80
Vietnam War, 87, 91, 106, 192
Virtue, xxi, xxxiii–xxxiv, 1, 11
Volpe, Justin, xxxvii
Voluntary membership associations, 248–49
Volunteering, 253–54
Voter turnout, 246, 247, 255
Voting, xxxv–xxxvi, 244–55, 268
    disenfranchisement, 249–52
    qualifications for, 250–51
    reasons for, 247–49

Wackenhut, xxxvi
Waksal, Sam, 98, 100
Walker, John, 289*n*
Walker, Lawrence, 69
Wall Street, conflicts of interest on, 141–42
Wall Street Journal, 48
Ward, Lloyd, 35
Wardlaw, Exavier, 19
Ware, James, 102–3
Warnock, G. J., 62, 63
War on Terrorism, 85–86
Warren, Earl, 20, 133
Washington, D.C., Metropolitan Police, 103
Washington Post, 43, 171
Washington v. Glucksberg, 219
Watergate, 91, 101
Watkins, Sherron, 31, 266

Watson, James, 153

Wattleton, Faye, 188

Weakness of will, 9–10

Weathers, Patricia, 179–80, 296*n*

Weber, Max, 109

Web plagiarism, 31–34

Webster, William, xxiii

Weinbaum, Barry, 134

Welfare, 110–11

Wellbutrin, 177

Wertheimer, Roger, 103–4

Westmoreland, William C., 91

Weyerhaeuser Company, 133

Wharton School of Business, 98

Wheeler Air Force Base, 86

Whistle-blowers, 31, 37, 266–67

White, Mary Jo, 133–34

Whitehead, Mary Beth, 158–59

White House Council on Bioethics, 144, 159

Why Johnny Can't Tell Right from Wrong (Kilpatrick), 83–84

Wild Blue, The (Ambrose), 43

Willpower, 9–10

Wills, 210–11

Winfrey, Oprah, 183

Wings of Morning, The (Childers), 43

Winthrop, Maggie, 112, 115

Winthrop, Don, 112, 115

Winthrop, Samuel, 112

Winthrop, Zach, 112

Wittgenstein, Ludwig, 65

Wolf, Susan M., 162

Wolfson, Freda, 263

Wolpe, Paul Root, 144

Women's Athenaeum, 128, 130

Women's rights, 91

Won't power, 9–10

Work ethic, 109–27

   sex and, 117–23

Work/home firewall, 112–27

Workplace intimacy, 111–27

Work week, 110

WorldCom, 30, 31, 129, 266

World Trade Center attacks (2001). *See* 9/11 terrorist attacks

World War II, 65, 96, 219, 225, 231, 232, 234

Wright, James Skelly, 207

Wrongful life, 167, 204, 205

Wyeth, 181

Xerox Corporation, xxiii

Yale Law School, 215

Yale Medical School, 3

Yale University, 118

Youk, Thomas, 216–17

Young, Lee Eric, 208, 210

Yugoslavia, 106

Zavos, Panayiotis "Panos," xxix, 155–56